Soil microbiology

Waksman, Selman A. (Selman Abraham), 1888-1973

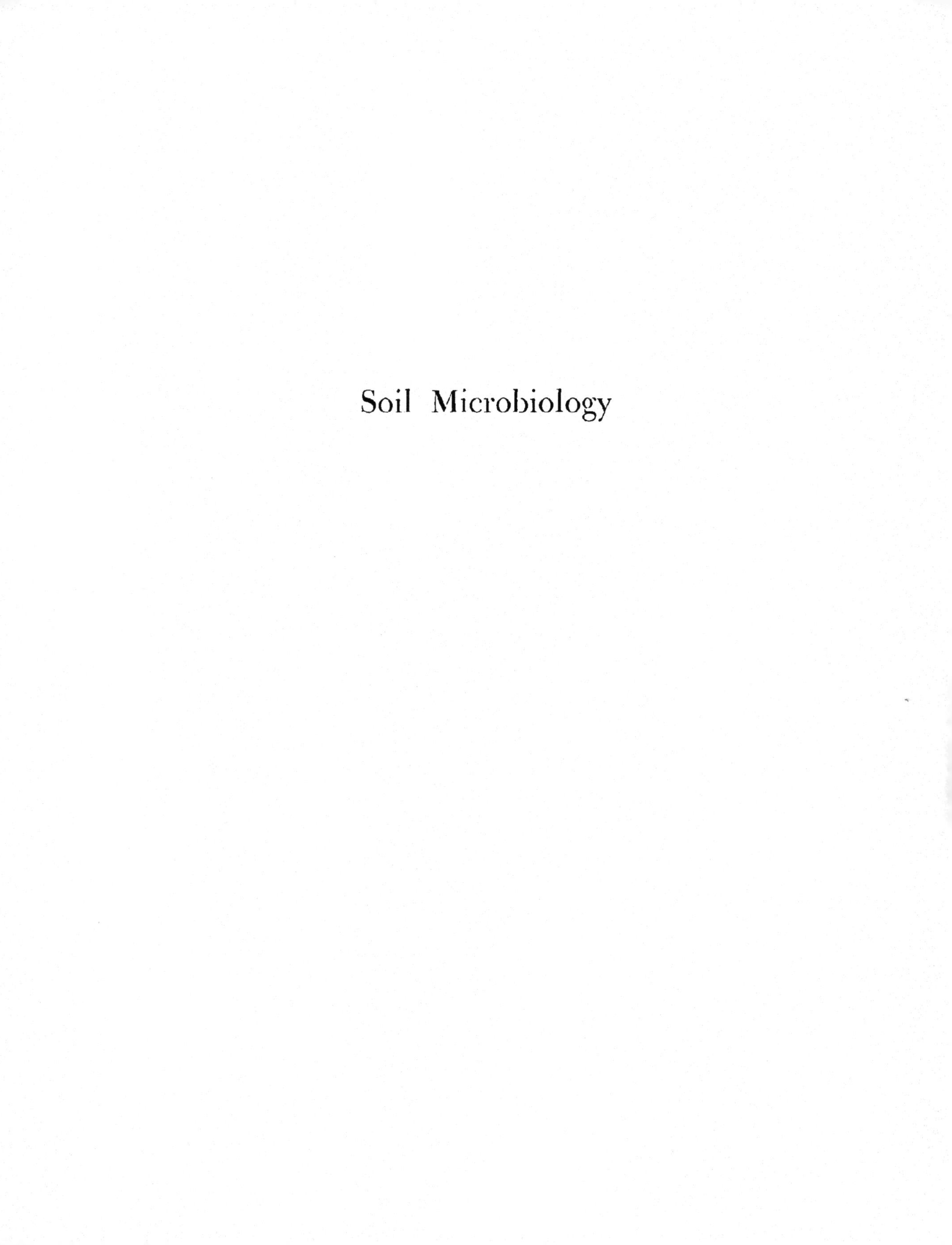

Soil Microbiology

Soil Microbiology

SELMAN A. WAKSMAN

Professor of Microbiology
Rutgers University

JOHN WILEY & SONS, INC., NEW YORK
CHAPMAN & HALL, LIMITED, LONDON

Library of Congress Catalog Card Number. 52-9965

PRINTED IN THE UNITED STATES OF AMERICA

Preface

This is a book about the life in the soil, the soil under our feet, the soil in which our cultivated and uncultivated plants grow and from which they derive most of their sustenance, and which in their turn support animal life, including that of man himself. This book deals with the numerous biological, physical, and chemical processes which continuously go on in the soil and in which microbes are involved. Without soil microbes, life on this planet would soon come to a standstill

The soil is not a mass of dead debris, merely resulting from the physical and chemical weathering of rocks; it is a more or less homogeneous system which has resulted from the decomposition of plant and animal remains It is teeming with life The numerous living forms which spend all or part of their life in the soil range from the submicroscopic viruses and phages, through the microscopic bacteria, actinomycetes, fungi, algae, and protozoa, to the lower animal forms, the worms, insects, and rotifers, many of which can be seen and recognized with the naked eye These organisms comprising both the living forms and their dead bodies, as well as the products of their decomposition, such as carbon dioxide and organic acids, interact with the rock constituents to give rise to soil The soil thus gains the characteristic properties that make it a suitable medium for plant and animal life.

The aims of this book are to survey the nature and abundance of microorganisms in the soil, to review the important role that they play in soil processes, and, so far as possible, to show the relation between them and soil fertility (including plant nutrition and crop production). I have attempted to point out some of the more promising lines of advance in the field of soil microbiology and to suggest some likely paths for future study

This book presents broadly a discussion of the soil microbiological population, the general flora and fauna of the soil, and the mutual interrelationships among microorganisms, the decomposition of plant and animal residues and the formation of humus; the transformation of various elements essential for plant growth, and the general applications of soil microbiology to other fields of knowledge, especially soil formation and plant nutrition. It should not be considered a reference book, but rather a textbook No attempt has been made to give complete bibliographies. Appended to each chapter, however, are references to some of the more important papers and books available in the English language, where the student and general reader can find up-to-date, concise statements concerning the problems discussed in the respective chapters and dealing with the various phases of soil microbiology

This book follows along the general lines of two previous volumes, *Principles of Soil Microbiology* (Williams & Wilkins Co, 1st Ed, 1927, 2nd Ed, 1932) and *The Soil and the Microbe* (John Wiley & Sons, 1931). I have drawn heavily upon the texts as well as upon the tables and illustrations of these earlier publications. This book may, therefore, be looked upon as a logical outgrowth of the older volumes, standing midway between the one that was more detailed and the other that was more concise and even more elementary.

In the preparation of this book, no attempt was made to cover in a comprehensive manner every aspect of the subject of the microorganisms inhabiting the soil, or of the various processes for which they may be responsible, or of the importance of these in soil fertility. It may even appear to some of those who will read this book that some aspects of the subject are treated rather sketchily, whereas others are discussed in great detail. This was bound to be so in a book covering such a vast subject as the complex microbiological population of the soil and its role in soil fertility and plant growth. My intention was to present here a broad outline of the subject, one might even say a philosophy of soil microbiology The supplementary books and papers recommended at the end of each chapter will help to fill the gaps and suggest additional sources of information on the various aspects of the subject to those who are eager to enlarge upon the information supplied in this volume.

SELMAN A. WAKSMAN

New Brunswick, New Jersey
June, 1952

Contents

· 1 ·

Historical

It has been recognized since the dawn of microbiology that the soil is inhabited by a living microscopic population which is responsible for the numerous reactions that take place in the soil and that affect the life and economy of man in many ways. Some of these reactions brought about by the microorganisms in the soil are highly beneficial, such as the destruction of various dead plant and animal residues that find their way into the soil, other reactions are injurious to plant and animal life, such as development of organisms which serve as potential sources of many plant and animal diseases. Within recent years, our knowledge of microbes in general and of soil microbes in particular, as they affect the cycle of life in nature, has been greatly advanced to a point where the role of these organisms in the transformation of matter and their importance in soil processes and plant growth have been appreciated.

Less than a century ago a battle was in progress among chemists, plant physiologists, agronomists, and microbiologists. The controversy centered about the role of microbes in the decomposition or "fermentation" processes and in a number of other important reactions that occur in nature, such as the effect of legumes on the subsequent growth of cereals.

The chemists, as typified by Justus von Liebig, as well as by Berzelius and Wohler, maintained that the evolution of carbon dioxide that takes place during the disintegration of sugars and other organic materials was a purely chemical reaction, which was described as "eremacausis." Liebig wrote: "All plants and vegetable structures undergo two processes of decomposition after death. One of these is named fermentation, the other decay, putrefaction, or eremacausis. Decay is a slow process of combustion, a process, therefore, in which the combustible parts of a plant unite with the oxygen of the atmosphere" Berzelius believed that yeast was not a living organism but a noncrystalline chemical substance similar to a precipitate of alumina The chemists looked with contempt upon the experiments of the biologists as frivolous and nonscientific. Fermentation was considered a mysterious catalytic force

The plant physiologists, as typified by Dumas and Boussingault, also failed to recognize the role of microbes in the cycle of life in nature They considered the animals and the plants the only living forms that participate in this cycle They stated, "Tout ce que l'air donne aux plantes, les plantes le cédent aux animaux, les animaux le rendent à l'air, cercle éternel dans lequel la vie s'agite et se manifeste, mais où la matière ne fait que changer de place" (*Chemical Statics of Organized Bodies*) Matter was thus believed to be in a state of change between plant and animal bodies

It was Pasteur, the microbiologist, who emphasized the microbiological nature of the processes of transformation of organic matter in nature. He established beyond question that, in addition to plants and animals, a third group of living forms, the microbes, participate in the cycle of life, they bring about the mineralization of residues of both plant and animal life and retransform the elements into forms available for fresh plant growth

Since the epoch-making contributions to the new science of microbiology by Pasteur and others, there have gradually emerged two distinct phases of this science, the medical and the biochemical These have frequently overlapped and just as frequently diverged from one another. Their attitudes toward the role of microorganisms in natural processes can be summarized from their respective viewpoints.

1. Microorganisms as Disease-Producing Agents. The role of microorganisms as causative agents of disease gave rise to a branch of microbiology which is usually described by the terms "medical bacteriology," "medical mycology," and "plant pathology." It deals with the causation of disease, with infections and epidemics, among human beings and other animals, as well as among plants This newly acquired knowledge has revolutionized our whole concept of public health and disease

2 Microorganisms as Chemical Reagents. A study of the chemical activities of microorganisms led to the development of microbial physiology and biochemistry. It has resulted in numerous applications of microbiology to various fields of human endeavor, as indicated by the terms "dairy bacteriology," "soil microbiology," "sewage bacteriology," "microbiology of foodstuffs," and "industrial micro-

biology." These sciences are based on the application and practical utilization of the activities of microorganisms. They also deal with the cycle of life in nature, notably the numerous decomposition processes whereby microorganisms liberate products that are useful

Fig. 1. Sir John Lawes established the Rothamsted Experimental Station, in which the most continuous experimental studies on soil fertility have been carried out for more than a century. Some of the fundamental studies of the microorganisms of the soil have been carried out at that institution.

or even essential for the growth of plants and animals. The knowledge thus gained has revolutionized many agricultural practices and has contributed to the discovery of many new processes, ranging from industrial fermentations to the manufacture of chemotherapeutic or disease-combating agents.

Pasteur established the fact that the mechanism of decomposition of organic matter by microorganisms depends not only upon the nature of the organisms but also upon the environmental conditions under which the process is taking place. In the presence of oxygen, or under aerobic conditions, a carbohydrate will be completely destroyed with the production of carbon dioxide In the absence of oxygen, or under anaerobic conditions, the carbohydrate will be only incompletely attacked, with the formation of alcohols, organic acids, and certain gases, such as hydrogen, methane, and carbon dioxide. The latter process, resulting from "life without air," came to be known as "fermentation," although this term has often been applied, quite incorrectly, to microbial life as a whole.

The Concept of Soil Microbiology

With the growing recognition of the numerous processes carried out by the bacteria, fungi, and other microbes in the soil, there gradually emerged a branch of microbiology which came to be known as "soil microbiology." This deals with the microscopic population of the soil, its role in the various transformations taking place in the soil, and its importance in plant nutrition and crop production. It concerns itself not only with the enumeration and classification of soil-inhabiting microorganisms, but also with the measurement of their activities in the soil, notably the decomposition of organic substances that are present in the soil or that find their way into the soil, with the production of ammonia and nitrates, with the fixation of nitrogen, and with numerous other transformations. The soil microbiologist is thus concerned with the isolation, identification, and description of the important groups of microbes occurring in the soil, as well as with the part they play in the physical and chemical changes that are brought about in that complex natural substrate.

Four distinct phases of soil microbiology have gradually emerged:

1. The ecological phase, which comprises the study of the quantitative and qualitative composition of the microscopic and ultramicroscopic soil population.

2. The experimental or physiological phase, which includes the study of the physiology and the biochemistry of the organisms, their role in the cycle of life in nature, and their utilization for the formation of valuable metabolic products.

3. The agronomical phase, or the application of microbiological activities to soil fertility and crop production

4 The pedological phase, or the importance of microorganisms in soil formation and soil structure.

From the point of view of their economic value, the numerous soil-inhabiting microorganisms include forms which are useful and highly important for plant and animal life; these take part in the decomposition of organic residues and in the liberation of the nutrient elements

FIG. 2. Sir Henry Gilbert, the first chemist of the Rothamsted Experimental Station.

in available forms, as well as in numerous other transformations of various elements and compounds which are essential for the continuation of life on this planet. Other groups of soil-inhabiting microorganisms include other forms of economic importance which are injurious to plant and animal life; this effect may either be direct, by attacking and destroying the higher forms of life, or indirect, by transforming certain chemical compounds into substances injurious to living processes. Here belong the numerous plant and animal pathogens that find in the soil a permanent or temporary habitat.

Our knowledge of the microbiological population of the soil and its importance in the continuation of life on this planet has been gradually accumulating during the last two and a half centuries, but it is only during the last seventy-five years that rapid progress has been made in dealing with this important branch of biology. Various groups of investigators have contributed to this progress.

FIG. 3. J. B. J. D. Boussingault initiated during the first half of the nineteenth century some of the most comprehensive investigations in agricultural chemistry and physiology.

The medical bacteriologists were interested in the soil as a medium for the growth and survival of disease-producing organisms. The agricultural chemists were interested in the soil processes that are important for the growth of cultivated plants and that result from the activities of microorganisms. The general bacteriologists, botanists, and zoologists were interested in certain special groups of organisms found in the soil, because they presented special problems in microbiology, either from theoretical consideration or from the point of view of practical utilization, as illustrated in the recent search for antibiotic-producing organisms. Finally, the soil microbiologists proper studied the soil population, either independently of any practical applications or in an attempt to solve certain practical problems. Thus the science of soil microbiology came into being.

Beginnings of Soil Microbiology (?–1860)

Although the beginnings of soil microbiology are attributable to farm practices, on the one hand, and to the growing knowledge of plant nutrition and of soil transformations, on the other, ample reference is found among the writings of the ancients and of the naturalists of the Middle Ages to the presence in the soil of certain minute living organisms that affect, in various ways, our own life, as well as that of our cultivated plants and animals

First historical mention of the possible presence in the soil of microscopic organisms which may directly influence the life of man is usually credited to a Roman writer who said that swamps give rise to minute animals which infect the air and cause human diseases Columella wrote about 60 B C of the marshes throwing up "noxious and poisonous steams" and breeding "animals armed with poisonous stings," whereby "hidden diseases are often contracted, the causes of which even physicians cannot properly understand."

Actual observations of the presence of microorganisms in the soil were reported in 1671 by Athanasius Kircheus, who wrote, "That the air, water, and soil are inhabited by numerous insects is so certain that it can be recognized with the naked eye; it was also known that worms are formed on putrefying bodies, but only since the wonderful discovery of the microscope has it become recognized that all rotting bodies swarm with a numerous mass of worms not recognized with the naked eye. I would have never believed that myself, had I not been convinced by experiments frequently repeated during many years" He cautioned about marshy lands near a home as follows: "If they become dry, certain animalcules which the eye cannot discern get into the body by the mouth and nose and propagate obstinate diseases."

This report was soon followed by the classical studies of van Leeuwenhoek, the "father of bacteriology," who used his now-famous microscope to examine various materials for the presence of "animalcules" These were found in rain water, in scum on teeth, and in other materials

The next one hundred years brought forth various investigations of bacteria and other microorganisms found in nature, but these studies dealt primarily with the development of the microscope, with determination of the size and shape of bacteria, and with attempts at rudimentary classification. The activities of the organisms and their role in natural processes either were not mentioned at all or were merely a subject for speculation, although the important relation of the lower organisms to the higher forms of life, namely, plants and animals, was gradually established.

It is sufficient to refer in this connection to the detailed knowledge that existed concerning the production of nitrates in soils and in

FIG. 4. G. J. Mulder investigated in detail the chemistry of soil organic matter, or humus, and its role in soil fertility.

composts. When, after the Revolution, the French Republic found itself blockaded by the English Navy and deprived of the possibility of importing nitrate from India, instructions were given to French farmers to accumulate nitrate by the proper composting of their stable manure. These instructions were so clear cut, and the biological processes involved so well understood, that it is obvious that nearly a century before the nitrate-forming bacteria were isolated their activities and importance were well appreciated.

By the middle of the last century, it was definitely established that stable manure becomes a nutrient to plants only after it has undergone a period of decomposition, or "fermentation," although the exact nature of this process was hardly understood. The production of ammonia and the liberation of heat, which are now recognized to be the important phases of protein decomposition and of energy transformation by microorganisms, were, however, looked upon as two distinct characteristics of the first stage of manure decomposition.

The beginning of our systematic knowledge of soil microorganisms

FIG. 5. Justus von Liebig contributed fundamental information to our knowledge of soil processes and plant nutrition.

had to wait until the birth of general systematic bacteriology. In 1836–1839, several distinct contributions appeared which had an indirect bearing upon knowledge of the activities of the microbial population of the soil. These were the first careful studies on the role of microorganisms in the decomposition of organic matter and in the formation of alcohols and acids. The work of Schwann and of Cagniard-Latour on the fermentation of wine and on the various "putrefactions" due to living organisms was soon followed by that of Kutzing, in 1837, on the production of acetic acid In 1841, Boutron and Fremy studied the formation of lactic acid from sugar, in 1844, Pelouze and Gelis studied the formation of butyric acid under anaerobic conditions, and, in 1850, Mitscherlich made a careful investigation of the decomposition of the cell wall of plants by microorganisms.

Although Mitscherlich emphasized in 1843 that the two well-known decomposition processes, designated as "fermentation" and "putrefaction," were brought about by two different groups of microorganisms, the first by yeasts and the second by vibrios, it remained for Pasteur to elucidate clearly in 1857 the principle of anaerobiosis or life without atmospheric oxygen. These two men thus clearly indicated the role of microorganisms, especially of bacteria, in a number of processes which are found to be of the greatest importance in the soil. Mitscherlich emphasized the role of bacteria in the decomposition of carbohydrates, and Pasteur the role of bacteria and other microorganisms in the decomposition of urea and other nitrogenous materials, processes of great importance in the degradation of plant and animal residues in soils and in composts.

Foundation of Soil Microbiology (1861–1890)

About the middle of the last century three distinct biological processes had been clearly outlined and were partly understood. These were decomposition of organic matter, nitrification, and nitrogen fixation.

Organic matter decomposition was known to give rise to humus, which was believed to be one of the fundamental factors in soil fertility Some investigators considered that humus was only an intermediary product and not a plant food Organic matter was believed by chemists to decompose slowly by chemical oxidation. The work of Wollny and others finally led to a better understanding of the microbiological nature of the process.

The accumulation of nitrates in the soil as a result of decomposition of organic matter was known in the seventeenth and eighteenth centuries, but only Boussingault and Schloesing connected this process with soil fertility Thus began a series of studies on nitrification which was to have an important effect upon our knowledge of soil microbiological processes

The use of legumes for enrichment of the soil was known to the ancient Romans. Berthelot was the first to suggest that nitrogen fixation may be accomplished also by nonsymbiotic bacteria. The

Fig. 6. Louis Pasteur established the role of microorganisms as causative agents of diseases and fermentations.

organisms concerned both in nitrification and in nitrogen fixation were not isolated until toward the close of the last century.

Thus, the work of the bacteriologists and chemists, of plant physiologists and agricultural chemists, contributed to the understanding of the cycle of life in the soil and laid the foundation for soil microbiology. Microbes, especially bacteria, were found to occur abundantly in the soil and to be responsible for many soil transformations.

Attention may be directed, for example, to the work of Kette, who emphasized in 1865 that the importance of addition of stable manure to the soil was due to the fact that the manure could not be replaced by inorganic nitrogen compounds and minerals or by purely vegetable matter, because these lack "a true vibrion fermentation."

FIG. 7. Ferdinand Cohn laid the basis for the classification of bacteria, including many that occur in the soil.

Robert Koch introduced in 1881 the gelatin plate for the study of bacteria, thus laying the basis for a systematic study of soil microorganisms. The gelatin was soon replaced by agar-agar as a solidifying agent for bacteriological media. Those who followed Koch were medical men who were more interested in public health and hygiene than in soil processes. They limited themselves to a study of various soil layers for the presence of bacteria and fungi that would develop on the gelatin plate. Any organism that did not develop on the plate was considered to be of no importance. The occurrence of specific bacteria was studied primarily for the purpose of establishing whether the soil contained pathogenic organisms. The pure-culture techniques that were thus developed made, however, an important contribution to bacteriology and had a significant effect upon the study of soil bacteria.

In a study of the purification of sewage water, Pasteur made the passing suggestion in 1862 that nitrification was due to bacterial action. Schloesing and Müntz found that, when a stream of sewage was allowed to pass very slowly through a column of sand and limestone, the ammonia in the sewage was at first unaffected, but, after twenty days, it became converted into nitrate, so that later the ammonia disappeared and nitrate was found in its place. Addition of a little chloroform vapor stopped the process completely; when the

FIG. 8. Robert Koch introduced the gelatin plate method for the enumeration of bacterial population of the soil and made other important contributions to microbiology.

chloroform was removed and a little soil suspension added, the process was started again. The role of "organized ferments" in the process of nitrification was thus established.

The enrichment culture method was introduced by Beijerinck. It consisted in using a selective medium containing special nutrients, for the purpose of stimulating the development of specific bacteria, which were then isolated in pure culture. This method was utilized by many bacteriologists, especially Winogradsky, and resulted in the isolation of a number of organisms concerned in important soil processes. This method contributed greatly to the solution of several important problems in soil microbiology.

Among the numerous soil microbiological processes, none is of greater importance than the fixation of nitrogen by leguminous plants. This has an important historical background, which can be separated into the following stages: (1) Our knowledge that legumes enrich the soil, which dates back to the time of the Romans. (2)

FIG. 9. J. J. T. Schloesing demonstrated the biological nature of the process of nitrification.

Boussingault's emphasis in 1838 that the favorable action of legumes upon the soil is due to their power to fix atmospheric nitrogen. (3) Lachmann's demonstration in 1858 and Woronin's in 1866, to be followed by those of various other botanists, that nodules are formed on the roots of leguminous plants. (4) Frank's demonstration in 1879 that the nodules on the roots of the plants are formed as a result of inoculation with microorganisms. Hellriegel and Wilfarth found in 1885 that, whereas the growth of nonleguminous plants is proportional to the amount of nitrate added to the soil, there is no such relationship in the case of leguminous plants. There was no gain in nitrogen when the nitrogen content of the plant was added to that of the sand in which nonleguminous plants were growing, but there was a considerable gain in combined nitrogen by the leguminous plants. Hellriegel and Wilfarth concluded, therefore, that the legumes took the nitrogen from the air through the agency of bacteria existing in the nodules of their roots. (5) Schloesing and Laurent's discovery that the weight of the nitrogen absorbed from the air by the leguminous plant is about equal to the gain in nitrogen by the plant and the soil. (6) The final isolation, by Beijerinck, of the organism responsible for the formation of nodules.

Numerous other important contributions to our knowledge of the microbiological population of the soil were made during this period. The work of Adametz on the fungus flora of the soil, of Miquel and others on urea bacteria, of Gayon and Dupetit on denitrifying bacteria, of Hoppe-Seyler and others on anaerobic cellulose decomposition, and of Warington and others on the bacteria concerned in the process of nitrification may serve as examples.

Determination of the role of microorganisms in decomposition processes, unfortunately, did not make such rapid progress. The clear and logical ideas of Pasteur were not always successfully followed by the bacteriologists and especially by the chemists, who attempted to apply them to various natural processes. They were very frequently confused, especially by the introduction of numerous terms to explain processes that were but vaguely understood. This is best illustrated by the ideas of Wollny, who summarized the status of the knowledge of decomposition of organic matter at the end of the nineteenth century. According to Wollny, there were three different classes of decomposition, as follows:

a. Decay or Aerobic Decomposition. This process was considered to be virtually a chemical "slow-burning" or "direct oxidation" of the organic matter. It was believed to be similar to the "fire-fanging" of manure, carried out "with or without the aid of minute organisms" and "leaving essentially ash behind." The organic substances were said to be volatilized, the nitrogen changed to ammonia, the carbon to carbon dioxide, the hydrogen to water, and the sulfur to sulfuric acid.

b. Putrefaction. When the oxygen tension was low, the processes were supposed to be different. Instead of carbon dioxide, water, ammonia, and minerals, various gaseous products consisting largely of methane, hydrogen, carbon dioxide, hydrogen sulfide, nitrous oxide, and nitrogen gas were believed to be formed, and the organic material left behind was described as rather dark colored and highly resistant to further decomposition. This residual material was reported to contain, in addition to nitrogen-free compounds (various fatty acids such as formic, butyric, acetic, propionic, valerianic), various nitrogen compounds (leucin, tyrosin, indol, skatol, amines, amides, as well as ammonia and sometimes nitrite); the minerals were said to be found largely in unassimilable forms

c. OTHER DECOMPOSITION PROCESSES. These were frequently placed between the two previously mentioned categories, as in the case of "Vermoderung," which was said to occur in nitrogen-poor substances with a moderate water content and in the presence of air. "Decay" and "putrefaction" were believed to take place at times side by side, according to the oxygen content of the various layers, as in manures. The various alcoholic and acid "fermentations" were also included in these intermediary reactions.

These confusing ideas took no consideration of the microbes as living organisms which possess a distinct metabolism and which use organic matter as a source of energy and of nutrients. This confusion carried over to more recent times. It was particularly evident in the ideas current even as late as the end of the second decade of this century, concerning the "humification" of organic matter in nature, especially in soil, in peat bogs, and in coal formation.

THE GOLDEN AGE OF SOIL MICROBIOLOGY (1891–1910)

Once the foundation for soil microbiology was laid, the field was open for contributions dealing with the population of the soil, especially the bacteria and its role in soil processes. Numerous organisms were described and many important soil processes were elucidated Among the outstanding investigators during this period, especially during its early phases, were M. W. Beijerinck and S N Winogradsky, who laid the foundation for much of the subsequent work. A number of chemical processes involved in the various transformations of nitrogen in soils and in composts were studied in detail. This element was recognized as frequently limiting plant growth. It was established that the transformation of nitrogen in nature is largely dependent upon the activities of various groups of soil microorganisms, especially the processes of ammonification, nitrification, and nitrogen fixation These comprise the liberation of nitrogen, in an available form as ammonia, from complex organic nitrogenous substances; the oxidation of ammonia to nitrate; and the fixation of atmospheric nitrogen by microorganisms when an available source of energy is supplied. The final elucidations of these processes were made, respectively, by Marshal and by Muntz and Coudon in 1893, by Winogradsky in 1891, and by Winogradsky and Beijerinck in 1893 and 1901.

The fixation of nitrogen by the association of bacteria and leguminous plants formed an important chapter of its own which was begun in the previous period and which has continued to the present.

Fig. 10. S. N. Winogradsky first isolated in pure culture the bacteria concerned with the processes of nitrification and nitrogen fixation, and later made a comprehensive study of the microbiological population of the soil.

The brilliant contributions of the earlier investigators were followed by numerous studies that led to the solution of this important problem, which has a significant bearing upon microbiology, plant physiology, and agronomy.

Among the most interesting investigations carried out during this period should be listed the attempts to coordinate the activities of bacteria with soil fertility. It was believed that a full appreciation of this relationship not only would modify our outlook upon soil economy, but also might revolutionize the whole agricultural practice. The agriculturist, as typified by Caron in 1895, believed that knowledge of the soil bacteria would do for soil management what knowledge of disease-producing bacteria had done for medicine.

In 1902, Remy attempted to utilize some of the soil microbiological processes as a measure of the sum total of activities of the microbial population of the soil and to develop methods for measuring soils of different fertility. The assumption was made that the fertility of the soil is directly correlated with the activities of its microbiological

Fig. 11. M. W. Beijerinck first isolated some of the most important soil bacteria, including the root-nodule organisms of leguminous plants, *Azotobacter chroococcum, Thiobacillus thioparus,* and numerous others.

population and that, by inoculating proper organisms into soil or by controlling the population by proper treatment of soil, the fertility of the latter could be regulated. Culture solutions containing proteins or their derivatives as a source of energy were used to favor the development of protein-decomposing organisms and the accumulation of ammonia. Such cultures were inoculated with soils of different fertility and the amounts of ammonia produced after a given incubation period were measured. The amounts of ammonia were thought to correspond to differences in the fertility of the soils. These methods were further developed and improved by Löhnis in 1904–1905.

Unfortunately, detailed studies of these methods have shown that a liquid culture medium in the laboratory does not present conditions comparable to those that exist in normal soils. The soil itself was then substituted for measuring the rate of chemical change that could be produced in a given substance. Such substance was added to the soil and was allowed to remain there for a definite period of

FIG. 12. V. L. Omeliansky first isolated the anaerobic cellulose-decomposing bacteria.

time under favorable temperature and moisture conditions. This led to the development of the "tumbler" or "beaker" method by J. G. Lipman and P. E. Brown. To measure the rapidity of ammonia formation from an organic nitrogenous material, a protein or a protein-rich substance, such as dried blood or peptone, was added to the soil. *To measure the rapidity of nitrate formation, ammonia in the* form of one of its salts or an organic nitrogenous substance was added to the soil. To measure the nitrogen-fixing capacity of a soil, a soluble carbohydrate was used; the soil was brought to optimum moisture condition and allowed to incubate for 7–30 days; the amount of nitrogen fixed was then measured.

These methods were variously modified, according to the nature of the substances added to the soil and the processes studied. Nitrates were utilized for stimulating the growth of nitrate-reducing organisms, which produced nitrite, ammonia, or gaseous nitrogen. Cellulose was used to bring about the development of cellulose-

FIG. 13. F. Löhnis wrote the first comprehensive book on soil bacteriology; he also studied the methods for the evaluation of the role of bacteria in soil fertility.

decomposing bacteria. The evolution of ammonia and the formation of nitrates also found application in determining the liberation of nitrogen from fertilizer materials, especially of organic origin. Hopes were aroused that the results thus obtained would find application in the measurement of soil fertility. It was believed that such methods could be utilized for routine examination of soils to foretell their potential productive capacity.

Unfortunately, the results obtained by those methods did not justify the expectations. After thousands of tests had been made and correlated with crop yields, the arbitrary conditions of the tests were found to limit their value, and the methods have now been largely abandoned.

The appearance in 1910 of Löhnis' monumental work, *Handbuch der landwirtschaftlichen Bakteriologie*, tended to summarize the developments in this subject and to point a way to future investigations. This book was followed in 1911 by Lipman's somewhat different volume, *Bacteria in Relation to Country Life*.

Fig. 14. Jacob G. Lipman first initiated in the United States a comprehensive study of the microbiological population of the soil and its role in soil processes.

Soil Microbiology as an Independent Science (1911–1940)

The thirty-year period from 1911 to 1940 brought forth extensive developments in the field of soil microbiology. Particular emphasis was laid not only on the bacterial population of the soil, but also on the other groups of microorganisms inhabiting the soil, notably the fungi, actinomycetes, algae, protozoa, nematodes, and insect larvae. Attention was also focused upon the complex interrelationships among the various groups of microorganisms and their significance in soil fertility.

It was at first believed that the bacteria are the all-important agents concerned in soil fertility. Information began to accumulate, however, indicating that other groups may also have important functions. Ehrenburg had shown in 1839 that the soil contains numerous protozoa. Darwin directed attention in 1881 to the role that earthworms play in certain soil processes. Adametz found in 1886 that fungi occur abundantly in the soil, and the abundance of actinomycetes was studied by Hiltner and Stormer. Algae and other organisms had also received their share of attention as important groups of soil-inhabiting microorganisms. It thus gradually became established that the soil harbors an extensive population representing all the foregoing groups in varying degrees of abundance. The activities of these organisms were found to result in products which are essential for plant growth. Some are important agents of decomposition, whereas others may exert injurious effects, such as causing plant and animal diseases.

This complex soil population can be considerably modified by soil treatment, such as liming, cultivation, addition of organic matter, and partial sterilization. Some of the soil processes, for example nitrification, nitrogen fixation, and sulfur oxidation, are carried out by specific groups of organisms, whereas other processes, such as decomposition of proteins, cellulose, and complex plant residues, are carried out by a variety of organisms or by large groups of organisms.

The complexity of the relationships between various microorganisms inhabiting the soil can best be illustrated by the theory of Russell and Hutchinson. According to this theory, protozoa are able to consume bacteria and thus exert a controlling effect on the bacterial processes in the soil and thereby on soil fertility. Any treatment that leads to elimination of the protozoa would, theoretically, result in an improvement of soil fertility. Although subsequent studies did not confirm this theory, the abundance of protozoa in the soil was definitely established.

Other important soil microbiological processes received much consideration. Among these was the decomposition of cellulose by microorganisms. In spite of the fact that cellulose makes up 20–50 per cent of most plant residues, little was previously known about the nature of the organisms concerned in decomposition of this important material. As late as 1902, when Omeliansky published his studies on the anaerobic cellulose bacteria, no consideration was given to the role of fungi or other microorganisms in this process.

Most of the discussion following Omeliansky's work was concerned with the question of purity of the cultures and with the uncertainty as to whether aerobic or anaerobic bacteria were more important and which group was the primary agent in cellulose decomposition.

Numerous studies demonstrated that a large number of fungi are capable of decomposing cellulose. In fact, under certain conditions, as in acid soils or in composts, fungi may be more important than

Fig. 15. Charles Thom made a detailed study of the fungus population of the soil; he is responsible for the identification of numerous soil organisms, notably members of the genera *Penicillium* and *Aspergillus.*

bacteria. Actinomycetes may also play an important part in cellulose decomposition, especially in high-temperature composts. Even protozoa may be able to transform cellulose. Considerable knowledge of the aerobic bacteria capable of bringing about cellulose decomposition was also obtained. The nature of the material, the nature of the soil or compost, and the conditions of decomposition, especially aeration and temperature, determine which organisms will attack the cellulose in soils, in peat bogs, in sewage, or in composts of manures and various plant materials.

The work of Jensen, Goddard, Waksman, and others on the fungi of the soil, which was followed later by the studies of Melin and Rayner on mycorrhiza fungi; the studies of Krainsky, Conn, Waksman, and Curtis on the actinomycetes of the soil; and the work of

Cutler on the soil protozoa and of Pringsheim, Robbins, Esmarch, Chodat, and Bristol on the soil algae, opened new fields for the study of the microbial population of the soil. These investigations and numerous others soon following broadened the subject of soil microbiology and reaffirmed the great abundance in the soil of

FIG. 16. E. B. Fred made a comprehensive study of the root-nodule bacteria of leguminous plants.

various groups of organisms besides the bacteria. In spite of the broadened scope of investigations, however, the bacteria were not neglected. It is sufficient to mention the work of Topping, Lochhead, Conn, and Winogradsky on the general composition of the bacterial population; of Ford and N. R. Smith on the spore-forming bacteria; of Hutchinson and Clayton, Krzemieniewska, Issatchenko, and others on the aerobic cellulose-decomposing bacteria; of Khouvine, Pochon, and Fred on the anaerobic cellulose-decomposing bacteria; of Lipman, Waksman, and Starkey on the sulfur-oxidizing bacteria; of Löhnis, Hänsen, Fred, Baldwin, McCoy, Stapp, and others on the specificity of legume bacteria, of Virtanen, P. S. Wilson, F. E. Allison, and others on the chemistry of the nitrogen-fixation process; of Lohnis on the life cycle of *Azotobacter*, and of Christensen, Gainey, and others on the influence of environmental conditions, such as reaction, upon the growth and activities of these bacteria in the soil.

This period was also marked by new methods for the study of soil microorganisms, notably the soil-staining, contact slide, and direct soil examination, introduced, respectively, by H. J. Conn and Winogradsky, by Rossi and Cholodny, and by Kubiena. These methods yielded additional information on the soil microscopic population.

The appearance in 1927 and in 1932 of *Principles of Soil Microbiology* by Waksman closes this chapter in the history of the subject, just as Lohnis' and Lipman's books closed the previous chapter.

Recent Developments and Perspectives (1940–1950)

World War II disorganized the normal course of development of many sciences, including that of soil microbiology. When the plowshare was set aside for the sword, peaceful pursuits had to give way to those which would help in winning the war and in alleviating human suffering. The soil microbiologist did not set aside his microscopes and his test tubes, his Petri dishes and his retorts, he used them for other purposes. Chief among these were studies resulting directly or indirectly from the war effort. The search centered on finding (*a*) methods for combating fungi causing spoilage of supplies and essential materials, (*b*) means of meeting possible attacks from the enemy, who might be tempted to utilize poisonous gases and bacterial warfare or to use microorganisms for killing cultivated plants, and finally (*c*) microorganisms capable of producing chemical substances which could be used as chemotherapeutic agents for combating infections and epidemics.

In the development of antibiotics, the soil microbiological population has contributed more than its share. It is to the soil that the microbiologists came in search of new antibacterial agents. In the isolation of the numerous antibiotics, organisms were utilized that came either directly from the soil or indirectly through the dust of the atmosphere. Thus came gramicidin and tyrocidine, as well as the many other bacterial products, penicillin, gliotoxin, clavacin, and other fungus products, actinomycin, streptothricin, streptomycin, chloramphenicol, aureomycin, terramycin, and neomycin, produced by actinomycetes. This field is still far from exhausted, and, although the significance of these studies in terms of soil fertility processes and plant growth still remains to be determined, the great importance of these findings to human health is beyond question.

Where is soil microbiology headed now? What are its problems and what is its future? One of the great masters of soil microbiology,

FIG. 17. Sir John Russell, Director of the Rothamsted Experimental Station, stimulated the study of the protozoa in the soil and their role in soil fertility and of numerous other microbiological processes in the soil.

Winogradsky, considers that what is called at the present time "soil microbiology" is nothing but a chapter of general microbiology, the treatment of microorganisms isolated from the soil and hypothetically admitted as taking part in some of the processes which are characteristic of the soil. He considers the information available at the present time merely an introduction to soil microbiology, not soil microbiology itself. Insufficient attention is believed to be paid to the study of the biological agents responsible for various soil processes, as they take place in nature, in the original soil and under specific soil conditions. General microbiology is based upon the obligatory pure culture method and upon the reactions carried out by these cultures under various conditions. In view of the fact that a specific organism has to compete in a certain process in the soil with numerous other organisms, some of which are much more active and more specialized, the ability of a given organism to carry out a certain function under laboratory conditions and in pure culture is no proof that the organism will carry out the same function in the soil Stress should be laid on the crude cultures of an elective character, arranged in a manner to allow the observation of the biological activities in the soil itself.

It thus becomes evident that the scope of soil microbiology cannot be narrowed down to one or two specific methods for determining the nature and abundance of the microbiological population, or to one or two processes for measuring the activities of one or more members of this population. The scope of the science is much broader. It avails itself of the methods of the botanist, the zoologist, the mycologist, and the bacteriologist, for determining the nature of the organisms present in the soil and their abundance. It avails itself of the methods of the chemist and of the physicist, for measuring the nature of the processes carried out by these organisms. It attempts to correlate the information thus obtained with that of the soil chemist, the soil physicist, and the agronomist, thus contributing its share to the building up of our knowledge of the science of the soil.

Like every other science, soil microbiology calls upon some of the older and some of the closely related sciences for specific methods and for the elucidation of its results Soil microbiology is not and cannot be merely a theoretical or a strictly applied science, as believed by some It is a science in itself with many theoretical phases and practical applications From this point of view, one is hardly justified in saying that up to now we have had only contributions to general microbiology and that the applied science of soil microbiology is still to come. One might be more justified in saying that up to now the general ecological and biochemical phases of soil microbiology have been dominant and that the application of this science to our knowledge of the soil is still of limited significance Even this, however, would hardly be fully justified, since considerable information has been accumulated concerning the interrelations between the soil processes and the microscopic population of the soil.

Selected Bibliography

1 Beijerinck, M W, *Verzamelde Geschriften,* 6 vols, Delft, Holland, 1921–1946

2 Bulloch, W, *The History of Bacteriology,* Oxford University Press, London and New York, 1938

3 Lohnis, F, *Handbuch der landwirtschaftlichen Bakteriologie,* Borntraeger, Berlin, 1st Ed, 1910, 2nd Ed, 1938.

4 Medical Research Council, *A System of Bacteriology in Relation to Medicine,* Vol 1, London, 1930.

5 Waksman, S A, *Principles of Soil Microbiology,* Williams & Wilkins Co, Baltimore, 1st Ed, 1927, 2nd Ed, 1932

6. Waksman, S. A., *Humus, Origin, Chemical Composition and Importance in Nature,* Williams & Wilkins Co., Baltimore, 1st Ed, 1936, 2nd Ed., 1938

7 Waksman, S A, Three decades with soil fungi, *Soil Sci*, 58 89–115, 1944

8 Waksman, S A, Soil microbiology as a field of science, *Science,* 102 339, 1945

9. Waksman, S. A., Sergei Nikolaevitch Winogradsky; the story of a great bacteriologist, *Soil Sci*, 62 197–226, 1946

10 Winogradsky, S N, *Microbiologie du sol, problèmes et méthodes,* Masson et Cie, Paris, 1949.

· 2 ·

The Microbiological Population of the Soil as a Whole

Composition of the Soil

The soil represents a medium or substrate in which numerous microorganisms live and bring about a great variety of processes which are responsible for continuation of the cycle of life in nature. A normal soil is made up of solid, liquid, and gaseous constituents. These can be broadly divided into five groups

1 Mineral Particles These vary greatly in size and in the degree of their mechanical and chemical disintegration They include particles ranging from large pebbles to fine sand, clay, and silt.

2. Plant and Animal Residues These comprise the freshly fallen leaves and other plant stubble and dead remnants of a variety of insects and other animal forms Some of the materials are largely undecomposed, still others are partly or thoroughly decomposed, so that the original structure can no longer be recognized. In the last state they are spoken of as humus or humified materials

3. Living Systems These include the living roots of higher plants, the great number of living animal forms, which range from protozoa, insects, and earthworms to rodents, as well as the numerous algae, fungi, actinomycetes, and bacteria.

4. Water The liquid phase of the soil, comprising both free and hygroscopic water, contains in solution varying concentrations of inorganic salts and certain organic compounds.

5. Gases The soil atmosphere consists of carbon dioxide, oxygen, nitrogen, and a number of other gases in more limited concentrations.

The composition of a typical podzol soil is shown in Table 1

The microbiological population which inhabits the soil, together with the roots of higher plants and with animal forms, makes the

TABLE 1 COMPOSITION OF A GRAY FOREST OR PODZOL SOIL (from Glinka)

Soil Constituent	Horizon A_1 Organic-Matter-Rich Material	Horizon A_2 Bleached Whitish Horizon	Horizon B Brownish Yellow Layer	Horizon C Granitic Base
	per cent	*per cent*	*per cent*	*per cent*
Loss on ignition	12.78	5.02	6.00	1.21
Organic matter	10.94	1.25	2.29	
SiO_2	66.86	74.01	63.60	74.87
Al_2O_3	13.38	13.78	17.10	13.82
Fe_2O_3	1.71	1.95	4.50	1.92
Mn_3O_4	0.04	0.04	0.08	0.04
CaO	1.38	0.92	0.69	0.63
MgO	0.14	0.13	0.45	0.40
K_2O	2.36	2.28	4.12	3.96
Na_2O	1.56	1.75	3.46	2.62

soil a living system and not a mere dead mass of mineral matter and organic residues. This can be clearly seen in Fig. 18.

The quantitative composition of the population and its qualitative nature depend largely upon the origin and nature of the soil and the relative composition of its inorganic and organic constituents. The prevailing climate and the growing vegetation also influence greatly the nature and abundance of the microorganisms that inhabit the particular soil. Among the other factors that have a marked effect upon the relative composition of the microbiological population, it is sufficient to mention the reaction of the soil, its moisture content, and the conditions of aeration.

MICROBIOLOGICAL POPULATION OF THE SOIL

Study of the soil population has progressed along several distinct lines. Some investigators have devoted their major attention to the quantitative composition of the microbiological population, others were interested in the nature of the organisms making up this population; still others were concerned with the chemical processes brought about in the soil by the various organisms and their importance in soil fertility and in plant growth.

The methods for the enumeration of bacteria and other microorganisms in the soil have undergone various changes during the last fifty years. The same is true of the concepts concerning the relative importance of the various constituent groups of microorganisms inhabiting the soil. These facts, as well as the discovery that certain groups of organisms occur in some soils and not in others, as affected by various cultural and environmental conditions, have all influenced the prevailing ideas concerning the nature and abundance of the microbiological population of the soil and its importance in the transformation of organic and inorganic materials. They have

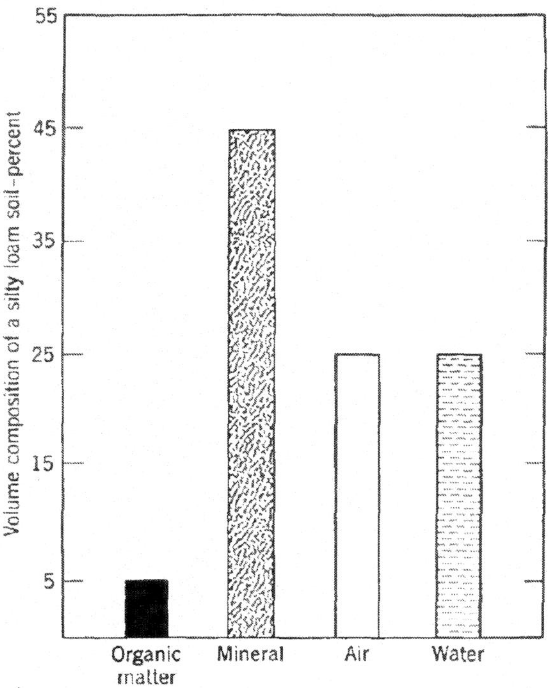

Fig. 18. The relative distribution of materials that compose a soil under conditions favorable to plant growth (from Waksman and Starkey).

modified considerably our understanding of the various processes which go on in the soil and determine its fertility.

At first, a general belief prevailed among agronomists and soil chemists that it was sufficient to count the numbers of bacterial colonies developing from a suspension of a given soil upon an agar or gelatin plate to obtain an accurate idea not only of the relative abundance of the particular organisms, but even of the composition of the soil microbiological population as a whole. The introduction of elective culture methods for the study of soil microbiological processes permitted a broader insight into the nature and activities of this population. These methods had also certain serious limitations. When artificial culture media are inoculated with small amounts of soil, they allow the development of only a small part of the microorganisms which are present in a particular soil, depending on the composition of the medium and conditions of incubation. The results thus obtained tended to obscure the importance of the microbiological population in the various soil processes The information obtained by these simple cultural methods gave, therefore, only a limited insight into the composition of the complex population, into the numerous processes for which this population was responsible, and into the complex associative and antagonistic interrelationships among the various soil-inhabiting microorganisms.

At first, bacteria were considered to comprise the all-important group of microorganisms, the various processes which influence soil fertility and for which microbes were known or were believed to be responsible were associated with the occurrence and abundance of bacteria. When it was recognized that various other groups of microorganisms must receive attention, and their importance in numerous soil processes could no longer be ignored, there came a change in the general concept of the population and its importance

These changes in our understanding of the nature of the soil population were also accompanied by a growing realization of the relation of this population to soil processes In order to measure the activities of the population in the soil, a small amount of soil was at first added to aqueous solutions containing varying concentrations of different substances, such as peptone, cellulose, ammonium salts, or nitrates. These solutions were incubated for a few days in the laboratory, and the chemical changes that took place in the composition of the specific substance were determined by various analytical procedures. The results thus obtained were believed to serve as a measure of the activities of the microbiological population in the soil It was later found that the chemical changes brought about in the solution cultures might not have been due at all to the important groups of organisms, but only to those forms that could adapt themselves more readily to the artificial conditions created by the particular selective media This tended to give to such organisms an exaggerated importance, out of all proportion to the part that they actually play in soil processes. The more predominant and perhaps the more important groups of microorganisms frequently had great difficulty in developing in the artificial media and under the artificial conditions of culture

The "solution" methods were gradually replaced by the "soil" methods, whereby a small amount of a known substance was added to a given quantity of soil, the moisture adjusted to optimum, and the soil kept in the laboratory for a given time The chemical changes that took place in the soil as a result of such treatment were analyzed by simple techniques. These procedures were often called "beaker" or "tumbler" methods after the container in which the soil was kept. The chemical changes brought about in the added substance by the soil microbiological population also gave an incomplete idea of the importance of certain groups of organisms, others may not have been recognized at all.

The introduction of microscopic methods for the examination of soil microorganisms proved to be a valuable tool in supplying information concerning the distribution of microorganisms in the soil and the nature and abundance of special groups of organisms These methods, usually based upon the staining and microscopic observation of a small amount of soil, were likewise subject to certain limitations and did not necessarily convey a true picture of the population, especially from the point of view of its importance in soil processes The greatest difficulty thereby encountered was that some of these methods could not be developed as routine laboratory procedures They could be used only by specialists, and the results thus reported varied so considerably, especially when different modifications of the methods were employed, that the information obtained proved to be of but limited value This is brought out by the fact that, after long experimentation, the conclusion was reached that the direct microscopic methods can, at best, supplement but not replace the plate and culture methods for evaluating the abundance and activities of the soil population. Among the microscopic methods, the contact slide proved to be most valuable, since it could present a picture of the microbiological state of the soil under given conditions of treatment.

Various discrepancies have been encountered in an attempt to correlate the presence of certain groups of microorganisms with the part that they were believed to play in certain soil processes When such organisms were isolated from the soil and grown in pure culture, it was found that the chemical reactions brought about by them under those conditions did not necessarily correspond to similar reactions taking place in the soil itself The importance of the actual or potential activities of such organisms in the soil under various conditions of cultivation was, therefore, questioned.

Studies made of the effect of various soil treatments and changes in environment demonstrated that the microbiological population in the soil is far from constant, that it undergoes a number of variations and changes which may be seasonal and even more frequent, and that these changes are subject to a variety of influences. Thus the many discrepancies in the interpretation of results obtained by different investigators, using different methods, were due more frequently to the procedure employed than to underlying fundamental differences in the soil population. The depth of the soil was found (Tables 2 and 3) to influence not only the total number of organisms, but especially the distribution of the various constituent groups

TABLE 2 DISTRIBUTION OF MICROORGANISMS IN THE DIFFERENT HORIZONS OF A PODZOL SOIL PROFILE (from Gray and Taylor)

Microorganisms in thousands per gram dry soil

Horizon	Moisture	Organic C	Bacteria	Actinomycetes	Fungi
	per cent	*per cent*			
A_1	73 3	22 7	9,792	1,104	191
A_2	16 8	0 9	369	53	10
B_1	14 1	0 4	400	<1	<1
B_2	19 0	0 9	1,006	<1	<1

TABLE 3 BACTERIA AND ACTINOMYCETES AT VARIOUS DEPTHS OF SOIL (from Waksman)

Numbers in thousands per gram, determined by plate method

Depth	Bacteria		Actinomycetes	
inches	*numbers*	*per cent*	*numbers*	*per cent*
1	7,340	91	743	9
4	5,300	85	933	15
8	2,710	82	612	18
12	950	80	239	20
20	259	51	246	49
30	124	35	240	66

COMPOSITION OF THE SOIL MICROBIOLOGICAL POPULATION

As has been pointed out, most of the investigators who devoted themselves, as late as the beginning of this century, to the study of occurrence and activities of soil microorganisms looked upon the bacteria as responsible for the most important, if not all, soil processes. A mere reading of the papers dealing with soil microorganisms, published during the final decade of the last century and the first decade and a half of this century, will tend to prove this generalization This is illustrated by the work of Russell and Hutchinson in England, of J G Lipman, H J Conn, and E. B Fred in this country, of Lohnis and others in Germany. Little attention was paid to the other groups of soil microorganisms The protozoa were looked upon merely as "injurious forms" or as "enemies of bacteria", the fungi were considered either nuisances or "dust contaminants"

Admittedly, it has been known since the time of Ehrenburg, in 1839, that the soil harbors numerous protozoa; since Darwin, in 1881, that earthworms may play an important role in certain soil processes, since Adametz, in 1886, that fungi are found in great abundance in the soil, and since Hiltner and Stormer, in 1904, that actinomycetes form an important constituent group of the soil population, as could be measured by simple plating procedures None of these organisms, however, were given sufficient consideration in any systematic study of the soil population; if they were considered at all, only feeble attempts were made to coordinate their occurrence and activities with important soil processes.

It has become definitely established only during the last three and a half decades that the soil is characterized by a distinct microbiological population, which is made up of specific groups. These exert a great variety of associative and antagonistic effects upon one another. These activities markedly influence the fertility of the soil and the growth of cultivated and uncultivated plants.

The following major groups make up the soil microbiological population, or its flora and fauna.

1 BACTERIA These include spore-forming and non-spore-forming rods, cocci, vibrios, and spirilla They vary considerably in size, shape, oxygen requirements (aerobic and anaerobic), energy utilization (autotrophic and heterotrophic), slime formation, and relation to plants and animals (saprophytic and parasitic).

2 ACTINOMYCETES Three of the genera of actinomycetes are well represented in the soil. Species of *Nocardia* are closely related to some of the bacteria, especially the mycobacteria and corynebacteria Species belonging to the genera *Streptomyces* and *Micromonospora* are more closely related to the true fungi Actinomycetes vary greatly in their biochemical properties, in their relation to higher plants and animals (saprophytic vs parasitic), and in their effect upon soil bacteria (associative and antagonistic interrelations)

3 FUNGI These include large groups of organisms, known as Phycomycetes, Ascomycetes, Hyphomycetes or Fungi Imperfecti, and Basidiomycetes. They produce extensive mycelium and spores

in soils and in composts. Their growth throughout the soil may be so extensive as to hold the mass of particles together by means of a very fine microscopic network of mycelium and its excretion prod-

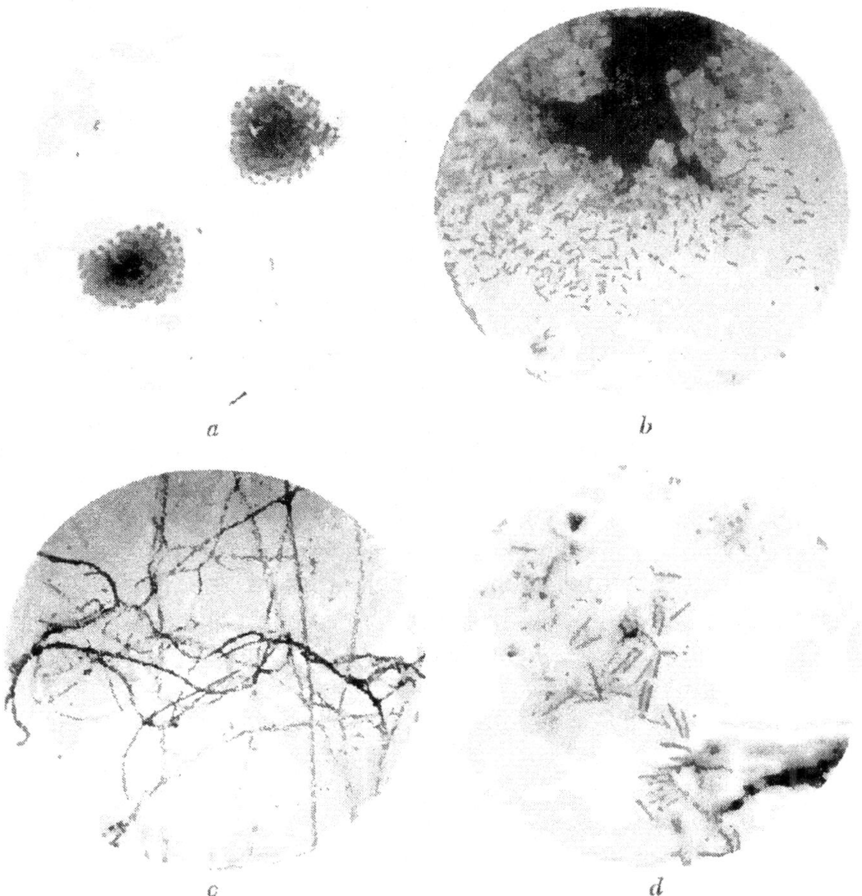

Fig. 19. Microbiological population of soil, as shown by contact slide method: *a, b, d,* different types of bacteria; *c,* fungus mycelium (from Cholodny).

ucts. Fungi vary greatly in their relation to higher forms of life, notably plants (saprophytic vs. parasitic), to soil bacteria (formation of antibiotic substances), and to other members of the soil population.

4. Algae. These organisms comprise the grass-green Chlorophyceae, the blue-green Cyanophyceae, and the Diatomaceae. Their

ability to produce chlorophyll makes their life in the soil, especially on its surface, independent of the presence of organic matter

5. PROTOZOA These comprise amoebae, flagellates, and ciliates The vegetative vs cyst condition of the protozoa in the soil has attracted considerable attention This is true also of their relation to the bacteria, since it was suggested at one time that protozoa function in the soil as the natural enemies of the bacteria By feeding upon bacteria, protozoa exert, it was believed, a controlling effect upon the abundance of bacteria, thus affecting adversely a variety of soil processes

6. HIGHER ANIMAL FORMS. These include nematodes, rotifers, earthworms, and larvae of insects These organisms have a variety of functions in the soil The ability of some of the soil-inhabiting insects to attack certain higher plants frequently makes them of great economic importance The action of earthworms as "soil cultivators" places them in an important category The fact that some of the injurious insects spend part of their life cycle in the soil suggests certain methods of control.

7. FILTERABLE ORGANISMS These include phages and other viruses Although our knowledge of the importance of these forms in soil processes is still very limited, their ability to attack both lower and higher forms of life, ranging from the bacteria and actinomycetes to cultivated and wild plants and animals, makes them of great potential importance

8 HIGHER PLANT FORMS In addition to the microscopic and ultramicroscopic organisms, the soil also harbors the root systems of higher plants The activities of these are frequently dovetailed with those of the microorganisms

Although the soil-inhabiting organisms form only a very small part of the total soil mass, they are responsible for the major changes that take place in the soil These organisms are distributed throughout the soil, primarily in the upper layers, where the plants send down their roots and where they obtain their necessary nutrients. When the roots die, they are rapidly decomposed by the fungi, bacteria, and other groups of organisms The constituent chemical elements, notably the carbon, nitrogen, and phosphorus, are thereby returned to circulation and again made available for the growth of new roots and new plants In these processes of decomposition, microorganisms build up extensive cell substance, which contributes to the organic matter of the soil or the soil humus The microbial cells not only serve as a reservoir for the further activities of microorganisms, but also act as binders for the soil particles.

Many of the groups of microorganisms found in the soil are cosmopolitan in nature, whereas others are of only limited occurrence Some are found in a number of soil types, and others only in certain soils and under specific environmental or cultural conditions Among the bacteria, the *Bacillus subtilis* and the *B. mycoides* groups are cosmopolitan in nature, whereas the *Rhizobium leguminosarum* is limited largely to soils in which specific legumes are growing. *Azotobacter chroococcum* is found only in soils that have a *p*H above 6 0, whereas *A. indicum* can withstand much more acid reactions Fungi are more abundant in acid soils, and actinomycetes in alkaline Many organisms are controlled by the nature and abundance of the organic matter, by climatic conditions, aeration, and reaction, and by the specific vegetation The mycorrhiza fungi and the various plant-pathogenic fungi and bacteria are particularly influenced by vegetation

The associative and antagonistic effects among microorganisms are often believed to exert a controlling influence upon the specific nature of the soil microbiological population. The inhibition of many bacteria, notably of the spore-forming rods and cocci, by antibiotic substances produced by fungi, the feeding of certain fungi upon nematodes and protozoa, the feeding of many protozoa upon bacteria; the attack of many bacteria and fungi upon insect larvae, the ability of various phages to attack bacteria—all contribute to the modification of the soil population

The addition of large amounts of organic matter, especially fresh plant and animal residues, to the soil completely modifies the nature of its microbiological population. The same is true of changes in soil reaction which are brought about by liming or by the use of acid fertilizers, by the growth of specific crops, notably legumes, and by aeration of soil resulting from cultivation The results of fertilization and liming upon the microbiological population, as determined by the agar plate method, are brought out in Table 4. Liming of soil favors the bacteria and actinomycetes, but not the fungi Acid mineral fertilizers, like ammonium sulfate, favor the fungi, but not the other two groups Manure favors all groups

Often a sequence of forms occurs after a certain treatment, one group of organisms following another. The addition of cellulose-rich materials, for example, first favors the development of fungi, notably species of *Chaetomium, Fusarium, Aspergillus, Penicillium,*

TABLE 4. INFLUENCE OF SOIL TREATMENT ON NUMBER OF MICROORGANISMS IN THE SOIL (from Waksman)

Numbers in thousands per gram

Treatment of Soil *	Soil Reaction *p*H	Bacteria	Actinomycetes	Fungi
Unfertilized	4.6	3,000	1,150	60
Lime alone	6.4	5,210	2,410	22
Minerals	5.5	5,160	1,520	38
Manure and minerals	5.4	8,800	2,920	73
Minerals and ammonium sulfate	4.1	2,690	370	111
Minerals, ammonium sulfate, and lime	5.8	7,000	2,520	39
Minerals and sodium nitrate	5.5	7,600	2,530	46

* Minerals = 320 pounds KCl and 640 pounds acid phosphate per acre every year

and *Trichoderma,* and of bacteria, especially myxobacteria and species of *Cytophaga,* these organisms may be followed by the growth of various spore-forming bacteria and finally by actinomycetes. The sequence of various groups of microorganisms can best be studied in composts, since the changes in temperature and the degree of decomposition of the materials in the compost greatly influence the nature of the organisms present: first bacteria begin to multiply rapidly, accompanied by the nematodes, the protozoa, and certain fungi notably the mucorales; these are followed by other filamentous fungi such as penicillia and aspergilli, finally the actinomycetes appear, and certain bacteria notably the thermophilic types

METHODS OF STUDYING THE SOIL POPULATION

To understand the theoretical and practical significance of the results, a critical evaluation of the methods used in determining the nature and abundance of this population is of the greatest importance.

Some of the methods, like the agar plate method and various liquid culture methods, supply information concerning the abundance of viable or reproducible members of the population, they also indicate the nature of the biochemical processes for which these organisms are responsible in the soil These methods are based upon the development of the living cells in the form of colonies on the agar plate or upon their growth in specific culture media The numbers of organisms obtained by either of these methods are commonly reported to range from 1 to 50 millions per gram of soil These numbers may represent only a very small fraction of the total soil population, such as 1 per cent or even less This is due to the fact that many organisms actually present in the soil in a living state are unable to develop in the artificial culture media employed for their evaluation. In some cases, very special procedures have to be devised before one is able to determine even the presence of a certain organism in the soil.

On the other hand, the microscopic methods may give a highly exaggerated picture of the abundance of the microbiological population, since the counts may include not only living but also dead cells of various organisms Hence counts of 1–10 billions of bacteria per gram of soil (Table 5), as frequently reported by use of these

TABLE 5 MICROORGANISMS IN 1 GM OF SOIL AS DETERMINED BY THE DIRECT MICROSCOPIC METHOD (from Richter)

Numbers in thousands per gram.

Type of Soil	Depth	Bacteria Cocci	Bacteria Bacilli	Bacteria *Azotobacter* Cells	Pieces of Fungus Mycelium
	cm				
Forest	0	1,379,000	1,212 000	1,000	47,000
	10	991,000	166,000	31,000	34,000
	20	281,000	169,000		7,000
Brown loam	0	870,000	376,000	84,000	5,000
	10	569,000	106,000	1,000	3,000
Sandy soil	0	519,000	192,000	79,000	3,000
	10	407,000	153,000	23,000	19,000
	20	269,000	139,000	8,000	3,000

methods, may not be fully correct These and similar methods may, therefore, also be open to criticism, since they do not give an accurate picture of the soil microbiological population.

Whatever the methods used, however, for evaluating the numbers of soil microorganisms, it may well be recognized that the actual living mass of microorganisms in the soil is considerable. Most of the organisms found in the soil are indigenous members of the population Some are found there because they seek shelter and protection beneath the soil surface. Others are carried into the soil by dead and dying plants and animals, by wind, or by rain, to live or to die there. Numerous groups of organisms pass their whole life in the soil, find their food there, and eventually leave their bodies to become a part of the soil mass, just as the roots of the higher plants penetrate and ramify throughout the whole of its surface area, and leave their remains to decompose in the soil. In the many changes that take place in the life cycle of the various microorganisms in the soil, a definite equilibrium has become established between the various groups. This equilibrium is not stable, however, but undergoes many changes as a result of the treatment that the soil undergoes.

The methods most commonly used for the enumeration of microorganisms found in the soil are commonly divided into several groups:

- I Microscopic methods
  1 Staining of soil and direct microscopic examination
  2 Contact slide method
  3 Direct examination of unstained soil
- II Culture methods.
  1 Plate culture methods
  2 Elective culture methods
  3 Soil enrichment methods

The numbers and types of organisms vary considerably, depending upon the method. Each one of these methods has its advantages and limitations. Some of the methods may have to be further modified in the study of a specific problem, or for the purpose of establishing the presence or abundance of a particular type of organism under a particular set of conditions.

Microscopic Examination of Stained Soil Preparations. This method consists in the preparation of a suspension of soil in a dilute fixative solution, one or two drops of the suspension is spread upon a clean slide, which is then dried and stained with an acid dye, and finally examined with a high-magnification microscope. The fixative solution is prepared by dissolving 0.15 gm of gelatin in 1 liter of distilled water. The staining solution consists of 1 gm erythrosin or rose-bengal dissolved in 100 ml of a 5 per cent aqueous solution of phenol, containing sufficient $CaCl_2$ (0.001–0.1 per cent) to give a very faint precipitate of the calcium salt of the dye.

The process of staining is carried out by placing a loopful of the soil suspended in the fixative solution upon a glass slide and spreading out with a needle until it covers a known area. The smear is allowed to dry over a boiling water bath. A drop of the staining solution is added to the smear and allowed to remain for 1 minute, while the slide rests on the bath. The stain is then washed off with water and the preparation allowed to dry.

Various modifications of the above method have been proposed. In one such modification, a measured amount of soil is suspended in a molten agar gel. Small drops of the agar are removed, placed in a hemacytometer slide of known depth, and allowed to solidify. The films are dried and stained in a solution of acetic-aniline blue, followed by dehydration in alcohol and mounting in euparal. Differential counts of a measured area of the film will give a quantitative

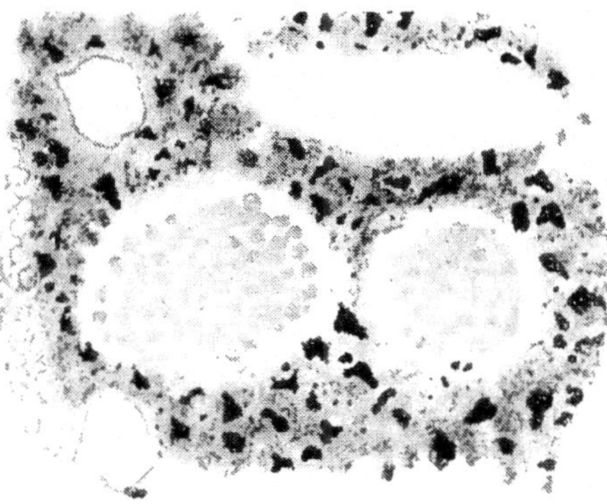

Fig. 20. Soil examination by direct microscopic method (from Winogradsky).

estimation of the microorganisms present in a given amount of soil. By adding a known suspension of bacteria to sterile soil, Jones and Mollison were able to recover 95.7–98.4 per cent. According to this method, the numbers of bacteria per gram of soil varied from 2,275 to 5,420 millions. The method will also detect large amounts of mycelium and spores of fungi and actinomycetes.

Thornton mixed a soil with a known amount of indigotin; by establishing the relation between the numbers of erythrosin-stained bacteria and indigotin particles, he was able to measure the abundance of microorganisms in the soil. He found that 1 gm of soil contained 1–4 billions of bacteria, whereas only 2 per cent of these bacteria are measured by the plate method. Detailed studies of stained soil preparations have established the fact that the numbers of bacteria in the soil are far greater than those that have been obtained by the plate culture methods.

Cholodny believed, however, that the direct staining methods cannot give a complete picture of the soil population in its natural habitat, because the shaking of soil with water allows the distribution of the organisms in a manner not comparable with their existence in the natural soil itself An especially distorted picture is thus obtained of the actinomycetes in the soil

CONTACT SLIDE METHOD. Rossi and Cholodny proposed a method, designated as "contact slide," "soil plate," or "surface growth plate" This method consists in making a slit in the soil with a sharp knife and inserting into the slit a clean cover slide The soil is then pressed gently to bring it in contact with the slide, which is left in position for 1–3 weeks. The slide gradually becomes covered with some of the soil solution and with soil particles When the slide is removed from the soil, it is cleaned on one side with a cloth to remove the soil particles and allowed to dry in the air. The preparation is fixed by passing the slide over a flame, it is then washed gently in tap water to remove the coarse soil particles, followed by distilled water, and stained with phenol erythrosin for 30 minutes, at room temperature. The slide is finally washed, dried, and examined under the microscope.

The microscopic population observed on the contact slide may not be exactly the one that may be found in the soil at a given moment, since it results from the development of specific organisms on the slide in contact with the soil. In experiments on decomposition of organic matter in soil, Jensen found that the results obtained by the direct method agreed with those secured by the plate method, hence the two methods were believed to be able to compensate each other

In their physical relation to the soil, the microorganisms are found chiefly upon the solid soil particles, only a small number of organisms are found in the liquid phase, chiefly because of the adsorption of the organisms by the soil particles. Thus the mechanical composition of the soil, its chemical nature, especially its reaction, and the nature of the base in the adsorbing complex are all significant in determining the degree of adsorption of soil organisms

Conn found that an increase in the moisture content of the soil results in a rapid change from a natural flora of fungi and actinomycetes to one in which bacteria predominate. In a natural soil and under normal conditions of wetting and drying, filamentous organisms are active, especially in acid soils high in colloidal material With an increase in the moisture content of such a soil, due to excessive rainfall, bacteria became more active, such increased activity is even greater than that following addition of lime.

The contact slide method was found to offer great possibilities not only for the quantitative evaluation of the soil microscopic population, but also for establishing certain important qualitative changes in the population, such as those resulting from fertilization of soil or use of antiseptics. It was also suggested that this method is effective for determining the influence of important plant nutrients, notably nitrogen, phosphorus, and potassium salts, upon the numbers of microorganisms in soil The method also lends itself readily to the study of the influence of soil treatment upon the rhizosphere or the relationship between plant roots and microorganisms.

In spite of these favorable results, various investigators reported that the microscopic examination of soil, either by direct staining or by the contact slide method, is inadequate for determining the functions of microorganisms in the soil These methods were believed, therefore, to be of importance only as supplements to the plate and other culture methods.

Among the limitations of the contact slide method is the fact that bacteria produce zooglea upon the glass To overcome this, Cholodny proposed the "soil chamber" method, which consists in placing fine particles of soil upon moist slides, keeping the slides in moist chambers, and examining microscopically the organisms growing out of the soil

Direct Examination of Soil by Microscope Kubiena developed a special microscope for the direct examination of soil in an undisturbed condition. The microbiological population may thus be observed in a natural state. Special surface illumination is attached to the microscope By means of micromanipulators, some of the larger organisms, notably the fungi, can be removed from the soil for staining purposes and for closer study. This method has not been used very extensively, and only limited information, dealing primarily with the fungi, is so far available

The nature of the soil population, as determined by the direct microscopic method, has been summarized by Jones and Mollison. The soil bacteria are largely coccoid and adherent to the humic matter, few or none being attached to mineral particles They may be in the form of large zoogleal colonies or may consist of smaller clumps or single individuals. Frequently groups of large cocci resembling *Azotobacter* cells are seen. Long rods are but rarely observed in fresh soil Fungal mycelium shows variable staining. There is, in fact, strong evidence of correlation of intensity of staining with viability. Progressive loss of the protoplasm from the hyphae, due either to decomposition or to its migration to the hyphal tip, can be frequently observed most of the hyphal fragments lacking organized contents. Such hyphae are stained purple in contrast with the deep blue coloration of those filled with protoplasm. This was confirmed by inoculating sterilized soil with fungal mycelium, allowing it to incubate for several days, and making films from a sample of this soil, on these films only deeply stained fungal fragments were seen. In normal soils, mycelium is scanty, and because of its filamentous nature and very variable length is not amenable to accurate statistics, though useful comparative results may be obtained. There were significantly fewer pieces of mycelium present in the soils receiving mineral fertilizer than in those receiving farmyard manure.

Lengths of well-stained mycelium frequently have organic matter adherent to their walls, probably through secreted mucilage. This may have an important bearing on the formation of soil crumbs. Few fungal spores are seen. Fibers may be distinguished from hyphae by their lack of staining and their polarization colors under crossed nicols. Other plant tissue absorbs but little dye and, at most, has a greenish hue. Stained nematodes are sometimes seen, and what are thought to be earthworm setae can be distinguished from fragments of mycelium by their tapering apices.

Plate Culture Methods. The gelatin plate followed by the agar plate was the first method used for the enumeration of soil organisms. It still remains the one most commonly employed. The method consists in suspending a given portion of soil in a given volume of sterile tap water, and making a series of dilutions, such as 1:100, 1:1,000, to 1:10,000,000. The final dilutions of soil are prepared in such a manner as to allow 40–200 colonies to develop on each plate. One-milliliter portions of the final dilutions are placed in plates to which suitable agar media are then added, the contents of the plates are carefully mixed; the plates are then incubated at 28–30°C, and the colonies counted after varying periods of time.

The plate method is very convenient, but its chief limitation lies in the fact that it allows the development of only the heterotrophic aerobic bacteria, certain yeasts, molds, and actinomycetes. Frequently, special media are used for the enumeration of fungi, whereby bacterial development is suppressed either by acidifying the medium or by the addition of antibacterial agents. This makes possible the use of much lower dilutions of soil than those required for the enumeration of the larger numbers of bacteria.

The plate method, supplemented with other methods, has made it possible to establish that different soil types possess characteristic microbiological populations. Correlations between microbial activities and crop yields have been derived only for certain soils. Definite relations have been observed between optimum conditions for the

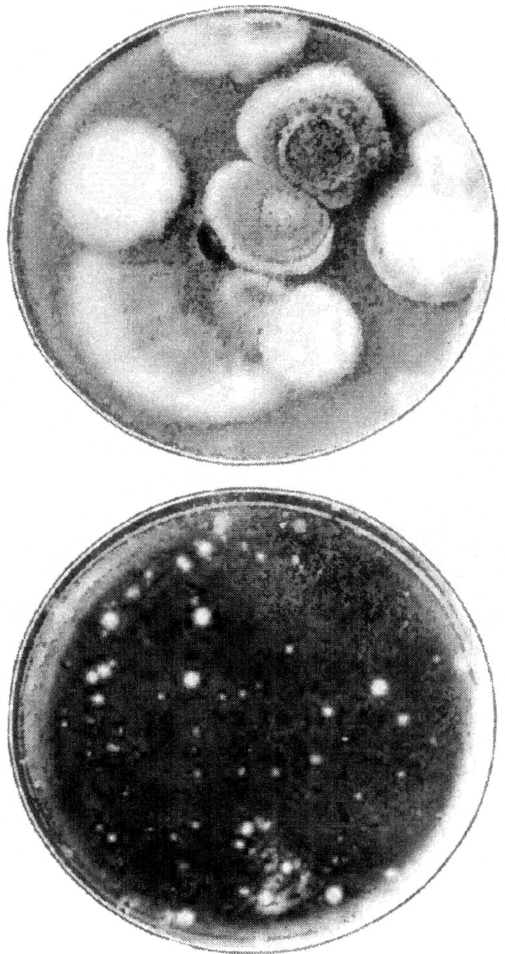

Fig. 21. Colonies of bacteria, actinomycetes (*lower plate*), and fungi (*upper plate*), developing on plates used in counting these organisms in soils (from Waksman and Starkey).

growth of higher plants and for microorganisms. The possibility of correlating the numbers and activities of certain groups of microorganisms and soil conditions, notably moisture and temperature, has also been indicated.

By use of the plate method, it was possible to demonstrate that an extensive microbiological population is found in field and garden soils, in forest soils, in peat bogs, and even in the ash of volcanoes and in desert sands.

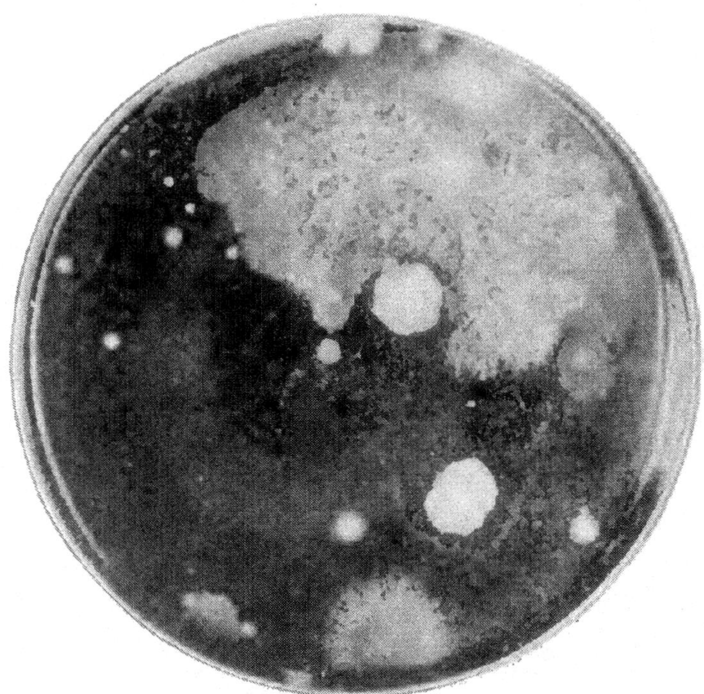

FIG. 22. Plate preparation, showing development of spreading colonies of bacteria (from Lipman).

The results obtained by the plate method, fully substantiated by other methods, emphasize the fact that the various groups of microorganisms are largely concentrated in the surface layer of the soil. This is true particularly of podzol soils, in which the surface layer corresponds to the A_1 horizon. In cultivated soils, the changes in the numbers of microorganisms with depth of soil are more gradual. Although bacteria and actinomycetes diminish with an increase in depth, the proportional reduction is far greater for the bacteria than for the actinomycetes; whereas at a depth of 1 inch the actinomycetes make up only 9.2 per cent of the organisms developing on the plate, their proportion may be increased to 65.6 per cent at a depth of 30 inches.

Among the various factors which influence the abundance of microorganisms in the soil, the most important are organic matter, reaction, moisture, temperature, aeration, and nature of crop grown. The distribution of microorganisms in the soil is, therefore, controlled by numerous ecological factors, comprising climatic or atmospheric, edaphic or soil, and biotic or living. Although no important relation has been found between the numbers and kinds of microorganisms and the climatic conditions, the edaphic and biotic factors are of great significance. The amount of organic matter in the soil influ-

Fig. 23. Colonies of fungi and bacteria, as determined by plate method (from Löhnis and Fred)

ences markedly the numbers of all groups of microorganisms, whereas the reaction governs largely the ratio of the fungi to the bacteria and actinomycetes. According to Feher, the total number of bacteria in the soil diminishes as one proceeds northward; however, the proportion of fungi to bacteria increases. This change was found to be correlated with a reduction in *p*H value and a change in temperature. There is also a decrease in numbers of bacteria with increasing altitude.

The effect of moisture is well illustrated in Table 6. With an increase in moisture from a fairly dry state to 80 per cent saturation, there is an increase in the number of bacteria; at the saturation point, there is again a decrease.

Among the other soil treatments that modify greatly the microbiological population of the soil, additions of organic matter are of greatest importance. Addition of manure favors bacteria and actinomycetes. Addition of acid fertilizer, such as ammonium sulfate, favors fungi and is detrimental to bacteria and actinomycetes; lime has the opposite effect.

TABLE 6 INFLUENCE OF MOISTURE CONTENT OF SOIL ON THE NUMBERS OF BACTERIA (from Engberding)

Numbers of bacteria in thousands per gram dry soil

Moisture Content	Percentage of Moisture-Holding Capacity	Total Bacteria	Relative Numbers
per cent			*per cent*
6 5	30	9,980	33
10 9	50	11,890	40
14 1	65	16,410	55
17 4	80	29,960	100
21 7	100	25,280	84

The numbers of microorganisms in the soil vary with the season of year, being highest in spring and fall and lowest in summer and winter The abundance of the individual constituent groups of bacteria may also vary with the season of year Hiltner and Stormer reported that actinomycetes make up 20 per cent of the microbial population developing on the plate in spring, 30 per cent in autumn, and 13 per cent in winter Conn found larger numbers of bacteria in winter, even in frozen soil, than in summer, he explained this by the existence of two types of bacteria, "winter" and "summer" Further studies suggested a simpler explanation for this observation the freezing of the soil and subsequent thawing result in the breaking up of the clumps of bacteria usually present, this gives an apparent increase in numbers, as determined by the plate method.

In addition to seasonal variations, there are also short-term variations among the microorganisms in the soil These are believed to arise from different competitive factors among the microorganisms The long-term fluctuations reflect the seasonal changes in climatic conditions, as affecting the supply of energy for microorganisms provided by plant materials. These variations offer a more logical explanation than the "inherent urge" concept suggested by some soil investigators The abundance and distribution of microorganisms in soil, as well as the composition of the population of different soil types, are influenced primarily by additions of organic matter

The bacteria of the soil are capable of adapting themselves readily to changes in temperature A definite correlation was found between the average yearly temperature of the air and soil and the optimum temperature for bacterial development, this optimum temperature is considerably higher than the soil temperature even during the warm periods of the year

Elective Culture Methods. These methods consist of diluting the soil with sterile water and adding definite volumes, such as 1-ml portions of the final dilutions, to special nutrient media adapted for the growth of specific groups of microorganisms. The highest dilution which allows positive growth permits the calculation of the

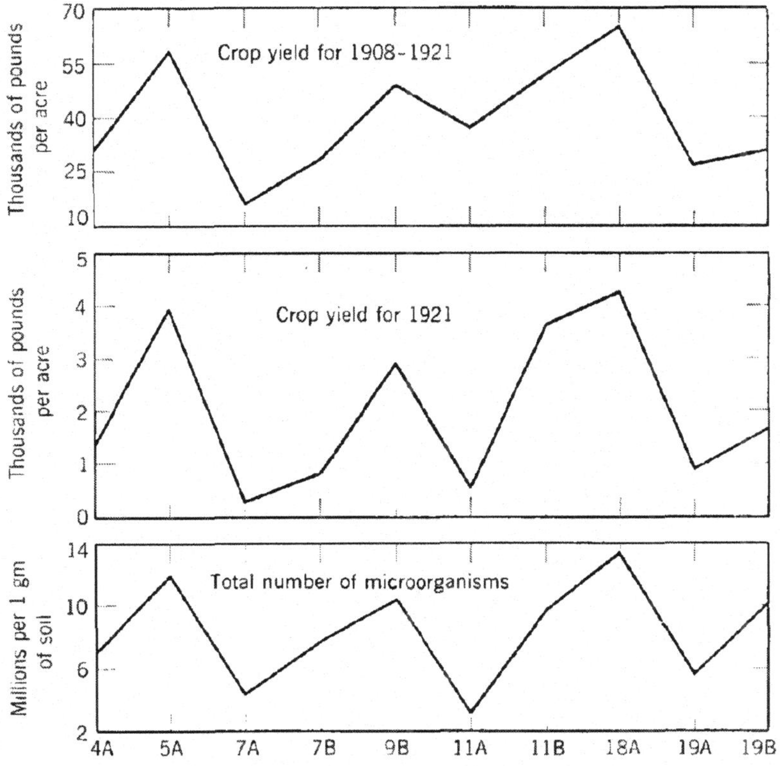

Fig. 24. Crop yields and bacterial numbers (from Waksman).

approximate number of specific organisms present in the particular soil. Thus, if a dilution of soil of 1:100,000 placed in a pectin medium allows the decomposition of the pectin, whereas a dilution of 1:200,000 does not, one may conclude that the soil contains 100,000 pectin-decomposing organisms per gram.

These methods are rather cumbersome, since they involve the preparation of a large number of media for the development of various physiological groups of organisms, and the need for a number of containers for making the various dilutions. Furthermore, the

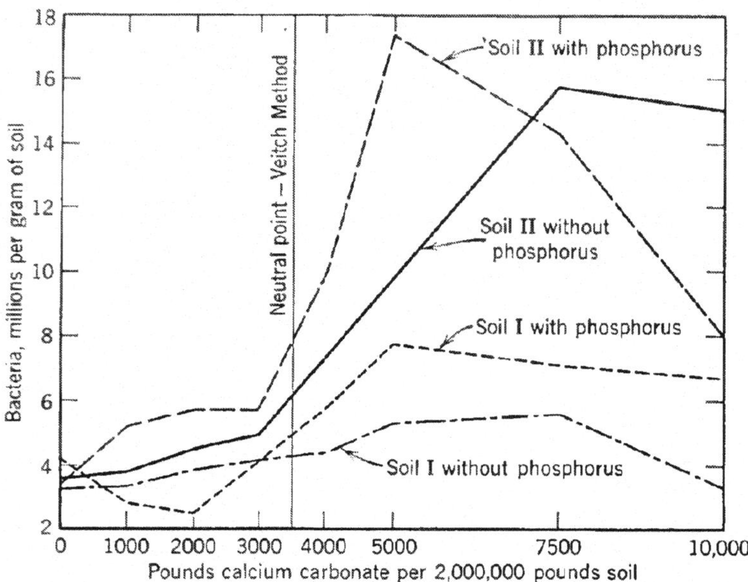

FIG. 25. Effect of $CaCO_3$ upon bacterial numbers in soil (from Bear).

results show great variability. These methods, however, may find certain applications in the solution of special problems.

TABLE 7. ABUNDANCE OF PHYSIOLOGICAL GROUPS OF BACTERIA IN SOIL

Numbers per gram soil.

Bacterial Group	After Hiltner and Störmer	After Löhnis
Peptone-decomposing	3,750,000	4,375,000
Urea-decomposing	50,000	50,000
Nitrifying	7,000	5,000
Denitrifying	50,000	50,000
Nitrogen-fixing	25	388

Table 7 shows the results obtained by two investigators. They are rather consistent and tend to throw some light upon the relative abundance of different physiological groups of bacteria in the soil.

SOIL ENRICHMENT METHODS. These methods consist in adding various organic and inorganic nutrients to portions of soil placed in beakers or tumblers. The soil is adjusted to moisture and kept in an incubator for varying periods. The chemical changes that have been brought about in the particular substance by the microorganisms in the soil are then determined The extent of change is used as a measure of the activity of the microbiological population of the soil.

These methods, whatever their value for measuring the rate of certain soil processes, do not lend themselves readily to the quantitative enumeration of soil microorganisms

Further details of the abundance of specific groups of bacteria will be found in the respective chapters.

Microorganisms in Manure and in Composts

The microbiological population of manures and composts can be studied by methods similar to those used for the study of the soil microorganisms.

By the direct microscopic method, manure was found to contain 37,600 millions of bacteria per gram, the greatest number occurring in stable manure kept in heaps, and the smallest number in the manure that was undergoing a "hot fermentation" process A definite correlation was found in the microbiological population of composted manure, whether determined by the plate or by the contact slide method

The numbers of bacteria and other microorganisms in stable manure vary greatly, depending on the composition of the manure, especially on the nature and amount of solid excreta, and on the degree of its decomposition. During the decomposition of manure, a marked change takes place in the nature and abundance of its microbial population. Fresh manure is very rich in cells of *E coli* and other enteric bacteria. During the process of composting, these soon disappear. At first, multiplication of various bacteria takes place, to be followed later by a reduction in numbers The temperature at which the decomposition of the manure is taking place exerts a marked influence upon the nature and abundance of the microbiological population, at different stages of decomposition, as shown in Table 8.

The addition of manures and other organic materials greatly increases the numbers of microorganisms in the soil There may also be a shift in the relative abundance of different groups An increase in numbers of saprophytic organisms may be accompanied by a reduction in numbers of plant-disease-producing fungi and bacteria

Table 8. Influence of Temperature upon the Microbiological Population of Manure Composts (from Waksman, Cordon, and Hulpoi)

Numbers per grain of moist compost

Temperature of Decomposition	Period of Decomposition	Bacteria and Actinomycetes	Fungi
°C	*days*	*millions*	*thousands*
28	0	1,600	200
	2	14,000	0
	8	175	
	21	85	11,000
	39	50	600
50	0	1,600	200
	2	100	
	8	2,000	
	39	6	1,000
65	0	1,600	200
	2	100	0
	8	106	0
	39	8	0
75	0	1,600	200
	8	4	0
	21	2	0

It was at first believed that the increase in bacterial numbers following the addition of manure was due to the introduction of organisms present in the manure. The value of addition of manure to the soil was even ascribed, at least partly, to its bacterial content. It was later demonstrated, however, that when manure is sterilized before its addition to the soil the effect upon the bacterial population is similar. It is the organic materials in the manure which serve, therefore, as nutrients for the bacteria and other microorganisms and which are responsible for their multiplication. Certain bacteria, however, such as the thermophilic forms, may be introduced into the soil by the manure.

The influence of organic materials in controlling the development of disease-producing bacteria and fungi in the soil is due to the fact that the antagonistic organisms favored by the manure play an important role in suppressing the growth of plant parasites, as will be shown later.

Distribution of Fungi and Other Nonbacterial Microorganisms in the Soil

Fungi are important constituent groups of the soil population They are widely distributed, certain forms being characteristic of one type of soil as a natural medium for their development, and others of other soils Fungi exist in the soil in the form of vegetative mycelium and of spores A colony of a fungus developing on the agar plate may thus represent either a spore or a piece of mycelium The latter produces a fine network around the soil particles. The mycelium is sensitive to drying of soil, as a result of which dry soil contains fewer fungi.

The mycelium of some fungi does not break up readily into fine particles, so that each of these would develop into a colony on the plate. Because of this, the plate method does not give a fair idea of the abundance or distribution of various fungi in the soil A high plate count of certain fungi may merely indicate a high sporulating capacity of these organisms. This is true particularly of species of *Aspergillus* and *Penicillium,* the mycelium of which also breaks up readily. On the other hand, the mycelium of the mucorales does not break up readily, which accounts for their relatively low numbers as determined by the plate method. Although it has been definitely demonstrated that the normal fungus population in the soil is present extensively in the mycelial state, the question is still raised. to what extent does the plate count represent the actual abundance of fungi in the soil?

Brierley found that the plate count of fungi is open to certain criticisms. (1) The slow-growing Basidiomycetes are almost all eliminated in plating the soil and are not found among the colonies developing on the plate (2) The same is true of some of the slow-growing Ascomycetes and Fungi Imperfecti. (3) Some of the Phycomycetes require special techniques for their isolation and do not develop on the plate at all. Most of the published lists of fungi found in the soil, especially when determined by the plate method, thus represent only a fraction of the total fungus population.

There is no basis for comparing the relative abundance of the bacterial and fungus flora of the soil with their potential activity in the soil, especially when it is not known whether the fungi represent mycelium or spores The presence in a given amount of soil, as measured by the plate method, of a thousand fungi may indicate a far greater degree of potential activity than the presence of a million bacteria. This is particularly true when a certain process, such as cellulose or protein decomposition, is studied. If the number of fungus colonies is a result of development of inactive spores, the significance of such a comparison may be further questioned.

Among the factors which control the abundance of fungi in the soil, the reaction occupies a prominent place. An acid medium, ad-

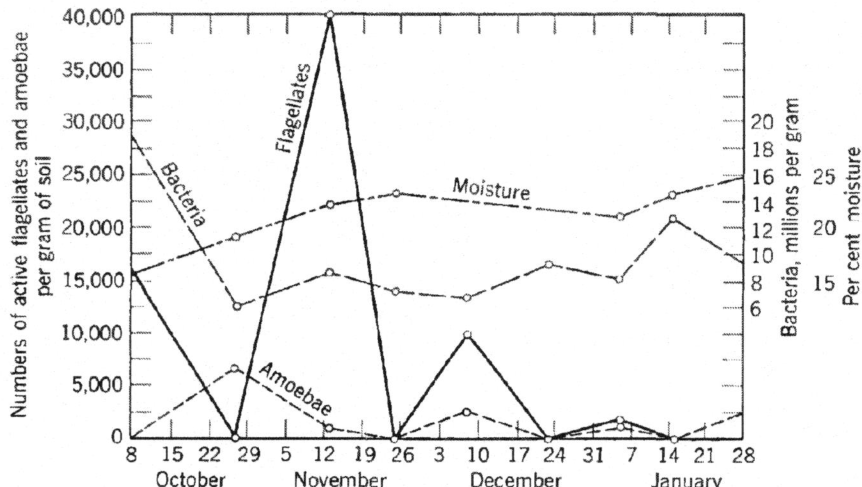

Fig. 26. Changes in numbers of bacteria and flagellates in soil (from Cutler and Crump).

justed to pH 4.0, is frequently used for determining the numbers of fungi in soil, since at that reaction most of the bacteria are eliminated. This reaction is not the optimum for the growth of fungi, which lies rather at pH 4.5–5.5. As the acidity of the soil decreases, the number of fungi decreases and the actinomycetes and bacteria increase.

Singh found a direct correlation between soil fertility and the number of fungi and actinomycetes in the permanent mangel and wheat fields at Rothamsted. The evidence concerning the periodicity of these organisms was inconclusive, the numbers being usually lower in winter. The nature of the crop did not exert a dominant effect, the actinomycetes being relatively higher in the wheat fields and the fungi in the mangel fields.

Protozoa are also abundant in the soil, their numbers and distribution being influenced greatly by the soil and environmental factors that influence the bacteria. Among the various counts reported, the following may serve as an example the flagellates ranged from 100,000 to 1,000,000 per gram, the amoebae from 50,000 to 500,000, and the ciliates from 50 to 1,000 per gram. Plots of soil treated with manure and with organic fertilizers had much larger numbers of amoebae than untreated plots, as shown in Table 9.

TABLE 9 INFLUENCE OF SOIL FERTILIZATION UPON THE NUMBERS OF AMOEBAE IN SOILS (from Singh)

Numbers per gram soil

	Amoebae	
Soil Treatment	Barnfield Soil	Broadbalk Soil
Manure	34,000	72,000
Artificial fertilizer	26,000	48,000
Untreated	8,000	17,000

The distribution of algae in the soil is controlled largely by humidity and by depth of soil. Although the subterranean numbers of algae appear to bear no relation to the abundance of carbon and nitrogen compounds in the soil, manuring was found to have a decided influence upon the development of specific types The effect of manure upon the distribution of algae in different depths of soil is illustrated in Table 10

TABLE 10 INFLUENCE OF MANURE AND SOIL DEPTH UPON THE DISTRIBUTION OF ALGAE IN SOIL (from Bristol-Roach)

Numbers per gram soil.

Depth *inches*	Unmanured	Manured
0–1	16 000	62,000
1–2	10 000	28,000
3–4	28 000	56,000
5–6	4 000	15,000

Earthworms and nematodes are also widely distributed in the soil A typical enumeration of nematodes in different soils is given in Table 11

TABLE 11 ABUNDANCE OF NEMATODES IN DIFFERENT SOILS (from Cobb and Steiner)

Numbers per acre of soil

Location and Nature of Soil	Thousands of Nematodes in Surface 6 Inches
Missouri corn field	648,000
New Jersey corn field	129,600
New Hampshire corn field	99,600
Vermont corn field	580,000
Acid forest soil in Virginia	320,000 *
Utah sugar-beet field	12,044,000 †

* Surface 3 cm

† Surface 2 feet.

Selected Bibliography

1 Brierley, W B , *The Microorganisms of the Soil,* E J Russell, Longmans, Green and Co., London, 1923.

2 Cholodny, N , Über eine neue Methode zur Untersuchung der Bodenmikroflora, *Arch Microb* , 1 620–652, 1930

3 Conn , H J , The microscopic study of bacteria and fungi in soil, *N. Y. Agr Expt. Sta. Tech. Bull* 64·1918, also 129 1927, 204 1932, *Soil Sci* , 26 257–260, 1928, *J. Bact* , 17.399–405, 1929.

4 Feher, D , *Untersuchungen uber die Mikrobiologie des Waldbodens,* J. Springer, Berlin, 1933

5 James, N., and Sutherland, M. L , The accuracy of the plating method for estimating the numbers of soil bacteria, actinomyces, and fungi in the dilution plates, *Can J Research,* C, 17 72–86, 1939

6 Jones, P. C. T , and Mollison, J E , A technique for the quantitative estimation of soil microorganisms, *J Gen Microb* , 2.54–69, 1948

7 Kubiena, W , Ein Bodenmikroskop fur Freiland- und Laboratoriumgebrauch, Internatl Soc Soil Sci , *Soil Research,* 3.91–102, 1932, *Arch Mikrob* , 3 507–542, 1932.

8 Rossi, G , Preliminary note on the microbiology of the soil and the possible existence therein of invisible germs, *Soil Sci* , 12 409–412, 1921

9 Russell, E J , and Hutchinson, H B., The effect of partial sterilization of soil on the production of plant food, *J Agr Sci* , 3.111–144, 1909, 5 152–221, 1913.

10 Russell, E J , *et al* , *The Microorganisms of the Soil,* Longmans, Green and Co , London, 1923

11 Singh, B N , Selection of bacterial food by soil flagellates and amoebae, *Ann Appl Biol* , 29 18–22, 1942, *J Gen Microb* , 3 204–210, 1949

12 Starkey, R L, Some influences of the development of higher plants upon the microorganisms in the soil VI Microscopic examination of the rhizosphere, *Soil Sci*, 45 207, 1938

13 Taylor, C. B, Short-period fluctuations in the numbers of bacterial cells in soil, *Proc Roy Soc*, B, 119.269–295, 1936

14 Thornton, H G, and Gray, P H H, The numbers of bacterial cells in field soils as estimated by the ratio method, *Proc Roy Soc*, B, 115 522–543, 1934

15 Waksman, S A, Microbiological analysis of soil as an index of soil fertility III Influence of fertilization upon numbers of microorganisms in the soil, *Soil Sci*, 14 321–346, 1922

16 Waksman, S A, *Principles of Soil Microbiology* Williams & Wilkins Co, Baltimore, 1st Ed, 1927, 2nd Ed, 1932

17 Waksman, S A, *The Actinomycetes,* Chronica Botanica Co, Waltham, Mass, 1950

18 Waksman, S A, Cordon, T C, and Hulpoi, N, Influence of temperature upon the microbiological population and decomposition processes in composts of stable manure, *Soil Sci*, 47 83–113, 1939

19 Winogradsky, S, Etudes sur la microbiologie du sol I Sur la méthode, *Ann Inst Pasteur,* 39 299–354, 1925.

· 3 ·

Occurrence of Specific Microorganisms in the Soil

The soil microbiological population has been divided by Winogradsky into two broad groups. (*a*) the *autochthonous* or native microbes, which are characteristic of the particular soil and which may be expected always to be found there; (*b*) the *zymogenic* microbes, or those which develop under the influence of specific soil treatments, as addition of organic matter, fertilization, or aeration. To these two groups, another may be added, (*c*) the *transient* microbes, comprising organisms that are introduced into the soil intentionally, as by legume inoculation, or unintentionally, as in the case of agents producing animal and plant diseases, these may die out rapidly or may survive in the soil for varying periods, especially in the presence of plant or animal hosts

Very few organisms can be identified while they are still living in the soil or in the compost It is necessary to isolate them in culture, and preferably in a purified state. For physiological studies, pure cultures of organisms are absolutely essential. Certain fungi, actinomycetes, and heterotrophic bacteria can easily be isolated and cultivated in pure culture by means of ordinary bacteriological procedures and simple media In the case of other organisms, however, isolation of pure cultures involves considerable skill, use of special techniques, and expenditure of much time This is true, for example, of the autotrophic bacteria, most of the protozoa, and certain fungi. The methods to be used in the isolation and study of different microorganisms must, therefore, be adapted to the nature and nutrition of the organisms

For identification of different microorganisms, known treatises, such as Bergey's manual, or special monographs, such as Waksman's *Actinomycetes* and Gilman's *Soil Fungi*, are used

Soil Bacteria

For the classification of soil bacteria, the Bergey system is now almost universally used. It will also be adopted here, with certain slight modifications. The following five orders are now recognized

I Simple and undifferentiated forms, not producing any threads and not branching under normal conditions of culture — Eubacteriales

II Rod-shaped, clubbed, or filamentous cells, with decided tendency to true branching — Actinomycetales

III Filamentous, largely aquatic forms, some showing false branching — Chlamydobacteriales

IV Cells enclosed in a slimy mass, forming a pseudoplasmodium-like aggregation before passing into a cyst-producing resting stage — Myxobacteriales

V Cells slender, spiral, flexuous — Spirochaetales

Another system of classification of bacteria based upon their physiological activities has frequently been employed in soil studies

A Autotrophic and facultative autotrophic bacteria, deriving their carbon primarily from the CO_2 of the atmosphere and their energy from the oxidation of inorganic substances or simple compounds of carbon

- I Bacteria using simple nitrogen compounds, ammonia and nitrite, as sources of energy
- II Bacteria using sulfur and simple inorganic sulfur compounds as sources of energy
- III Bacteria using iron (and manganese) compounds as sources of energy
- IV Bacteria using hydrogen as a source of energy
- V Bacteria using simple carbon compounds (CO, CH_4) as sources of energy

B Heterotrophic bacteria deriving their carbon and energy from organic compounds

- I Nitrogen-fixing bacteria, deriving their nitrogen from the atmosphere as gaseous atmospheric nitrogen
  - 1. Nonsymbiotic nitrogen-fixing bacteria
    - *a*. Anaerobic, butyric acid organism
    - *b*. Aerobic *Azotobacter*, *Radiobacter*, *Aerobacter*, etc.
  - 2 Symbiotic nitrogen-fixing, or root-nodule, bacteria
- II Bacteria requiring combined nitrogen
  - 1 Aerobic bacteria
    - *a* Spore-forming bacteria
    - *b* Non-spore-forming bacteria·
      - (1) Gram-positive bacteria
      - (2) Gram-negative bacteria
  - 2 Anaerobic bacteria, requiring combined nitrogen

AUTOTROPHIC BACTERIA

Autotrophic bacteria are characterized by certain physiological properties that differentiate them sharply from all the other bacteria. The principles originally laid down by Winogradsky for the growth of these bacteria still hold today with only slight modifications. The characteristic properties of these organisms can be summarized as follows:

1. Their development in nature takes place in strongly elective mineral media, which contain specific oxidizable inorganic substances.

2. Their existence is connected with the presence of such inorganic elements or simple compounds, which undergo oxidation as a result of the life activities of the organisms.

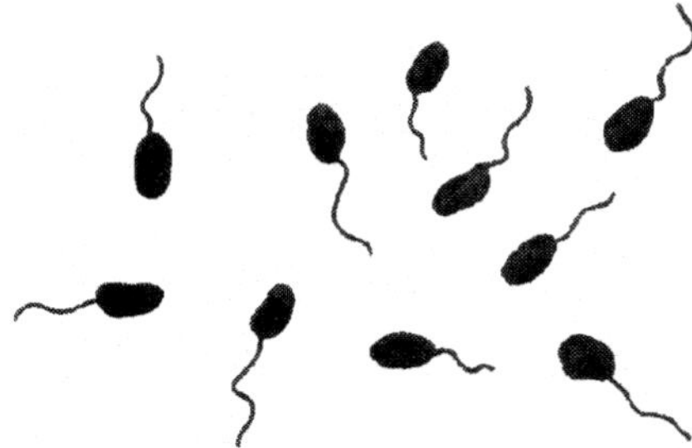

FIG. 27. Nitrite-forming bacterium, *Nitrosomonas europea* (from Winogradsky).

3. The oxidation of the inorganic substances supplies the only source of energy for the growth of these organisms.

4. They do not need any organic nutrients either for cell synthesis or as a source of energy.

5. They are almost incapable of decomposing organic substances and may even be checked in their development by certain compounds.

6. They use carbon dioxide as an exclusive source of carbon, which is assimilated chemosynthetically.

The isolation of autotrophic bacteria forms one of the most fascinating chapters not only in the history of soil microbiology but also in the history of microbiology as a whole.

NITRIFYING BACTERIA. Among the autotrophic bacteria, the nitrifying organisms have received the greatest consideration, because of the importance of the process of nitrification in the soil, in composts, in sewage-disposal systems, and in fresh and salt waters. During the last three decades of the nineteenth century, the elucidation of the process of nitrification engaged the attention of some of the most brilliant minds in the fields of agronomy, soil science, and microbiology. These studies culminated in the isolation by Winogradsky in 1891 of the organisms concerned

Various purely chemical theories were at first suggested to explain the formation of nitrates in nature. Pasteur was the first to suggest that the oxidation of ammonia to nitrate is accomplished by the agency of microorganisms. This view was confirmed in 1877 by Schloesing and Muntz. When a soil capable of transforming ammonia to nitrates was heated to 100°C or treated with antiseptics, such as chloroform, the process of nitrification was prevented. When a fresh portion of soil was added to the soil that had been heated or chloroformed, its power to transform ammonia to nitrate was restored.

Aeration was found to be essential to nitrification. Proper aeration could be obtained either by bubbling air through the medium or by placing the medium as a thin layer over the bottom of the container It was soon established that the quantity of oxygen consumed during nitrification bore a definite ratio to the amount of nitrogen nitrified. The addition of calcium carbonate or alkaline carbonates in low concentrations (0 2–0 5 per cent) had a favorable effect.

The conditions commonly utilized in saltpeter heaps were thus found to correspond to the essential factors favorable for the activities of the nitrifying organisms These are. (*a*) presence of nitrogenous compounds, (*b*) thorough aeration, (*c*) proper moisture content, (*d*) presence of bases, like calcium or magnesium carbonate Nitrate formation was noticeable at 5°, became prominent at 12°, and reached a maximum at 37°C Higher temperatures, such as 45°C, exerted an injurious effect, and at 55°C the process came to a standstill

These observations of the French investigators concerning the biological nature of the nitrification process were confirmed by Warington A dilute aqueous solution of ammonia, containing chalk and sodium-potassium tartrate, proved to be a favorable medium, addition of sugar to replace the tartrate exerted an injurious effect upon the process of nitrification Upon inoculation with soil, the ammonia was first oxidized to nitrite, and the latter to nitrate. When organic nitrogenous compounds or nitrogen-rich materials, such as urine, milk, and asparagine, were added to the medium, they could be nitrified only after they were first converted to ammonia. The process of ammonia formation was, however, sharply distinguished from that of ammonia oxidation, the latter being an essential part of the nitrification process, although the existence of two different organisms was not suspected at first.

The various reactions involved in nitrification of nitrogenous compounds were clearly elucidated toward the middle of the ninth decade of the last century. All efforts to isolate the specific organisms concerned in the process failed, however. This was chiefly due to a lack of recognition of the specific mode of nutrition of the organisms concerned in nitrification. As long as the characteristic manner of energy utilization by these organisms was not understood, no suitable methods could be developed for their isolation. Although numerous investigators asserted that certain organisms, some even pathogenic in nature, were able to produce nitrates, the observations were not fully confirmed. It is even doubtful whether the results obtained were properly interpreted, the traces of nitrate observed in these experiments may have come from the atmosphere, and the nitrite reported may have been a result of the reduction of nitrate present in the medium. Many of the investigators who approached this problem were primarily chemists or agronomists, whereas the bacteriologists were at that time so much under the influence of the gelatin plate method of Robert Koch that the fact that an organism produced no growth on this medium was sufficient to justify the conclusion that such an organism did not exist.

Winogradsky was fully prepared to undertake this study by his previous investigations of sulfur and iron bacteria, carried out in 1885–1888, which brought out the fact that these organisms were able to derive their energy from inorganic compounds. He reasoned by analogy that the nitrifying bacteria could probably use the ammonia as a source of energy. These organisms might, therefore, possess properties similar to those which have the capacity to oxidize other elements or simple inorganic substances. The principle of elective culture was used, with ammonium salts as the only available source of energy. Conditions were thereby made unfavorable for the development of all those microorganisms that are unable to oxidize ammonium salts and utilize the energy thereby liberated.

Flasks containing a salt solution free from organic carbon compounds and with an ammonium salt were inoculated with soil. Bacterial growth took place after 4–5 days' incubation at 25–30°C, sometimes a longer period was required. Manured and cultivated soils contained nitrifying organisms in greatest abundance, especially in the upper layers Warington showed that the process of nitrification consists of two stages (*a*) the oxidation of the ammonium salt to nitrite; (*b*) the oxidation of the nitrite to nitrate.

In crude cultures prepared from soil, the nitrite-forming bacteria are present together with the nitrate-formers, and, even when the development of the former reaches its maximum, the latter may still be dormant. As soon as all the ammonia has been transformed into nitrite, the nitrate-formers become active. When transfers are made from the crude cultures thus obtained into fresh media, the stage of oxidation of the ammonium salt will influence the type of organism that will be prevalent in the subsequent culture If transfers are made at an early stage of oxidation, when the ammonium ion is still present, the nitrate organism may be entirely eliminated from the culture even after only a few such consecutive transfers If, however, nitrite is substituted for the ammonium salt in the medium, which is then inoculated with soil or with a previous culture at an active stage of nitrate formation, the nitrite-forming organism may be entirely eliminated The two bacteria can thus be separated from one another when their characteristic metabolism is recognized.

The culture media in which these organisms develop show at first no turbidity or pellicle formation, because of the scarcity of growth of the corresponding organisms After repeated additions to the media of ammonium salt or of nitrite, a bluish slime is produced on the bottom and on the wall of the flask. When this slime is examined microscopically, it is found to consist of a layer of minute rods staining with difficulty After several transfers into fresh media, the culture becomes sufficiently enriched so that plates can be prepared for the isolation of pure cultures

All soils that are not very acid in reaction contain bacteria capable of oxidizing ammonium salts to nitrites and the latter to nitrates. The limiting acidity for the development of these bacteria is *p*H 4 0–3.7, whereas their optimum reaction is at *p*H 6 8–7 3 When a soil more acid in reaction than the minimum and lacking the nitrifying organisms is treated with lime, the organisms will gradually appear, although inoculation with a good fertile soil is often practicable, so as to introduce the organisms immediately This is true of acid peat soils and certain acid forest soils.

The nitrifying bacteria are not very sensitive to drying, but steam or volatile antiseptics are highly injurious, resulting in their rapid destruction in the soil.

Several types of nitrite-forming organisms are found in various soils. These bacteria were classified by Winogradsky into four groups.

1 *Nitrosomonas* Free, motile forms, present in the soil as cocci or as rods with rounded ends. Optimum reaction is at *p*H 8.6–8.8, some strains may have their optimum at *p*H 9.1–9.2, and others at *p*H 7.5–7.8, growth ceases at *p*H 6.0.

2. *Nitrosocystis* Masses of cocci surrounded by a membrane. Optimum *p*H 7.4–7.8.

3 *Nitrosospira* Spiral-shaped forms.

4. *Nitrosogloea* Zoogloea-producing organisms.

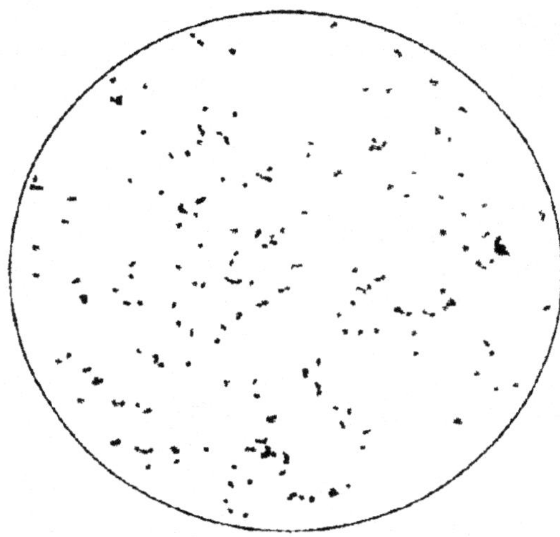

Fig 28 Nitrate-forming bacterium, *Nitrobacter* sp. (from Fred and Davenport)

Not all the various types of nitrite-forming bacteria occur in all soils, the last group is found, for example, only in uncultivated soils. They differ greatly in their activity, the *Nitrosomonas* being most active and the *Nitrosospira* least The *Nitrosocystis* is found in forest soils, including both mull and raw-humus soils.

The numbers of the nitrifying bacteria per gram of soil vary greatly, from a few cells to as many as 24,000. The dilution method is commonly used for this determination In view of the fact, however, that many cells are usually added to a liquid medium before growth can take place, since the artificial conditions of culture are not so favorable for their development as in normal soil, the actual number of living cells in the soil is far greater than indicated by this method In humid soils, the nitrifying bacteria are present in the upper few inches and rapidly disappear in the subsoil. In arid soils, they occur to a depth of many feet.

SULFUR BACTERIA. The sulfur bacteria, or those bacteria which are capable of obtaining the energy necessary for their growth from the oxidation of sulfur or its compounds, should be distinguished from other bacteria taking part in the sulfur cycle, such as those liberating hydrogen sulfide in the hydrolysis of proteins or in the reduction of sulfates.

The sulfur bacteria do not form any uniform morphological or physiological group of organisms, as do the nitrifying bacteria. Morphologically they are found among the Desmobacteriaceae and among the Bacteriaceae. Physiologically they oxidize hydrogen sulfide and other sulfides, elementary sulfur, or thiosulfate; they act either in an acid or in an alkaline reaction. Some are obligate autotrophic and some are facultative. They are widely distributed in nature, occurring in water basins, soils, and other natural substrates. Those sulfur bacteria that are found in normal, fertile soils, or that become active in such soils when introduced, are limited chiefly to the genus *Thiobacillus.*

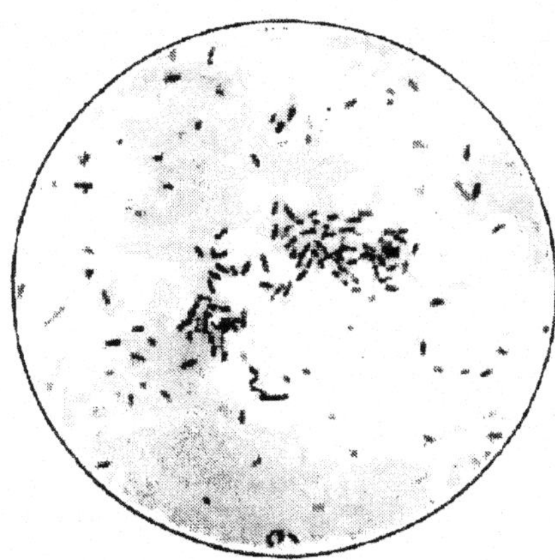

FIG. 29. Sulfur-oxidizing bacterium, *Thiobacillus thiooxidans* (from Waksman and Joffe).

At least eleven species of *Thiobacillus* are found in the literature, and twelve others have been described but not named. There is considerable overlapping among the various forms, many of them having been only incompletely described. Some, like *Th. thiooxidans,* also oxidize sulfur and are obligate autotrophic. The thiosulfate-oxidizing bacteria have been separated into the strictly autotrophic (*Th. thioparus*), facultative autotrophic (*Th. novellus*), and heterotrophic (*Pseudomonas fluorescens*) forms: the first two groups increase the acidity of the medium, and the third group decreases its acidity.

When sulfur is mixed with soil, it is oxidized slowly at first and then, as the soil becomes acid, more rapidly. If powdered rock phosphate is added to the mixture of soil and sulfur, the insoluble phosphate is transformed into soluble forms by the acid produced from the sulfur A direct correlation has been found between the acid formed and the amount of phosphate going into solution. When a fresh mixture is inoculated with some material from an old compost, the reaction goes on more rapidly, indicating the biological nature of the process

By inoculating, with some of the above compost, a medium containing sulfur as the only source of energy, certain mineral salts, and tricalcium phosphate as a neutralizing agent, the culture of a bacterium capable of oxidizing sulfur to sulfuric acid is obtained The acid produced interacts with the tricalcium phosphate and transforms it into calcium sulfate and monocalcium phosphate and finally into phosphoric acid

By use of very acid media, with an initial reaction of *p*H 2 0 and a high dilution of the crude culture (1 100,000), a pure culture of an organism was obtained from such composts. This culture gave no growth when inoculated into broth or other media favorable for the growth of bacteria and fungi Microscopic examinations further established the purity of the organism described as *Th thiooxidans* It is a small, nonmotile rod, 0 75–1 0 by 0.5–0.75 μ; it produces cloudiness throughout the medium but does not form any pellicle.

The organism is strictly aerobic, the particles of sulfur in the culture being surrounded by the bacterial cells The medium becomes very acid In the presence of calcium phosphate or carbonate, the sulfuric acid produced in the medium interacts with the calcium to give crystals of $CaSO_4$ $2H_2O$, which hang down from the particles of sulfur floating on the surface of the medium; gradually they fill the flask with gypsum crystals

The organism forms no spores and is destroyed at 55–60°C in several minutes The limiting reactions are *p*H 6 0 and 1 0. It is possible, however, to accustom the organism to a neutral and even an alkaline reaction, when transferred from one soil to another before the reaction becomes too acid.

Most of the other sulfur bacteria, especially the filamentous forms (*Beggiatoa, Thiothrix*), occur largely in water basins

Van Niel has shown that the metabolism of purple and green sulfur bacteria (Thiorhodaceae) is a truly photosynthetic process of the general reaction:

$$CO_2 + 2H_2A = CH_2O + H_2O + 2A$$

The green bacteria dehydrogenate the H_2S only to S, whereas the purple bacteria oxidize H_2S, S, sulfite, and thiosulfate to sulfate. In the absence of oxidizable sulfur compounds, the purple bacteria can develop in the presence of organic compounds under anaerobic conditions, but only in the presence of radiant energy.

OTHER AUTOTROPHIC BACTERIA. Among the other autotrophic bacteria should be mentioned those that oxidize hydrogen, carbon monoxide, and ferrous iron; not all of these bacteria are strictly soil inhabitants, although certain conditions make some of them abundant in the soil.

HETEROTROPHIC BACTERIA

Heterotrophic bacteria comprise the great majority of soil organisms. They depend on organic materials for their energy sources, and are primarily concerned with the decomposition of cellulose and hemicelluloses, starches and sugars, proteins and other nitrogenous materials, fats and waxes. These bacteria vary greatly in structure and physiology, in abundance, and in importance. Some are aerobic; others are anaerobic. Some are spore-forming; others are non-spore-forming. Some are Gram-positive; others are Gram-negative. Some are able to fix atmospheric nitrogen; others depend upon fixed forms of organic or inorganic nitrogen.

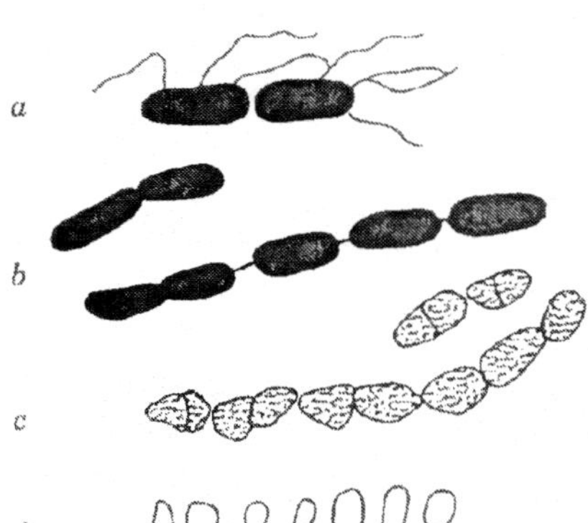

FIG. 30. Heterotrophic, spore-forming bacterium, *Bacillus megatherium*: *a*, young cells showing flagella; *b*, young cells showing connections into chains of rods; *c*, older cells; *d*, variations in size and shape of spores (from Conn).

SPORE-FORMING BACTERIA. The soil harbors a large number of spore-forming bacteria. The three most common forms can be readily recognized by the gelatin plate method. *Bacillus mycoides* is a rapidly liquefying form; it produces large filamentous to rhizoid colonies. *Bacillus cereus* liquefies gelatin almost as rapidly and usually forms round colonies with entire edges; the surface membrane contains granules that tend to be arranged concentrically. *Bacillus megatherium* liquefies gelatin more slowly; its colonies are seldom more than 1 cm in diameter and are characterized by a flocculent center composed of white opaque granules, surrounded by a zone of clear liquefied gelatin; the smaller colonies have no surrounding zone and are recognized only by their granular structure The occurrence of different spore-forming bacteria in the soil is illustrated in Table 12

TABLE 12. OCCURRENCE OF SPORE-FORMING BACTERIA IN DIFFERENT SOILS (from Ford *et al*)

Organism	Presence in Number of Soil Samples	
	Baltimore Soil	Nazareth Soil
B petasites	73	116
B cereus	134	41
B megatherium	29	13
B subtilis	24	9
B mesentericus	9	11
B vulgatus	12	6
B mycoides	15	2
B mesentericus var *flavus*		9
B cereus var *fluorescens*	3	
B fusiformis	3	2
B brevis		3
B simplex	1	
B cohaerens	1	2
B agri	2	
Total isolations	306	214

NON-SPORE-FORMING BACTERIA The aerobic, heterotrophic, non-spore-forming bacteria usually produce punctiform colonies on agar and gelatin, they are chromogenic or nonchromogenic, motile or non-motile; some liquefy gelatin rapidly, whereas others do it only slowly or not at all The most important representative of the group of rapid-liquefying organisms is *Pseudomonas fluorescens*. The whole group is often spoken of as the *fluorescens* group, although many of the organisms never produce any fluorescence

Conn divided these organisms into five groups on the basis of their growth upon synthetic media

1 Organisms forming small short rods, usually less than 0 5 μ in diameter, nonmotile or having one or possibly two polar flagella; no tendency to change in morphology but very variable in physiology, such as liquefaction of gelatin and gas formation from nitrate *Bacterium parvulum* belongs to this group

2 Organisms that appear, for a day or two after inoculation on a new medium, as small short rods, less than 0 5 μ in diameter, then

shorten and begin to look like micrococci. All liquefy gelatin slowly. *Bacterium globiforme* can be considered a representative of this group, it is most abundant in the soil, its presence was believed to be a good index of the availability of the soil nitrogen

3. Small short rods, with a tendency to produce long filaments, usually unbranched, but frequently branched.

4 Organisms consisting mostly of branching forms, especially in young cultures; they are apparently produced by the germination of small spherical arthrospores The branching types disappear in a few days, leaving the coccoid forms.

5 Organisms occurring normally as cocci, but with a tendency to produce rods and filaments after a few days of growth on ordinary media This group is more abundant in manure than in soil

Topping suggested classification of the non-spore-forming, non-acid-fast, rod-shaped soil bacteria into four groups

1 Gram-positive, motile bacteria, capable of producing branching variants.

2*a*. Gram-positive, nonmotile, rod-shaped bacteria.

2*b* Gram-positive, nonmotile, mycelium-shaped bacteria

3 Gram-negative bacteria (motile and nonmotile)

Some of the forms included under 2*b* are identical with *Nocardia corallinus*, which Jensen placed between *Corynebacterium* and *Nocardia* The forms included in 2*a* are related to the *Nocardia* but are classified with *C liquefaciens*

Thermophilic Bacteria. Miquel was the first to isolate, in 1879, bacteria capable of developing at 72°C. These organisms were found in river mud, sewage, animal excreta, dust, and soil. It was soon established that various bacteria capable of growing at 50–70°C, but not at room temperature, are found in the soil. Organisms capable of growing at temperatures up to 79 5°C were also found in stable manure The self-heating and burning of hay, cotton, peat, and manure are caused by bacteria which Schloesing designated in 1892 as "thermogenic bacteria." Some of these organisms may be rather thermotolerant than strictly thermophilic Their distribution depends on the nature of the soil the sands of the Sahara Desert contain such organisms, but forest soils do not The nature and amount of manure and fertilizer applied to the soil have a marked effect: heavily manured garden soils may contain 1–10 per cent thermophilic forms, as measured by the plate method, field soils contain only 0 25 per cent or less of these bacteria, uncultivated soils may be entirely free from them.

In addition to the bacteria, other groups of microorganisms also contain thermophilic forms. This is indicated by such names as *Thermomyces, Thermoactinomyces,* and *Actinomyces thermophilus*

Myxobacteria Myxobacteria occur abundantly in manure and in soil The total number of these organisms depends upon the nature of the soil Some are found only in alkaline, neutral, or faintly acid (*p*H 8.0–6.0) soils, others in very acid soils (*p*H 3.7–5.9), and still others are independent of the reaction. Moist soils are more favorable for their development than dry soils, cultivation of soil has also a favorable effect. Peat bogs and moist forest soils contain a specific flora of myxobacteria

To demonstrate their presence, balls of rabbit manure, previously moistened with water and sterilized, are placed on the surface of the soil. As many as 7–10 species may thus be obtained from a single soil sample Certain myxobacteria can be isolated by the use of living fungus mycelium, such as *Verticillium,* growing in a dish the bacteria cause the destruction of the mycelium

Some of the myxobacteria play an important role in the decomposition of vegetable residues in soil, notably the cellulose. It has even been suggested that the very active cellulose-decomposing group *Cytophaga* represents a group of myxobacteria (*Myxococcus*)

Denitrifying Bacteria. A large number of microorganisms are able to reduce nitrates to nitrites or to ammonia. Only specific bacteria, however, can reduce, under certain conditions, the nitrate to elementary nitrogen and to oxides of nitrogen, which can thus escape into the atmosphere Under anaerobic conditions, the nitrate may serve as a source of oxygen for these bacteria, with organic carbon compounds as sources of energy This process is usually referred to as complete denitrification, and the bacteria are spoken of as denitrifying bacteria

Various denitrifying bacteria have been isolated from horse manure, cattle excreta, and soil Van Iterson demonstrated the presence in soil of organisms designated as *B stutzeri, B denitrofluorescens,* and *B vulpinus* The same soil which favors nitrification under aerobic conditions will favor denitrification in absence of free oxygen

Several organisms reducing nitrates are capable of obtaining their energy from inorganic compounds *Thiobacillus denitrificans,* an organism widely distributed in the soil, oxidizes sulfur and reduces nitrate to nitrogen gas Thiosulfate can be oxidized under anaerobic conditions only in the presence of nitrate as a source of oxygen The energy obtained by oxidation of hydrogen gas has been utilized for reduction of nitrates by *Hydrogenomonas agilis.*

Decomposition of cellulose in the soil may be due to the symbiotic action of two bacteria, one reducing nitrate to atmospheric nitrogen and the other decomposing cellulose; the products of the cellulose-decomposing bacteria are used by the other organism as sources of energy, thus enabling it to reduce the nitrate, whereas the oxygen thus liberated makes it possible for the cellulose-decomposing organism to live under anaerobic conditions.

FIG. 31. Sulfate-reducing bacterium, *Spirillum desulfuricans* (from Beijerinck and Omeliansky).

SULFATE-REDUCING BACTERIA. Several organisms capable of reducing sulfate to hydrogen sulfide have been described. *Vibrio desulfuricans* was isolated from soil and other substrates. It is a strictly anaerobic, Gram-negative form, growing at 30–55°C, and able to use salts of organic acids as sources of energy. The cultures grown at the lower temperature (30°) consist of small vibrios or spirals, motile by means of one or two polar flagella, and asporogenous; at higher temperature (55°C), the cells are largely vibrios, containing granules. Starkey found that they form spores and suggested that the name be changed to *Sporovibrio desulfuricans.*

UREA-DECOMPOSING BACTERIA. Pasteur was the first to recognize, in 1860, that ammonia formation from urea is brought about by a living organism, which he designated as *Torula ammoniacale.* It was later established that organisms capable of decomposing urea are found in most families of bacteria, actinomycetes, and fungi, but that only certain specific bacteria, whose metabolism is closely connected with the transformation of this substance, are termed "urea bacteria." These are divided into cocci and bacilli; the former are usually destroyed at 60–70°, whereas the latter, because of their ability to form endospores, can withstand heating at 90–95° for several hours. The optimum temperature is about 30°C. These organisms usually thrive best in media containing urea (2 per cent), particularly when made alkaline with ammonium carbonate. The accumulation of ammonia from the hydrolysis of the urea in the culture is so great as to kill, in many instances, the organisms themselves. Rapid urea decomposition does not necessarily accompany rapid growth The urea bacteria differ in their oxygen tension: most of them are aerobic, although the amount of oxygen required may be rather small.

The urea bacteria have a *p*H limit of 6.6 for *Urobacillus duclauxii*, 7.0 for *Ur. maddoxii*, and 8.1 for *Ur. pasteurii* The favorable effect of acid peat in preventing losses of ammonia from manure is believed to be due to the checking of the growth of the urea bacteria.

ANAEROBIC BACTERIA By selective culture methods, Duggeli found the following numbers of anaerobic bacteria per gram of soil. 1,000–1,000,000 butyric acid, 0–1,000 cellulose-decomposing, 100–1,000,000 nitrogen-fixing, 100–1,000,000 protein-decomposing, and 100–1,000,000 pectin-decomposing forms By the deep tube method, only between 19,000 and 900,000 anaerobic bacteria were found per gram of soil. No single solid medium can be devised which would be favorable for the development of all anaerobic bacteria.

These bacteria take an active part in the composting of manure in the heap, whenever there is an insufficiency of aeration The phenomenon of "putrefaction" is chiefly a result of the decomposition of proteins under anaerobic conditions, due to incomplete oxidation resulting from insufficient aeration. The absence of air in the deeper layers of the manure pile, the slightly alkaline reaction, and the presence of large amounts of undecomposed organic substances make conditions favorable for the development of anaerobic bacteria. Various anaerobic urea bacteria and thermophilic organisms also find conditions in the composting manure heap favorable for their development

Well-rotted horse manure contains spore-forming, anaerobic, thermophilic bacteria, the limiting temperature for their growth being 60–65°C and the thermal death point 110–120°C. Some of these organisms are actively proteolytic. A number of anaerobic spore-bearing bacteria are no doubt brought into the soil in great abundance with the feces; certain types have been found in intestinal excreta.

The role of anaerobic sulfate-reducing bacteria in bringing about iron corrosion appears to be very important Localized anaerobiosis is believed to exist in the vicinity of buried pipes; in the presence of sulfate and a certain amount of organic matter, the bacteria are able to bring about the formation of hydrogen sulfide, which will precipitate the iron dissolved from the pipe to give iron sulfide

Various anaerobic pathogenic bacteria are able to survive in the soil *Clostridium welchii* was demonstrated in 100 per cent of all soils examined, *Cl. putrificus verucausus* in 71 per cent, *Cl. putrificus tenuis* in 21 per cent, *Cl. amylobacter* in 65 per cent, *Cl. tetanomorphum* in 14 per cent, and *Cl. tetani* in 11 per cent of the soils.

CELLULOSE-DECOMPOSING BACTERIA. Cellulose decomposition in nature is carried out by numerous groups of microorganisms. Among

FIG. 32. Anaerobic, cellulose-decomposing bacterium, *Bacillus cellulosae dissolvens* (from Khouvine).

these, bacteria occupy a prominent place. The anaerobic bacteria were at first believed to be the most important agents in the decomposition of cellulose. It was later found, however, that aerobic bacteria and various fungi are far more important than the anaerobic bacteria. In peat bogs, however, and in the digestive tracts of animals, the anaerobic bacteria are most active. In addition to these, certain special groups of bacteria are often recognized, such as the thermophilic forms, actively concerned with the decomposition of cellulose in manure, and the denitrifying forms which decompose cellulose only in the presence of nitrates.

Omeliansky found that the gases liberated in the decomposition of cellulose by anaerobic bacteria contained either hydrogen or methane. On further study, he observed that these two gases seemed to be produced by two different organisms: when the inoculum was added without preliminary heating, methane was formed; when the inoculum was heated for 15 minutes at 75°C, conditions favored the development of bacteria which formed hydrogen. The spore of the methane organism germinated earlier than that of the hydrogen form. When the culture was transferred, the former organism predominated and the latter could finally be eliminated. By heating the inoculum of a young culture, the vegetative cells produced from the spores of the methane form, which had already germinated, were killed, whereas the ungerminated spores of the hydrogen form survived and proceeded to develop. By heating the culture several times, at an early stage of development, the hydrogen-producing type could be obtained free from the methane-producing form.

Kellerman and associates could not confirm the results of Omeliansky. They isolated from Omeliansky's cultures an aerobic cellulose-decomposing organism and suggested that the cellulose was decomposed by aerobic bacteria, the anaerobic organisms accompanying the aerobic bacteria were able to form gas from the products of cellulose decomposition. This interpretation has not been universally accepted, however.

Khouvine isolated from the intestine of man an obligate anaerobic organism, *B. cellulosae dissolvens,* capable of decomposing cellulose vigorously, especially in mixed culture. The vegetative cells were 2.5–12.5 μ long and produced no flagella, the spores were 2.5 by 2 μ. The organism was cultivated upon a medium containing fecal matter as a source of nitrogen. The spores were killed only on boiling for 45–50 minutes. Cellulose was decomposed at a range of 38–51°C.

Werner isolated from the intestinal tract of the larvae of *Protosea cuprea* an anaerobic organism, *B. cellulosam fermentans,* capable of attacking cellulose but no other carbohydrates. The anaerobic nature of the cellulose-decomposing bacteria in the digestive tract of horses, cattle, termites, and insect larvae was fully confirmed. Under anaerobic conditions, cellulose decomposition is carried out entirely by bacteria. The mechanism of cellulose decomposition, especially in relation to the nutrition of herbivorous animals, has been studied in detail by Woodman. Methane was produced by unheated cultures and was probably due to accompanying forms. The thermophilic organisms occupy an important place among the anaerobic bacteria.

Probably no other group of bacteria has been so much confused as the aerobic cellulose-decomposing organisms. Many names have been proposed for different members of this group, one organism receiving a number of names from different investigators. In 1918, Hutchinson and Clayton reported the isolation from the soil of an organism which develops first as a sinuous filamentous cell (3–10 μ by 0.3–0.4 μ) and which goes through several phases in its life cycle, terminating in the production of a spherical body or sporoid. This body differed in a number of respects from the true spores of bacteria. Germination of the sporoid gave rise to a filamentous form which possessed perfect flexibility and was feebly motile, although no flagella were observed. This organism was named *Spirochaeta cytophaga*.

Fig. 33. Aerobic, cellulose-decomposing bacterium, *Cytophaga lutea* (from Winogradsky).

A detailed systematic study of various aerobic cellulose-decomposing bacteria found in the soil has been made by Winogradsky, who divided these organisms into three genera:

1. *Cytophaga:* slender, flexible filaments, 3–8 μ long, and pointed at each end; only cellulose can be used as a source of energy; the cellulose is changed into a colloidal gel, colored yellow, orange, rose, red. Four species of this organism were described, including *Cyt. hutchinsoni,* the organism previously described by Hutchinson and Clayton.

2. *Cellvibrio:* slender, bent rods with rounded ends, 2–5 μ long; actively motile, with one flagellum; cellulose decomposition is not invariably specific; cream- to ocher-colored pigment, readily diffusing; very abundant, although only two species were described.

3. *Cellfalcicula:* spindle- or sickle-shaped cells, not exceeding 2 μ in length, with pointed ends; motile, with one flagellum; paper stained

green and cream-colored, never distinctly yellow, red, or orange, as the first two genera are, three species were described.

According to Krzemieniewska, *Cyt. hutchinsoni* is a totally different species from *Sp. cytophaga*, since the former does not form microcysts and the latter does. *Spirochaeta cytophaga* is believed to be quite distinct from other species of *Cytophaga* in its life cycle, which resembles more closely that of the *Myxococcus* of the myxobacteria. The name *Cyt. myxococcoides* was suggested for this organism. Germination of the microcysts and their transformation into rods are influenced by the reaction of the medium, temperature, and oxygen tension. Similar results concerning the life cycle of this organism were obtained by Issatchenko, who suggested, however, that the name given by Winogradsky be reserved for the organism. Another organism belonging to this group was described by Rippel under the name *Itersonia ferruginea*. Under certain conditions, the cellulose bacteria are adapted to a specific mode of nutrition, as shown for the organisms found in rice fields or iron-rich soils; these bacteria require a certain amount of iron to make their optimum growth. Their optimum *p*H is 8.0; growth ceases at *p*H 4.5 even in presence of sufficient iron.

Other Bacteria. Many other groups of bacteria are found abundantly in the soil. Among these are mycobacteria, corynebacteria, various anaerobic bacteria in addition to those listed above, and a host of other bacteria characterized by specific physiological or morphological properties. Some of them are adapted to a special mode of nutrition and may possess various biochemical properties which render them of great economic importance. These include the nitrogen-fixing bacteria, which are treated in detail elsewhere (p. 191), antibiotic-producing bacteria, like *B. subtilis*, *B. brevis*, and *B. polymyxa*, bacteria capable of decomposing the capsular material of the pneumococcus and of oxidizing *p*-aminobenzoic acid and anthranilic acid, and various coliform bacteria.

Actinomycetes

Actinomycetes form, taxonomically, a link between the bacteria, through the genera *Mycobacterium* and *Corynebacterium*, and the true fungi. They are characterized by the formation of a unicellular mycelium, composed of hyphae, which show true branching, similar to that of fungi. The hyphae are rather long and are usually

0.5–0.8 μ in diameter. The mycelium develops either in the substrate or on the surface of the substrate as aerial growth. The mycelium breaks up into short fragments, which may look like bacterial rods and resemble true bacteria in their protoplasmic properties. When examined directly under the microscope, the aerial mycelium is found to consist of very fine, characteristic, long or short branching hyphae, with distinct spore-bearing hyphae.

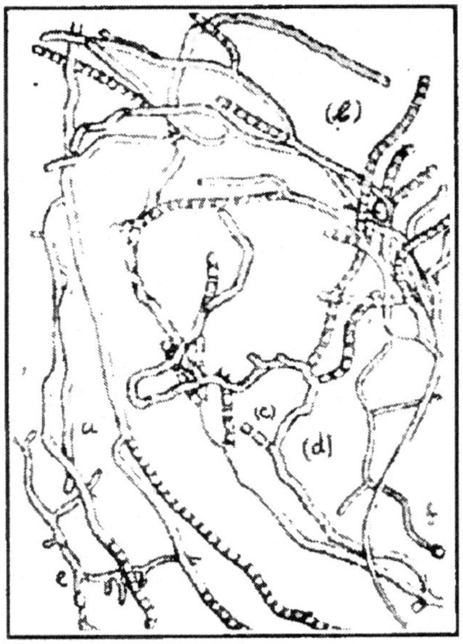

Fig. 34. *Streptomyces griseus*, with a short mycelium and abundant branching: *a, b, c,* portions of aerial mycelium; *d, f,* spores germinating with one and two germ tubes, respectively (from Drechsler).

The reproductive conidia, which are characteristic of the genus *Streptomyces*, are produced by a simultaneous division of the protoplasm in the sporogenous hyphae, progressing from the tip toward the base. The spores possess a somewhat greater power of resistance to environmental factors than the vegetative hyphae. They resemble bacteria in size, shape, and staining properties, are 0.5–1.5 μ in diameter, 1–2 μ long, oval to rod-shaped.

All actinomycetes, particularly in young preparations, are Gram-positive. In stationary liquid media, they never cause turbidity, but grow either on the surface of the medium or in the form of flakes or small colonies throughout the medium; they may sink to the bottom of the container or adhere to the glass. The surface colonies may grow together to form a smooth or wrinkled surface membrane. The colonies on solid media are usually tough, leathery, smooth or wrinkled, often growing high above the surface of the medium, and are broken up only when appreciable effort is applied. When transferred to suitable media, the spores germinate readily. The older the mycelium, the more reduced is the germinating power of the individual fragments. In shaken cultures, they grow in the form of "clumps" or "colonies" throughout the medium. This mass of growth can easily be removed by filtration, leaving a clear fluid.

The aerial mycelium may be white, gray, lavender, red, yellow, brown, green, or of some other type of pigmentation. The aerial hyphae may be short, giving the growth a chalky appearance, or long, forming a thick mat over the surface of the vegetative growth; or

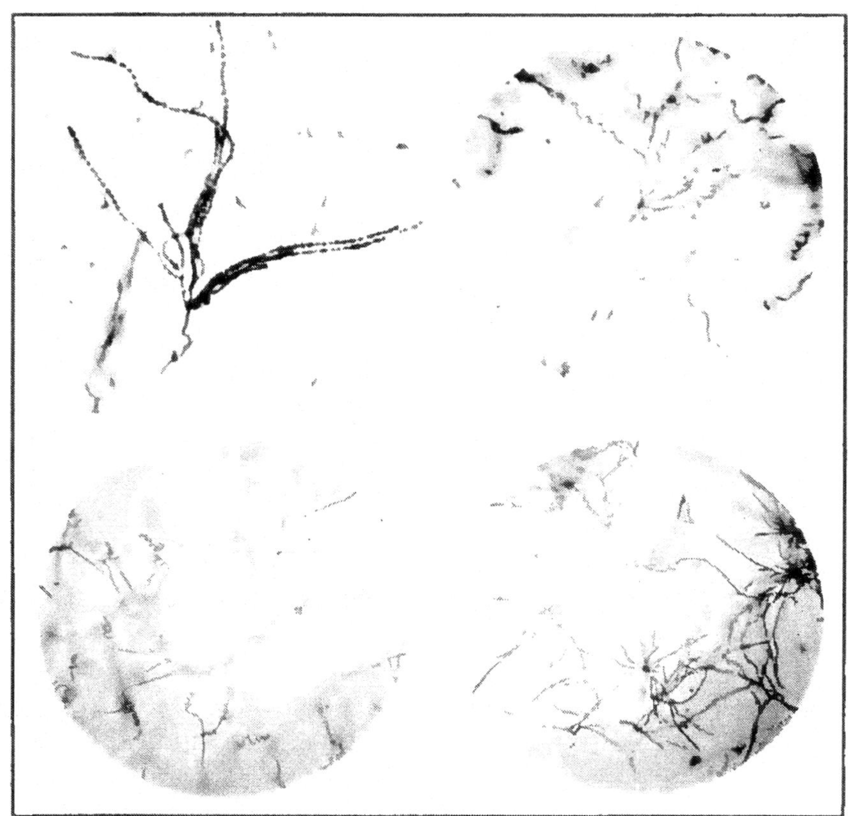

Fig. 35. Soil actinomycetes showing different types of sporulation.

they may form a fine network. The colonies are often brilliantly colored. Some cultures produce soluble pigments which vary in color and intensity in accordance with the effect of the composition of the medium. Most species are characterized by the production of a peculiar sharp odor, characteristic of the soil (earthy odor). All species of *Streptomyces* liquefy gelatin; the rapidity of liquefaction depends upon the nature of the organism and previous cultivation. Most of the actinomycetes produce active diastatic enzymes; fewer produce invertase; still fewer produce tyrosinase, which enables

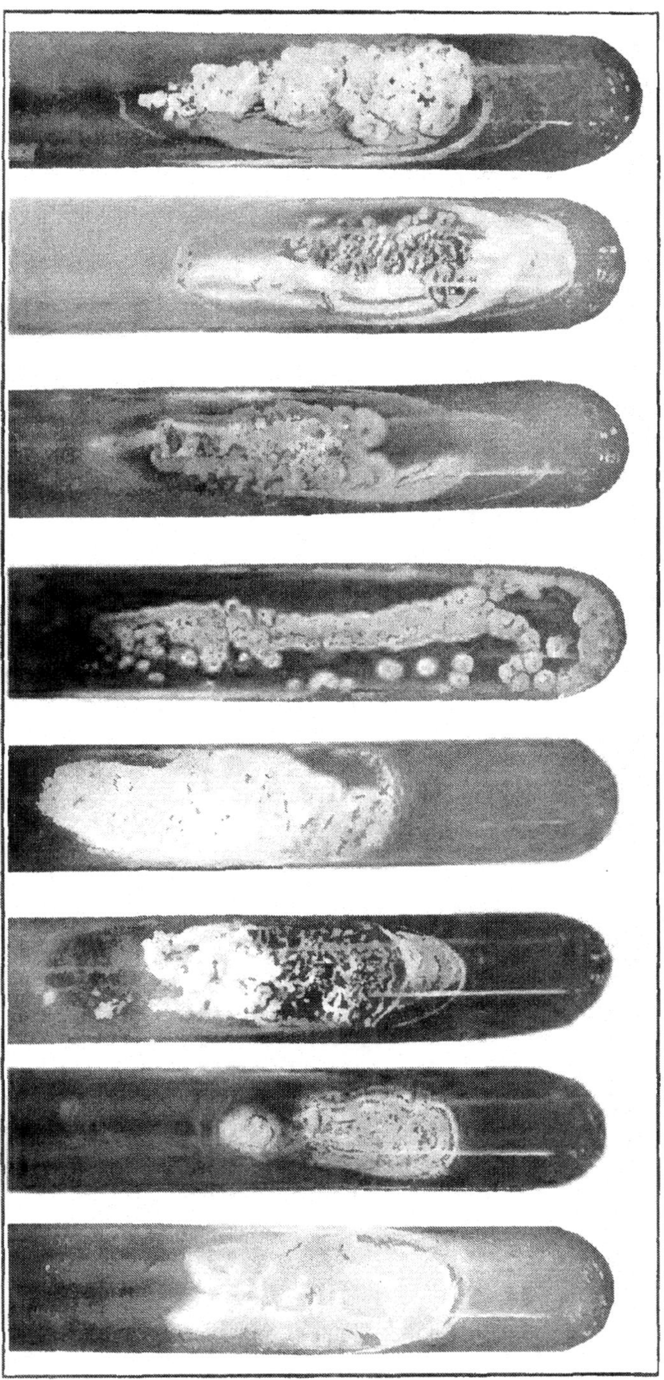

Fig. 36. Soil actinomycetes growing on agar slants.

them to convert the tyrosin of the protein molecule into dark-colored melanins.

The numerous species differ primarily in the length of their vegetative mycelium, nature of their aerial mycelium, absence or presence of spores, method of spore formation, shape and color of colony, pigmentation of colony and formation of soluble pigment, oxygen requirement, production of diastatic and proteolytic enzymes, and

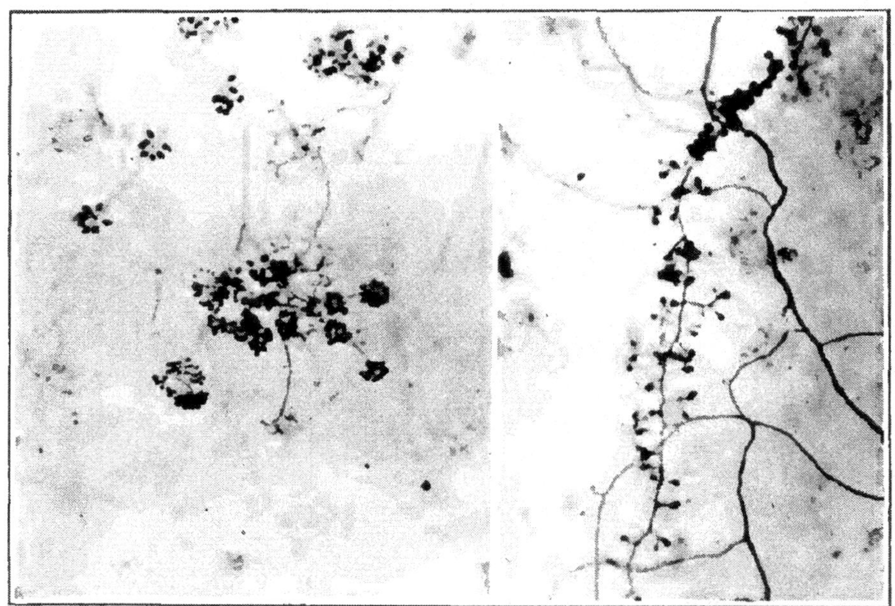

FIG. 37. Growth of two typical strains of *Micromonospora.*

a number of other morphological and physiological characters. These vary in quantity as well as in quality, not only under the influence of environmental conditions but even on continued cultivation under the same conditions. The characteristic pigments produced by many species may be lost or changed in kind; the color of the aerial mycelium may be modified, and even the very property of forming such mycelium may be lost.

The ability of actinomycetes to produce antibiotics has recently attracted considerable attention. Nearly seventy-five compounds or preparations have now been obtained. They vary greatly in chemical composition, toxicity to animals and to plants, *in vivo* activity, and chemotherapeutic potentialities. Some, like streptomycin, chloramphenicol, aureomycin, terramycin, and neomycin, have found extensive application in human and in animal therapy. Their function in soil processes is still unknown.

According to the system of classifying actinomycetes proposed by Waksman and Henrici and adopted in Bergey's manual, four genera are now recognized: *Actinomyces*, *Nocardia*, *Streptomyces*, and

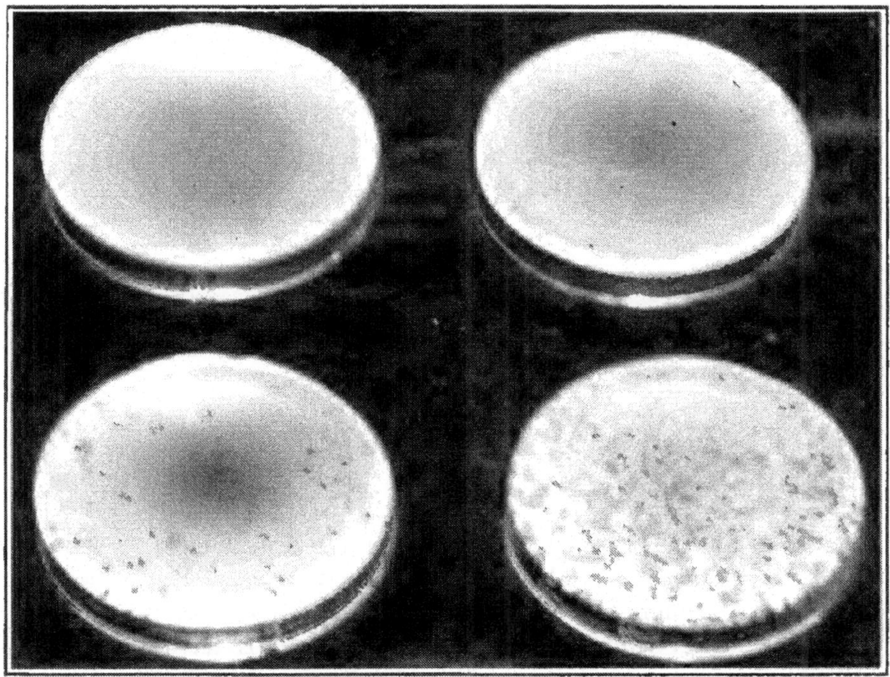

FIG. 38. Effect of actinophage upon *Streptomyces griseus* (from Reilly, Harris, and Waksman).

Micromonospora. The first genus includes the animal pathogens; the second comprises both parasites and saprophytes; the third embraces most of the soil forms, including the plant-pathogenic scab producer; and the fourth is the most abundant in lake bottoms and in high-temperature composts.

SOIL FUNGI

Although fungi are not represented in the soil by so many physiological groups as are the bacteria, many thousands of species find in the soil a temporary or permanent habitat. Of the various genera of fungi found in the soil, the most common, both in the number of species and in the frequency of occurrence, are *Zygorhynchus*, *Mucor*, *Rhizopus*, *Penicillium*, *Aspergillus*, *Trichoderma*, *Fusarium*, and *Cladosporium*. The wide distribution of different genera of fungi in the soil is demonstrated in Table 13. Brierley tabulated sys-

Table 13. Isolation of Common Genera of Soil Fungi by Different Investigators (from Waksman)

Genus	Koning	Dale	Jensen	Goddard	McLean and Wilson	Waksman
Acrostalagmus	*		*	*		*
Alternaria	*	*	*		*	*
Aspergillus	*	*	*	*	*	*
Cephalosporium	*					*
Cladosporium		*	*	*	*	*
Fusarium		*		*		*
Mucor	*	*	*	*	*	*
Penicillium	*	*	*	*	*	*
Rhizopus		*	*	*	*	*
Trichoderma	*	*	*	*	*	*
Verticillium		*		*		*
Zygorhynchus	.	*	*		*	*

* Found to be present.

tematically all the fungi which have been found in the soil. Of these, 56 species belonged to 11 genera of Phycomycetes, 12 species belonged to 8 genera of Ascomycetes, 197 species belonged to 62 genera of Fungi Imperfecti. Many more groups have since been added from all parts of the world. Niethammer and Gilman published comprehensive summaries of the fungi isolated from various soils.

When fresh plant materials are added to the soil, the fungus population is greatly stimulated. There is usually a sequence of forms, depending on the chemical composition of the materials and the extent of their decomposition. On the basis of their relation to organic matter, the fungi were divided into seven groups: (1) *humicolous* forms, which grow on practically pure humus, (2) *terrestrial* (*geophilic, terricolous*) forms, which grow in soil containing more or less organic matter, (3) *coprophilic* (*fimicolous*) forms, growing on manure, (4) *hypogeous* forms, which grow below the surface of the soil, (5) *lignicoleous* forms, growing on the lignins of plant materials, (6) *pseudoparasitic* forms, which are wound parasites, mycorrhiza-formers, facultative parasites; and (7) *true parasites*.

Garrett divided the root-infecting fungi into soil inhabitants and soil invaders, the former being primitive or unspecialized parasites with a wide host range and widely distributed in the soil, and the latter including the specialized parasites which depend upon the host plant.

From an ecological point of view, one may recognize certain specific groups of fungi, depending on the nature of the substrate or the particular nutrients in the substrate which favor their development. Thus, one may speak of (1) "sugar fungi" (comprising largely Phycomycetes); (2) "cellulose-decomposing fungi" (comprising various Ascomycetes and Fungi Imperfecti); (3) "lignin-decomposing fungi" (comprising some Basidiomycetes); (4) "humus fungi"; (5) "root-inhabiting fungi"; (6) "soil-inhabiting parasitic fungi"; (7) "coprophilous fungi"; (8) "predaceous fungi"; etc. When a fresh supply of nutrients is made available in the soil, as by the penetration and subsequent death of plant roots, there is a rapid sequence in the flare up of the various groups of fungi, the "sugar" forms coming first and the "lignin-decomposing" types last (Garrett).

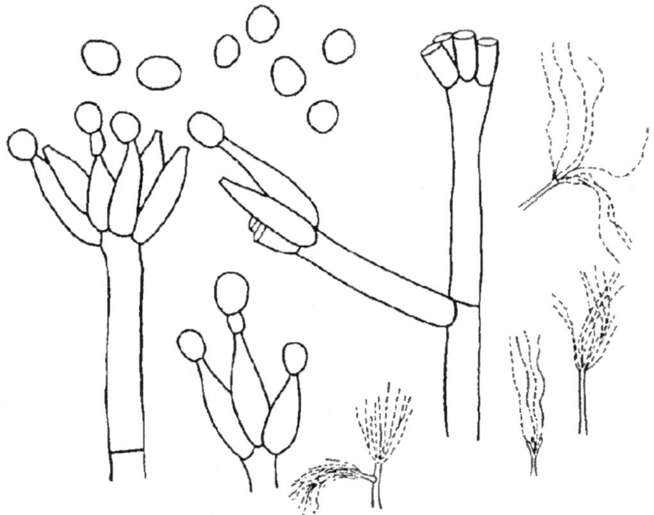

Fig. 39. Microscopic structure of a soil *Penicillium* (from Thom).

The effect of lime and manure upon the numbers of fungi in the soil is shown in Table 14.

TABLE 14 INFLUENCE OF CELLULOSE UPON THE NUMBERS OF FUNGI IN SOIL (from Waksman and Starkey)

Numbers per gram of soil

Nature of Soil	Reaction of Soil pH	$NaNO_3$ Added to Cultures	Numbers of Fungi: Soil without Cellulose	Numbers of Fungi: Soil with 1 Per Cent Cellulose
Unlimed, unmanured	5.1	−	115,700	160,000
Unlimed, unmanured	5.1	+	115,700	1,800,000
Limed, unmanured	6.5	−	20,000	17,000
Limed, unmanured	6.5	+	20,000	290,000
Unlimed, manured	5.5	−	87,300	320,000
Unlimed, manured	5.5	+	87,300	3,100,000

HIGHER FUNGI

The occurrence of Basidiomycetes in soil has been studied largely by observations with the naked eye, and findings are not based upon isolations from soil and cultivation in the laboratory. Hence, only those fungi which produce fruiting stages visible to the naked eye have been reported. Gilbert found that the nature and the concentration of organic matter in the soil are the most important factors influencing the development of these fungi. Reaction, moisture content, light, temperature, season of year, topography, and nature of higher plants are among the other factors of importance in this connection. Some of the organisms are highly specialized, growing only under specific conditions and upon very few organic materials, whereas others are less specific, growing under a great variety of conditions.

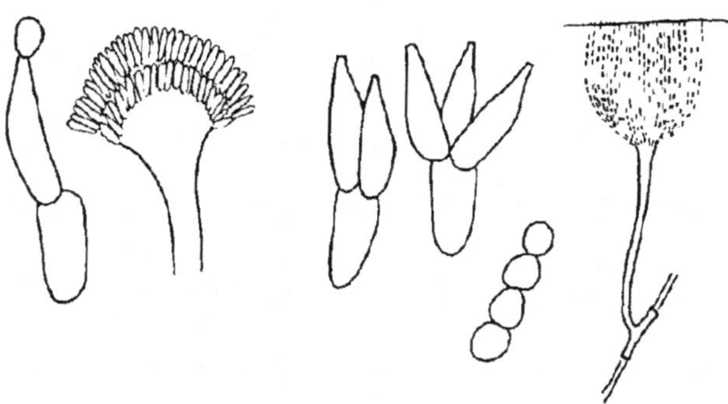

FIG. 40. Microscopic structure of a soil *Aspergillus* (from Thom)

The higher fungi have been divided into two general groups. (1) *Calcofilic fungi*, including *Amanita ovoidea*, *Lepiota granulosa*, *Clitocybe geotropa*, *Tricholoma album*, *Russula maculata*, *Cortinarius fulgens*, *Boletus satanas*, *Clavaria flava*, and *Lycoperdon caelatum* (2) *Calcofugic fungi*, including *Amanita virosa*, *Lepiota procera*, *Clitocybe clavipes*, *Lactarius turpis*, *Russula amoena*, *Cortinarius mucosus*, and *Boletus bovinus*

Cellulose-Decomposing Fungi

The addition of cellulose to the soil brings about an extensive development of fungi, most of which possess very strong cellulose-decomposing power. These include various species of *Penicillium*, *Aspergillus*, *Trichoderma*, *Sporotrichum*, *Fusarium*, *Chaetomium*, and other forms McBeth suggested that the fungi play a much more important part in cellulose decomposition in moist soils, particularly in humus soils, than in dry soils Daszewska found *Verticillium cellulosae*, *V glaucum*, *Sporotrichum olivaceum*, and various other sporotricha, fusaria, monosporia, alternariae, and moniliae among the strongest cellulose-decomposing fungi in the soil. She also concluded that the Hyphomycetes play a much more important part than the bacteria in the decomposition of cellulose in the soil, the color of the humus being due to the color of the mycelium and the spores of fungi. Sugars and alcohols were formed as intermediary products

More recent studies have fully confirmed these observations. It may now be concluded that the fungi play a highly important part in the decomposition of cellulose in soils and in composts. Their part in the decomposition of cellulosic materials under tropical conditions became particularly important during World War II.

Mycorrhiza Fungi

The mycorrhiza fungi form a special group of organisms. They are capable of attacking the subterranean organs of plants, feeding upon their organic constituents. The plant cells may recover, however, and in their turn digest the fungus mycelium. In this instance, the subterranean part of the plant and the fungus mycelium form an association which is frequently of benefit to both, this union being known as *mycorrhiza* or *fungus-root.*

Frank divided the mycorrhiza into two groups· (1) *Ectotrophic mycorrhiza*, in which the fungus produces an external investment of the root, in the form of a crown of hyphae, without penetrating into cells other than those of the epidermis; there is an extensive intercellular development between the cortical cells of the roots which is especially characteristic of forest trees. (2) *Endotrophic mycorrhiza,* in which the hyphae of the fungus penetrate to the inner parts of

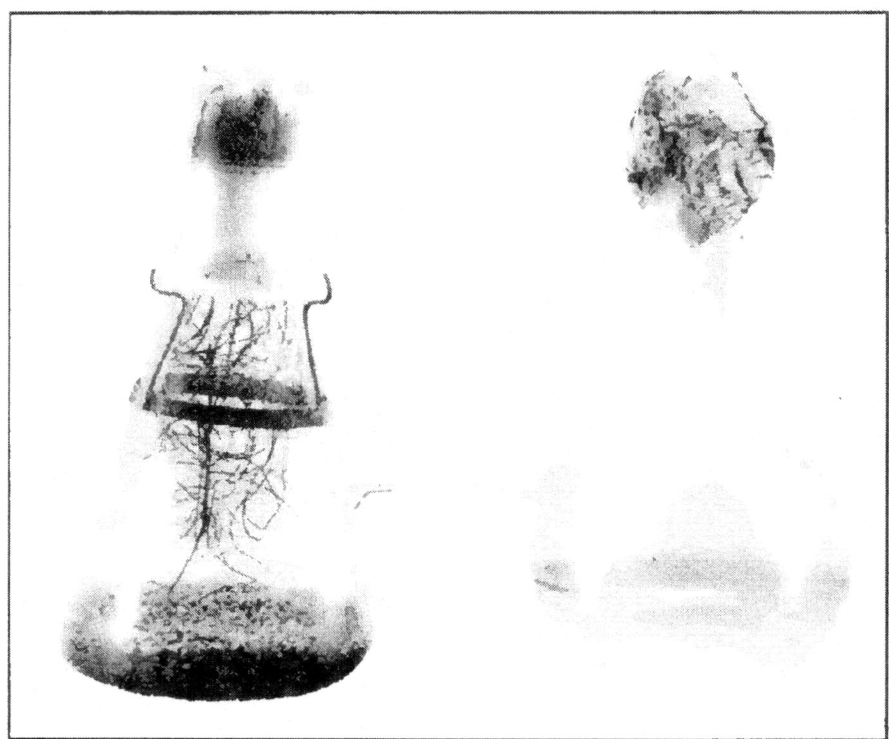

Fig. 41. Ectotrophic mycorrhiza growing in flask culture (from Melin).

the roots, into definite root layers, and into the cells, and have little connection with the mycelium in the soil. This is true of plants belonging to the Orchidaceae, Ericaceae, and Eparidaceae, and is now known also for many other plants. Root hairs are frequently absent in ectotrophic mycorrhiza and are replaced by hyphae of fungi.

Melin described three types of mycorrhiza formations on pine trees: (1) *Forked mycorrhiza,* best developed in the presence of an abundant layer of raw humus; it is golden-brown to black in color. (2) *Tuber mycorrhiza,* which is pale at first and later becomes gray to brownish gray. (3) *Simple mycorrhiza,* or the unbranched form characteristically found on the pine; this may be a young stage of the forked or tuber type, or it may be a result of conditions unfavorable for optimum growth of the fungus. Melin also recognized *pseudomycorrhiza,* which are endotrophic in nature but are not comparable to the true endotrophic forms in orchids; the hyphae are not digested and the fungus is largely parasitic.

The stimulating effect of fungi on the growth of Ericaceae is believed to be due to inactivation, destruction, or absorption of toxic substances in the rooting medium, rather than to the secretion of substances stimulating to the higher plants. Rayner claimed that *Phoma radicis* is capable of bringing about systemic infection and results in an obligate mycorrhizal relationship with ericaceous plants. This concept has not been confirmed.

Numerous species of fungi, nearly all Basidiomycetes, largely Agaricineae, are capable of forming mycorrhiza. Many of the mycorrhiza fungi are especially adapted to certain trees, some are less specific, and still others grow without association with the living tree. When a forest is removed, the obligate mycorrhizal fungi disappear from the soil and reappear only when a new crop begins to develop. The spores of these fungi do not germinate on artificial media, and the mycelium and the fruiting bodies do not develop when not connected with living tree roots.

Algae

Algae are widely distributed in the soil. Although they are largely confined to the surface layer and are controlled by the moisture content, they may also be found below the surface and even in fairly dry soils. Since they depend on sunlight for their growth, the subterranean forms must either lead heterotrophic existence or remain there largely in an inactive state.

The soil algae comprise the Myxophyceae, or the blue-greens, the Chlorophyceae, or the grass-greens; and the Bacillariaceae, which include the diatoms. Some of the blue-greens are able to fix atmospheric nitrogen. The grass-greens are very abundant in acid soils.

Protozoa

Protozoa are unicellular organisms, varying in size from a few microns to 4–5 mm. Some protozoa are also able to form colonies which consist of numerous individuals. The majority of species, particularly the soil forms, are microscopic and can be studied in detail only with the highest magnifications. Their protoplasm is in a colloidal state and contains chromatic or nuclear substance, generally forming nuclei readily distinguishable from the protoplasmic body,

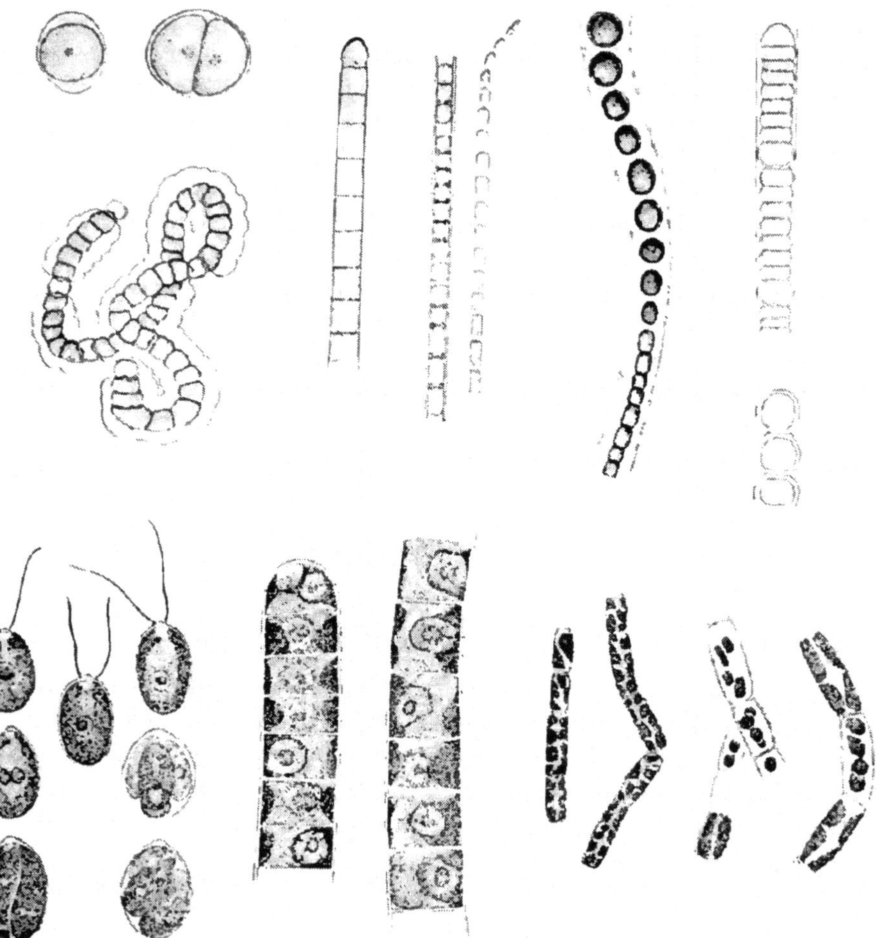

FIG. 42. Different types of soil algae (from Bristol).

which is either naked at the surface or enclosed by a cell membrane. Usually one or two nuclei are present; in some cases, several. Contractile vacuoles, when present, are for the elimination of waste fluids or possibly for the adjustment of the osmotic pressure of the protoplasm. Some *Mastigophora* contain in their endoplasm green, yellow, or brown chromatophores. The most important constituents of the cell are the complex proteins, particularly the nucleins and nucleoproteins. In addition to these, carbohydrates, lipoids, and enzymes are always present in the living cell. Also found in the protozoa are undigested food particles, waste materials, or foreign elements, which take no part in the physiology of the organism; algae and bacteria may often be present in the endoplasm, either as ingested food or as a result of a certain symbiotic relationship. Many species of protozoa are subject to attacks by parasitic organisms.

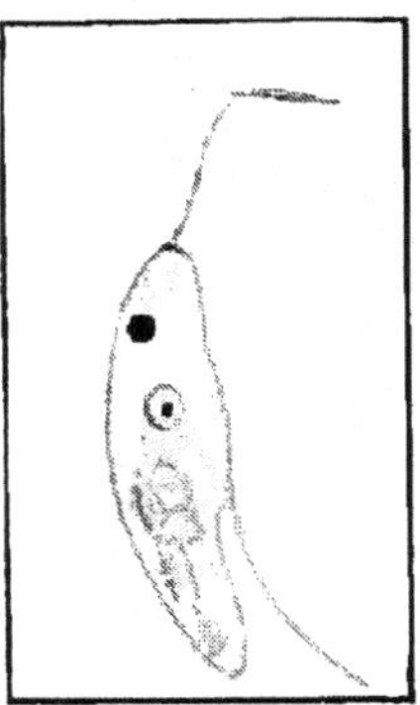

FIG. 43. Flagellate, *Bodo caudatus* (from Martin and Lewin).

The protozoa are classified on the basis of locomotion, as follows:

1. *Sarcodina* or *Rhizopoda.* Motility by means of pseudopodia, which are extensions of the protoplasm of the cell body. The pseudopodia are broad, blunt, finger-like or filiform, simple, or branched. In some, the ray-like pseudopodia are usually supported by axial filaments. Some of the rhizopods are naked. Others form shells, which are composed of secreted materials, as chitin, silica, and calcium carbonate; they may also be constructed from foreign materials, as diatoms, sand grains, and clay particles. Some shells are delicate, transparent, whereas others are composed of distinct plates, arranged more or less regularly.

2. *Mastigophora* or *Flagellata.* Motility by means of flagella. These flexible whip-like processes are usually attached at one end of the body. Either one or more flagella may be present. When single, the flagellum is usually directed forward and draws the body forward by its movement. When more than one flagellum is present, one or more may be directed backward. Some low flagellates can form pseudopodia.

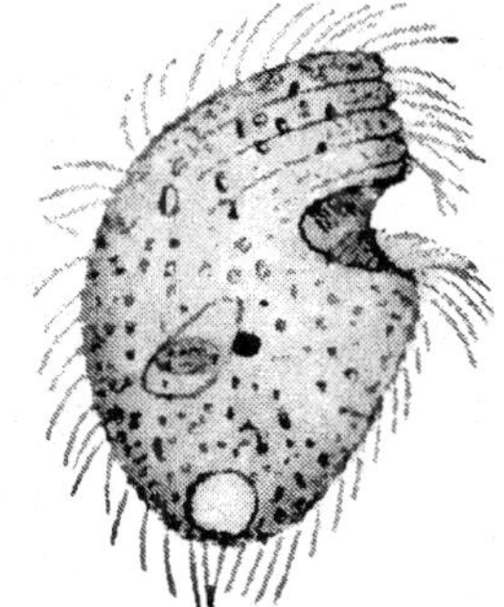

FIG. 44. Ciliate, *Colpoda steinii* (from Goodey).

3. *Ciliata* or *Infusoria.* Motility by means of numerous cilia or short hair-like processes present during the entire existence of the protozoa or during their embryonic stage only. The cilia are either evenly distributed over the surface of the organisms or restricted to certain regions. Large spine-like cirri or setae, or vibrating membranelles, may be formed from fusion of cilia. Most ciliates are free swimming; some are attached by rigid or flexible stalks or pedicels.

4. *Sporozoa.* These are parasitic forms, the motility of which is greatly reduced.

Ciliates are present in the soil largely in an encysted condition and cannot, therefore, function as a factor limiting bacterial activity in the soil, a property often ascribed to protozoa. Smaller amoebae and flagellates were at one time believed to play the most important part in the phenomenon of "sick" soils. The limiting factor as regards their activity in the soil is the quantity of water. An extensive protozoan fauna normally occurs in the soil in a trophic state; this fauna is most readily demonstrated in moist soil well supplied with organic matter, like heavily manured soils, sewage soils, and especially greenhouse "sick" soils. The forms predominating in the soil are not necessarily the same as those that develop on artificial media, such as hay infusions inoculated with soil.

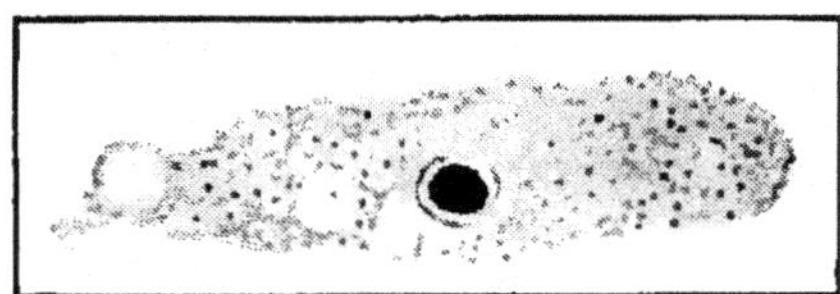

Fig. 45. Soil amoeba, *Vahlkampfia soli* (from Martin and Lewin).

Protozoa that are present in the soil in the form of cysts, especially after a continuous dry period, will be rapidly transformed into a trophic state by the first rain that brings the moisture content of the soil to optimum. Some protozoa are found in an active state even in soils containing a low percentage of water. The flagellate *Cercomonas crassicauda* is capable of excysting and reproducing in air-dried soils brought to one-sixth of their water-holding capacity. Various other common protozoa behave normally in soil previously dried and restored to one-half to one-third of its water-holding capacity.

Some investigators have reported that ciliates and flagellates are more abundant in the soil than are amoebae; others have found amoebae and thecamoebae to be most prevalent. The discrepancy may be due to the difference in methods used, especially in view of the sensitiveness of the amoebae and thecamoebae to the composition of the medium. The largest numbers of protozoa are present in the soil in spring, after the thawing of snow, or in summer, after heavy rainfall; only cysts are found in dry soils.

The protozoan fauna is largely confined to the top 6 inches of soil. In arid regions, especially in poor sandy soils, protozoa are found in greatest abundance somewhat below the surface. Irrigation of arid soils stimulates considerably the development of numerous protozoa. The richer the soil is in organic matter, the richer it is in protozoa, especially in amoebae and thecamoebae.

The majority of soil protozoa are cosmopolitan, since they are found throughout the world, although not all the species are found in every soil.

Cutler and associates found six species of protozoa occurring constantly in the soil in sufficient numbers to admit the application of statistical methods to the results These are (1) *Dimastigamoeba gruberi*, (2) a small limax amoeba, (3) *Heteromita* sp resembling *Bodo repens*, (4) a small soil flagellate, 3–6 by 2–3 μ, (5) *Cercomonas* sp, and (6) *Oicomonas termo.*

Sandon found the following average number of species of protozoa in 107 soils examined· 7 2 flagellates, 3 4 ciliates, 2 45 amoebae, and 2 0 testaceous rhizopods Some species grew in all media employed, others developed only in special media In all, Sandon recorded 250 species of protozoa, some of which were observed in every soil, often in very large numbers The flagellates *Heteromita globosus, Oicomonas termo,* and *Cercomonas* sp.; the ciliates *Colpoda cucullus* and *C. steinii;* and the limax amoebae *Naegleri gruberi* and *Hartmanella hyalina* were most common and most abundant. Most protozoa found in the soil are also present in various other habitats, such as standing and flowing fresh waters, sea water, and plankton, a few are found only in the soil. The extreme climate of arctic land is not in itself an obstacle to the abundant development of protozoa, provided the soil is well manured and in good condition

In general, the soil contains an extensive population of protozoa, consisting largely of amoebae and flagellates, and to a lesser extent of ciliates These organisms are specifically adapted to a terrestrial form of life. The protozoa, in comparison with other groups of microorganisms, form only a small part of the microbial population of the soil. Their ability to reduce the numbers and control the activities of other groups of microorganisms in soil is very limited Some protozoa feed only upon certain types of bacteria, others consume protozoa, and still others take an active part in the decomposition of plant and animal residues, even by consuming certain specific bacteria, they may favor the process for which these bacteria are responsible Partial sterilization of soil does not destroy all the protozoa.

Other Animal Forms

Animal forms larger than protozoa also occur abundantly in the soil. They range from microscopic nematodes to large earthworms and insect larvae. Some nematodes (*Heterodera schachtii*) and certain insects are parasitic on plants; some (hookworm larvae) are parasitic on animals; others, such as nematodes that attack Japanese beetle larvae, parasitize plant parasites and are thus beneficial. Many are saprophytic; these comprise the earthworms, which macerate the soil, mix the organic with the inorganic contents, and thus greatly improve soil fertility.

Fig. 46. Parasitic nematode (from Cobb).

Viruses and Phages

Certain viruses and various phages exist independently in the soil. The mosaic virus of wheat can be transmitted from the soil. Heating the soil for 10 minutes inactivates this virus. The survival in the soil

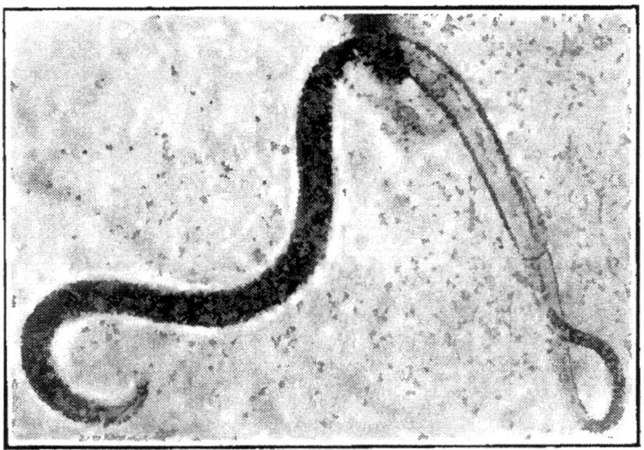

Fig. 47. Saprophytic nematode attacking parasitic form (from Cobb).

of phages active upon legume bacteria may become an important economic problem in successful legume inoculation; the selection of phage-resistant strains of bacteria may be the answer. Various actinophages have also been demonstrated in the soil.

Selected Bibliography

1. *Bergey's Manual of Determinative Bacteriology,* Williams & Wilkins Co., Baltimore, 6th Ed., 1948.
2. Cutler, D. W., and Crump, L. M., *Problems in Soil Microbiology,* Longmans, Green and Co., London, 1935.
3. Darwin, C., *The Formation of Vegetable Mould through the Action of Worms, with Observations on Their Habits,* John Murray, London, 1881.
4. Garrett, S. D., *Root Disease Fungi,* Chronica Botanica Co., Waltham, Mass., 1944.
5. Garrett, S. D., Ecological groups of soil fungi. A survey of substrate relationships, *The New Phytologist,* 50: 149–166, 1951.
6. Gilman, J. C., *A Manual of Soil Fungi,* The Collegiate Press, Ames, Iowa, 1945.
7. John, R. P., An ecological and taxonomic study of the algae of British soils. I. The distribution of the surface-growing algae, *Ann. Botany,* N. S., 6: 323–349, 371–395, 1942.
8. Melin, E., *Untersuchungen über die Bedeutung der Baummykorrhiza,* G. Fischer, Jena, 1925.
9. Niethammer, A., *Die Mikroskopischen Bodenpilze,* N. V. Van de Garde & Co., Drukkerij, Zaltbommel, 1937.
10. Rayner, M. C., *Mycorrhiza,* Wheldon and Wesley, London, 1927.
11. Russell, E. J., *et al., The Microorganisms of the Soil,* Longmans, Green and Co., London, 1923.
12. Sandon, H., *The Composition and Distribution of the Protozoan Fauna of the Soil,* Oliver and Boyd, London, 1927.
13. Smith, N. R., Gordon, R. E., and Clark, F. E., Aerobic mesophilic sporeforming bacteria, *U. S. Dept. Agr. Misc. Pub.* 559, 1946.
14. Starkey, R. L., Products of the oxidation of thiosulfate by bacteria in mineral media, *J. Gen. Physiol.,* 18: 325–349, 1935; Isolation of some bacteria which oxidize thiosulfate, *Soil Sci.,* 39: 197–220, 1935.
15. Van Niel, C. B., *Advances in Enzymology,* pp. 263–328, Interscience Publishers, New York, 1941; The culture, general physiology, morphology, and classification of the non-sulfur purple and brown bacteria, *Bact. Revs.,* 8:1–118, 1944.
16. Waksman, S. A., *Principles of Soil Microbiology,* Williams & Wilkins Co., Baltimore, 1st Ed., 1927, 2nd Ed., 1932.
17. Waksman, S. A., *The Actinomycetes,* Chronica Botanica Co., Waltham, Mass., 1950.
18. Winogradsky, S. N., *Microbiologie du sol, problèmes et méthodes,* Masson et Cie, Paris, 1949.
19. Wolf, F. A., and Wolf, F. T., *The Fungi,* 2 vols., John Wiley & Sons, New York, 1947.

·4·

Decomposition of Plant and Animal Residues in Soils and in Composts

For dust thou art, and unto dust shalt thou return. Genesis III.19

Nature of Plant and Animal Residues

With the exception of autotrophic bacteria, the green or chlorophyll-bearing plants are the only living forms on this planet capable of synthesizing organic matter out of inorganic elements and simple compounds. These essential nutrients are obtained partly from the atmosphere and partly from the soil. By utilizing the photosynthetic energy of sunlight, plants are able to produce, from carbon dioxide and water, sugar and starch, which serve as the starting point for the synthesis of numerous other carbohydrates, fats, proteins, and various other compounds. The soluble forms of nitrogen and the minerals required by the plant for synthetic purposes are obtained from the soil; certain few plants, the legumes, are able, in association with root-inhabiting bacteria, to obtain their nitrogen from the elementary form in the atmosphere.

Plant materials are partly used for animal feeding and are partly returned to the soil in the stubble and other plant residues. The animals and their excretion products also find their way, sooner or later, into the soil. These materials are subject to decomposition by numerous groups of microorganisms and thereby contribute to the soil organic matter. The various organic residues which undergo decomposition in soils and in composts can be classified as follows:

1. Plant and animal remains decomposing on the surface of the soil; here belong the leaves, needles, branches and twigs of all plant life.

2 Plant residues plowed into the soil, these include plant stubble and special crops which are grown specifically for this purpose, as cover crops or green manures

3 Stable manures; these consist of the solid and liquid animal excreta and bedding

4. Artificial manures and composts

5 Organic commercial fertilizers, these include a variety of animal and plant products such as bone meal, dried blood, tankage, cottonseed meal, linseed meal, peat

6 Microorganisms and their dead bodies

The plant residues are made up of three groups of constituents water, organic materials, and inorganic compounds. The water content of plant residues varies from 50 to 95 per cent, depending on the nature and degree of maturity of the plant, usually about 80 per cent for young and 60 per cent for mature plants The water-free plant material consists of 88–99 per cent organic matter, and 1–12 per cent mineral or inorganic matter. The organic constituents comprise a large number of chemical compounds containing the elements carbon, hydrogen, oxygen, and nitrogen and, in lesser amounts, sulfur, phosphorus, potassium and a variety of others, some of which are usually present in mere traces.

When the organic matter synthesized by the plants undergoes digestion by herbivorous animals, many of the constituents are destroyed and the elements changed back into simple gases or inorganic compounds such as CO_2, H_2O, NH_3, phosphates, sulfates, potassium salts. Out of the plant materials, directly or after they have been transformed into simpler compounds, the animals synthesize their own tissues. These animal bodies may now be used, in their turn, as food by other animals The bodies of these omnivorous or carnivorous animals also undergo a series of transformations; part of the elements and compounds which they consumed as nutrients are liberated as waste products, in the form of gases (CO_2, NH_3), as simple organic compounds (urea, organic acids), or as complex organic materials comprising the residual and partly digested plant and animal residues found in the feces.

Animals depend upon plants and some of them upon other animals for their necessary energy, for the organic nitrogenous compounds, for some of the fatty substances, and for the vitamins. On the other hand, animals are able to synthesize, out of the complex materials supplied to them by the plants and other forms of life, new organic compounds, largely of a protein and fatty nature. Some of the plant constituents, such as the sugars, starches, fats, and proteins, are utilized by animals for their own metabolism and for supplying their energy needs. Other plant constituents, like the hemicelluloses, cellulose, lignins, and waxes, are used not at all in the animal system or only to a very limited extent The cow and other ruminant animals are able to digest a large part of the cellulose, with the help of bacteria living in their digestive tracts. The undigested residues are excreted by the animals and sooner or later find their way into the soil

The bacteria and certain protozoa may play an important part in the digestive mechanism in the animal body: (*a*) by digesting the cellulose and certain other carbohydrates to organic acids, they make these constituents available to the animal for its nutrition, (*b*) by synthesizing certain vitamins and other complex substances in the animal, they supply nutrients which the animal is unable to synthesize; (*c*) they may also form certain products that are undesirable or even toxic to the animal body

The plant and animal residues find their way into the soil either directly or after preliminary decomposition in composts or on the surface of the ground These residues comprise either the whole plant, stems, leaves, and seed, or only certain parts of the plant, needles and leaves, surface stubble, and subsurface roots. The surface portion of certain crops, such as grasses used for pasture, cereals, and corn, may be largely removed for cattle food or for other purposes In some cases the straw may be returned to the soil, either as such or as a constituent part of the stable manures. In crops like peas and beans, only the seed may be removed from the land, whereas the rest of the plant may find its way into the soil In still other crops, used for soil cover or as green manures, the whole plant may be returned to the soil In pastures and in forests, where the soil is not plowed at all, the plant residues are attacked by microorganisms either in the soil itself or on the surface of the ground; the products of decomposition gradually find their way into the soil through leaching or by land cultivation.

Thus the cycle of life is completed, from the soil back to the soil In this broad cycle, numerous secondary cycles occur, in which one or more elements are concerned In the transformation of each one of these, microorganisms play a highly important part Without them, life would soon come to a standstill, upon their activities, the continuation of life on the planet depends

Abundance and Chemical Composition of Plant Residues

Sachs calculated that the leaves of an ordinary sunflower plant, having a surface area of 1.5 square meters, absorb two-thirds of a liter or 1.3 gm of CO_2 per hour. If the growing day is taken to be 10 hours, the plant will absorb 400 gm of CO_2 a month. On the basis of a million plants per square kilometer of land and a 3-month growing period, the sunflower will consume annually 1,200,000 kg of CO_2. In view of the fact that the CO_2 content of the atmosphere is very small, only 0.03 per cent, the available supply of this essential plant nutrient would soon become exhausted if it were not for the continuous liberation of the CO_2 from the soil by the action of microorganisms upon the plant and animal residues and upon the soil organic matter.

According to Lundegårdh, the amount of CO_2 produced in the soil by microorganisms approaches that which is required by the plants for the photosynthesis of organic matter. If it is assumed that the average content of the organic matter in the upper 15 cm of soil is 2–4 per cent, an acre of soil will contain 20,000–40,000 kg of organic matter. Since the carbon content of the latter is 58 per cent, it is possible to conclude that the average amount of organic carbon in an acre of soil is 10,000–22,000 kg. In some soils, like prairie and peat soils, the organic matter content may be considerably higher (10 per cent or more), whereas, in poor sandy soils, it may be 1 per cent or less.

A study by Waksman and Starkey of the evolution of CO_2 from soil revealed that, under favorable moisture and temperature conditions, 1 kg of soil may give off, in 24 hours, 5–30 mg of carbon as CO_2. Taking an average of only 10 mg of carbon and a period of active annual decomposition of 4 months, we find that an acre of soil containing 10,000 kg of carbon will give off during the warm months 1,000 kg of carbon in the form of CO_2. Under these conditions of decomposition, the soil organic matter would become exhausted within 10 years. If it were not for the constant addition of plant, animal, and microbial residues to the soil, the amount of available CO_2 from the above source would soon also become a limiting factor in plant growth.

Ebermeyer calculated that the vegetation on 1 hectare of field soil consumed annually 2,000 kg of carbon and on 1 hectare of forest soil 3,000 kg, corresponding to 7,300–11,000 kg CO_2. The plant vegetation of the whole earth (allowing for 25 per cent of the earth surface as being unproductive), covering 10,160 million hectares, will require an annual consumption of 90 billion kg of CO_2. The whole atmosphere contains 2,100 billion kg of CO_2, thus allowing only for about 25 annual crops, a very small figure indeed. Others have calculated, however, that the green plants consume annually only one-seventeenth of the CO_2 of the air in 1 year, which amounts to 30 billion kg annually. Ebermeyer further reported that, out of the 3,000 kg of carbon synthesized by 1 hectare of forest, 1,491–1,792 kg was converted to wood and 1,196–1,167 kg to litter. The latter is returned immediately to the soil and becomes subject at once to decomposition by microorganisms.

Chemical Nature of Plant and Animal Constituents

The plant and animal bodies are made up of numerous organic compounds. Attention will be directed to only the more important and more abundant substances, the decomposition of which by microorganisms has been studied in greater detail and contributes to our knowledge of the cycle of life in the soil.

1. Fats, oils, waxes, sterols, and terpenes.

2. Carbohydrates, including the simple sugars of the mono-, di-, and tri-saccharides, the starches, the hemicelluloses (comprising the pentosans and hexosans), the polyuronides (pectins, gums, and mucilages), and true cellulose.

3. Organic acids, including saturated fatty acids, oxy-fatty acids, and unsaturated acids.

4. Aldehydes, ketones, and alcohols, including aliphatic, polyvalent, and unsaturated alcohols.

5. Lignins, compounds which are frequently spoken of as "incrustants." They are believed to form definite chemical or physical compounds with the celluloses. Some believe, however, that cellulose and other carbohydrates do not form any chemical compounds with lignins and may not even form any homogeneous mixtures. This concept is substantiated by the fact that the lignin content of plants varies considerably, depending on the plant and on the stage of growth, and may even vary in the different tissues of the same plant.

6. Cyclic compounds, including hydrocarbons, phenols, quinones, tannins.

7. Alkaloids and organic bases, including purine bases, pyridine, and piperidine compounds.

8. Proteins, polypeptides, amino acids, amines, and other nitrogenous compounds.

9. Enzymes, hormones, vitamins, pigments, antibiotics, and other important products of living systems, the exact chemical nature of some of which still remains unknown.

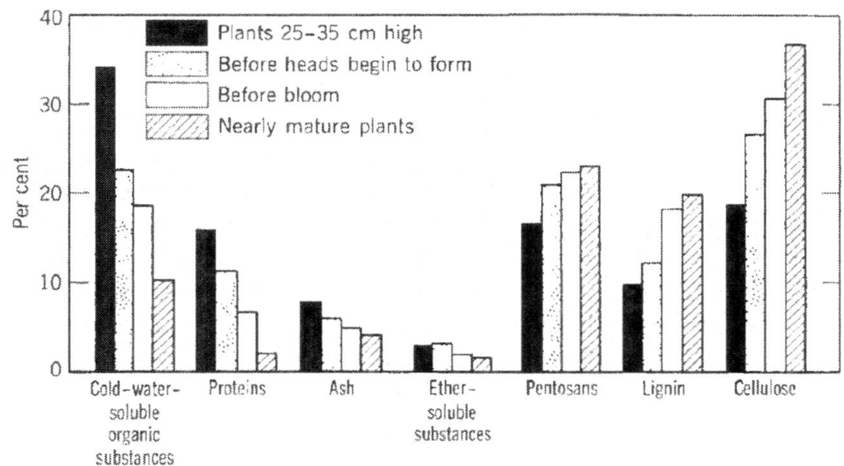

FIG. 48. Influence of age upon the chemical composition of rye plants (from Waksman and Tenney).

10. Mineral constituents: phosphates, silicates, sulfates, carbonates, chlorides, nitrates, and potassium, sodium, calcium, magnesium, and other salts.

It is almost impossible to make a complete quantitative analysis of plant and animal materials, whereby all the chemical constituents are accounted for. For most purposes, it is sufficient to account for some of the more important groups of compounds, to obtain a fairly good idea of the chemical composition of the materials which undergo decomposition. Such an analysis need be only proximate in nature. It may be supplemented by special determinations of certain compounds which are either characteristic of a given material or essential for the understanding of a certain process. In a proximate analysis, only those compounds which occur most abundantly in the plant and the decomposition of which is best understood are taken into consideration. The common foodstuff analyses are not of sufficient value for this purpose, since they give a rather limited concept of the chemical composition of the plant materials that find their way into the soil.

A series of analyses of various plant materials, as obtained by the proximate method, is given in Table 15. The chemical composition of the plant varies not only with its nature, but also with its age and with conditions of growth and nutrition. Tables 16 and 17 indicate the effect of age upon the chemical composition of rye and corn plants. At an early stage of growth, plants are rich in water-soluble substances, including sugars and amino acids, in proteins, and in mineral constituents, the older the plants become, the less is the proportion of these constituents and the greater is the concentration of cellulose and lignin and, to some extent, of the hemicelluloses and polyuronides. This change in composition has an important bearing upon the rapidity of decomposition of the plant materials. In leguminous plants, such as alfalfa, the protein content also decreases with the maturity of the plant, and the cellulose and lignin contents increase. This affects both the digestibility of the plant materials by animals and their decomposition in soil.

Decomposition Processes

When plant and animal residues are added to the soil or are placed in composts under favorable conditions of moisture and aeration, they are attacked by a great variety of microorganisms, including bacteria, fungi, actinomycetes, protozoa, worms, and insect larvae. As a result of the activities of these organisms, considerable portions of some of the constituent chemical elements in the residues, notably the carbon, nitrogen, phosphorus, and potassium, are rapidly liberated in forms available for plant growth. The process is at first rapid but gradually slows down; the rate of decomposition depends upon the nature of the residues and upon the conditions under which decomposition is taking place. If the residues are low in nitrogen, as in straw, this element will not be liberated for some time and is, therefore, not made available for plant growth.

This is illustrated in Table 18, where the formation of nitrate in the soil is used as a measure of liberation of the nitrogen in an available form. A definite quantity of root material obtained from several

TABLE 15. CHEMICAL COMPOSITION OF A SERIES OF PLANT MATERIALS (from Tenney and Waksman)

Per cent of air-dry material.

Constituent	Young Rye Plants	Mature Wheat Straw	Soybean Tops	Alfalfa Tops	Young Corn Stalks	More Mature Corn Stalks	Young Pine Needles	Old Pine Needles	Oak Leaves Green	Oak Leaves Mature, Brown
Fats and waxes	2.35	1.10	3.80	10.41	3.42	5.94	7.65	23.92	7.75	4.01
Water-soluble constituents	29.54	5.57	22.09	17.24	28.27	14.14	13.02	7.29	22.02	15.32
Hemicelluloses	12.67	26.35	11.08	13.14	20.38	21.91	14.68	18.98	12.50	15.60
Cellulose	17.84	39.10	28.53	23.65	23.05	28.67	18.26	16.43	15.92	17.18
Lignin	10.61	21.60	13.84	8.95	9.68	9.46	27.63 *	22.68	20.67	29.66
Protein	12.26	2.10	11.04	12.81	2.61	2.44	8.53	2.19	9.18	3.47
Ash	12.55	3.53	9.14	10.30	7.40	7.54	3.08	2.51	6.40	4.68

* The higher lignin content in the younger pine needles is due to the fact that this preparation has not been extracted with alcohol and is thus high in oils and waxes.

TABLE 16. INFLUENCE OF AGE OF RYE PLANTS UPON THEIR CHEMICAL COMPOSITION (from Waksman and Tenney)

Per cent of dry material

	Age of Plant			
Constituent	10–14 Inches (I)	Just before Head Formation (II)	Just before Bloom, Stems and Leaves (III)	Mature Plants, Stems and Leaves (IV)
Fats and waxes	2.60	2.60	1.70	1.26
Cold-water-soluble	34.24	22.74	18.16	9.90
Pentosans	16.60	21.18	22.71	22.90
Cellulose	18.06	26.95	30.59	36.29
Lignin	9.90	11.80	18.00	19.80
Ash	7.66	5.90	4.90	3.90
Total nitrogen	2.50	1.76	1.01	0.24

TABLE 17. COMPOSITION OF INDIAN CORN AT DIFFERENT STAGES OF GROWTH (from Morrison and Henry)

Pounds per acre

Stage of Growth	Dry Matter	Ash	Crude Protein
Four feet high, July 24	731	90	149
First tassels, Aug. 6	2,245	195	360
Silks drying, Aug. 28	4,567	272	436
Milk stage, Sept. 10	6,174	328	544
Glazing stage, Sept. 24	8,104	389	566
Silage stage, Oct. 1	8,929	369	660
Ready to shock, Oct. 8			
corn and cobs	5,186	76	492
stalks and blades	4,226	307	199
Total	9,412	383	691

plants and containing 0.6 gm of nitrogen was added to 13 kg of soil, the nitrate produced during 3 months was measured. With an increase in the nitrogen content of the plant material, there is an increase in the formation of nitrate. Only when the nitrogen content is 1.7 per cent is the rate of decomposition sufficient to supply the requirements of the microorganisms for cell synthesis. The lower the nitrogen content of the plant residues, the more nitrogen is required by the microorganisms from an outside source, the soil, and, therefore, the lower is the nitrate content of the soil itself or the amount of nitrate available for plant growth.

TABLE 18 INFLUENCE OF NITROGEN CONTENT OF PLANT RESIDUES ON THE LIBERATION OF NITROGEN AS NITRATE (from Lyon, Bizzell, and Wilson)

Nature of Root Material	Nitrogen Content of Roots	Weight of Roots Used	Nitrogen Found as Nitrate
	per cent	*gm*	*mg*
Control soil		0	946 6
Oats	0 45	133 3	207 3
Timothy	0 62	96 8	398 4
Corn	0 79	75 9	510 6
Clover	1 71	35 1	924 4

To hasten the decomposition of straw and of similar plant materials, some available nitrogen and phosphorus may have to be added in the form of inorganic salts. The microorganisms bringing about decomposition of the plant and animal residues are living systems. They grow and multiply, they require considerable amounts of energy and nutrients. In the straw and in the stubble of cereals and other plants, they find sufficient energy but not enough essential nutrient elements, especially nitrogen and phosphorus. Hence, these must be added to favor the activities of the organisms which thus bring about the rapid destruction of the plant materials. When green plants, however, such as young rye and clover, or plant and animal residues high in nitrogen and in phosphorus are added to the soil, the microorganisms are able to decompose them rapidly, without the addition of inorganic salts; the plant nutrients are liberated.

The results presented in Table 19 fully confirm those given in Table 18, even though totally different types of material are used. Plant substances high in nitrogen decompose rapidly, a large part of the nitrogen is liberated as ammonia, and comparatively little

TABLE 19 PRODUCTS OF DECOMPOSITION OF RYE PLANTS HARVESTED AT DIFFERENT STAGES OF GROWTH (from Waksman and Tenney)

Stage of Growth of Plant	CO_2 Given Off	Nitrogen Liberated as Ammonia	Nitrogen Consumed from Ammonium Salt Added to Soil
	mg C	*mg N*	*mg N*
I *	286 8	22 2	0
II	280 4	3 0	0
III	199 5	0	7 5
IV	187 9	0	8 9

* See Table 16

humus is left. Materials low in nitrogen decompose slowly, liberating at first no available nitrogen and leaving a large amount of humus. This is illustrated in Fig. 49. There are many exceptions to this rule, depending on the nature of the residues and their treatment and on the nature of the soil.

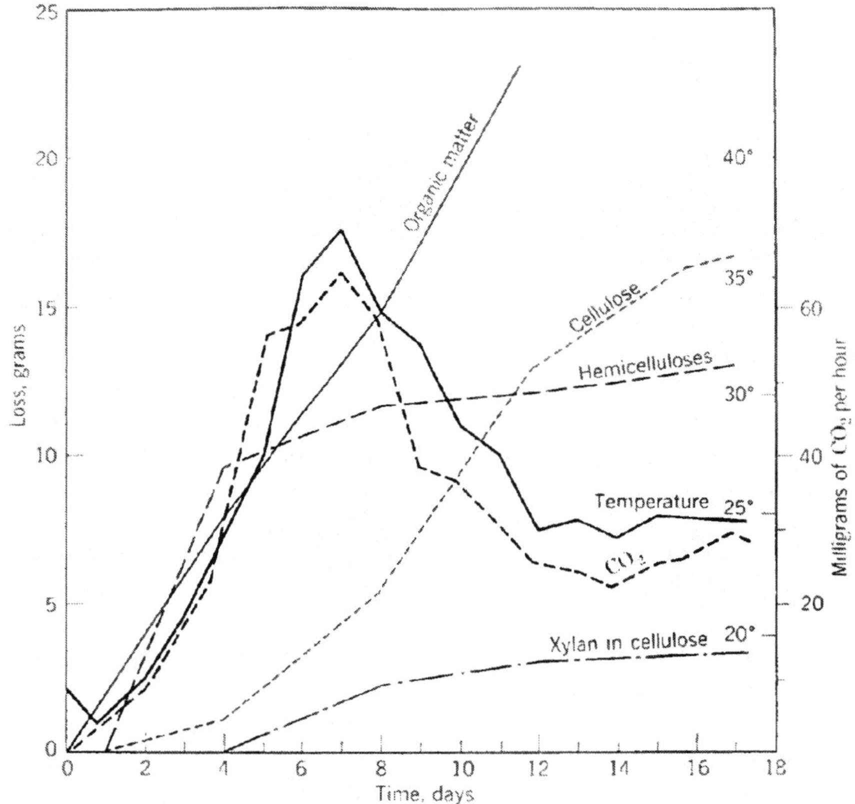

Fig. 49. Decomposition of oat straw (from Norman).

Straw, stubble, and forest litter, unless properly supplemented with essential nutrients, are useful primarily as sources of humus and less as fertilizing materials for plant growth; they may leave, after 3–10 months of decomposition, as much as 50–60 per cent humus.

In the process of humus formation from plant residues, three distinct phases are recognized: (*a*) rapid decomposition of some of the chemical constituents by microorganisms, (*b*) synthesis of new substances by these organisms, (*c*) formation of resistant complexes by various processes of condensation and polymerization. During the process of decomposition, a considerable amount of microbial cell substance is synthesized This substance is later attacked again by other microorganisms. The processes of decomposition are continued until most of the organic complexes in the original plant materials are gradually changed into simple elements or inorganic compounds. The final processes of decomposition of organic matter by microorganisms and the final liberation of the elements in mineralized form complete the cycle of transformation of the essential chemical elements which are used for the building up of organic life in nature. The microbes thus tend to complete the cycle begun by plants.

The plant and animal residues do not decompose as a whole The various chemical constituents are attacked at different rates. The sugars and starches, some of the hemicelluloses, and some of the proteins undergo a most rapid decomposition by a great variety of microorganisms. The cellulose, certain hemicelluloses, and some of the fats, oils, and other plant constituents are decomposed more slowly and, commonly, by specific organisms The lignins and some of the waxes and tannins are most resistant to decomposition, some of the lignins may even affect the decomposition of the proteins by rendering the latter more resistant to attack. This is illustrated in Table 20

TABLE 20 CHEMICAL CHANGES IN CORN STALKS AS A RESULT OF DECOMPOSITION BY MICROORGANISMS (from Tenney and Waksman)

On basis of dry material.

Chemical Constituent	Original Corn Stalks	After Days of Decomposition			
		27	68	205	405
	per cent	*per cent*	*per cent*	*per cent*	*per cent*
Ether-soluble	1.80	2.22	0.80	0.64	0.25
Cold-water-soluble	10.58	3.43	5.27	3.96	4.59
Hot-water-soluble	3.56	2.45	3.20	5.36	8.71
Hemicelluloses	17.63	15.56	16.41	10.68	10.39
Cellulose	29.67	23.80	21.93	6.28	5.05
Lignin	11.28	17.70	19.12	23.83	21.30
Crude protein	2.50	4.81	6.84	10.93	12.13
Ash	7.53			26.12	29.43

The rate of decomposition of plant and animal materials can be measured by a number of different methods. These are based upon the products of decomposition; the disappearance of specific plant and animal constituents, such as the sugars, the cellulose, the pentosans, or some of the nitrogenous bodies; the formation of resistant products of decomposition, such as accumulation of lignins and their transformation into humus compounds. As shown in Table 20, the accumulation of the ash may be used as a measure of total decomposition.

Products of Microbial Decomposition

When plant and animal residues undergo decomposition in the soil and in composts, the various constituent elements, especially the carbon, nitrogen, sulfur, and phosphorus, are liberated in mineralized forms.

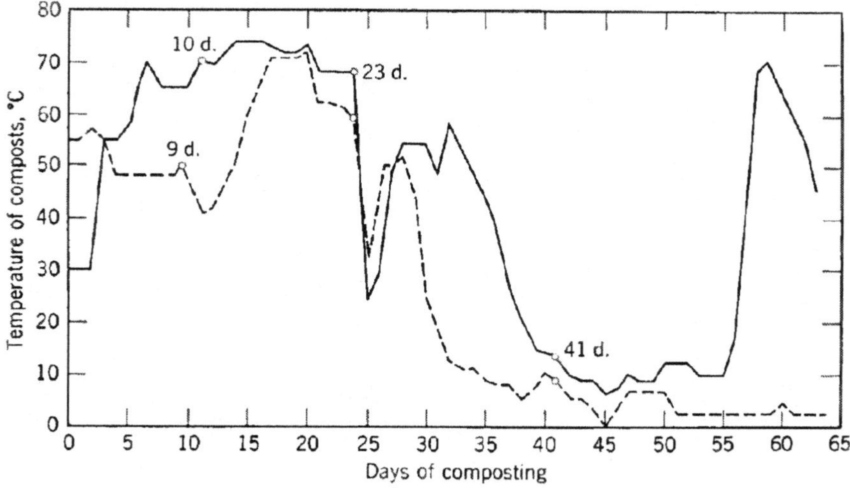

Fig. 50. Course of decomposition of stable manure as measured by temperature changes (from Waksman and Nissen).

The carbon is liberated, under aerobic conditions, as CO_2, and under anaerobic conditions, as methane, organic acids and alcohols, and CO_2. Even under the most favorable conditions of decomposition, however, the carbon of the organic matter is not all transformed to CO_2 at once. This is due to the assimilation of a large part of the carbon by the microorganisms concerned in the decomposition process, for the synthesis of their cell material. The decomposition of 100 gm cellulose (containing 40 per cent carbon) in the form of straw or other plant material, for example, gives rise to 20 or 30 gm carbon as CO_2; the rest of the carbon may be tied up in the synthesized bodies of the bacteria and fungi. Under anaerobic conditions, not more than 10 gm of the carbon may be liberated as CO_2, whereas the larger part of it may be left in the form of organic acids or methane

When proteins undergo decomposition, they are first hydrolyzed, by proteolytic enzymes produced by microorganisms, to polypeptides, amino acids, and other nitrogen derivatives These are further acted upon by a variety of organisms. The nitrogen is finally converted to ammonia, the amount thus liberated depends upon the abundance of the proteins and also upon the other constituents of the plant material, especially the carbohydrates. In a comparison of the decomposition of rye plants harvested at different stages of growth, young plants were found to decompose very rapidly, as shown by the evolution of CO_2; some of the nitrogen was liberated as ammonia, as shown in Table 19 As the plants grew older, they decomposed more slowly, and less nitrogen was liberated as ammonia, until a point was reached at which additional nitrogen was required to hasten decomposition of the plant materials

When plant residues contain more than 1.5 or 1.7 per cent of nitrogen, some of it will be liberated as ammonia, the actual amount depending upon the original concentration of the nitrogen in the plant residues. When the nitrogen content is less than 1 5 per cent, however, very little ammonia will be liberated, even after several months of decomposition The decomposition of cereal straw, which contains only 0 2–0 5 per cent nitrogen, requires the addition of available nitrogen to enable the microorganisms to decompose the carbohydrates in the straw This process is utilized in the preparation of artificial manures, as shown later.

The ammonia which is produced in the soil in the decomposition of plant and animal residues does not accumulate there except under very special conditions, but is rapidly oxidized by the nitrifying bacteria to nitrate Some of the ammonia may also be consumed by various microorganisms responsible for the decomposition of the carbohydrates

Decomposition of Carbohydrates

The mechanism of decomposition of carbohydrates by microorganisms depends entirely upon the nature of the carbohydrate, the nature of the organisms, and the conditions of decomposition, especially the oxygen supply. Thus, if glucose is attacked by fungi, the following reactions are involved:

$$C_6H_{12}O_6 + 1\tfrac{1}{2}O_2 = \underset{\text{Citric acid}}{C_6H_8O_7} + 2H_2O$$

$$C_6H_{12}O_6 + 4\tfrac{1}{2}O_2 = \underset{\text{Oxalic acid}}{3C_2H_2O_4} + 3H_2O$$

$$C_6H_{12}O_6 + 6O_2 = 6CO_2 + 6H_2O$$

If the glucose is attacked by anaerobic bacteria and by yeasts, the following reactions are involved:

$$C_6H_{12}O_6 = \underset{\text{Lactic acid}}{2C_3H_6O_3}$$

$$C_6H_{12}O_6 = \underset{\text{Alcohol}}{2C_2H_5OH} + 2CO_2$$

$$C_6H_{12}O_6 = \underset{\text{Butyric acid}}{C_4H_8O_2} + 2CO_2 + 2H_2$$

If the glucose is attacked by anaerobically growing fungi, another reaction may take place

$$\underset{\text{Glucose}}{C_6H_{12}O_6} + 2H = \underset{\text{Fumaric acid}}{C_4H_6O_4} + \underset{\text{Alcohol}}{C_2H_5OH} + H_2O$$

Under aerobic conditions, the alcohol is further oxidized, through the acetic acid stage, to fumaric acid.

$$C_2H_5OH + 2O = CH_3COOH + H_2O$$

$$2CH_3COOH + O = C_4H_6O_4 + H_2O$$

Starch is first hydrolyzed by diastatic enzymes, to give rise to dextrins, and finally to maltose and glucose:

$$\underset{\text{Starch}}{(C_6H_{10}O_5)_{2n}} + (n - 1)H_2O = \underset{\text{Maltose}}{nC_{12}H_{22}O_{11}}$$

$$\underset{\text{Maltose}}{C_{12}H_{22}O_{11}} + H_2O = \underset{\text{Glucose}}{2C_6H_{12}O_6}$$

Starch is readily decomposed by a large number of microorganisms Among the fungi, certain species of *Aspergillus,* such as *A. oryzae,* and, among the bacteria, various spore-formers, such as *B. amylovorus, B. mesentericus,* and *B macerans,* are particularly capable of attacking starch The products of starch hydrolysis are further broken down by microorganisms, through some of the reactions shown above for the sugars In addition to the highly specialized starch-decomposing organisms capable of producing powerful diastatic or amylolytic enzymes, numerous other fungi, bacteria, and actinomycetes are also capable of utilizing starch

Decomposition of Cellulose

Cellulose, like starch, is a polymer of glucose Because of its specific physical structure, however, and its resistance to most enzymes and chemical reagents, it presents distinct problems as regards decomposition in soils and in composts. The formation of specific cellulolytic enzymes can be demonstrated only with great difficulty. Cellulose represents chemically a single type of compound. Because of differences in the nature of the accompanying impurities, celluloses of different origin may show distinctly different physical properties

Cellulose predominates in fibrous and woody materials, such as straw, stubble, weeds, grasses, leaves, branches, and twigs. In young and succulent plants, the cell-wall material is proportionally low, whereas the sugars, proteins, and soluble minerals are high In mature plants, the straw, stems, leaves, and twigs are high in cellulose. Cellulose is resistant to various oxidizing agents and is hydrolyzed only by concentrated acids It is also resistant to attack by the great majority of soil-inhabiting microorganisms It can be decomposed readily, however, by certain specific organisms found among the bacteria, fungi, actinomycetes and lower animals.

Various systems have been proposed for classifying the cellulose-decomposing organisms. They can be divided into a number of distinct groups, on the basis of either morphological or physiological differences One such system comprises (1) aerobic bacteria, (2) myxobacteria, (3) anaerobic bacteria, including thermophilic forms, (4) actinomycetes, (5) filamentous fungi, (6) higher or mushroom fungi, (7) protozoa, (8) insects and other animal forms.

The mechanism of the breakdown of cellulose by microorganisms depends entirely upon the nature of the organism and the conditions of decomposition. The aerobic bacteria and fungi break down the cellulose completely, producing only CO_2, some slimy material, certain pigments, and a considerable amount of microbial cell substance. As much as 30–40 per cent of the cellulose decomposed may be converted into the cell material of the organisms decomposing the cellulose.

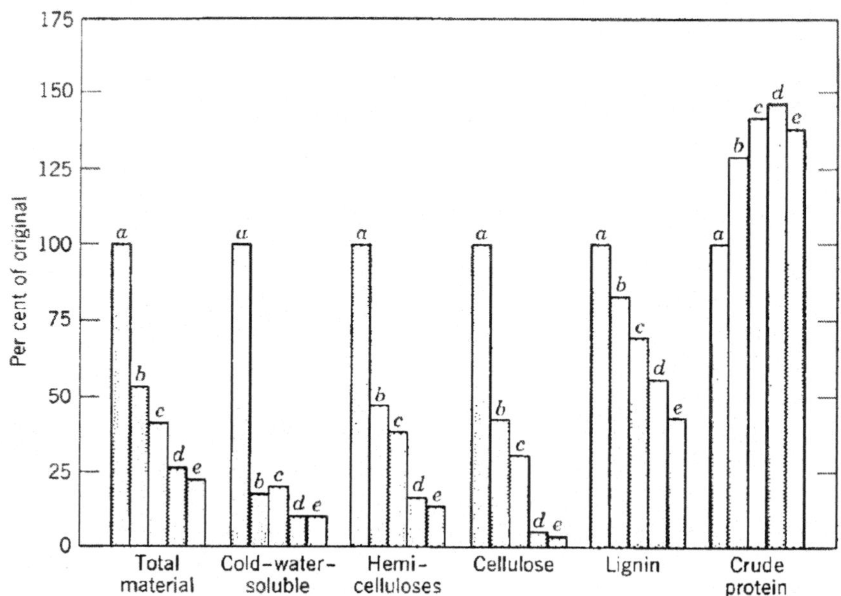

FIG. 51. Course of decomposition of various chemical constituents of corn stover under aerobic conditions (from Tenney and Waksman).

Anaerobic bacteria, however, decompose the cellulose with the formation of various organic acids and alcohols in accordance with the following reactions:

$$\underset{\text{Cellulose}}{(C_6H_{10}O_5)_n} + (n - 1)H_2O = \underset{\text{Glucose}}{nC_6H_{12}O_6}$$

$$C_6H_{12}O_6 = \underset{\text{Lactic acid}}{C_3H_6O_3} + \underset{\text{Ethyl alcohol}}{C_2H_5OH} + CO_2$$

$$\underset{\text{Ethyl alcohol}}{2C_2H_5OH} = \underset{\text{Acetic acid}}{C_2H_4O_2} + \underset{\text{Methane}}{2CH_4}$$

The animal forms capable of utilizing cellulose as a foodstuff range from termites and other wood-destroying insects to herbivorous animals, especially the ruminants The latter carry out the digestion largely by means of an extensive population of bacteria and protozoa that inhabit their digestive tracts The breakdown products of cellulose, the sugars, alcohols, and organic acids, are utilized by the animals for their nutrition Association or symbiosis is thus established, the animal providing a habitat or shelter for the microbes, and the latter digesting the food for the host. Whether this association holds true also for shipworms and other mollusks capable of digesting cellulose in wood still remains to be determined

Among the environmental factors that influence the nature of the microorganisms concerned in the destruction of cellulose under a particular set of conditions, the most important are moisture, reaction, aeration, temperature, and a sufficient supply of nitrogen and other nutrient elements

A high moisture content (80–95 per cent) favors the development of anaerobic bacteria and is injurious to the growth of fungi and of most actinomycetes A medium moisture (50–75 per cent) is favorable to filamentous fungi and to aerobic cellulose-decomposing bacteria; some of the fleshy fungi, like the wood-destroying forms, develop at a lower moisture than the filamentous forms. A very low moisture (10 per cent or less) completely stops the activities of most cellulose-decomposing organisms, although some, such as insects, may still be able to make a certain amount of growth; destruction of paper in books and in paper files takes place at a rather low moisture

The reaction of the medium also has a marked influence upon the nature of the microbiological population responsible for the process of cellulose decomposition. The aerobic bacteria belonging to the *Cytophaga* group are able to grow at *p*H 6.1–9 1. Soils more acid than *p*H 6 0 may be lacking in this group of organisms entirely, although other cellulose-decomposing bacteria are able to develop at *p*H 5 0–6 0 Actinomycetes grow at *p*H 5.5–9.5, whereas fungi develop within much wider reaction ranges, at *p*H 3 0–9.5. Some cellulose-decomposing fungi, like *Trichoderma,* are able to grow even at as high an acidity as *p*H 2 1–2 5 A slightly alkaline reaction (*p*H 7 5) favors, therefore, the growth of bacteria, whereas an acid reaction is injurious to bacteria and is favorable to fungi Addition to the soil of acid-reacting fertilizers, which results in a low *p*H, favors the development of fungi concerned in cellulose decomposition, addition of alkaline fertilizers, especially lime, reduces considerably the numbers of fungi and leads to the development of bacteria which are responsible for decomposition of the cellulose

The aerobic cellulose-decomposing bacteria have their temperature optimum at 20–28°C; the anaerobic organisms grow best at 37°C, the thermophilic fungi at 45–55°C, and the thermophilic bacteria and actinomycetes at 50–65°C. Different temperatures may, therefore, favor the development of different groups of organisms

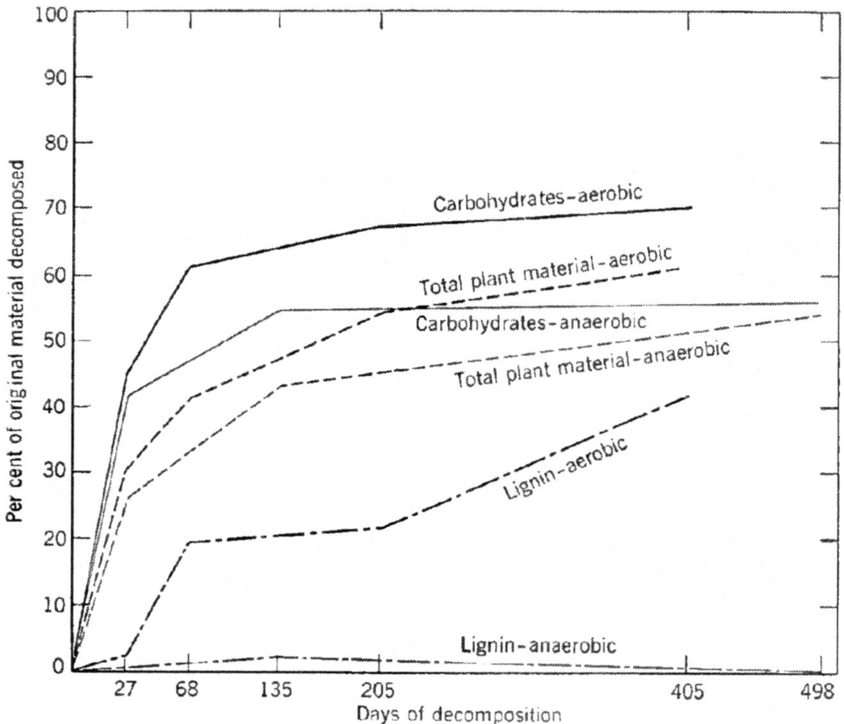

Fig. 52. **Influence of aeration upon the decomposition of the whole alfalfa plant, the total water-insoluble carbohydrates, and the lignins under aerobic and anaerobic conditions** (from Tenney and Waksman).

and thus modify the nature and extent of the process of cellulose decomposition.

The oxygen supply also influences the nature of the cellulose-decomposing microorganisms developing in a given substrate, as well as the speed of their activities. If horse manure is to be stored for some time before it is needed for the preparation of composts for mushroom production, it is kept in a well-compacted state; this creates anaerobic conditions and results in comparatively little cellulose decomposition. When the manure is needed for the mushroom house, it is thoroughly aerated; this leads to active cellulose decomposition, which is accompanied by a rise in temperature.

Jensen made a detailed study of cellulose decomposition in lab-

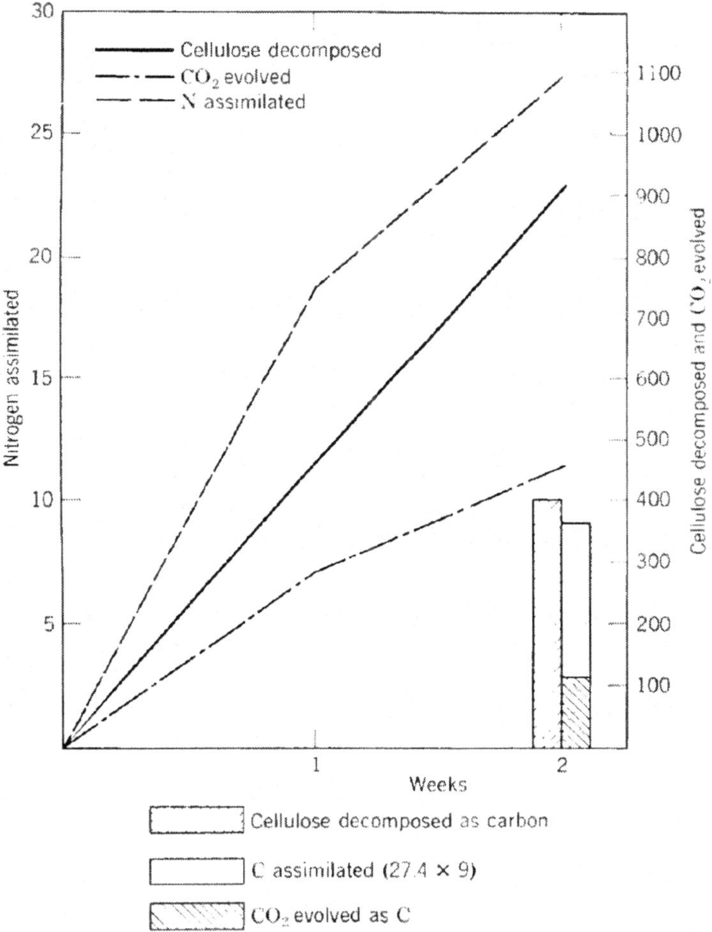

Fig. 53. Relation between cellulose decomposition by microorganisms and nitrogen assimilation, or its transformation into microbial cell substance (from Waksman and Heukelekian).

oratory experiments, using well-manured soil. He reached certain general conclusions concerning the course of decomposition and accompanying microbiological processes:

1. When farmyard manure was added to neutral (*p*H 6.5–7.0) soils, cellulose-decomposing organisms of the genus *Vibrio* devel-

oped When the reaction of the soil was acid (*p*H 5.7–6.2), the vibrios were reduced and *Spirochaeta cytophaga* grew abundantly At a still greater acidity, fungi were the only cellulose-destroying forms, among these *Trichoderma* and *Penicillium* were most active The fungi found in neutral soils included *Mycogone nigra, Stachybotrys, Coccospora agricola,* and *Botryosporium*

2. The cultures of bacteria isolated from the various soils behaved in pure culture in a manner similar to that in the natural soil Four species of *Vibrio* were not active upon cellulose below *p*H 6.4 but gave optimum growth at *p*H 7.1–7.6 *Spirochaeta cytophaga,* however, was able to grow at *p*H 5.6–6.0.

3 All cultures thus isolated were able to decompose not only pure cellulose but also lignified cellulose of straw

4 The nitrogen required for cellulose decomposition varied from 1 part nitrogen to 25–54 parts cellulose

5 The cellulose-decomposing bacteria did not produce any humus-like substances The fungi *Mycogone nigra* and *Stachybotrys* gave rise to humus

Dubos used a simple mineral salt solution for studying cellulose-destroying aerobes This medium consisted of 0.5 gm $NaNO_3$, 1.0 gm K_2HPO_4, 0.5 gm $MgSO_4 \cdot 7H_2O$, 0.5 gm KCl, 0.01 gm $FeSO_4$ $7H_2O$, and 1,000 ml water Strips of filter paper were placed in the tubes containing this medium, and the tubes were inoculated with various dilutions of soil This method proved to be very favorable for the isolation of *Cytophaga* and other cellulose-destroying bacteria The medium could also be used for determination of the quantitative distribution of cellulose-decomposing bacteria in soil.

Decomposition of Hemicelluloses

Hemicelluloses represent a great variety of chemical compounds, usually divided into polysaccharides, or those compounds which give on hydrolysis simple sugars ($C_6H_{12}O_6$, $C_5H_{10}O_5$), and polyuronides, or those that give on hydrolysis sugar acids ($C_6H_{10}O_7$) or mixtures of sugars and sugar acids The designation of individual hemicelluloses is based on the sugar produced on their hydrolysis by acids or enzymes. On hydrolysis, pentosan gives pentose sugar, araban yields arabinose, xylan gives xylose, hexosans yield hexose sugars, galactan giving galactose and mannan giving mannose

The polyuronides are more complex Pectin is an abundant constituent of fruits and vegetables and is made up of galactose, arabinose, galacturonic acid, acetic acid, and methyl alcohol Some polyuronides are simple polymers of uronic acid, $(C_6H_{10}O_6)_n$, whereas others are even more complex than pectins.

Hemicelluloses are attacked by a great variety of bacteria and fungi, they can also be digested by most animal forms There is greater variation in the digestibility and in the rate of decomposition of the hemicelluloses than of cellulose, because of greater differences in chemical nature between various hemicelluloses Some, like the mannans, are attacked readily, similarly to the starches, whereas others, like the galactans, are more resistant to decomposition and can be attacked only by highly specific organisms. In the rotting of fruits and vegetables, either in a growing state or in storage, the breakdown of the pectins is particularly important This is carried out first by a group of enzymes, designated as pectase, pectinase, and pectolase, as follows.

$$\underset{\text{Pectin}}{C_{41}H_{60}O_{36}} + 9H_2O = \underset{\text{Galactose}}{C_6H_{12}O_6} + \underset{\text{Arabinose}}{C_5H_{10}O_5} + \underset{\text{Acetic acid}}{2CH_3\ COOH} + \underset{\text{Methyl alcohol}}{2CH_3OH} + \underset{\text{Galacturonic acid}}{4C_6H_{10}O_7}$$

Similar reactions are involved in the retting of flax and other fibers by aerobic bacteria and fungi, anaerobic bacteria change the sugars and sugar acids of the pectin to alcohols and lower acids.

Since arabans and xylans make up 20–30 per cent of cereal straw, of corn cobs, and of other plant residues, their breakdown in composts and in soil is of great importance. They are usually attacked by a variety of organisms somewhat more readily than is cellulose Hemicelluloses also form an important group of constituents of microbial cell substance (capsular material) and may thus contribute materially to the humus produced.

The decomposition of cellulose and hemicelluloses in oat straw harvested at different stages of growth is brought out in Table 21 When the plant is young, and its cellulose and lignin contents are low, it decomposes very rapidly. as much as 56 3 per cent of the total material has been destroyed by the microorganisms in 59 days As the plant grows older and as its cellulose and lignin contents increase, its rate of decomposition decreases, that this is due largely to an unbalanced nitrogen condition is brought out by the fact that, when a soluble nitrogen compound is added, the mature plant material decomposes as rapidly and as extensively as the young plant.

TABLE 21 INFLUENCE OF AGE OF PLANT (OATS) UPON THE DECOMPOSITION OF ITS CONSTITUENT CARBOHYDRATES (from Gerretsen and Waksman)

Per cent of decomposition after 125 days

Constituent	Age of Plant, days 59	86	112
Hemicellulose	15 3	17 4	19 3
Cellulose	24 6	34 5	39 1
Lignin	6 7	11 7	15 7
Total decomposed no nitrogen added	56 3	37 4	27 1
Total decomposed + $(NH_4)_2HPO_4$		62 8	60 2
Hemicellulose decomposed	14 4	12 6	10 4
Hemicellulose decomposed + $(NH_4)_2HPO_4$		16 0	17 3
Cellulose decomposed, no nitrogen added	20 8	24 3	20 1
Cellulose decomposed + $(NH_4)_2HPO_4$		31 8	36 0

The effect of the added nitrogen is largely concerned with the greater decomposition of the cellulose and hemicelluloses

Numerous other transformations take place in the process of decomposition of complex plant materials

Decomposition of Proteins and Other Nitrogenous Substances

Proteins make up 1–20 per cent of all plant residues They are complexes of amino acids They contain, on an average, 50–55 per cent carbon, 15–19 per cent nitrogen, 6–7 per cent hydrogen, 21–23 per cent oxygen, and small amounts of sulfur, some proteins also contain phosphorus

Proteins vary considerably in nature and in functions, depending upon their amino acid make-up On hydrolysis by specific enzymes or by chemical reagents, the proteins are split first into various polypeptides and finally into simple amino acids. The latter are further attacked by a great variety of bacteria and fungi, giving rise to ammonia, carbon dioxide, and various organic acids and alcohols Under anaerobic conditions, various amines and mercaptans are also formed, these are responsible for the "putrefactive" odors produced in the decomposition of protein-rich materials.

The great majority of soil organisms are capable of attacking proteins. The amount of nitrogen finally changed to ammonia depends upon the nature of the organism, nature of the protein, presence of available carbohydrates, and soil conditions Since in the decomposition of proteins and amino acids energy is also liberated, a certain amount of cell material will be synthesized by the organisms. Some of the nitrogen will thus be consumed and transformed into

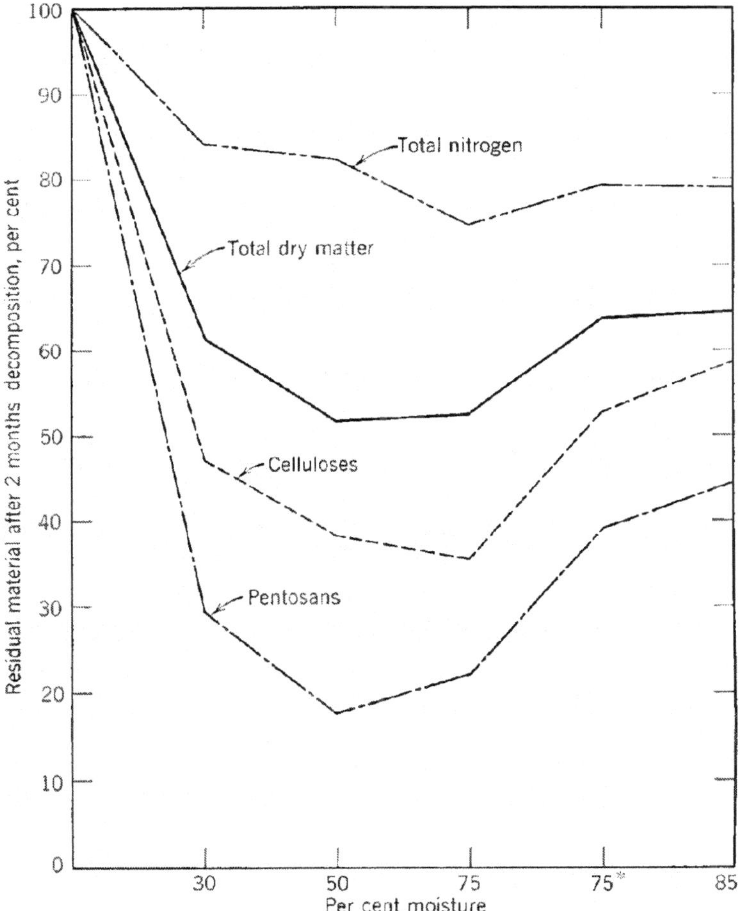

FIG. 54. Influence of moisture and aeration upon decomposition of horse manure (from Egorov).

microbial cell substance. The amount of ammonia liberated in the decomposition of protein will thus be a resultant of the breakdown of the protein and the destruction of the amino acids, on the one hand, and of cell synthesis, on the other. The amount of ammonia finally liberated may thus range from 50 to 80 per cent of the total nitrogen of the protein decomposed. In the presence of carbohydrates, more of the ammonia will be consumed by the organisms;

therefore, the greater the relative concentration of the carbohydrates to the proteins, the less ammonia will be liberated.

The decomposition of different proteins by pure cultures of different microorganisms is brought out in Table 22 In comparison

TABLE 22 FORMATION OF AMMONIA (MG) BY MICROORGANISMS FROM 0.5 GM OF PROTEINS IN 40 DAYS (from Waksman and Starkey)

Protein	Organism			
	Proteolytic Bacterium	*Bacillus subtilis*	*Streptomyces coelicolor*	*Rhizopus* sp
Gelatin	25.45	42.82	39.99	18.98
Casein	37.57	23.43	21.81	18.58
Gliadin	29.91	14.55	21.41	18.59
Fibrin	19.76	18.55	16.12	18.55
Albumin	15.75	14.54	15.35	11.31
Zein	25.86	7.68	8.89	2.43

with the fungus and actinomyces cultures, the bacterium synthesized less cell material and liberated the greatest amount of ammonia.

Plant and animal residues contain, in addition to proteins, various other nitrogenous substances, such as urea, purine bases, hippuric acid, lecithin, choline, cyanamide, cyanide, alkaloids and chitins These compounds are also decomposed by a great variety of microorganisms in soils and in composts, the mechanism of their decomposition depends upon the nature of the organism and conditions of decomposition (Table 23).

Cyanamide is first changed in the soil to urea, which is decomposed further, it may also polymerize to give dicyanodiamide, which is toxic to some bacteria, such as the nitrifying forms Choline is transformed to trimethylamine by a variety of bacteria. Urea is decomposed to ammonia

$$CO\begin{matrix} \diagup NH_2 \\ \diagdown NH_2 \end{matrix} + H_2O = 2NH_3 + CO_2$$

DECOMPOSITION OF LIGNINS

Lignins are complex plant materials characterized by a benzol ring structure with certain side chains This is shown by the following formula·

$$C_{40}H_{30}O_6(OCH_3)_4\ (OH)_5\ CHO$$

TABLE 23 DECOMPOSITION OF VEGETABLE AND ANIMAL PROTEINS BY DIFFERENT MICROORGANISMS (from Waksman and Starkey)

Period of decomposition, 9–15 days.

Protein	Organism	Dry Weight of Residue	Nitrogen Content of Residue	NH_2-N	NH_3-N
		mg	*mg*	*mg*	*mg*
Edestin	Control	978	164.2	0	Trace
	T. koningi	604	85.1	28.3	32.6
	S. viridochromogenus	862	140.8	4.5	11.7
	B. cereus	408	65.0	22.8	40.1
Gliadin	Control	954	135.0	0	0
	T. koningi	271	28.0	36.8	32.8
	S. viridochromogenus	792	109.8	3.5	15.2
	B. cereus	51	7.3	36.2	42.6
Zein	Control	966	144.8	0	0
	T. koningi	718	97.3	14.0	26.8
	B. cereus	128	17.9	27.8	46.5
Casein	Control	. .	140.2	7.5	1.2
	T. koningi	232	17.2	12.6	44.7
	S. viridochromogenus	95	10.2	13.3	19.2
	B. cereus	105	12.3	38.9	40.9

This formula is not generally accepted. Certain investigators proposed the formula of substituted phenyl-propane groups linked together. The phenyl group has a hydroxyl in the *para* position and a methoxyl in the *meta*. The propane may have a double bond, thus becoming a propene, and a hydroxyl. It is also claimed that nitrogen is present as a tertiary amine in a linkage similar to that in pyridine. Bondi and Meyer claimed that lignins of various plants are built out of three of these units, having a molecular weight of about 650. They formed two methoxyls in grass lignins and one methoxyl in leguminous lignins, each lignin containing two phenolic hydroxyls and one aliphatic.

Lignins are found in virtually all plants in varying concentrations, depending upon the nature of the plant and the degree of its maturity, usually to the extent of 5–30 per cent. The more mature the plant, the higher its lignin content; young plants have comparatively little lignin, whereas mature plants have a high lignin content.

In the decomposition of plant materials under natural conditions, lignin tends to accumulate, since it is more resistant to decomposition than are the carbohydrates and proteins (Table 24). Fir wood,

TABLE 24. CHANGES IN THE CHEMICAL COMPOSITION OF WOOD AS A RESULT OF ITS DECOMPOSITION (from Rose and Lisse)

On basis of dry wood

Chemical Constituent	Cellulose	Pentosan	Methoxyl Groups	Alkali-Soluble	Methyl-pentosan
	per cent	*per cent*	*per cent*	*per cent*	*per cent*
Fresh wood	58.96	7.16	3.94	10.61	2.64
Partly decomposed wood	41.66	6.79	5.16	38.10	3.56
Fully decomposed wood	8.47	2.96	7.80	65.31	6.06

for example, lost all or nearly all of its cellulose constituents, but still contained 85.55 per cent lignin, after considerable decomposition.

When plants are attacked by soil microorganisms, the lignins are affected only to a very limited extent, especially when present in mature plants and under anaerobic conditions of decomposition. As a result, lignin contributes considerably to the formation of humus in soils, in composts, and in certain types of peat bogs.

Under aerobic conditions, lignin is not absolutely resistant to decomposition but can be gradually oxidized. The exact nature of the organisms concerned in the oxidation of the lignins in soils and the nature of the products formed are not yet clearly understood. It is known, however, that certain organisms, like some of the higher or fleshy fungi, including some of the wood-destroying forms, are capable of attacking lignins very rapidly. Falck distinguished two processes in the decomposition of wood by fungi, namely, "destruction" and "corrosion." In "destruction," cellulose is decomposed, whereas the lignin accumulates, organisms like *Merulius lacrymans* and species of *Coniophora, Poria,* and *Lenzites* are concerned in this process. In "corrosion," the lignin as well as the cellulose is attacked. *Polyporus annosus* is responsible for this process in spruce wood. *Trametes pini* attacks the lignin in pine wood. In the "destruction" of wood, the cellulose diminished from 56 per cent in the original material to 7.8 per cent, whereas the lignin increased from 23.5 to 56.5 per cent, in "corrosion," the lignin diminished from 23.5 to 15.1 per cent and the cellulose from 56.0 to 48.2 per cent. Several other fungi, like *Stereum rugosum,* are also capable of attacking lignins. *Agaricus nebularis* destroys lignin, cellulose, and pentosan, whereas *Coniophora cerebella* is able to decompose cellulose but not lignin.

The common edible mushroom, *Psalliota campestris,* is capable of utilizing lignin for its nutrition. In 51 days, 18 per cent of the lignin in a compost and only 14.5 per cent of the cellulose were decomposed. Other fleshy fungi, like *Coprinus*, are also capable of attacking lignin, from fresh horse manure, *C. radians* removed, in 51 days, 22 per cent of the total lignin and 70 per cent of the cellulose.

Decomposition of Other Plant Constituents

Plant and animal materials contain organic compounds that undergo rapid or slow decomposition by microorganisms. Of particular importance are the oils, fats, and waxes, the sterols and alcohols, the organic acids and tannins, the paraffins, cutins, and gums, and a variety of compounds that occur in varying concentrations from a fraction of 1 per cent to more than 2 per cent. These are all decomposed, sooner or later, giving rise to numerous products. Oils and fats, for example, are hydrolyzed to glycerol and fatty acids; the glycerol is readily oxidized to CO_2 and water, and the fatty acids may give rise to certain resistant and, sometimes, toxic products.

The transformation of fatty substances under anaerobic conditions is a process that is believed to have contributed materially to the origin of petroleum. *Clostridium perfringens*, for example, has been shown to form, from alkaline oleates prepared from olive oil, a black combustible liquid immiscible with water and resembling a petroleum fraction.

Decomposition of Plant Materials as a Whole

Rapid decomposition of plant materials is favored by the following conditions.

1. A low lignin and wax content of the plant material
2. The presence of an adequate supply of available nitrogen
3. A fine state of mechanical disintegration
4. A favorable *p*H
5. Favorable aeration and an adequate supply of moisture. Anaerobic conditions result in a restricted bacterial population, with lower nitrogen requirements
6. A high temperature, usually within the range of 30–45°C

Mixed materials frequently decompose more quickly than single types of materials. This is true, for example, of a mixture of straw and alfalfa, bedding and excreta in animal manures, and mixed litter from several species of trees.

Selected Bibliography

1 Dubos, R J, The decomposition of cellulose by aerobic bacteria, *J Bact*, 15 223–234, 1928

2 Jensen, H L, Microbiology of farmyard manure decomposition in soil II Decomposition of cellulose, *J. Agr Sci*, 21 81–100, 1931

3 Lundegårdh, H, *Environment and Plant Development*, Edward Arnold & Co, London, 1931

4 Norman, A G, *The Biochemistry of Cellulose, Polyuronides and Lignin*, Oxford University Press, New York, 1937

5 Pringsheim, H, *The Chemistry of the Monosaccharides and of the Polysaccharides*, McGraw-Hill Book Co, New York, 1932

6 Smith, F. B, and Brown, P E, Decomposition of lignin and other organic constituents by certain soil fungi, *J. Am Soc Agron*, 27 109–119, 1935

7 Waksman, S A, *Principles of Soil Microbiology*, Williams & Wilkins Co, Baltimore, 2nd Ed, 1932

8 Waksman, S A, and Diehm, R A, On the decomposition of hemicelluloses by microorganisms I Nature, occurrence, preparation, and decomposition of hemicelluloses, *Soil Sci*, 32.73–95, 1931.

9 Waksman, S A, *Humus*, Williams & Wilkins Co, Baltimore, 2nd Ed, 1938

10 Wise, L E, *Wood Chemistry*, Reinhold Publishing Corp, New York, 1944

• 5 •

Humus: Nature and Formation

What Is Humus?

In the past, various meanings attached to the term "humus." Some used this term to designate a certain fraction of the organic matter in soils and in composts, others used it to indicate all the organic matter of the soil, still others recognized as humus the organic materials of natural origin in advanced stages of decomposition, whether in soils, in composts, or in peat bogs, and whether plant or animal in nature. Fresh plant roots and stubble, fresh stable manures and green manures, fresh kitchen wastes and garbage, undecomposed bodies of worms and insects, fresh tankage and fish, and numerous other products of plant and animal life, when their origins are still recognizable, are not in a humified or in a humus state All these serve as sources of humus, upon their decomposition by microorganisms, humus is produced

When various plant and animal residues are plowed into the soil or are made up into composts, they are immediately attacked by numerous microorganisms, including bacteria, actinomycetes, fungi, protozoa, and worms. As a result of their decomposition, some of the constituents of the fresh materials are volatilized, others are used by the microorganisms for the building of microbial cell substance, and still others are gradually transformed into a uniform, dark-colored, amorphous mass, which is designated as "humus." The rate of formation of humus and the amounts produced depend upon the physical and chemical nature of the residues, the nature of the soil or of the compost in which decomposition is taking place, the nature of the microorganisms concerned, and the environmental conditions, notably temperature, moisture supply, aeration, and reaction. In humus, the products of decomposition can no longer be distinguished from the original plant and animal materials from which they have been formed

This broad concept of humus must be differentiated from its narrow definition, whereby only certain constitutents of the organic matter of soils, composts, and peats, possessing characteristic properties, such as dark pigment, solubility in alkalies, and insolubility in certain oxidizing agents, are designated as humus. Frequently, the narrow definition does not differentiate between "humus" and "humic acid," another ill-defined term, occasionally used to designate the alkali-soluble or the alcohol-soluble humus constituents A highly complex terminology has been introduced for distinguishing a number of "humic acids" on the basis of their solubility in certain reagents. In view of the great confusion that has resulted from this definition, this concept of the "humic acids" can no longer be accepted in classifying humus types and humus constituents.

By the use of selective adsorption techniques, Forsyth separated four fractions from humus. (1) a fraction that is usually present in small quantities and contains water-soluble organic compounds, such as sugars and amino acids; (2) a fraction containing phenolic glycosides or tannins, (3) a polyuronide of the glucuronic acid type containing *d*-glucose, *d*-xylose, *l*-rhamnose, and another sugar, this fraction seems to have a composition independent of the soil from which it has been extracted, and may be of bacterial origin, (4) a fraction rich in nitrogen and containing pentose sugars and organic phosphates

Bremner used neutral pyrophosphate for dispersing the humic fractions of the soil humus The proportions of the fractions appeared to depend on the treatment. These results indicate that artifacts are produced by hydrolysis of the humus material, especially when sodium hydroxide solution is used for dispersion. Other side reactions may also be brought about.

The so-called humins in the soil are not dispersed in caustic soda They appear to be polymerization products of some of the humus constituents and also contain some of the undecomposed or partially decomposed plant and microbial residues

Certain constituents of humus or even certain types of humus are frequently designated as "true humus" or "pure humus," especially in speaking of organic materials in advanced stages of decomposition. This is true of various peats, forest litter, well-composted plant materials, and the humus of mineral soils. These must not be considered superior forms of humus, but merely types of humus, or designations of certain humus forms Under different conditions, a variety of different humus types is produced One can thus speak of field, orchard, and garden soil humus, of pasture soil humus; of forest humus, comprising not only the litter, but also the underlying humus layers, of highmoor, lowmoor, and forest peat humus, of composts produced from stable manures and from other farm residues, of sewage sludge and garbage humus, and of water humus or marine humus, that form of organic matter which is found in flowing and in standing fresh- or salt-water basins.

Some plant residues decompose very rapidly in the soil but leave comparatively little humus, whereas others decompose much more slowly and leave large amounts of humus. Not only the nature of the plant material but also its age or degree of maturity influences the rapidity of its decomposition. Among the soil factors that influence formation of humus from the plant residues, the mechanical composition of the soil, its physical conditions, notably its texture, and its chemical properties, especially reaction and presence of available nutritive elements, are most important. The formation and nature of humus are also influenced by the system of crop rotation, by fertilizer treatment, by utilization of green manures, by abundance of animals on the farm, by climatic conditions, and by other factors.

Humus may be considered the more or less final and stable product into which some of the plant and animal residues are transformed in the process of decomposition Humus is not an absolutely resistant product, since it is also decomposed, but only very slowly, in the soil The rate of its destruction, however, is far less than that of the plant and animal materials from which it originated

Humus thus represents a natural organic system, in a state of a more or less dynamic equilibrium. Since humus originates from plant, animal, and microbial residues, its composition depends upon the chemical nature of these residues. Since humus is formed as a result of various decomposition processes, its composition will also depend upon the microorganisms concerned in the decomposition of the residues, and upon the conditions under which this process takes place. Because of these factors, a number of humus types are present in nature One is thus able to differentiate between the humus of lowmoor and of highmoor peats, between the humus in coniferous and deciduous forests, between the humus found in mineral soils, notably of the podzol, chernozem, and gray-desert types, and between the humus present in lake and in marine bottoms Although all these forms of humus vary markedly in chemical composition, they represent a type of organic matter which has a number of common physical, chemical, and biological properties. An appreciation of the chemistry of humus is based largely upon a knowledge of the processes of decomposition of plant and animal residues under natural conditions.

Fig. 53. Humus podzol (from Thom).

Nature and Functions of Humus

Humus possesses certain properties that distinguish it from the plant and animal materials from which it has been formed. These properties of humus can be briefly characterized as follows: it is dark brown to black in color; it is virtually insoluble in water, although a part of it may go into colloidal solution in pure water; it dissolves to a large extent in dilute alkali solutions, especially on boiling, giving a dark-colored extract; a large part of this extract precipitates when the alkali solution is neutralized by mineral acids.

Certain constituents of humus may also dissolve in acid solutions and may be precipitated at the isoelectric point, which is at pH 4.8

Chemically, humus contains a somewhat larger amount of carbon than do plant, animal, and microbial bodies; the carbon content of humus is about 55–60 per cent, usually averaging 58 per cent. Humus contains considerable nitrogen, from 3 to 6 per cent, these figures may frequently be lower, as in certain highmoor peats, which contain only 0.8–1.0 per cent nitrogen; they may also be higher, especially in certain subsoils, where they may reach 10–12 per cent.

Humus contains the elements carbon and nitrogen in a ratio which is close to 10 1; this is true of many soils and of the humus in sea bottoms. This ratio varies somewhat with the nature of the humus, the stage of its decomposition, the nature and depth of soil from which it has been obtained, and the climatic and other environmental conditions under which it has been formed Humus is not chemically static or nonvariable, but is rather in a dynamic condition, since it is constantly formed from plant and animal residues and is continuously decomposed further by microorganisms Humus serves as a source of energy for the development of various groups of microorganisms, and as a result of its decomposition a continuous stream of carbon dioxide and ammonia is given off.

Humus possesses a high capacity for base exchange, the ability to combine with various other inorganic soil constituents, to absorb water, and to swell. It is also characterized by other physical and physicochemical properties that make it a highly valuable constituent of natural substrates, such as soils, which support plant and animal life.

The importance of humus in the soil is manifold. it serves as a source of nutrients for plant growth; it modifies, in various ways, the physical and chemical nature of the soil, it regulates and determines the nature of the microbial population and its activities, by supplying various organic and inorganic nutrients essential for growth of these organisms and by making the soil a more favorable substrate for their development. An abundance of humus in the soil is practically equivalent to a high rate of fertility of the soil Humus characterizes the soil type, since differences in its origin, abundance, and chemical nature result in the development of a particular type of soil.

Humus may be looked upon as a storehouse of important chemical elements essential for plant life, especially of carbon and nitrogen, and to a less extent of phosphorus, calcium, magnesium, iron, manganese, and many others The utilization of some of these elements held in the inorganic fraction of the soil is also influenced by the soil humus, through its chemical interaction with the inorganic complexes. One should consider further the colloidal effects of humus on the soil; its buffering properties, which modify the soil reaction, its combining power with bases, its influence upon the oxidation-reduction potential of the soil; its adsorption of certain toxic materials injurious to plant growth, its ability to supply certain catalytic agents and small quantities of various trace elements essential for plant growth, its influence upon soil structure, upon the moisture-holding capacity of the soil, and upon soil temperature. Humus also brings about in the soil numerous other reactions which are of direct or indirect importance to plant growth.

The functions of humus in the soil may thus be considered threefold: (1) *physical,* thereby modifying the color, texture, and structure of the soil, as well as its moisture-holding capacity and aeration, (2) *chemical,* influencing the solubility of certain soil minerals, forming compounds with some of the elements, such as iron, which thus become more readily available for plant growth, and increasing the buffering properties of the soil; (3) *biological,* by serving as a source of energy for the development of microorganisms, by making the soil a better medium for the growth of higher plants, and by supplying certain essential nutrient elements and compounds required by higher plants.

The Nature of the Clay-Humus Complex

Among the important aspects of humus in the soil, the most significant is its interaction with the clay constituents, which gives rise to clay-humus. In this respect, two types of soil are frequently recognized in one the clay and humus particles are held together by calcium ions in the other, iron, and possibly also manganese and aluminum, may replace calcium, although aluminum has not yet been demonstrated to play this part. Tiulin classified the soil colloids into two groups in one (group II colloids) the iron acts as a cement, holding the clay and humic particles together, iron, and possibly also aluminum, appear to be responsible for the binding of the humus to the sand particles in the B horizon of a podzol The organic matter dispersed from the B horizon is rich in iron and possibly also in aluminum, it is comparable to the β-humus of Waksman. When dispersed in acid solutions, these substances may become negatively charged, act as cations, and move toward the cathode during the electrodialysis of soils. They are usually not considered to confer a favorable structure on the soil.

The group I colloids of Tiulin comprise the clay-humus complex which is held together by calcium ions. Agriculturally, it is believed to be the most important type. This complex is largely responsible for the favorable physical conditions found in various soils and composts. The clay appears to have an appreciable base-exchange capacity. The presence of calcium is essential if only for ensuring the formation of the correct type of humus.

Increasing the amount of soil organic matter in this combination is of great importance. The addition of clay to sandy soil may be as important as the addition of organic matter itself. A certain quantity of stable manure or compost or mass of plant residues can be converted into this type of complex only when it is composted with a certain type of clay before it is applied to the soil.

A third organic-inorganic colloid has been prepared, although it has not been isolated from field soil. Ensminger and Gieseking found that proteins can be strongly adsorbed by bentonites through their basic groups acting as an exchangeable base; this process of adsorption renders the protein more resistant to proteolytic enzymes. In view of the fact that only little is known about the nitrogenous constituents of the soil organic matter, it is difficult to postulate the formation of protein complexes and the reasons for their stability.

How Humus Is Formed

The various plant and animal residues on the farm and in the home, the crop wastes, and those crops which are specially grown as a source of humus, all vary considerably in chemical composition and in the rapidity of decomposition. The rate of liberation of the chemical elements, notably the carbon and the nitrogen, in forms available for crop growth, and the nature and amount of humus produced from these residues will, therefore, also vary. Among the sources of humus, plant stubble, stable manures, green manures, and artificial composts occupy a leading place.

Plant stubble includes the root systems of the plants, as well as the stems, leaves, and other residues left after the crop has been harvested. There is considerable variation in the amount and chemical composition of the stubble, depending on the nature and abundance of the crop, method of soil cultivation, and fertilizer treat-

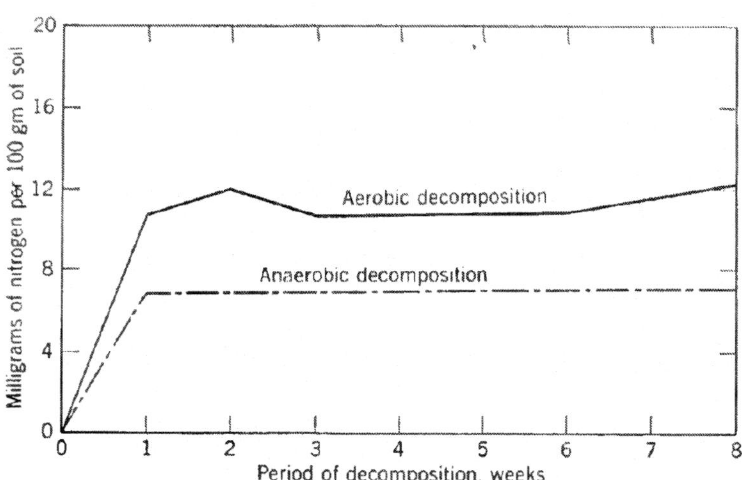

FIG. 56. Decomposition of sheep manure under aerobic and anaerobic conditions (from Joshi).

ment. Because of the difficulty in removing the mass of roots left by the crop, only the surface portions are usually determined. The root mass may equal if not exceed the surface stubble, as shown in Table 25, where the results obtained by Woods in 1888 are reported.

TABLE 25. AMOUNT OF STUBBLE AND ROOTS LEFT BY VARIOUS CROPS (from Woods)

Pounds (air-dry) per acre.

Plant	Weight of Tops	Weight of Stubble	Weight of Roots
Clover, in bloom	1,657	. . .	898
Clover, ripe	. . . . .	1,272	1,460
Wheat, heading	2,554	226	591
Wheat, ripe	7,092	595	591
Oats	5,037	216	293
Barley, heading	2,449	187	408
Barley, ripe	7,154	355	336
Timothy, ripe	5,254	2,056	5,215

The plant residues vary considerably in chemical composition, the stubble and roots of cereals containing about 0.5 per cent nitrogen, 0.1 per cent phosphorus, and 0.5 per cent potassium, whereas the corresponding concentrations of these elements in legume residues are 2–3, 0.5, and 2–2.5 per cent. The chemical composition of stable manures, green manures, and other sources of humus is given in Chap. 14.

In the decomposition of plant and animal residues by microorganisms in soils and composts, the materials are not attacked as a whole. Some of the organic constituents are decomposed very readily, others less quickly, and still others are fairly resistant and tend to disappear only very slowly. Some of the compounds are decomposed completely; others are transformed into various products which are more resistant. The sugars and starches are rapidly destroyed, followed by some of the hemicelluloses, the proteins, and the celluloses. The

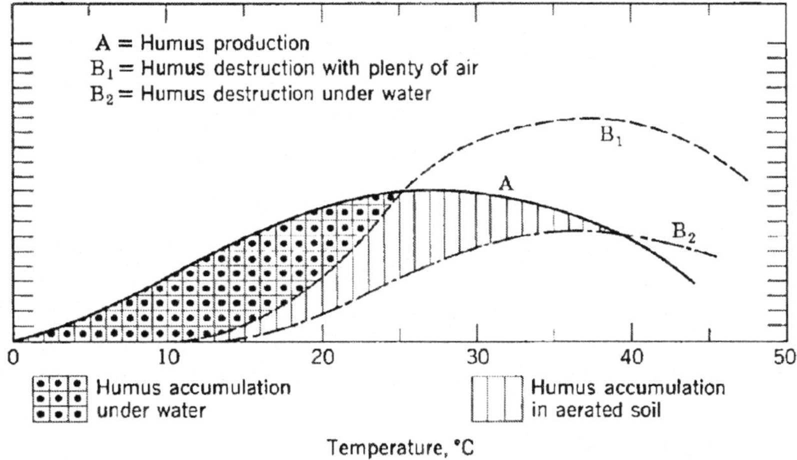

FIG. 57. Humus accumulation and humus decomposition in tropical soils (from Mohr).

lignins and some of their derivatives, certain proteins and hemicelluloses, as well as the waxes, tannins, and other materials, are more resistant to decomposition and therefore gradually accumulate. The processes of decomposition are accompanied by the synthesis of microbial cell substance comprising fungus mycelium, bacterial bodies, worms, and insects.

When plant and animal residues are added to the soil or placed in composts, rapid decomposition sets in at first. This is followed by consumption of oxygen, evolution of heat, liberation of considerable carbon dioxide and ammonia if the material is rich in nitrogen, and darkening of the residual material. As the decomposition progresses and as the more readily decomposable constituents disappear, the process becomes slower until a certain level is reached, when the residual mass has become brown to black.

This mass of slowly decomposing and decomposed material, together with the newly synthesized microbial cell substance, comprises the humus. Humus is formed from the plant and animal residues which have lost the readily decomposable constituents, have gained the synthesized microbial substances, and have accumulated the more resistant constituents. Humus is, therefore, chemically not always the same.

Humus accumulates under conditions not favorable to its further decomposition. This is true particularly when humus is formed in a water-saturated environment, as in peat bogs, or in an acid environment, as in raw humus layers in forest soils, or at very low temperatures, as in high altitudes, when it is frequently designated as "alpine humus."

Methods of Analysis of Humus

The total humus content can be determined by the loss on ignition, especially in peats, composts, and other humus-rich materials. In mineral soils, the best method of determining humus is to calculate it from the organic carbon content, by using the factor 1.724. The fact that humus is not simple in chemical composition and that it comprises a number of complex substances, both organic and inorganic, can be demonstrated by the proximate method of analysis, when it is possible to show that different types of humus have different chemical compositions (Tables 26 and 27). Not only does

Table 26. Chemical Composition of the Organic Matter in Different Mineral Soils

On basis of total dry soil, surface samples

Soil No.	Description of Soil	pH	Loss on Ignition	Total Carbon × 1.72	Total Nitrogen	C/N Ratio
			per cent	*per cent*	*per cent*	
4	Summit	6.8	7.9	4.5	0.24	11
6	Chernozem, Hays, Kansas	7.6	6.0	2.7	0.15	10
16	Chernozem, Edmonton, Alberta	6.4	17.1	11.2	0.67	10
18	Brown soil at Indian Head, Saskatchewan	8.3	10.3	6.2	0.33	11
21	Chernozem at Brandon, Manitoba	8.3	10.0	7.4	0.40	11
29	Carrington loam, dark colored prairie	7.8	10.2	6.5	0.32	12

forest humus vary from peat humus and from humus in composts, but all these vary considerably from the humus in mineral soils. The humus in the different layers of forest soils varies greatly in chemical composition.

Table 27. Chemical Nature of the Organic Matter of Soils Described in Table 26

On basis of total organic matter (C × 1.72).

Soil No.	Ether-Soluble	Alcohol-Soluble	Hemi-cellulose	Cellulose	Lignin-Humus Complex	Protein
	per cent	*per cent*	*per cent*	*per cent*	*per cent*	*per cent*
4	3.6	0.6	5.4	3.6	43.4	33.8
6	4.7	1.5	8.6	5.2	40.8	34.7
16	0.8	0.8	5.5	4.1	41.9	37.4
18	1.0	0.9	7.0	3.5	42.0	33.3
21	0.5	0.8	8.5	2.8	42.8	33.4
29	0.6	0.6	8.2	3.6	42.3	30.4

Peat as Humus

Peat represents a type of humus which has originated as a result of decomposition of plant materials in areas submerged in water. It comprises various organic formations spoken of also as "muck,"

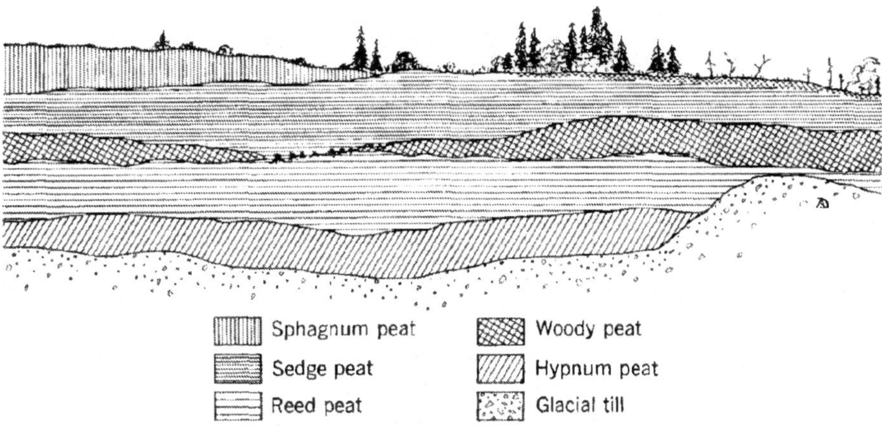

Fig. 58. Different layers in peat profile (from Stokes).

"turf," "peat moss," and "black humus." The physical and chemical differences found among the different types of peat are due largely to the nature of the plants from which they have been formed.

Lowmoor peat, frequently spoken of as "muck," is produced principally from reeds and sedges; it is slightly acid in reaction (*p*H 5.0–6.0) and contains 5–10 per cent mineral matter and 2–4 per cent nitrogen. Peat moss, or highmoor peat, is formed from sphagnum and other mossy plants; it is more fibrous in nature, very acid in reaction (pH 3.5–4.5), low in ash and nitrogen (less than 1 per cent). After proper drainage, the lowmoor peat, as well as a third type of peat, known as sedimentary, forms good agricultural soil. Lowmoor peat is also harvested and marketed for making lawns. Highmoor or sphagnum peat is used as litter in stables and for horticultural purposes. A number of other peats, intermediary in nature, are formed from different types of vegetation and under different environmental conditions.

Most peats are valuable as sources of humus, but they are poor as plant nutrients, and even the nitrogen in the peats is not so readily available for plant growth as is that in animal manures and green manures. Peat cannot, therefore, take the place of fertilizers for plant nutrition; it serves primarily to improve the physical condition of the soil. Peat is frequently mixed or composted with soil, before its application to the soil, in order to prevent the formation of layers and to improve the uniform structure of the soil.

The chemical composition of a group of peats is given in Table 28.

Table 28. Proximate Chemical Composition of Some Typical Peats

On basis of dry material (from Waksman)

Peat Constituent	Lowmoor, New Jersey	Saw-Grass, Florida	Lake Peat, Florida	Forest Peat, New York	Sphagnum Peat, Germany	Sphagnum Peat, Maine
	per cent	*per cent*	*per cent*	*per cent*	*per cent*	*per cent*
Ether-soluble	0.7	3.0	0.4	3.2	3.1	2.5
Water-soluble	3.1	1.7	0.7			
Hemicellulose	10.3	6.4	1.2	5.4	16.9	20.9
Cellulose	0	0.3	0	2.7	19.4	16.2
Lignin-like complex	38.4	46.1	35.2	60.7	34.0	25.4
Protein	22.5	23.1	15.1	14.3	5.2	5.7
Ash	13.2	10.0	39.6	3.9	1.7	1.8
pH	5.9	6.2	7.3	4.7	4.1	4.0

The marked variation in reaction, total organic matter content, and chemical nature of the organic matter is due to differences in the vegetation from which peat has been formed, the nature of the waters finding their way into the peat bogs, the topography of the region, and the climate.

Humus in Forest Soils

Forest humus varies with the nature of the vegetation and the soil. The forest floor usually consists of several distinct layers of

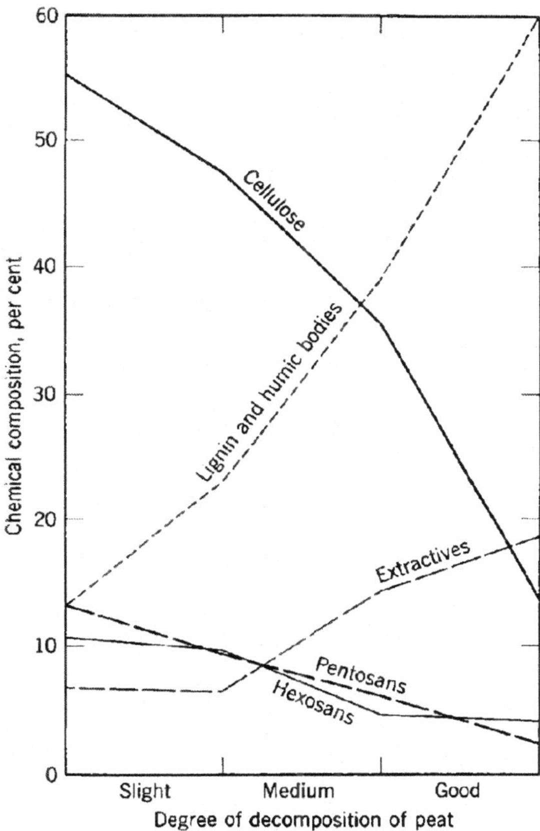

Fig. 59. Decomposition of plant constituents in the process of peat formation (from Maliutin).

vegetable remains. The surface layer, or litter, is made up of partly decomposed leaves, needles, roots, twigs, cones, and other tree residues. This layer is superimposed on another layer of partly decomposed plant residues and is underlain by a third layer of thoroughly decomposed material which is said to be completely humified. The total organic layer of the surface of forest soil is 0.5 to more than 6 inches deep. In evergreen forests, the largely organic surface layers are usually not mixed with the inorganic soil layers; the former are referred to as the "raw humus" or "duff." In deciduous forests, the organic residues and their decomposition products are well mixed with the inorganic part of the soil, giving rise to a type of soil known as "mull." This soil is less acid and is more active biologically.

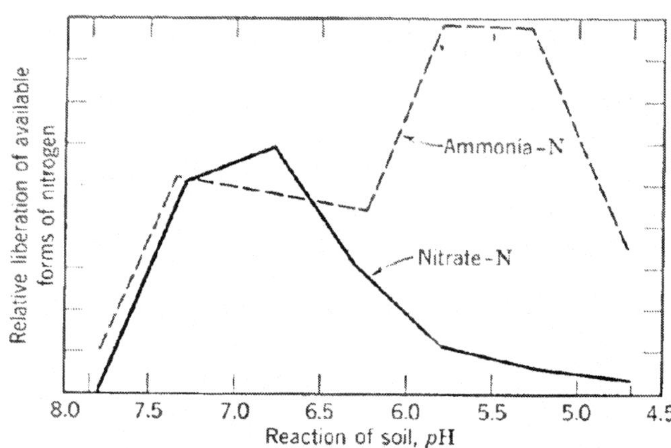

FIG. 60. Influence of reaction upon the nitrate and ammonia nitrogen liberation in forest soil (from Aaltonen).

DECOMPOSITION OF HUMUS

When compared with fresh plant residues, humus is rather resistant to decomposition; otherwise it would not accumulate at all in the soil, and it would certainly not persist there for long periods. Under favorable conditions, however, humus can decompose further. Were this not the case, the soil long ago would have become covered by a surface layer of organic debris of varying degrees of thickness, similar to that formed in peat bogs, in certain forests, and especially in coal. If humus in soil were as resistant to decomposition as humus in coal and in peats, the surface of the earth would have become organic and would not have remained predominantly inorganic in nature; the limited supply of available carbon would soon have become exhausted, making all further life impossible. In fact, under certain conditions, the decomposition of humus in the soil may be so rapid that the farmer experiences considerable difficulty in keeping up the supply, especially when he cultivates his soil year after year and does not return to it sufficient plant residues and organic manures, as in the growing of intertilled crops.

When the temperature, moisture, reaction, and aeration of the soil are favorable, the soil humus undergoes constant decomposition, as evidenced by the continuous stream of carbon dioxide given off into the air and by the nitrate that accumulates in the soil; the nitrogen is first liberated as ammonia, which is changed rapidly to nitrate by certain bacteria. The gradual disappearance of the humus becomes especially evident when the soil is kept fallow or free from all plant growth and no plant residues in any form are added to it.

In the cultivation of soil, the top layer, including both living and dead materials to a depth of 4–8 inches, is turned over. The rapidly decomposing organic residues, which previously were on the surface, are now placed under the surface. Root systems filling the upper layer of soil are thus killed and mixed with the residues already dead and decomposing. The lower layer of soil, which was hitherto protected by a surface layer, is in its turn brought to the surface. Harrowing, hoeing, or other cultivating brings this fresh soil into more or less intimate contact with air, sunlight, and the daily variation of heat, cold, and drought.

The whole mass of soil from the surface to the lower layer of the furrow-slice becomes an aerobic environment in which microorganisms find favorable conditions for development This results in great changes in the soil flora and fauna and in the soil organic matter. Smith and Humfeld, in their studies of decomposition of green manure, showed that great activities were localized wherever plant remains were left to decompose in such a mixture of materials

Humfeld demonstrated that the whole mass above the green manure is quickly flooded with carbon dioxide, due to the respiration of the dying vegetation and to the microbiological reactions When optimum moisture was present, the process was accompanied by the disappearance of the various fungi, and even by the partial suppression of the whole fungus flora. This was true especially of the brown- and black-walled fungi. With a low moisture content, certain fungi developed, the mycelium was colorless, however, and soft-walled, this was associated with a low content of lignin or related substances, which are characteristic of the flora of the surface decomposition process.

Under conditions of regular cultivation, as demonstrated by King and Doryland in Kansas, the organic matter content of the soil was gradually decreased by cultivation. Conditions were made favorable for decomposition of the soil organic matter. This was accompanied by a release of nitrogen, phosphorus, and potash As a result, crop production increased. Continuance of this system of cropping, however, without compensating return of organic manures, might be expected to deplete the humus supply of the soil.

Difficulties encountered in continuous cropping of soils in prairie areas led Alway and others to make extensive comparisons of the organic matter in various soils

When a virgin soil is brought under cultivation, the humus content is reduced, at first rapidly, and then more slowly, depending upon the soil, its climatic conditions, and the manner of cultivation. Although a crop, whether cultivated or uncultivated, leaves certain

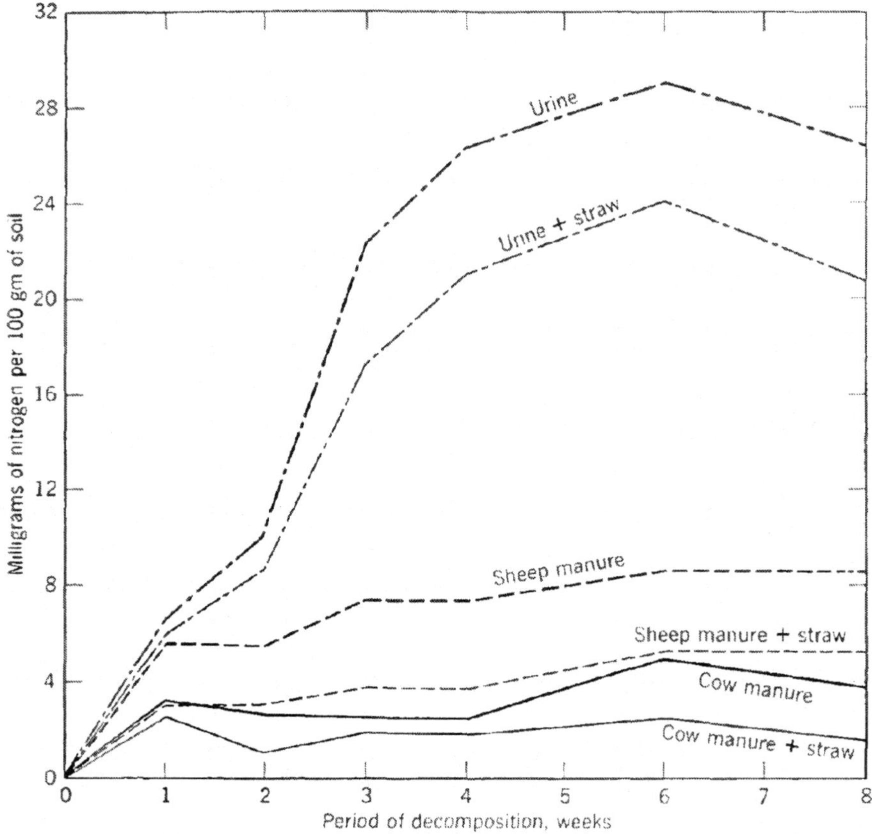

Fig. 61. Influence of straw upon the liberation of nitrogen as nitrate from urine and cow and sheep manure, in the process of decomposition (from Joshi).

residues in the form of roots and stubble, which are gradually changed to humus, the amount of humus decomposed as a result of cultivation is not fully compensated by the humus produced from these residues. To keep up the fertility of the soil in certain types of farming, it is essential to increase the humus content above that made possible by the residues of a cultivated crop grown on the soil. This can be done by growing a special crop to be plowed under for green manuring purposes, by adding stable manures, or by introducing special forms of humus, such as composts, forest litter, or peat. Addition of sufficient inorganic fertilizer will also result in an increase in the amount of plant residues, which will yield greater amounts of humus to replace, partly at least, the loss resulting from cultivation.

Shutt found that, on cultivating a virgin prairie soil, there was a loss of over 100 pounds of nitrogen per acre annually for 22 years;

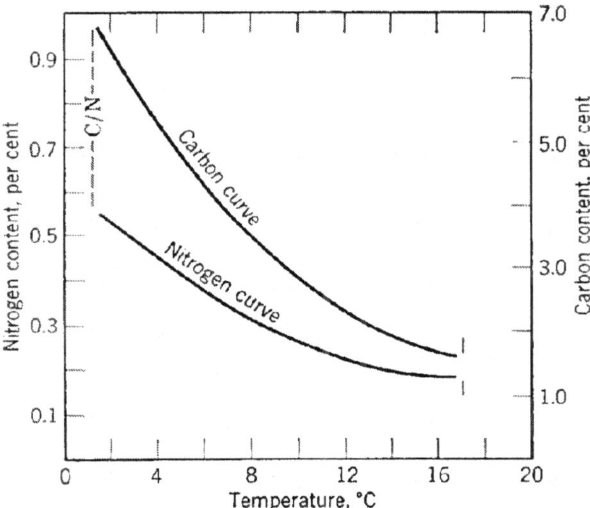

Fig. 62. Schematic representation of the widening C:N ratio of soil humus with decreasing temperature (from Jenny).

only one-third of the loss was accounted for by the crop grown. About 25 per cent of the total organic matter of the soil was lost as a result of cultivation during this time. Lipman and Blair also found an annual loss, for 20 years, of 70–100 pounds of nitrogen from a heavily manured soil. This loss could not be accounted for in the crop, but could be accounted for largely by the nitrogen in the drainage water. Some losses may also occur in the gaseous forms of nitrogen.

In dry-land farming, the most important soil problem, aside from that of water, is maintenance of organic matter. Russell calculated the loss of organic matter under dry-land farming to be 6.5 per cent during the first 3–7 years under cultivation, 12.4 per cent in 8–15 years, 26.8 per cent in 17–30 years, and 28.0 per cent in 45–60 years. The depletion of soil organic matter leads to erosion by wind and water. Greater losses of organic matter, up to 60 per cent in 40 years, have been reported under conditions of poor soil management.

The losses of organic matter as a result of cultivation are at first rapid, later becoming slower, until an equilibrium is attained after about 30 years, a base level of organic matter has then been reached, which is 25–30 per cent lower than that of the virgin soil Jenny calculated that the loss of nitrogen during cultivation of a virgin soil is 25 per cent the first 20 years, 10 per cent during the second 20 years, and 7 per cent during the third 20 years. Alway (Table 29)

TABLE 29 INFLUENCE OF CULTIVATION UPON LOSS OF ORGANIC MATTER FROM PRAIRIE SOILS (from Alway)

30–40 years in cultivation

Treatment	Organic Matter Content		Loss on Cultivation
	Cultivated Soil	Virgin Soil	
	per cent	*per cent*	*per cent*
15 years in wheat, 15 in corn	2.74	3.89	29.5
Corn, oats, and wheat	3.21	4.43	27.5
Alfalfa last 12 years	3.86	4.43	12.9
Alfalfa last 7 years	3.38	5.03	32.8
Alfalfa last 7 years, badly blown 1 year	2.47	5.03	50.9
Alfalfa last 12 years	4.29	5.41	20.7
Orchard, clean cultivation, last 7 years	2.76	5.41	49.0
Grass last 5 years	3.57	5.41	34.0
Heavily manured for 20 years	4.68	5.05	7.3

has shown that the growth of a legume or addition of stable manure reduces considerably the loss of organic matter. The greatest danger to the humus content of the soil was found in clean cultivation and in wind or water erosion

Detrimental changes in soil structure and tilth accompany losses of organic matter, which imparts stability to the soil granules. In analyzing the results of 50 years of field experiments at the Woburn Experimental Station, Russell and Voelcker came to the conclusion that soil deterioration under continuous cropping can be prevented only by a combination of farmyard manure with crop rotation. The plots receiving about 8 tons of manure a year showed no deterioration in crop yield and no loss of nitrogen from soil The fact that artificial fertilizers did not completely stop deterioration suggested that the latter was due to the exhaustion of some soil constituent necessary for plant growth under field conditions. By eliminating the possibility that minor elements were concerned, the conclusion was reached that exhaustion is associated with loss of organic matter The possibility was suggested that productiveness of a given soil rises and falls with the percentage of humus present.

The influence of treatment upon the rate of humus decomposition can be best illustrated when a peat bog is drained When the bog is saturated with water, humus accumulates, the rate of accumulation depending upon the nature of the vegetation, climate, topography, and chemical composition of the waters entering the bog When the bog is drained, humus ceases to accumulate and begins to disintegrate The rate of disintegration of the humus is controlled by the nature of the peat, climatic conditions, and the depth of the drainage system. The rapid rate at which certain peats decompose in warm climates points to the great danger of their rapid disappearance by improper handling.

In recent studies Broadbent and Norman used isotopic nitrogen and carbon compounds. They found that, when decomposable organic matter was added to the soil, a considerable increase took place in the rate of decomposition of the soil organic matter present. In one experiment they added 1 and 2 gm of sudan grass to 100 gm of soil, incubated the soil for 11 days, and measured the CO_2 produced. Since the sudan grass contained 2.67 per cent of the isotopic carbon, they could calculate the proportion of the CO_2 which resulted from the oxidation of the soil organic matter. When the soil alone was incubated, 49 mg CO_2 was produced from the soil organic matter; when 1 and 2 gm of sudan grass were added, 216 and 329 mg were produced, respectively, from the soil, in addition to the 418 and 651 mg of CO_2 from the decomposition of the sudan grass For every 100 mg of CO_2 produced from the sudan grass, an additional 40 mg was formed from the soil organic matter. No explanation could be given for the fact that soil organic matter became a better source of nutrient for the soil population when readily decomposable organic matter was added.

Abundance and Nature of Humus in Different Soils

The humus content of soils varies considerably, from extremely small amounts, as 0 1 per cent in some poor sandy soils, to as much as 20 per cent, in prairie soils, it may be even higher (50–80 per cent) in certain soils which have originated from peat bogs that have been brought under cultivation Light-textured soils contain less organic matter than soils of heavier texture. Typical analyses of sandy loams gave, on an average, 0.06 per cent nitrogen, which is equivalent to 1.03 per cent organic matter, clay loams in the same series of soils were found to contain 0.1 per cent nitrogen or 1 72 per cent organic matter The stage of development of a soil influences considerably its organic matter content.

Humus is not distributed evenly through the soil depth. It is largely concentrated in the upper 10 or 12 inches, or the surface soil layer, and decreases rapidly in the subsoil. In brown forest soil and in the red and yellow soils, there is a rapid drop in organic matter content below the upper 6 inches, it becomes very low at comparatively shallow depths. In prairie soils, chernozems, and chestnut-brown soils, there is a gradual decrease of organic matter with depth

It has already been emphasized that the accumulation of humus or its further decomposition depends entirely upon the vegetation, the soil, its topography, and the environmental conditions, especially the climatic, under which humus has been produced. These are the major factors which influence the abundance and nature of the humus In heavy soils, especially those rich in lime, humus will be fixed and will tend to decompose only very slowly. In light sandy soils, humus will not accumulate to so great an extent. Under favorable conditions, humus will decompose more rapidly, under certain conditions, it may also be readily leached out, as illustrated by the process of podzolization

The nature of the vegetation has a marked effect upon the accumulation of humus In pasture and prairie soils, where the land is covered by a growing crop and is not cultivated, the gradual disintegration of the roots in a soil environment lacking sufficient oxygen will give rise to a considerable amount of humus. If this soil is high in lime, the humus produced will be fixed and will gradually accumulate This results in the course of time in a type of soil which is designated as "chernozem" In forest vegetation, the annual drop of leaves, needles, and other tree residues will bring about an extensive accumulation of organic matter on the surface of the soil If this organic matter is gradually worked in with the underlying mineral part of the soil, a phenomenon brought about largely through the activities of the earthworms, insects, and other animals inhabiting some of these soils, a type of soil will result which is designated as "mull", this soil is characterized by one type of humus If the tree residues are not mixed with the underlying mineral layers, however, a soil will result which is designated as "raw humus", this may be due to the nature of the vegetation and type of soil. The surface layer of the raw humus soil may undergo considerable leaching, whereby certain of its organic and inorganic constituents are removed and are reprecipitated in the subsurface, a type of soil is thus formed which is designated as a "podzol."

A comparison of the chemical nature of the humus in different soil types shows that, in warmer regions, the carbon-nitrogen ratio of the humus tends to become narrower This is due to a greater decomposition of the carbohydrates and other nonnitrogenous constituents of the humus and the greater accumulation of the proteins, the latter originating largely through microbial synthesis.

The two major factors which control the abundance and nature of the humus in different soil types are, first, the formation and accumulation of the humus, as influenced by nature of vegetation, type of soil, aeration of soil, reaction, and environmental factors, especially temperature and rainfall; and, second, the decomposition of the humus, as controlled by the treatment of the soil, especially drainage and cultivation, farming practices, and climate

Humus and Soil Fertility

Among the various factors which contribute to the fertility of the soil, none occupies a more prominent place than soil organic matter. It has a fourfold effect upon the soil.

1. It serves as a storehouse of plant nutrients: the slow but gradual decomposition of the organic matter by microorganisms results in the liberation of a continuous stream of carbon dioxide, of available nitrogen as ammonia, which is soon changed to nitrate, of phosphorus, and of other elements essential for plant growth

2. It has important physical effects upon the soil it improves the soil structure, it provides better aeration, it has a binding effect upon the soil particles, it increases the water-holding capacity of the soil, it helps the soil to absorb more heat it increases the buffering properties of the soil, preventing rapid increases in acidity or alkalinity

3. It has certain chemical effects upon the soil constituents, such as rendering phosphorus and other elements more soluble, and neutralizing substances which tend to be toxic to plants, it has also a very high base-holding power.

4. It has an important effect upon the biological state of the soil, making it a more favorable medium for the development of the root systems of plants and for the growth of microorganisms essential for soil processes.

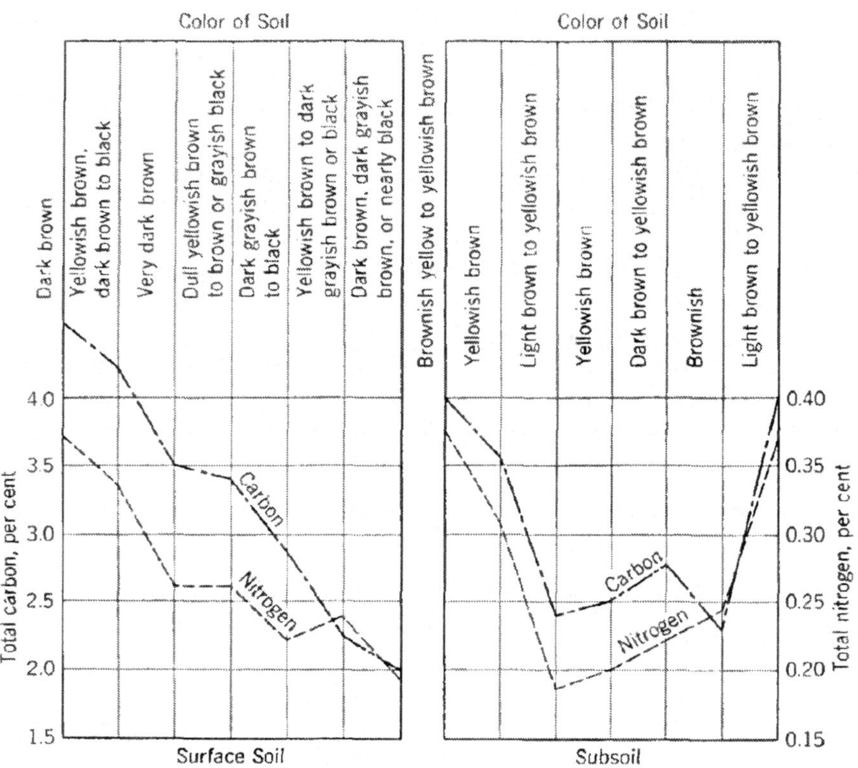

Fig. 63. Carbon and nitrogen content of different soils and subsoils (from Brown and O'Neill).

For countless generations, man depended upon the humus of the soil to supply the necessary plant nutrients, through the activities of the numerous microbes which inhabit the soil in thousands of millions per single gram. These nutrients were built up by the plants into plant tissues, which were partly consumed by animals, including man, and partly returned to the soil in the form of leaves, needles, stems, and roots. The animals and their excreta found their way, sooner or later, into the soil, to serve again as sources of humus, to be later again decomposed, with the liberation of the constituent nutrient elements for renewed plant growth. Humus can thus be considered the granary of plant nutrients in the soil. The benefits to plant growth resulting from an increase in the concentration of carbon dioxide about the leaves cannot be overemphasized. In addition to being an important source of plant nutrients, notably nitrogen and phosphorus, humus also has solvent effects upon relatively insoluble elements

The major effects of humus upon the soil and upon the growing plant are not associated with its direct fertilizing value, however important this may be. The physical and biological functions of humus are of great significance. The improvement in the physical condition of the soil as a result of addition of humus is associated with improved texture, structure, and tilth, better water and air relations, influence upon soil temperature and reaction, retention of plant nutrients, and neutralization of toxic effects of certain compounds formed in the soil Humus tends to make soils granular, causing the individual particles to form aggregates, thus preventing baking when the soil is dry and stickiness when it is wet The effects of humus are particularly evident on sandy soils and on heavy silt or clay soils. In the latter, a more open structure develops, which favors increased circulation of the air and more rapid movement of the water In the sandy soils, humus exerts a binding effect, thus retarding rapid percolation of water and giving to the soil the properties of heavier texture with higher moisture-holding capacity.

Soils receiving the proper amount of organic matter hold water to better advantage, because sufficiently large pore spaces are created to permit drainage of the excess water, while at the same time the moisture-holding capacity of the organic matter is sufficiently high to keep the soil from drying out too rapidly This enables the plants to resist drought not only because of the increased moisture content at the surface but also because of the deeper root penetration favored by the improved soil structure. Air circulation in the soil is essential for good root growth and plant development Root penetration may be favored by making the soil more porous, by improving the gas relationships in the soil, whereby the water table is lowered, root persistence is made possible. Soils receiving organic manures are also found to be less subject to seasonal variations than those receiving artificial fertilizers only, as brought out by the investigations of the Rothamsted Station.

In the presence of sufficient humus, plant nutrients are washed out from the soil less readily by the percolating waters. This is particularly true of the basic elements comprising a number of important compounds, such as ammonia and the salts of potassium, calcium, and magnesium. Rapid changes in reaction to either higher or lower acidity are also prevented by the "buffering" properties of soil organic matter. Plant poisons become less toxic in a soil high in humus, high salt concentrations are less injurious, and aluminum solubility, and thus its specific injurious action, are markedly decreased (Hester and Shelton). Plant deficiency diseases are usually less severe in soils well supplied with organic matter, not only because of the increased vigor of the plants but also because of antagonistic effects of the various soil microorganisms which become more active in the presence of an abundance of organic matter. Although some of these diseases may sometimes be controlled by treatment of the soil with organic matter, the effectiveness of this procedure cannot be fully relied upon in all cases.

Selected Bibliography

1. Albrecht, W. A., Methods of incorporating organic matter with the soil in relation to nitrogen accumulations, *Missouri Agr. Expt. Sta. Res. Bull.* 249, 1936.
2. Alway, F. J., Changes in the composition of the loess soils of Nebraska caused by cultivation, *Nebraska Agr. Expt. Sta. Bull.* 111, 1909.
3. Hester, J. B., and Shelton, F. A., Soil organic matter investigations upon coastal plain soils, *Virginia Truck Expt. Sta. Bull.* 94, 1937.
4. Jenny, H., Soil fertility losses under Missouri conditions, *Missouri Agr. Expt. Sta. Bull.* 324, 1933.
5. Lipman, J. G., and Blair, A. W., Nitrogen losses under intensive cropping, *Soil Sci.*, 12: 1–16, 1921.
6. Lyon, T. L., Bizzell, J. A., and Wilson, B. D., Depressive influence of certain higher plants on the accumulation of nitrates in soil, *J. Am. Soc. Agron.*, 15: 457–467, 1923.
7. Russell, E. J., *Plant Nutrition and Crop Production,* University of California Press, 1926.
8. Russell, E. J., and Voelcker, J. A., *Fifty Years of Field Experiments at the Woburn Experimental Station,* Longmans, Green & Co., London, 1936.
9. Russell, J. C., Organic matter problems under dry-farming conditions, *J. Am. Soc. Agron.*, 21: 960–969, 1929.
10. Shutt, F. T., Influence of grain growing on the nitrogen and organic matter content of the western prairie soils of Canada, *Can. Dept. Agr. Bull.* 44 N.S., 1925.
11. Smith, N. R., and Humfeld, H., Effect of rye and vetch green manures on the microflora, nitrates, and hydrogen-ion concentrations of two acid and neutralized soils, *J. Agr. Research,* 41: 97–123, 1930.

12 Sprague, H B, The value of winter green manure crops, *N J Agr Expt Sta Bull* 609, 1936

13 Waksman, S A, *Principles of Soil Microbiology*, Williams & Wilkins Co, Baltimore, 2nd Ed, 1932

14 Waksman, S A, *Humus, Origin, Chemical Composition and Importance in Nature*, Williams & Wilkins Co, Baltimore, 1st Ed, 1936, 2nd Ed, 1938

15 Waksman, S A, and Tenney, F G, The composition of natural organic materials and their decomposition in the soil II Influence of age of plant upon the rapidity and nature of its decomposition—rye plants, *Soil Sci*, 24 317–333, 1927

16 Woods, C D, Roots of plants as manure, *Conn (Storrs) Agr Expt Sta, 1st Ann Rept*, 1888, pp 28–43, Stubble and roots of plants as manure, *2nd Ann Rept*, 1889, pp 67–83

6

Decomposition of Soil Organic Matter and Evolution of Carbon Dioxide

Evolution of CO_2 in Decomposition of Plant and Animal Residues

Carbon makes up an average of about 50 per cent of all the elements in plant and animal tissues In certain carbohydrates and organic acids, it may be somewhat less than 40 per cent, and in fats and waxes it is above 60 per cent. In the decomposition of these residues by microorganisms, most of the carbon is liberated as CO_2, the evolution of this gas can, therefore, be taken as a measure of the rate and extent of the decomposition process Some of the carbon is assimilated by microorganisms for cell synthesis, whereas another part is left in the form of intermediary products, in both aerobic and anaerobic decomposition The total amount of CO_2 liberated depends on the nature of the material, the microorganisms concerned, and the conditions of decomposition

When cellulose, hemicelluloses, sugars, and starches are decomposed by fungi and by aerobic bacteria, as much as 50–80 per cent of the carbon is liberated as CO_2 In a comparative study of the decomposition of rye straw by pure and mixed cultures of microorganisms, the mixed soil population decomposed only about one-third as much of the total material in absence of added nitrogen as when ammonium salt was added The corresponding amount of carbon liberated as CO_2 was about one-fourth in absence of added nitrogen Of the total carbon in the material, 72 and 83 per cent were liberated as CO_2 Less CO_2 was liberated by pure cultures of fungi because of greater consumption of the carbon and greater quantities of intermediary products left

Plant materials in a young green state decompose much more rapidly than those in a mature state, and much more CO_2 is produced in a given time. The ratio of CO_2 liberated to the organic matter decomposed is similar, however, and depends on the organisms and conditions of decomposition. In nitrogen-rich materials, liberation of CO_2 is accompanied by production and accumulation of ammonia, which is soon changed in field and garden soils to nitrate; the ratio between the carbon and nitrogen liberated depends on the nitrogen

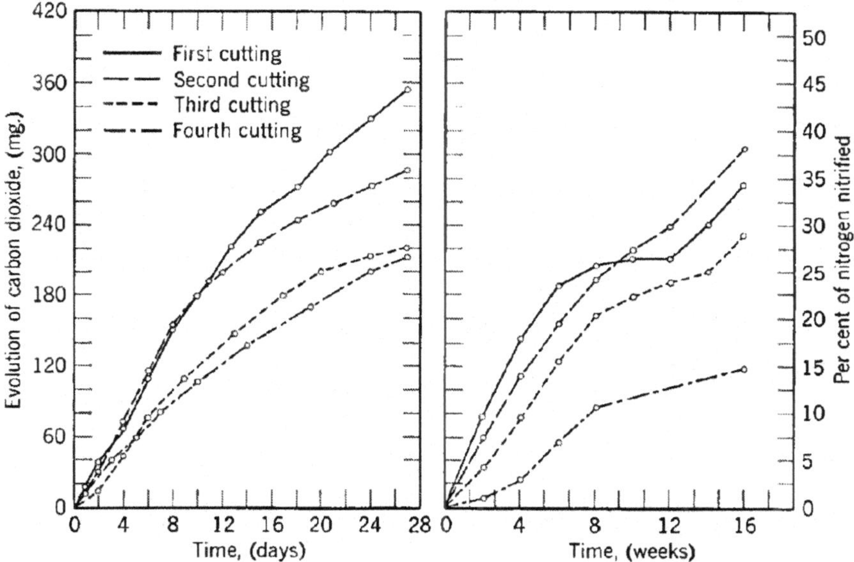

Fig. 64. Influence of age of plant (stems and leaves) on its decomposition in sand medium as indicated by the evolution of carbon dioxide (from Waksman and Tenney).

content of the material undergoing decomposition and on the rate of decomposition.

Decomposition of plant residues low in nitrogen is controlled by the amount of available nitrogen present. Ammonia is not liberated and may actually be consumed. The wider the carbon-nitrogen ratio in the plant and animal residues, the greater is the proportion of CO_2 to ammonia liberated, until the latter becomes a negative figure; then nitrogen must be added for active decomposition.

Figures 65–67 illustrate the course of CO_2 evolution in the decomposition of different plant materials under different conditions, both in soils and in composts.

Although some CO_2 may be formed by purely chemical processes in the soil and although considerable CO_2 is evolved by the roots of green plants during their respiration, in which the plants obtain their oxygen as a part of the soil air and return CO_2 to the gas mixture, most of the CO_2 is a result of decomposition processes carried out by microorganisms.

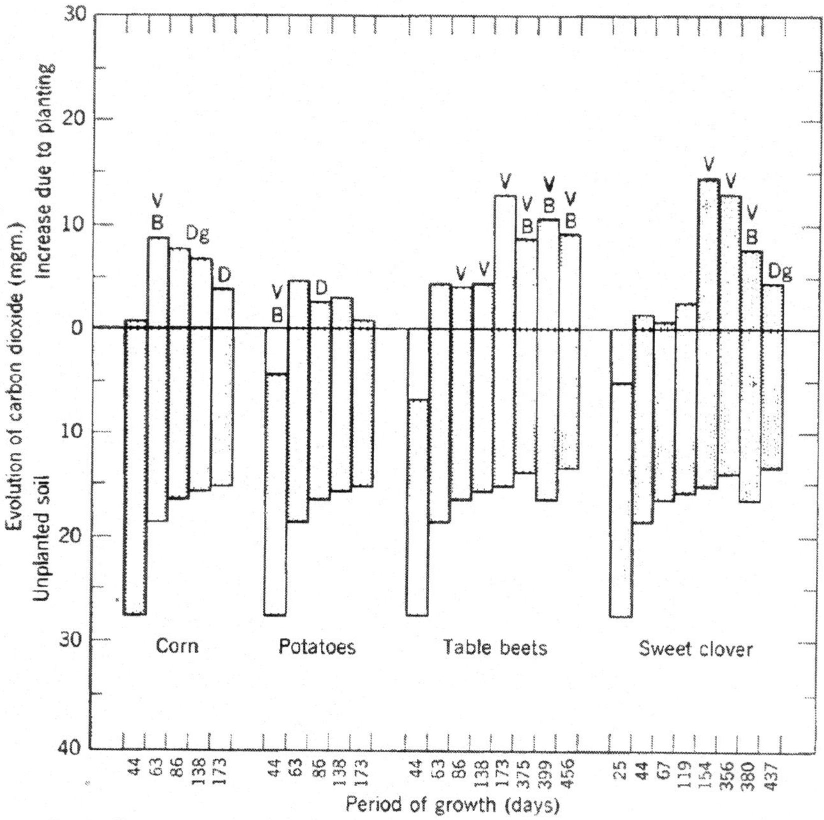

Fig. 65. Influence of plant development upon the evolution from the soil of carbon dioxide of microbial origin: V, height of vegetative development; B, blooming; Dg, degeneration; D, death (from Starkey).

The total CO_2 given off is a result of the decomposition of plant remains by microorganisms, chemically produced CO_2, and CO_2 given off during respiration by the roots of green plants. Lundegårdh calculated the percentage of total CO_2 due to respiration, and reached the conclusion that about 30 per cent of the total CO_2 was due to the presence of the roots. He believed that here, too, microorganisms associated with the roots had much to do with the CO_2 liberation. He concluded that, when oats were grown in sterilized soil, 45 per cent of the increase in CO_2 evolution due to the roots was microbial in origin, which would reduce the contribution of the oat roots to 16.5 per cent. One may thus conclude that about 85 per cent of the total CO_2 liberated from the soil is due to the activity of microorganisms.

Evolution of CO_2 from Soil Humus

The study of CO_2 evolution from soil has followed several lines, depending on the methods of determination. These are:

1. Methods based upon the extraction of gas from soil samples removed from the field and taken to the laboratory. Leather established that soil gases contain varying percentages of CO_2 ranging from 3.84 per cent to 15.29 per cent.

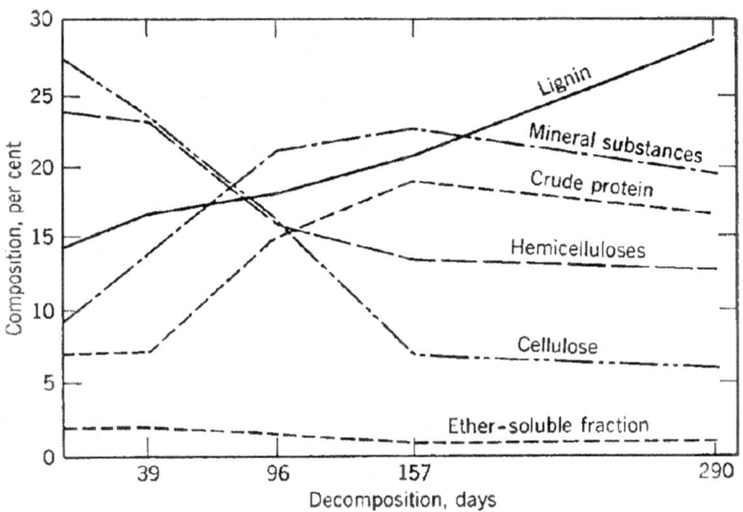

Fig. 66. Changes in composition of horse manure compost during different stages of decomposition (from Waksman and Diehm).

2. Methods in which an apparatus is placed on or thrust into the soil, and the gas present is extracted by suction, as measured by Appleman, by Russell and Appleyard, by Potter and Snyder, and by Lundegårdh.

3. Methods in which representative soil samples are taken and tested in the laboratory for capacity to evolve CO_2 under arbitrarily prescribed conditions, as done by Waksman and Starkey and by Marsh.

4 Methods in which the evolution of CO_2 from a measured area in a given time is determined in the field, as by Lundegårdh and by Humfeld

Some of the results may be summarized as follows:

When soil samples are taken in the field for extraction in the laboratory, the greatest precautions are necessary to devise apparatus for taking the sample without driving out the gases already present or allowing diffusion between the sample and the atmosphere.

Appleman devised a sampling tube for collecting the soil atmosphere This consisted of two brass tubes, the smaller fitting tightly inside the larger and extending about 1 inch at each end One end was grooved for a rubber tube, the other was fitted with a point the size of the larger tube, thus leaving a space between the point and the large tube, in which twelve holes were drilled to drain the soil gases from the free space The outer tube was slipped down over the holes, and the instrument was thrust into the soil to the desired depth, then the smaller tube was pushed in far enough to uncover the holes while the outer tube was stationary. Rubber tubing was then attached and suction applied. The first 100 ml of gas collected over mercury was discarded, then 250-ml samples were taken for analysis

In the cooler part of the season, between May 1 and June 1, the CO_2 from the soil varied from 0.13 to 0.38 per cent Later in the season, July 16, Appleman found 6 91 per cent in the soil under alfalfa; 2 97 per cent under cabbage leaves, 5 05 per cent in a check, and only 1 4 per cent in the soil between the rows The air 1 foot above the soil contained 0 03 per cent CO_2. When the plots high in CO_2 were cultivated, the total CO_2 dropped off 90 per cent in the first day, showing that cultivation brings aeration and dissipates the accumulated gas.

The difficulty of thrusting an instrument into the soil without opening channels, cutting across wormholes, insect burrows, or other cracks which bring atmospheric air to the instrument in but slightly changed condition, is readily seen

In the study of the capacity of a soil to evolve CO_2, the sample is collected as representative of the area It may be partly dried, at least to a known water percentage. It is crumbled or ground, sifted, and weighed, in lots of 50 or 100 gm, into flasks with or without the admixture of specific fertilizing or organic manuring substance. Water content is brought to a definite point, and the flask is connected into the collecting system to be held for a definite time at controlled temperature Marsh forced a stream of CO_2-free air through the mass of soil, whereas Waksman and Starkey placed the soil in a layer 2–3 cm deep in the bottom of an Erlenmeyer flask, through the stopper of which a tube brought CO_2-free air into the flask, while a second tube, reaching nearly to the surface of the soil, removed the CO_2-laden stratum of air as fast as it was formed. The CO_2 was absorbed by alkali and determined by titration.

The main weakness of these procedures is that conditions are arbitrarily chosen, they may not reproduce in any definite way the demands made upon a soil in the field They do not measure anything which is definitely found in nature.

Lundegårdh devised a zinc bell—a pyramidal cover with straight margins to be forced down into the soil, giving a collecting space of a known volume. After the collecting bell remains in position for a specified time, gas samples are pumped into containers and taken to the laboratory for analysis. By standardizing the operation of his collector, Lundegårdh found it possible to move from plot to plot across the field and take a sample every 20 minutes, accumulating the receiving tubes and taking them all back to the laboratory for microanalysis.

Lundegårdh's apparatus has the advantage of placing a known container over undisturbed soil for a brief period and collecting for analysis a part of the air and CO_2 mixture resulting from interruption of the diffusion of the CO_2 evolved during the period. The sample taken can be calculated to milligrams of CO_2 evolved per square meter of surface per hour or to any other desired unit. Whether confinement of the CO_2 evolved during that period results in delaying evolution of CO_2 may be questioned. If so, the results may be low. The work of Lundegårdh does, however, give a comparison, of actual CO_2 evolved, between different plots of ground in the field

In the studies reported by Humfeld, the collecting apparatus was modified in appearance from Lundegårdh's bell, into a box 3 by 8 inches and 3 inches high, with the open side pressed into the soil about 1 inch At one end a collecting tube about 1/4 inch in diameter was attached, and at the other a vent to which usually a tube was attached with its open end carried 2–3 feet above the soil to give a supply of atmospheric air to the collector. In this apparatus, the air passing over the soil carried CO_2, hence the extra tension of CO_2-free air was eliminated, but the percentage of the CO_2 present in the atmosphere was determined regularly and deducted from the totals found in the collection apparatus.

With this apparatus, one can list the rate of CO_2 evolution day by day over a season, or hour by hour through some special period. It requires no abstruse calculation but makes a demand for a continuous suction with a steady source of power; it also calls for regular attention.

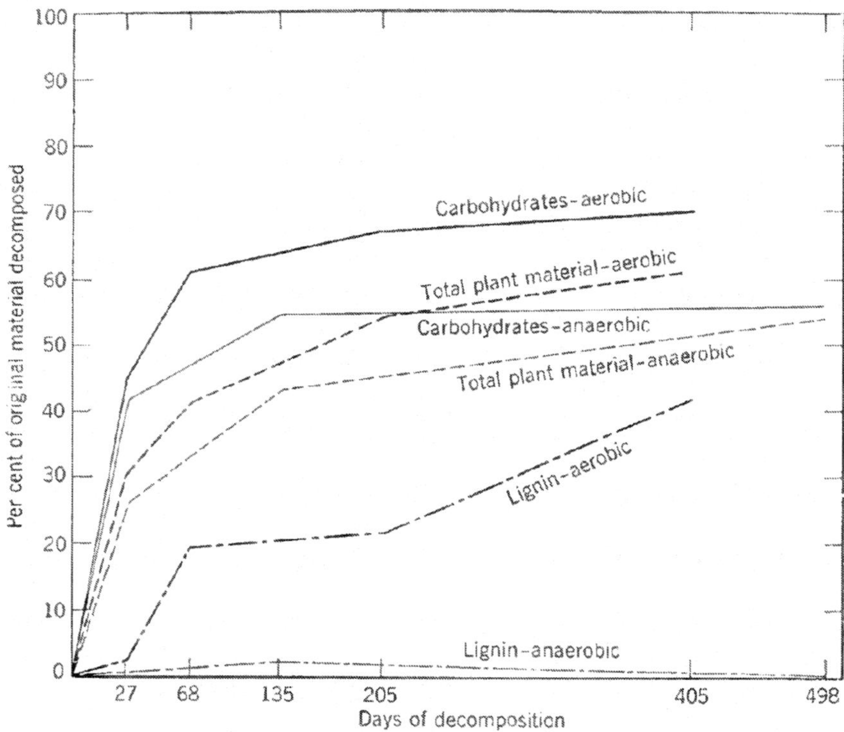

Fig. 67. Influence of aeration upon decomposition of alfalfa plant (from Tenney and Waksman).

This procedure has weaknesses such as the small size of the collecting box; the continuous position that interrupts processes that go on near or on the surface; the irregularity of suction apparatus; and inability to adjust absorbent, rate of flow, and frequency of changes to the great changes in rate of CO_2 evolution brought about by some types of fertilization. It is probably most valuable in following the effects of some soil treatment from the time of application for a period limited to a few days.

Smith and Brown emphasized that CO_2 diffuses downward into the soil from the area of biological activity as well as upward into the air; that absorption by soil solution with subsequent loss in drainage water carries away part of the CO_2 produced. Total production of CO_2 is, therefore, much greater than the amount which escapes into the atmosphere. Hence the amount of CO_2 collectible over a given area cannot be regarded as a measure of the CO_2 produced in the soil.

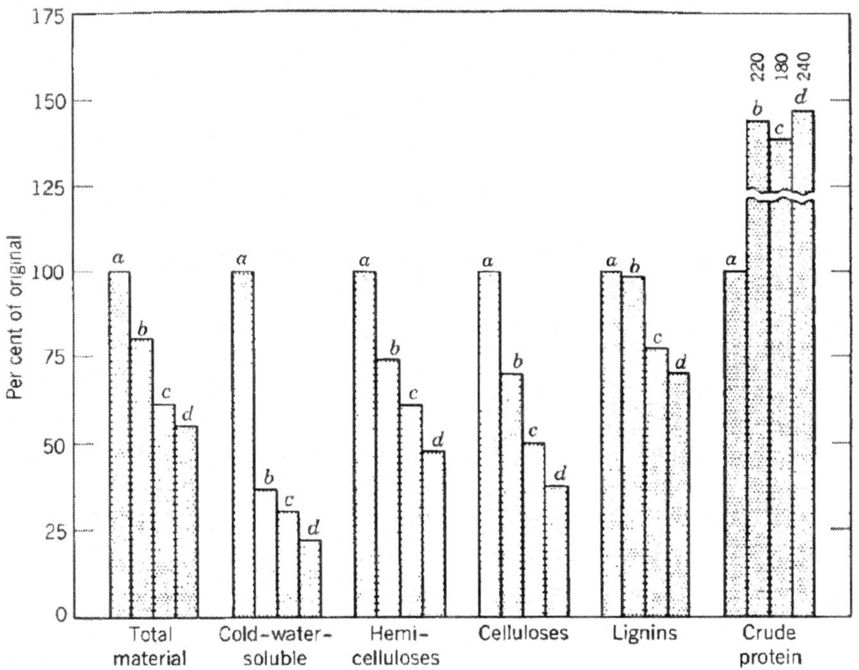

Fig. 68. Decomposition of various chemical constituents of rye straw with additional nutrient salts (from Tenney and Waksman).

As shown previously, the humus in the soil is not absolutely resistant to decomposition, but undergoes slow but continuous decomposition. The rate of evolution of CO_2, especially under aerobic conditions, is the most accurate and simplest method for measuring humus decomposition. This can be measured either (*a*) as total CO_2 arising from a given volume of soil during a certain period of time, or (*b*) as the amount of CO_2 found in the soil atmosphere. The mineralized nitrogen liberated as a result of humus decomposition can be measured as ammonia or as nitrate, or both; in most soils ammonia does not accumulate as such but is rapidly oxidized to nitrate. In addition to determining the products of humus decomposition, measurements may also be made of the actual disappearance of humus as a whole or of some of its specific chemical constituents This can be done by measuring the total carbon or nitrogen content of the soil or by making a proximate analysis of the humus The latter is of particular advantage in the study of peats, forest soils, and composts.

Other methods can be utilized to measure humus decomposition, as, for example, the change in calorific value of the humus in the soil or the evolution of heat accompanying processes of humus decomposition. These methods amply demonstrate the fact that humus is not stable, that it can disintegrate and disappear from the soil, but that the rate of its disappearance is rather slow Different farm practices may result in the preservation and even accumulation of humus or in its destruction. Which of these is more desirable depends entirely upon the nature of the soil, the nature of the crop grown, and general problems of soil utilization and soil conservation

As a result of extensive decomposition, humus may reach a definite chemical equilibrium, as shown by its more or less constant carbon-nitrogen ratio This equilibrium is particularly characteristic of humus in field and garden soils In this condition, further decomposition of humus results in a parallel liberation of carbon as CO_2 and of nitrogen as ammonia, rapidly oxidized to nitrate. In composts, forest soils, and peats, the ratio of CO_2 liberated to nitrate produced varies considerably, depending upon the nature of the material and the state of its decomposition

A distinct parallelism was thus found to exist between the abundance of microorganisms in the soil and the decomposition of the soil humus, the more fertile a soil is, the greater will be the amount of CO_2 liberated in a given time. Wollny reported in 1880 that the CO_2 content of the soil rises and falls with the amount of organic matter present.

One of the early accurate studies on humus decomposition was carried out by Déhérain and Demoussy They placed the soil under examination in closed glass containers and kept them at different constant temperatures At the end of a definite period of incubation, the gas was extracted from the soil and container and the CO_2 present determined These workers were among the first to demonstrate that the formation of CO_2 was due almost entirely to the action of microorganisms; it increased with an increase in temperature to about 65°C, then decreased, at 90°C, another increase in CO_2 formation took place, which was due to the chemical oxidation of the humus at this high temperature. A certain amount of moisture was required for the maximum production of CO_2 by microorganisms. The state of division of the soil and its aeration were found to affect greatly the rate of decomposition of the humus. Sterile soils produced only small amounts of CO_2; when a soil infusion was added, the process was increased twenty-five times. One of the most important points brought out in these investigations was the fact that sterilized and inoculated soil gave two to five times as much CO_2

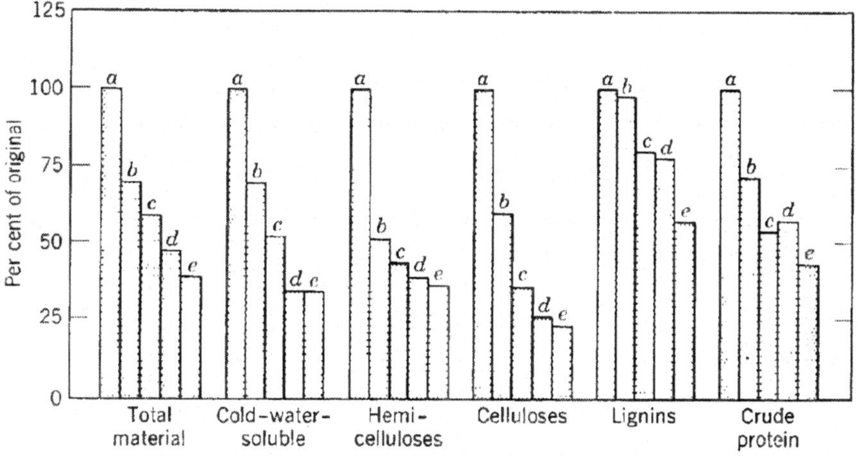

Fig. 69. Decomposition of various chemical constituents of alfalfa without additional nutrient salts (from Tenney and Waksman).

as unsterilized and uninoculated soil. This indicates definitely that the process of sterilization rendered the soil humus more susceptible to decomposition. There is also an optimum moisture content for the formation of CO_2; this is influenced by the state of division of the soil and its aeration.

A distinct parallelism was found to exist between the amount of oxygen absorbed and the amount of CO_2 produced from different soils. A similar parallelism was also found between CO_2 evolution and nitrogen accumulation in the form of ammonia and nitrate. Russell measured the amount of oxygen absorbed by the soil as an index of soil oxidation instead of determining the CO_2 produced. The rate of absorption of oxygen was found to increase with temperature, the amount of water (up to a certain point), and the amount of calcium carbonate present in the soil. Since these factors also paralleled soil fertility, Russell suggested the use of soil oxidation as a measure of the fertility of the soil. The amount of oxygen absorbed was thus believed to measure the total action of soil microorganisms, which are responsible for the decomposition processes in the soil.

Stoklasa and Ernest placed 1-kg portions of sieved soil in glass cylinders through which a current of air was passed at the rate of 10 liters in 24 hours. They observed that the evolution of CO_2 by a soil, under certain conditions of moisture and temperature, in a given time, can furnish a reliable and accurate method for the determination of bacterial activities in the soil, the presence of organic matter and the temperatures were found to be of greatest importance. The evolution of CO_2 was shown to be greatest in neutral or slightly alkaline soils abundantly supplied with readily assimilable plant nutrients and well aerated. The production of CO_2 from the soil was found to be in direct proportion to the available organic matter in the soil rather than to the total organic matter. The evolution of CO_2 was thus found to be an index of the availability of the soil humus, or of the ease with which it decomposes (Table 30).

TABLE 30. INFLUENCE OF SOIL DEPTH AND SOIL TREATMENT UPON THE DECOMPOSITION OF HUMUS, AS MEASURED BY THE RATE OF CO_2 EVOLUTION (from Stoklasa)

Soil Depth	Soil Treatment: Uncultivated, Unfertilized	Cultivated, Fertilized under Clover	Manured Fertilized, under Beets
cm	*mg*	*mg*	*mg*
10–20	16.5	38.6	47.5
20–30	19.4	38.8	49.7
30–50	9.8	20.2	28.5
50–80	3.3	6.3	6.6
80–100	2.1	2.7	2.3

Van Suchtelen passed a current of air, usually 16 liters in 24 hours, through 6 kg of soil placed on pure sand in a jar. The intensity of CO_2 production was much greater at the beginning of the experiment and decreased rapidly after a short time. The amount of CO_2 produced was measured until it reached a uniformly low level, the average amounts of CO_2 produced per unit time from the different soils served as a basis for comparison. The conclusion was reached that the determination of CO_2 formation from different soils furnishes a better means for estimating the bacterial activities in the soil than the numbers of bacteria. Cultivation, aeration, and nutritive salts exerted a stimulating effect upon CO_2 production, moisture and organic matter content of the soil are among the most important factors.

On comparing the curves for bacterial numbers, nitrate accumulation, and CO_2 content of the soil air, Russell and Appleyard found them to be sufficiently similar to justify the view that all these phenomena are related. A rise in bacterial numbers was accompanied by a rise in the CO_2 content of the soil air and somewhat later by a rise of nitrate in the soil. The rate of decomposition of organic matter in the soil, as measured by CO_2 evolution, was, therefore, looked upon as a function of bacterial activities. The rate of these activities in the soil attained maxima in late spring and autumn, and minima in summer and winter. In autumn the bacteria increased first, then the CO_2 content rose, and finally the nitrate increased.

Neller measured the CO_2-producing capacity of the soil by adding plant material to 200-gm portions of soil placed in tumblers under bell jars, and passing CO_2-free air for 16 days. On comparing two limed and two unlimed soils, he obtained distinct correlation between crop yield, nitrate accumulation, and numbers of bacteria, but these did not correlate with ammonia accumulation.

The evolution of CO_2 from soil resulting from the decomposition of humus was thus found to be the best index of the rate of decomposition of this humus. This is further brought out in Table 31,

TABLE 31. EFFECT OF LIMING UPON MICROBIOLOGICAL ACTIVITIES IN SOIL (from Neller)

Soil Treatment	Carbon Dioxide Evolution *	Nitrification	Nitrogen Fixation *	Bacterial Numbers †
	mg	*mg*	*mg*	*millions*
Unlimed	221	10.4	−0.02	2.5
Limed	320	21.3	+1.35	6.2
Unlimed	199	16.1	−0.90	5.1
Limed	333	39.9	+7.00	6.5

* Per 200 gm soil in 16 days.

† Per gram soil, as determined by plate method.

where the respiratory power of soils has been measured for a group of plots variously treated and of varying degrees of fertility. The curves for bacterial numbers, accumulation of nitrate, and evolution of CO_2 were found to be sufficiently similar to justify the view that they are closely related. A rise in bacterial numbers was found to be accompanied by an increase in the CO_2 content of the soil air and somewhat later by a rise in the amount of nitrate in the soil. The rate of decomposition of humus in the soil may, therefore, be looked upon as a function of microbiological activities. Cultivation, aeration, and presence of nutrient salts exert a stimulating effect upon these processes. Among the most important factors, however, are moisture content and abundance and nature of humus. A direct relation exists between temperature and humus decomposition, the process of humus decomposition goes on at temperatures below 0°C, but it is greatly hastened by a rise in temperature. Variations in the production of CO_2 with season of year are due largely to variations in temperature and to the available organic matter. The amount of CO_2 evolved in 24 hours from 1 square meter of soil was shown to range from 2 to 20 gm calculated as carbon, the actual amount of CO_2 liberated depends on the nature of the soil, treatment, season of year, and various other factors.

Since evolution of CO_2 from soil is a measure of the rate of decomposition of the humus, one may conclude that the rate of decomposition depends upon the abundance of humus in the soil, the physical and chemical nature of the soil, its treatment, and the crops grown (Table 32). In fertile soils, humus decomposes more readily, thus resulting in the liberation of a greater amount of CO_2 and ammonia. Those soils in which humus decomposes very slowly are called infertile. Frequently this condition can be corrected by addition of lime, by cultivation, by drainage, or by other special treatments. An increase in the rate of decomposition of humus will be accompanied by an increase in the fertility of the soil.

The decomposition of humus is brought about by the activities of a large number of bacteria, fungi, and other microorganisms inhabiting the soil. These activities are rather slow as compared with the decomposition of fresh plant and animal residues. The amount of humus decomposed in a season is usually between 2 and 5 per cent of the humus content of the soil. Under special conditions, the decomposition may be greater, under other conditions, it may be less.

Another early student of humus decomposition in soil, Boussingault, recorded, in 1873, observations on a humus-rich soil. He found that one-half of the total organic carbon in the soil became changed to CO_2 in 11 years; one-third of the nitrogen appeared as nitrate in that period. The more extensive experiments at Rothamsted, however, showed a loss of only one-third of the nitrogen in 50 years, from soils free from crops but cultivated. In prairie soils, a

TABLE 32. CHEMICAL AND BIOLOGICAL CONDITIONS OF THE SOILS AS RELATED TO THEIR CROP PRODUCTIVITY

Plot No.	Treatment	Reaction of Soil	Nitrogen Content	Carbon Content	Total Crop Yield per Acre for 24 Years	Numbers of Micro-organisms per Gram by Plate Method	CO_2-Producing Capacity	
							From 1 Kg of Soil, in 14 Days	From 200 Gm of Soil + 0.5 Gm Dextrose, in 48 Hours
		pH	*per cent*	*per cent*	*pounds*	*millions*	*mg*	*mg*
5A	Minerals + manure	5.5	0.146	1.7	69,300	13.0	999	196
7A	Untreated	4.9	0.083	1.0	15,464	5.6	241	47
9A	Minerals + $NaNO_3$	5.8	0.099	1.2	57,968	9.6	479	85
11A	Minerals + $(NH_4)_2SO_4$	4.4	0.106	1.2	41,754	5.3	418	161
5B	Minerals + manure + lime	6.7	0.143	1.7	59,754	12.5	1,100	226
7B	Lime only	6.5	0.087	1.2	30,160	9.8	489	126
11B	Minerals + $(NH_4)_2SO_4$ + lime	6.1	0.095	1.1	61,906	10.6	523	132

loss of one-third of the nitrogen was shown to take place in 22 years, as a result of cultivation; one-third of the nitrogen liberated during

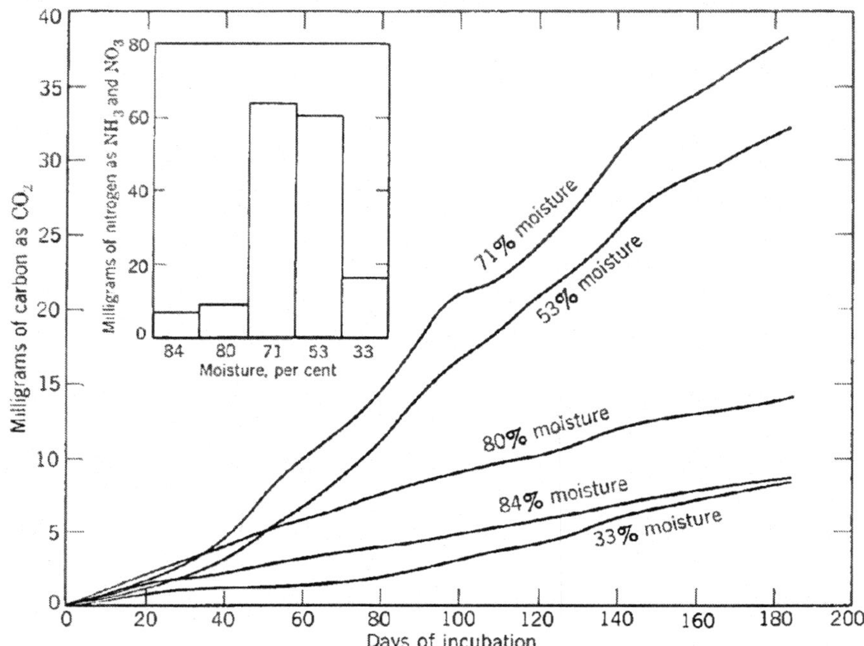

Fig. 70. Influence of moisture upon decomposition of peat (from Waksman and Purvis).

the decomposition was recovered in the crops. The nature and the treatment of the soil are of considerable importance in determining the extent of these changes (Table 32).

Table 33. Influence of Carbon-Nitrogen Ratio in Soil upon the Decomposition of Soil Organic Matter (from Sievers and Holtz)

Carbon	Nitrogen	C/N Ratio	Carbon Liberated as CO_2	Nitrogen Liberated as Nitrate	C/N Ratio of Mineralized Elements
per cent	*per cent*		*mg*	*ppm*	
0.91	0.09	10.0	120	15.4	7.8
1.68	0.14	11.8	188	18.3	10.3
1.86	0.16	12.0	168	17.6	9.5
2.89	0.23	12.4	231	26.3	8.8

Influence of CO_2 on Soil Minerals

An increase in the evolution of CO_2, as a result of the decomposition of plant and animal residues added to the soil or of the soil humus, leads to an increase in the CO_2 content of the soil atmosphere This results in an increase in the hydrogen-ion concentration of the soil

$$CO_2 + H_2O = H_2CO_3$$

$$H_2CO_3 = H^+ + HCO_3^-$$

The hydrogen ion will interact with the various soil minerals, especially the phosphate and silicates, and bring about their greater solubilization and availability for plant growth. This is shown in the following reactions.

$$Ca_3(PO_4)_2 + 2H_2CO_3 = 2CaHPO_4 + Ca(HCO_3)_2$$

$$Na_2SiO_3 + 2H_2CO_3 = 2NaHCO_3 + H_2SiO_3$$

$$H_2SiO_3 = H_2O + SiO_2$$

The CO_2 content of the soil atmosphere thus hastens the whole process of weathering of rock constituents of the soil It exerts an important solvent effect upon the soil minerals, bringing them into solution and making them more readily available for plant growth An increase in CO_2 concentration in the soil will thus influence the availability of various minerals essential for plant growth This affects first of all the solubility of the phosphates and silicates and also that of other anions (borates) It also results in bringing into solution greater concentrations of various cations, such as potassium, calcium, and magnesium.

Influence of CO_2 on Plant Growth

Carbon dioxide affects plant growth both directly and indirectly It has been definitely established by Lundegårdh and others that plants depend a great deal upon the CO_2 liberated from the soil humus for their nutrition, to supplement the CO_2 present in the atmosphere above the plants It has even been said that the major function of the addition of manure to soil is to increase the amount of CO_2 liberated, thus rendering larger concentrations of this important element available for plants

The microorganisms are thus found to act as regulators of the CO_2 tension in the atmosphere and of the amount of CO_2 available to plants. Were these organisms less active in the liberation of the CO_2 from the dead plants and animals or from the waste products of their metabolism, the earth would soon become covered with undecomposed plant and animal debris, while the limited supply of CO_2, having become exhausted, would gradually bring to an end all forms of life The activities of microorganisms which bring about the decomposition of this organic debris prevent its abundant accumulation and make available to plants a constant stream of CO_2, as well as of nitrogen and other nutrient mineral elements On the other hand, were these organisms more active in bringing about these decomposition processes, the surface of the earth would soon become covered with a layer of sand or clay free from all traces of organic matter, this would soon prevent the normal growth of the majority of economic plants by providing an unfavorable physical and chemical medium for plant growth, and even more by preventing any possible accumulation of nitrogen, which is also important for plant growth

Selected Bibliography

1 Appleman, C O Percentage of carbon dioxide in soil air, *Soil Sci*, 24 241–245, 1927

2 Humfeld, H, A method for measuring carbon dioxide evolution from soil, *Soil Sci*, 30 1–9, 1930

3 Lundegårdh, H, Carbon dioxide evolution of soil and crop growth, *Soil Sci*, 23 417–450, 1927

4 Marsh, F W, A laboratory apparatus for the measurement of carbon dioxide evolved from soils, *Soil Sci*, 25 253–260, 1928

5 Smith, F B, and Brown, P E, Soil respiration, *J Am Soc Agron*, 23 909–916, 1931, 24 577–583, 1932

6 Starkey, R L, Some observations on the decomposition of organic matter in soils, *Soil Sci*, 17 293–314, 1924

7 Waksman, S A, and Starkey, R L, Microbiological analysis of soil as an index of soil fertility VII Carbon dioxide evolution, *Soil Sci*, 17 141–161, 1924

·7·

Transformation of Nitrogen in Soil; Nitrate Formation and Nitrate Reduction

Nitrogen is added to the soil in organic and inorganic forms The organic forms are found largely in plant residues, such as stubble, weeds, leaves, and pine needles; green manure crops; stable manures and composts, and special organic fertilizers, such as dried blood and cottonseed meal The inorganic forms of nitrogen are added largely in the mineral fertilizers, these include mostly ammonium salts, cyanamide, and nitrates. Both organic and inorganic fertilizers are subject in the soil to various changes brought about by microorganisms

Decomposition of Proteins and Their Derivatives

The amount of protein in organic material is usually measured by multiplying the total nitrogen, as determined by the Kjeldahl method, by the factor 6 25 The protein content of plant and animal residues added to the soil varies from 1.5 per cent or even less, as in cereal straw and wood shavings, to 15 or even 20 per cent, as in legume plants, young rye plants, and certain animal manures, such as chicken manure. The protein content of certain defatted meals, such as cottonseed meal, or of certain animal residues, such as dried blood, may run to 30 or even 60 per cent.

The primary stage of the breakdown of proteins by microorganisms consists in the formation of smaller units known as peptides, and these in turn break down into the individual component amino acids. The enzymes produced by the organisms and responsible for these reactions are known as proteases or proteolytic enzymes The amino acids are then reduced to certain derivatives, depending on the organisms and the conditions of decomposition, and finally to ammonia (Table 34) The enzymes concerned in these reactions are known as deaminases and amidases.

TABLE 34 TRANSFORMATION OF PROTEIN NITROGEN INTO AMMONIA BY MICROORGANISMS

Organism	Per Cent	Organism	Per Cent
B mycoides	46	*B arborescens*	19
Bact vulgare	36	*Ps fluorescens liquefaciens*	16
B mesentericus vulgatus	36	*Cephalothecium roseum*	37
S lutea	27	*A terricola*	32
B subtilis	23	*Botryotrichum piluliferum*	24
B janthinus	23	*Stemphylium* sp	5
Ps fluorescens putidus	22	*Actinomyces* sp	21

Many proteins are present in various residues, especially in microbial products, in the form of compounds with nucleic acids, known as nucleoproteins. The composition of a typical protein is $NH_2 \cdot CHR\ CO \cdot (NHCHR \cdot CO)_n\ NH\ CHR \cdot COOH$. A typical nucleic acid has the composition $C_{36}H_{48}O_{30}N_4P_4$ and is made up of a purine or pyrimidine base, a carbohydrate (hexose or pentose), and phosphoric acid.

Proteins can be broken down by microorganisms through one or more of the following processes.

1. Hydrolytic deaminization The hydrolysis of an amino acid may result in the formation of a lower fatty acid and ammonia, or of an alcohol, CO_2, and ammonia, or of an aldehyde, lower acid, and ammonia, as shown by the general formulas

$$R\ CH\ NH_2\ COOH + H_2O = R\ CHOH\ COOH + NH_3 \quad (1)$$

$$R\ CH\ NH_2\ COOH + H_2O = R\ CH_2OH + CO_2 + NH_3 \quad (2)$$

$$R\ CH\ NH_2\ COOH + H_2O = R\ CHO + H\ COOH + NH_3 \quad (3)$$

2 Decarboxylation with amine formation.

$$R \cdot CH\ NH_2\ COOH = R\ CH_2\ NH_2 + CO_2 \quad (4)$$

$$R\ CH_2\ NH_2 + H_2O = R\ CH_2\ OH + NH_3 \quad (5)$$

3 Reductive deaminization.

$$R\ CH\ NH_2\ COOH + H_2 = R\ CH_2\ COOH + NH_3 \quad (6)$$

or

$$R\ CH\ NH_2\ COOH + H_2 = R\ CH_3 + NH_3 + CO_2 \quad (7)$$

4 Ammonia formation without reduction. Anaerobic bacteria may produce ammonia from amino acids, without reduction.

$$R\ CH_2\ CH\ NH_2\ COOH = R\ CH{:}CH\ COOH + NH_3 \qquad (8)$$

5. Oxidative deamination

$$R\ CH\ NH_2\ COOH + O_2 = R\ COOH + NH_3 + CO_2 \qquad (9)$$

This process is carried out by aerobic organisms, especially by fungi. As examples of this reaction, the transformation of leucine into isovaleric acid, as shown above, and of glutamic acid into succinic acid may be cited·

$$\underset{\text{Glutamic acid}}{COOH\ CH_2{\cdot}CH_2{\cdot}CH\ NH_2\ COOH} + O_2$$

$$= COOH{\cdot}CH_2{\cdot}CH_2\ COOH + NH_3 + CO_2$$

The decomposition of one amino acid may involve the reactions of oxidative deamination, decarboxylation, and reduction. The same organism may bring about a series of these reactions, while different results may be obtained by the same organism under different conditions.

The action of microorganisms on proteins and amino acids results in the formation of various indols, some of which, such as indolacetic acid, act as growth-promoting substances, hormones or auxins, upon plants. The favorable effect upon plant growth of organic manures and animal excreta may thus be due to the action of these plant hormones, or, as they have been called, "phytohormones." Certain fungi and probably bacteria are able to synthesize these hormones, as in the case of rhizopin.

In addition to proteins, other organic nitrogen compounds, like lecithin, methylated amines, purine bases, and other substances present in plant or animal tissues and found in the soil, are acted upon by microorganisms to form simpler compounds Ammonia is one of these.

Lecithin is first split to choline, glycerophosphoric acid, and fatty acids.

The choline is decomposed into ammonia, trimethylamine, carbon dioxide, and methane. Betaine, creatinine, guanidine, and purine bases, like uric acid, also undergo decomposition by microorganisms

Uric acid can also be decomposed by various bacteria according to the following reaction·

$$C_5H_4N_4O_3 + 8H_2O + 1\tfrac{1}{2}(O_2) = 4NH_4HCO_3 + CO_2$$

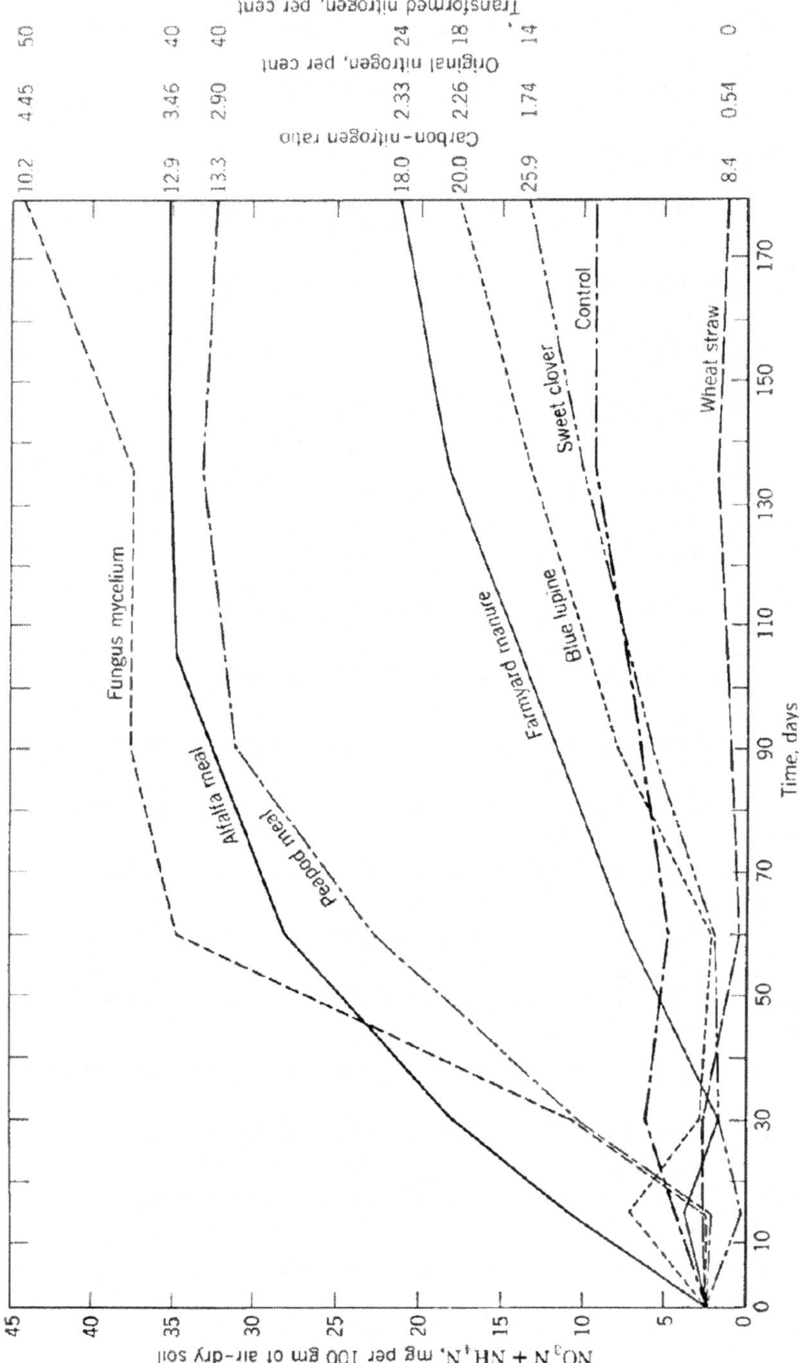

FIG. 71. **Liberation of nitrogen in decomposition of different materials** (from Jensen).

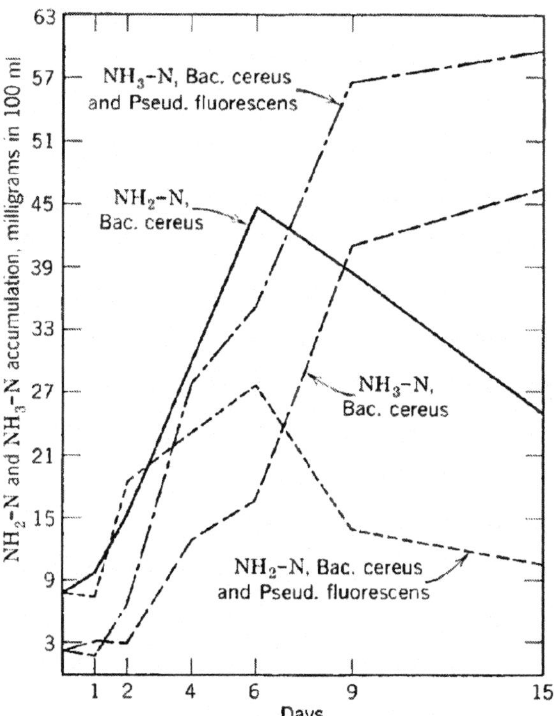

FIG. 72. Course of accumulation of amino- and ammonia-nitrogen from casein by *Bacillus cereus* and *Pseudomonas fluorescens* (from Waksman and Lomanitz).

A large number of microorganisms are able to use hippuric acid as a source of carbon and nitrogen. The acid is usually first hydrolyzed by an enzyme produced by these organisms:

$$\underset{\text{Hippuric acid}}{C_6H_5 \cdot CO \cdot NH \cdot CH_2 \cdot COOH} + H_2O = \underset{\text{Benzoic acid}}{C_6H_5 \cdot COOH} + \underset{\text{Glycocoll}}{NH_2 \cdot CH_2 \cdot COOH}$$

Urea is hydrolyzed, with the formation of ammonia, by a large number of soil microorganisms as well as by specific groups of bacteria, which utilize the energy liberated in the process:

$$CO\begin{matrix} \diagup NH_2 \\ \diagdown NH_2 \end{matrix} + 2H_2O = (NH_4)_2CO_3 = CO_2 + 2NH_3 + H_2O$$

The true structure of urea has been postulated, however, to be as follows:

$$HN = C\langle{}^{NH}_{O}$$

Cyanamide readily breaks down in the soil to ammonia, which is then nitrified virtually quantitatively. Cyanamide may first be

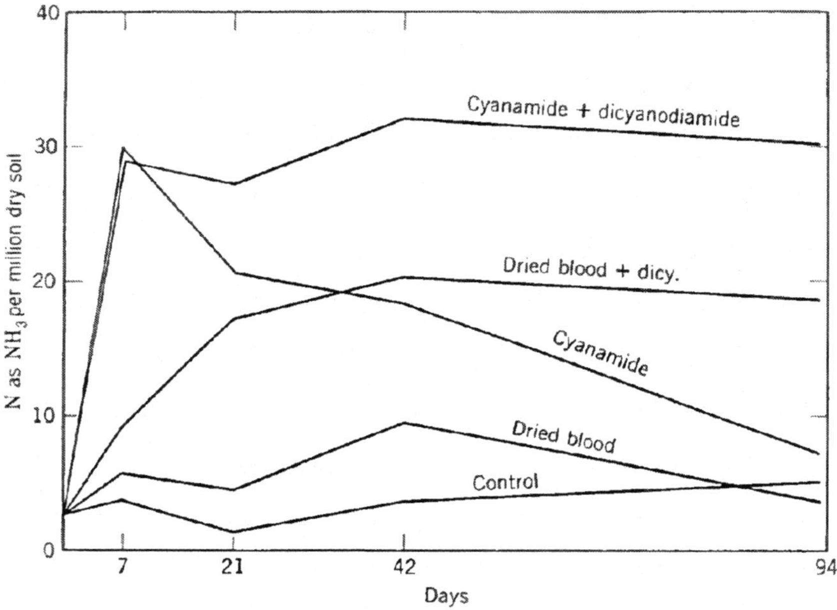

Fig. 73. Accumulation of ammonia from cyanamide and dried blood, as influenced by the presence of dicyanodiamide (from Cowie).

decomposed in the soil into urea by a purely chemical process, under the influence of catalyzers, or it may polymerize into dicyanodiamide (especially in the presence of catalyzers such as $ZnCl_2$).

Soils differ markedly in the rate with which they decompose calcium cyanamide, but very few are deficient in the required catalyst, which changes the cyanamide to urea. The urea is transformed in the soil to ammonia within a few days, especially in soils active microbiologically. Nitrate formation proceeds more slowly in soils treated with cyanamide, the retardation depending on the soil and the environmental conditions. A great many soil organisms are capable of decomposing dicyanodiamide.

Chitin is found among the synthesized constituents of the cells of microorganisms, especially fungi, and is constantly added to the store of soil organic matter It consists of one molecule of glucosamine and three molecules of acetyl-glucosamine, from which four molecules of water have been removed ($C_{30}H_{50}O_{19}N_4$)

Ammonia Formation by Microorganisms

The earlier investigators of bacterial metabolism, like Hoppe-Seyler, Bienstock, and Hauser, found that mixtures and pure cultures of bacteria, like *Proteus vulgaris, Bacillus subtilis, Serratia marcescens, Clostridium putrificus,* and *Pseudomonas fluorescens liquefaciens,* are capable of breaking down proteins with the formation of various end products, one of which is ammonia. Proteins of both plant and animal origin are decomposed by a number of bacteria, giving a great variety of products

Marchal used a solution containing 1 5 per cent nitrogen, in the form of egg albumin made insoluble by means of 0 01 per cent ferric sulfate, which was inoculated with various bacteria, ammonia was determined, after 20 days' incubation at 30°C, by distilling with MgO

Strains of *B mycoides* derived from different sources varied in their power to produce ammonia from proteins. With one strain, Marchal obtained a transformation of 58 per cent of egg-albumin nitrogen into ammonia, accompanied by a marked change of the reaction of the medium to alkaline The more dilute the solution of the protein, the greater was the transformation

The great majority of soil organisms developing on the plate were found to produce ammonia from proteins The gelatin-liquefying bacteria are capable of inducing greater protein decomposition with more abundant ammonia formation. Since the members of this group form at times more than 15 per cent of the total number of soil bacteria developing on the plate, they were believed to do the initial work in rendering soluble the protein nitrogen in the soil, so that it might be further decomposed by the same or other soil organisms

According to Conn, however, the non-spore-forming bacteria are much more active in manured soil than the spore-forming organisms *Bacillus cereus* was found to decompose proteins to amino acids, whereas *Ps fluorescens* acts largely upon amino acids In the presence of a mixture of the two organisms, the protein is rapidly changed to ammonia. Thus there is a possibility that different organisms take an active part in different stages of the process of protein decomposition; bacteria like *B. cereus* may be active in the first stages of hydrolysis, and bacteria like *Ps. fluorescens*, in the latter stages leading to the formation of ammonia.

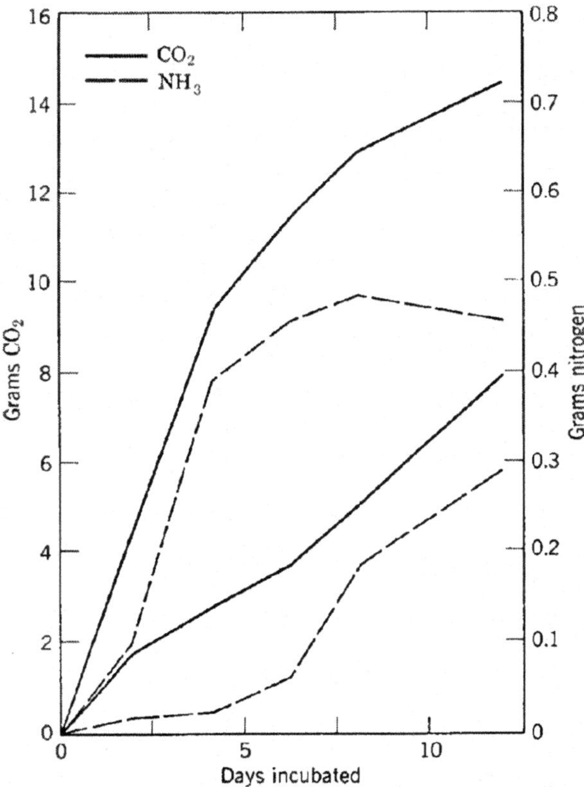

Fig. 74. Rate of decomposition of cottonseed meal in soil, as shown by the evolution of carbon dioxide and accumulation of ammonia (from Gainey).

The rapidity of ammonia formation from proteins by bacteria depends not only upon the nature of the organism but also upon the kind of protein. The process of ammonia formation from casein was completed in a few days, whereas it continued for more than a month from gliadin. The amino-nitrogen contents of the gliadin and casein media were 0.57 and 0.68 mg before hydrolysis; 42.56 and 99.31 mg after acid hydrolysis; and 17.03 and 46.00 after hydrolysis with *B. subtilis*. All the nitrogen forms of the protein molecule are changed more or less by the action of bacteria, the end product being ammonia; in no case, however, is one form of nitrogen completely destroyed. A similarity was found in the chemical changes produced by acid hydrolysis and by bacteria. Carbohydrates exert a depressing effect upon the liberation of ammonia from proteins (Table 35).

TABLE 35. INFLUENCE OF VARIOUS CONCENTRATIONS OF GLUCOSE ON THE FORMATION OF AMMONIA FROM CASEIN (from Doryland)

Organism	Incubation	Casein		Casein + 0.05 Per Cent Glucose		Casein + 0.1 Per Cent Glucose		Casein + 0.2 Per Cent Glucose	
	days	NH_3 *mg*	Bact.*	NH_3 *mg*	Bact.	NH_3 *mg*	Bact.	NH_3 *mg*	Bact.
B. subtilis	2	15.7	2.9	13.0	4.6	12.0	4.9	13.2	4.0
	4	25.1	11.4	20.0	22.8	15.9	30.9	13.0	33.0
	6	49.5	49.0	55.0	54.7	48.7	54.3	17.0	59.0
Pr. vulgaris	2	13.8	5.1	10.9	6.0	11.8	6.8	10.9	6.9
	4	20.2	21.1	22.0	39.2	13.7	48.3	15.0	50.1
	6	30.3	86.6	32.0	80.1	30.1	89.1	15.7	92.2
B. mycoides	2	22.6	4.7	14.8	4.4	13.9	3.8	14.0	4.8
	4	64.0	25.9	20.1	32.1	14.4	33.0	15.0	37.0
	6	69.6	63.2	60.0	65.9	52.0	66.7	11.9	66.1
S. lutea	2	12.9	1.9	11.2	2.0	11.9	2.8	10.8	3.1
	4	22.4	5.9	10.2	7.6	11.9	6.1	12.0	7.4
	6	26.1	7.9	20.0	19.0	11.3	10.7	11.0	8.9

* Bact. = bacteria in millions.

Fungi are able to decompose proteins very vigorously. Different species vary greatly in this respect; the nature of the protein, reaction of medium, and presence of available carbohydrates affect the process. A large part of the nitrogen may be left in the form of intermediary products. Organisms like *Aspergillus niger,* which produce large amounts of acid (oxalic and citric) from carbohydrates and even from proteins and which are thus enabled to neutralize the ammonia, accumulate only very small amounts of amino acids in artificial cultures; at the same time appreciable quantities of ammonia are formed in the medium. But when the oxalic acid is neutralized with $CaCO_3$, or when the formation of both oxalic acid and ammonia is prevented by means of insufficient aeration, amino acids accumulate.

When the protein is the only source of carbon available for fungi, a definite parallelism is found between the growth of the mycelium and the production of ammonia. Different protein derivatives are not utilized alike, and their nitrogen is not liberated alike in the form of ammonia. *Aspergillus niger* grows best with leucine, followed by peptone, asparagine, and glycocoll. The difference in the nature of the carbon compounds accompanying the proteins or of the protein carbon itself accounts for the difference in the amount of fungus growth and ammonia formation, because, in the absence of available carbohydrates, the fungus uses the protein both as a source of energy and as a source of nitrogen. The amount of nitrogen liberated as ammonia depends not only upon the nitrogen content of the protein, but also largely upon the availability of other sources of carbon. The nitrogen is then either liberated as a waste product, ammonia, or reassimilated and changed into microbial protein (Table 36).

TABLE 36. INFLUENCE OF COMPOSITION OF AMINO ACID UPON AMMONIA PRODUCTION BY MICROORGANISMS (from Waksman and Lomanitz)

Amino Acid	C/N	Organism	Dry Growth of Cells	NH_3-N	Growth / NH_3-N
			mg	*mg*	
Glycocoll	1.7	*Trichoderma*	50	24.28	2.0
Glycocoll	1.7	*Actinomyces*	59	30.46	2.0
Alanine	2.57	*Trichoderma*	80	21.98	3.6
Alanine	2.57	*Actinomyces*	126	39.17	3.2
Glutamic acid	4.28	*Trichoderma*	218	29.12	7.5
Glutamic acid	4.28	*Actinomyces*	169	28.36	5.9
Glutamic acid	4.28	*Ps. fluorescens*	128	28.50	4.5

NITROGEN TRANSFORMATION IN DECOMPOSITION OF ORGANIC MATTER

When nitrogenous organic substances are added to the soil, a group of complex reactions result, so far as the nitrogen is concerned.

(1) Hydrolysis of the proteins into polypeptides and amino acids, with liberation of some ammonia, takes place. (2) This is followed by the decomposition of the amino acids and other products of protein hydrolysis, with a further liberation of ammonia. (3) Synthesis of microbial protoplasm leads to a storing away of a part or the whole of the ammonia nitrogen, the greater the quantity of available non-nitrogenous organic matter accompanying the nitrogenous sub-

stances, the greater will be the synthesis of microbial protoplasm, leading to a greater assimilation of the nitrogen and to a smaller accumulation of ammonia (4) Various soil conditions, as well as differences in the composition of the nitrogenous and the accompanying non-nitrogenous organic substances, lead to the development of different microorganisms capable of decomposing the nitrogenous materials, the carbon-nitrogen metabolism of these microorganisms is different, this leads, therefore, to differences in the amounts of ammonia liberated in a free state.

These reactions result in a transformation of a larger or smaller part of the nitrogen of the organic complexes into ammonia, which, either as such or after it has been oxidized to nitrate, is available as a source of nitrogen for the growth of cultivated plants In view of the great economic importance of the liberation of ammonia, numerous contributions have been made to the subject, known as "ammonification." These studies have been chiefly limited to adding about 1 gm of the nitrogenous organic material to 100 gm of soil, mixing, placing in tumblers, then bringing the moisture content of the soil to optimum (60 per cent saturation), incubating for 4–14 (usually 7) days, then measuring the amount of ammonia present in the soil by distilling with MgO.

Thus, in the presence of available carbohydrates (Table 37), two

TABLE 37 INFLUENCE OF CARBOHYDRATE UPON AMMONIA FORMATION IN SOIL (from Kelley)

Nitrogen Source	Nitrogen Content	1 gm of Each Organic Material Added to 100 gm Soil NH_3-N	132 9 mg Organic Nitrogen plus Enough Starch to Make Equivalent Amounts of Carbon NH_3-N
	per cent	*mg*	*mg*
Casein	12 40	50 2	31 4
Dried blood	13 29	42 4	18 9
Soybean cake	8 28	40 9	34.1
Cottonseed meal	5 10	27 1	34 0
Linseed meal	5 00	26 0	34 1

factors are at work. first, less of the protein is decomposed, since the bacteria and fungi prefer the carbohydrate to the protein as a source of energy, second, the ammonia that has been formed from the decomposition of the proteins may be reassimilated by the microorganisms which utilize the carbohydrate as a source of energy. These microbes are, therefore, competing with higher plants for the available nitrogen compounds in the soil. As a result of these studies, Doryland defined ammonification as "an expression of an unbalanced ratio for microorganisms, in which the nitrogen is in excess of the energy-nitrogen ratio." If the available energy ma-

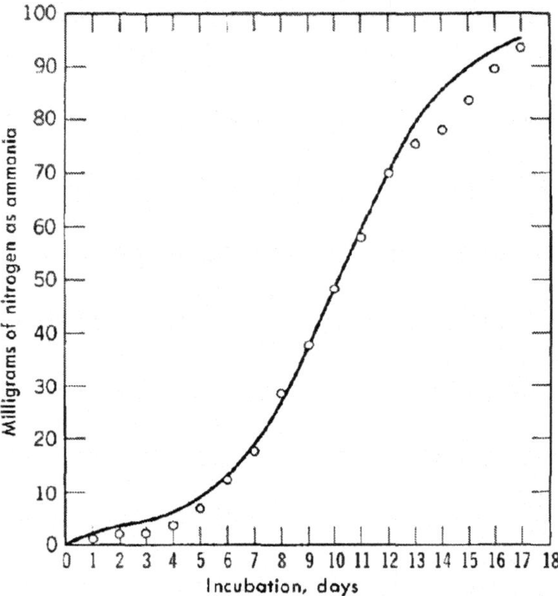

FIG. 75. Rate of ammonia formation from peptone by *Aspergillus niger* (from Waksman).

terial is equal to or in excess of the energy-nitrogen ratio required by the flora, the coefficient of ammonia formation tends to approach zero; it tends to approach a maximum if the available energy material is less than the energy-nitrogen ratio. Depending on the proportion of energy material to nitrogenous substances, "beneficial" bacteria may become "harmful."

The nature and the composition of the organic matter greatly influence its decomposition. The ratio between the carbon and nitrogen of the material used is of special importance in this connection. The same is true of the nature of the non-nitrogenous organic materials introduced into the soil in addition to the nitrogenous substances. Table 38 has been compiled from the results of Lipman and associates, who added different organic nitrogenous materials to 100-gm

TABLE 38 INFLUENCE OF CARBOHYDRATES UPON THE ACCUMULATION OF AMMONIA FROM NITROGENOUS ORGANIC MATERIALS (from Lipman)

Nitrogenous Substance *	Total Nitrogen in Material	Ammonia Formed			
		No Carbohydrate	Glucose 2 gm	Sucrose 2 gm	Starch 2 gm
	mg	mg	mg	mg	mg
Rice flour	46 4	1 26	1 30	1 48	0 87
Corn meal	51 2	1 18	1 30	1 04	0 69
Wheat flour	94 8	5 14	3 66	5 84	1 56
Cowpea meal	156 8	50 88	31.71	28 57	23 70
Linseed meal	247 0	110.69	96 01	60 73	63 34
Soybean meal	245 6	129 64	108 03	94 88	54 36
Cottonseed meal	246.1	123 63	99 67	97 23	54 54

* Four grams of organic material added to 100 gm of soil

portions of soil, the moisture content was brought to an optimum, and after the soils were incubated for 7 days, the ammonia was determined by distilling with MgO. Rice flour and corn meal, with a wide carbon-nitrogen ratio, allowed no accumulation of ammonia, either with or without additional carbohydrate. The substances rich in nitrogen allowed an accumulation of almost 50 per cent of the nitrogen as ammonia, but this was considerably reduced when more available energy in the form of carbohydrates was added (Table 39)

TABLE 39 INFLUENCE OF ADDED NITROGEN SALT UPON THE DECOMPOSITION OF RYE STRAW * AND ITS CONSTITUENT CARBOHYDRATES BY MICROORGANISMS

Units in milligrams

Organisms	Ammonium Salt Added	CO_2 Liberated	Total Plant Material Decomposed	Hemicelluloses Decomposed	Cellulose Decomposed	NH_3-N Assimilated
Control	−	37				
Control	+	37				
Trichoderma	−	333	231	190	47	
Trichoderma	+	648	504	280	327	25
Humicola	−	588	602	199	125	
Humicola	+	1,106	908	339	461	31
Soil inoculum	−	799	601	240	116	
Soil inoculum	+	2,964	1,940	609	1,079	53

* Five-gram portions

Nitrification in Soil

The production of nitrates from ammonia was known and utilized long before the microbiological nature of the process was understood. This is illustrated by the fact that during the Napoleonic Wars careful instructions were given to the French farmers for preparing composts of stable manure, favoring nitrate formation and

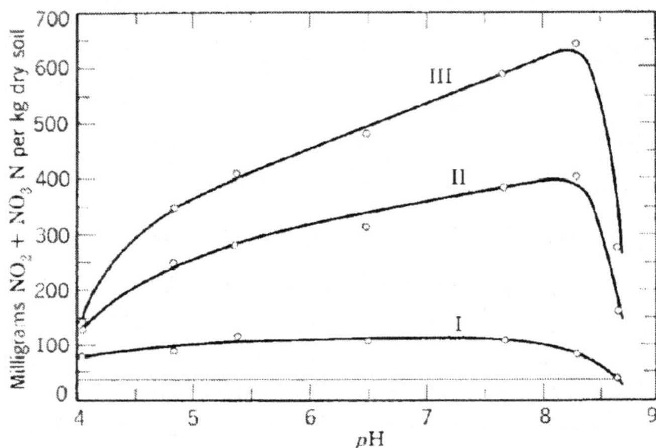

Fig. 76. Influence of reaction on nitrification in soil, after 11 days (I), 22 days (II), and 29 days (III) (from C. Olsen).

accumulation. During our own Civil War, especially in the South, "niter plantations" or "nitriaries" were common (Taber).

The decomposition of proteins and of other nitrogenous organic substances leads to the formation and often the accumulation of ammonia in the soil. Under favorable conditions, this is rapidly oxidized to nitrites and then to nitrates. Under certain conditions, when the nitrifying bacteria are killed, as in the partial sterilization of soil, or when conditions do not favor nitrification, as with excessive soil acidity, ammonia may accumulate in the soil.

The oxidation of ammonia to nitrate can be accomplished by three types of processes, namely, chemical, physicochemical, and, most important, biological.

At high temperatures and in the presence of catalysts, ammonia may be oxidized chemically to nitrate, as in the electrolytic oxidation of ammonia in the presence of copper oxyhydrate. Oxidation may also take place, to a limited extent, in an atmosphere saturated with ammonia and in the presence of ferric hydrate. Ammonia is also oxidized to nitrite by ultraviolet radiation. According to Weith and Weber, hydrogen peroxide and ammonia react with each other,

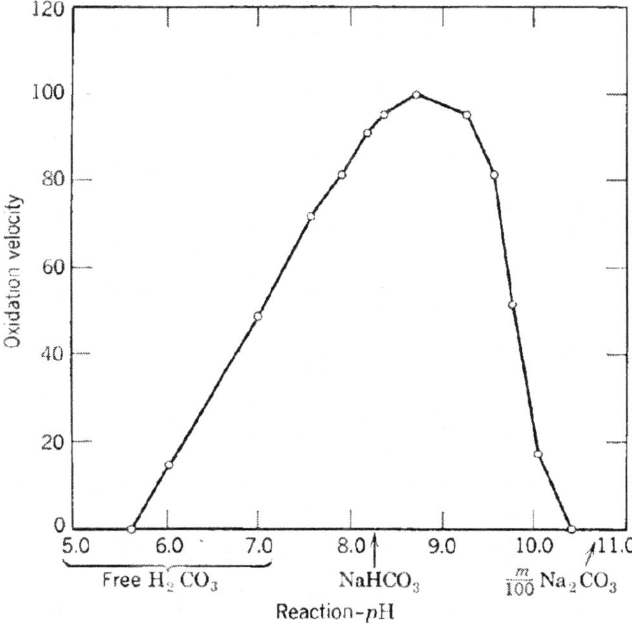

FIG. 77. Influence of reaction upon nitrate formation (from Meyerhof).

giving rise to nitrous acid. The interaction between ozone and ammonia to give ammonium nitrate has been known for several decades:

$$(NH_3)_2 + 4O_3 \rightarrow NH_4NO_2 + H_2O_2 + 4O_2$$

$$NH_4NO_2 + H_2O_2 \rightarrow NH_4NO_3 + H_2O$$

It has been reported recently that oxidation of ammonia and its salts in solution and in soil may be effected by sunlight, in the presence of certain photosensitizing substances, TiO and ZnO being most active; basicity favored oxidation and acidity impeded it (Table 40). It was believed that a part of the nitrification in soil is due at least to photochemical oxidation at the surface of various photocatalysts present in the soil. The process was believed to be of special importance in tropical countries, such as India (Dhar). Rossi also suggested that the process of nitrification is of a purely physico-

TABLE 40 RELATIONSHIP BETWEEN SOIL REACTION AND ABUNDANCE OF AMMONIA-OXIDIZING ORGANISMS (from Wilson)

*p*H	Abundance of Organisms
6.2	1,000
6.4	3,500
6.6	6,280
6.8	25,000
7.0	35,000

chemical nature at the very surface sod layer The evidence submitted to substantiate both these theories is still insufficient On further study, at least in tropical countries, negative results were obtained, the results obtained by Rossi were explained by the specific effect of drying upon the removal of nitrate already present in the soil Nath concluded that sunlight and ultraviolet light have no effect on the oxidation of ammonia in soil, actually nitrates are decomposed under these conditions

At best the quantities of nitrite and nitrate formed by chemical agencies are insignificant and of little importance in the soil. The biological process of nitrification, as established by Schloesing and Muntz, Warington, and Winogradsky, is by far the most important.

MECHANISM OF BIOLOGICAL OXIDATION OF AMMONIA Various reactions have been suggested to explain the mechanism of oxidation of ammonia to nitrite by the nitrite-forming bacteria The following two reactions are most probable

$$2NH_3 + 3O_2 \rightarrow 2HNO_2 + 2H_2O$$

$$2NH_3 + 3O_2 \rightarrow N_2O_3 + 3H_2O$$

The free energy efficiency of *Nitrosomonas* is usually taken to be about 6 per cent. Lees and Hofmann have recently calculated such energy for different stages of growth of the organism At the early stages of growth, the value was found to be about 50 per cent, falling rapidly as nitrite accumulated, with a nitrite concentration of 1.5 mg nitrogen per ml, it reached about 6 per cent This rapid fall in efficiency was believed to be due to an increased respiration loss following the maintenance of a low intracellular nitrite concentration with an increasing nitrite content Using paper chromatography, Hofmann found that the amino acid content of the protein of nitrifying bacteria is similar to that of the proteins of other organisms

Mechanism of Nitrite Oxidation. The oxidation of nitrite to nitrate takes place according to the following reaction:

$$NaNO_2 + \frac{1}{2}O_2 = NaNO_3$$

This was demonstrated by measuring the nitrite and oxygen consumption. With optimum concentration of the nutrients and proper aeration of the culture, the nitrate-forming organisms, in liquid culture, may oxidize 4–5 gm $NaNO_2$ per liter in 24 hours.

Winogradsky observed the interesting phenomenon that ammonium salts injuriously affect the growth of nitrate bacteria. This seemed rather strange in view of the fact that the nitrate bacteria are active side by side with the nitrite bacteria which use the ammonium salt as a source of energy. It was then suggested that the two processes follow in two successive periods in the soil, nitrate formation beginning only after all the ammonium salt is converted into nitrite. On decreasing the amount of Na_2CO_3, which would lead to a lower alkalinity, Boulanger and Massol found that the injurious effect of ammonium salt is less, and concluded, therefore, that the growth of nitrate bacteria is not injured by the salt but by free ammonia. This was confirmed by Meyerhof, who established that the injurious influence of ammonia and its derivatives (aliphatic amines) consists in the penetration of the base into the cell (which does not take place in the case of ammonium salt) and in a specific action of the NH_3 and NH_2 groups. Lipoid-insoluble amines, like the diamines, are not injurious. The injurious effect of amines and cations depends upon their ability to penetrate into the cell and upon the reaction of the media; respiration is usually less affected than growth. The intermediary products of the oxidation of sulfur (hyposulfite) are a decided deterrent to the process of nitrate formation in soil, the nitrifying bacteria as such are not injured, since the process is resumed as soon as these intermediary products have disappeared.

Schloesing compared the formation of nitrates from various ammonium salts added to the soil and found that the following relative amounts of nitrogen (in milligrams) are nitrified per day: NH_4Cl, 3.4; $(NH_4)_2SO_4$, 9.0; $(NH_4)_2CO_3$, 4.0. Ammonium salts of organic acids are also nitrified rapidly.

It was thought at first that organic matter can be nitrified directly. Muntz has shown, however, that organic matter has to be decomposed first, and ammonia liberated, before nitrates can be formed. Omeliansky later obtained negative results also for urea, asparagine, methylamine, dimethylamine, and egg albumin. He concluded that all forms of organic nitrogen have to be transformed first into ammonia before they can be nitrified This was found to hold true also for calcium cyanamide When the processes of nitrate formation from ammonium salts and from amino acids are compared, the latter is found to take place more slowly. This is probably due to the fact that the amino acids have to be changed first to ammonia and also to the fact that some of the nitrogen is stored away in the microbial cells which use the carbon of the amino compounds as a source of energy.

When ammonium sulfate is used as a source of nitrogen for nitrate formation and the reaction of the soil is acid to begin with, there will be an increase in acidity in absence of sufficient buffer or base, as a result of formation of nitric acid from the oxidation of the ammonia and the accumulation of the residual sulfuric acid Nitrate accumulation will proceed until the reaction of the soil has reached a *p*H of about 4.0. The amount of nitrate formed under these conditions depends upon the initial reaction of the soil and its buffer and base content, the higher the buffer and base content of the soil, the larger will be the amount of nitrate formed for a certain change of reaction. The continuous use of ammonium sulfate as a fertilizer without the addition of lime will, therefore, lead to a gradual increase in soil acidity. However, nitrates may be found even in very acid soils. This was explained by Hall and associates as due to the fact that, under acid conditions, nitrate formation takes place in films surrounding the small isolated particles of $CaCO_3$ The addition of $CaCO_3$ has, therefore, a decidedly stimulating effect on nitrate formation, particularly in acid soils. In alkaline soils which are deficient in organic matter, $CaCO_3$ may have the opposite effect, since it tends to liberate from ammonium salts free ammonia, which retards nitrification

Conditions that tend to promote nitrate formation in the soil are temperature of 27.5°C, an abundant supply of air (oxygen), proper moisture supply, a favorable reaction (*p*H greater than 4 6), presence of carbonates or other buffering agents, and absence of large quantities of soluble organic matter The nature of the crop grown also influences the nitrate content of the soil

Denitrification in Soil

Just as aerobic conditions in soil favor oxidation processes, so do anaerobic conditions (exclusion of free oxygen) favor processes of reduction. Either organic or inorganic compounds may be formed as a result of these processes, depending upon the composition of the medium. It is not necessary for the soil to be saturated with water for the conditions to be anaerobic. Winogradsky demonstrated, by the development of anaerobic nitrogen-fixing bacteria,

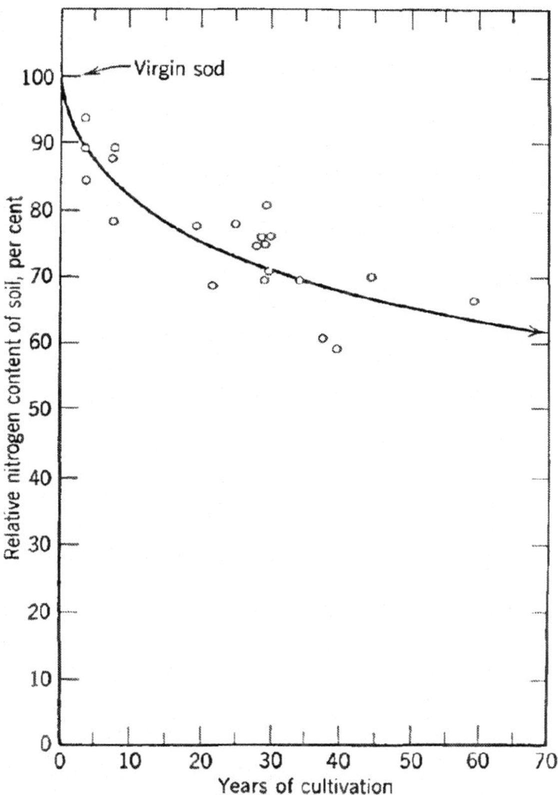

FIG. 78. Nitrogen level of soils cultivated for a number of years (from Jenny).

that, when a soil contains water equivalent to only about 40 per cent of its moisture-holding capacity, anaerobic bacteria find conditions favorable for their development even at the very surface of the soil.

The disappearance of nitrates in soil as a result of activities of microorganisms may be due to three groups of phenomena: first, direct utilization of nitrates by microorganisms as sources of nitrogen, in the presence of sufficient energy material; second, reduction of nitrates to nitrites and ammonia in the process of nitrate assimilation; third, utilization of nitrates as sources of oxygen (nitrates as hydrogen acceptors). In the last process oxygen is utilized by the organism for the oxidation of carbon compounds or inorganic substances, such as sulfur. The energy thus derived is used for the reduction of the nitrate to nitrite, to free nitrogen gas, to oxides of nitrogen, or to ammonia. The formation of nitrogen gas from nitrate may be so rapid under favorable conditions that the gas can actually serve as a measure of the amount of nitrate reduced.

The disappearance of nitrates in the soil due to the various processes of nitrate reduction and nitrate assimilation has often been referred to as "denitrification." However, the reduction of nitrates to nitrites and ammonia, as well as their assimilation by microorganisms, involves no losses of nitrogen, but merely indicates that the nitrates are for the moment taken out of circulation and changed into forms from which nitrate can be again produced. The nitrates may completely disappear without involving any loss of nitrogen, as in their assimilation by fungi and various bacteria in the presence of available energy. The term "denitrification" (or complete denitrification) should designate the complete reduction of nitrates to atmospheric nitrogen and oxides of nitrogen, whereas the other processes involving disappearance of nitrates may be referred to as "nitrate reduction" and "nitrate assimilation."

Certain bacteria are capable of reducing nitrates to nitrites, ammonia, and atmospheric nitrogen or oxides of nitrogen. Goppelsroder was the first to observe that nitrates are reduced in the soil to nitrites. He ascribed this property to the organic matter of the soil. Schoenbein in 1868 and Meusel in 1875 recognized the bacterial nature of the process. This idea was developed further by Gayon and Dupetit and others, as shown previously.

In absence of free oxygen but in presence of nitrate, various aerobic bacteria are capable of existing anaerobically. Some organisms bring about complete denitrification, others reduce the nitrate to the nitrite stage only, a smaller amount of oxygen thereby becoming available.

$$2HNO_3 = 2HNO_2 + O_2$$

When the nitrite is reduced to atmospheric nitrogen,

$$2HNO_2 = N_2 + 1\tfrac{1}{2}O_2 + H_2O$$

In the reduction of nitrate to ammonia, the following reaction takes place.

$$HNO_3 + H_2O = NH_3 + 2O_2$$

The more nearly complete the reduction of the nitrate, the more oxygen becomes available, and, therefore, the greater is the amount of carbohydrate that can be oxidized and the greater is the gain in energy. In the case of many aerobic microorganisms, nitrate can act as the hydrogen acceptor, whereby it is first reduced to the NO_2 ion, and this, through the hypothetical dioxyammonia (HON·HON),

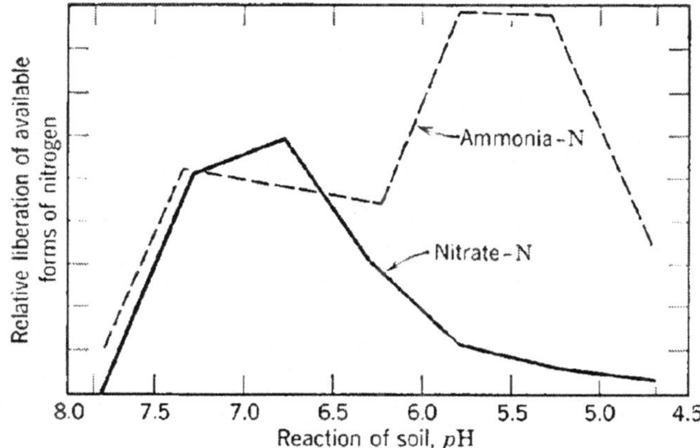

FIG. 79. Influence of reaction upon nitrogen liberation in forest soil (from Aaltonen).

to $NH_2 \cdot OH$ (hydroxylamine) and then to NH_3. The first stage of the reduction can be presented as follows:

$$HCOOH + HNO_3 \rightarrow CO_2 + HNO_2 + H_2O$$

Nitrate reduction can be brought about readily by a number of soil bacteria, under anaerobic conditions, when carbon complexes are available as sources of energy. Nitrates enable many facultative anaerobes to develop under anaerobic conditions, using sources of carbon which would otherwise not be available.

The reduction of nitrates to atmospheric nitrogen always goes through the nitrite stage. The following reaction was at first suggested to explain the complete reduction of the nitrate molecule:

$$5C_6H_{12}O_6 + 24HNO_3 = 24H_2CO_3 + 6CO_2 + 18H_2O + 12N_2$$

The carbohydrates or organic acids of the media are decomposed with the formation of carbon dioxide and nascent hydrogen; the nitrate is then used by the organism as the hydrogen acceptor, which results in the reduction of the nitrate. When tartaric acid is oxidized by atmospheric oxygen or by reduction of nitrates, nearly equal amounts of energy are liberated, since the reduction of nitrates to atmospheric nitrogen does not consume a large amount of energy.

Most of the denitrifying bacteria reduce nitrate to nitrogen gas and N_2O in varying proportions, *B. nitroxus* being particularly active in the process. A 5–12 per cent solution of nitrate inoculated with soil gives, at 20–37°C, a current of gas which is 80 per cent N_2O.

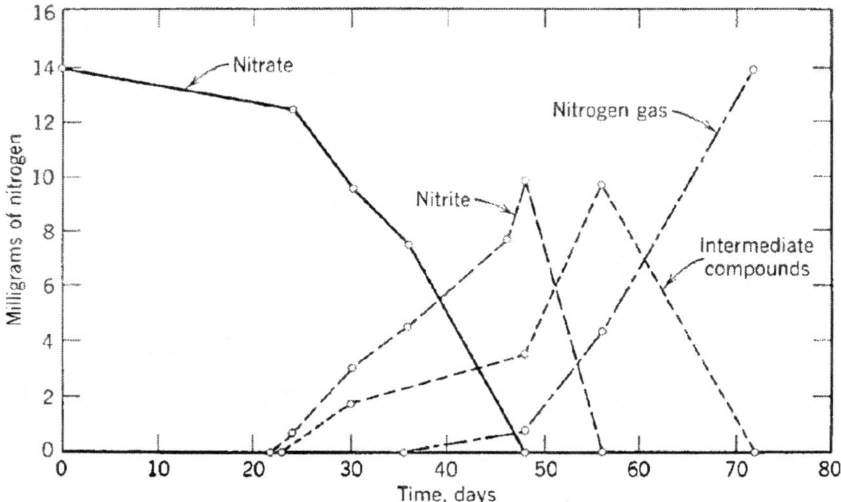

Fig. 80. Reduction of nitrate by microbes (from Korsakowa).

Various other denitrifying bacteria, like *Ps. aeruginosa* and *B. stutzeri*, give in solutions of nitrate (particularly NH_4NO_3) a gas rich in N_2O. Of 100 cultures of bacteria tested by Maassen, 31 were found capable of reducing nitrate to nitrite; the latter is then reduced to atmospheric nitrogen and various oxides of nitrogen. This process was rather slow and independent of the oxygen supply. Tacke found that 38 per cent of the gas mixture formed during the process of nitrate reduction by bacteria may consist of N_2O. The formation of nitric oxide in the reduction of nitrates has also been demonstrated by other investigators.

In general, the liberation of atmospheric nitrogen by reduction of nitrate depends upon changes in oxidation-reduction potential of medium, *p*H value, presence of nitrite, and nature of available carbon sources. The presence of certain growth-inhibiting substances is also of importance. The addition of KCN to a culture of *Micrococcus denitrificans* inhibited the formation of elementary nitrogen; the last stage in the reduction process, that of hyponitrite to gaseous nitrogen, was believed to be affected, the hyponitrite breaking up to the oxide of nitrogen and free base

The presence in the soil of bacteria capable of reducing nitrates to atmospheric nitrogen and oxides of nitrogen was definitely established in 1882 by Gayon and Dupetit and by Déhérain and Maquenne The same year, Lawes, Gilbert, and Warington pointed out that considerable quantities of nitrogen may be given off when a soil receives heavy applications of manure and is saturated with water or is improperly aerated Bréal announced in 1892 that many substances of organic origin especially straw, can serve as sources of energy which would enable the bacteria to liberate atmospheric nitrogen from nitrates In 1895, Wagner reported that the addition of manure to liquid cultures containing nitrates greatly increased denitrification, this observation led him to the conclusion that the same process takes place in the soil He found confirmation of this in field experiments where organic nitrogen and nitrates were added simultaneously before the crop was planted Wagner declared, on the basis of these experiments, that denitrification may take place extensively in cultivated soils, the application of manure (cow or horse) to the soil may often be not only unprofitable but even harmful. This was believed to be due to the fact that manure carries microorganisms which destroy the nitrates in the soil, not only nitrates added as such, but even those formed by the nitrifying bacteria.

These and similar other investigations created the impression that, when nitrates are added to the soil, denitrification sets in and may produce an injurious action by causing the transformation of the nitrate into gaseous nitrogen It was soon found that these results were greatly exaggerated Losses of nitrogen were found possible only when considerable amounts of organic matter were added together with the nitrate, but this is not commonly done. Pfeiffer and Lemmermann demonstrated that very little actual denitrification takes place in the soil as a result of addition of manure The lack of nitrogen often observed is due to other causes rather than to the loss of nitrogen Nitrate reduction sets in when the soil is saturated with water. Only in the presence of a great abundance of organic manures is there any fear of loss of nitrate nitrogen in a gaseous form from the soil When soils are submerged in water, the nitrates are rapidly reduced Nitrites may be formed not at all or only in too small amounts to cause plant injury. Ammonia is formed in some cases. As a result of this reduction, the reaction of the soil becomes more alkaline. A similar increase in alkalinity is observed when green manures are applied to flooded soils. In high-moor peat soils, the addition of lime leads to active nitrification; when the nitrates are reduced by denitrifying bacteria, the nitrogen in the soils is rapidly depleted.

Great losses of nitrogen may take place in a humid, hot climate; the rate of loss is increased by liming, bare fallows in rainy season were found to be especially wasteful because of the leaching of nitrates in drainage waters. There is little danger from denitrification in normal soils. The partial reduction of nitrates to nitrites and ammonia, which is more extensive and carried out by larger numbers of microorganisms, does not involve any actual losses of nitrogen. The nitrates may completely disappear from the medium without loss of nitrogen. The products formed from the nitrates (nitrites and ammonia) can be further acted upon by nitrifying bacteria, the part of the nitrate assimilated by microorganisms is merely stored away in the soil in an organic form.

It is often observed that addition of large quantities of undecomposed organic matter to a soil particularly rich in carbohydrates and poor in nitrogen injures crop growth. This is not due to denitrification, to which it has often been ascribed, but to the fact that, in the presence of an excess of available organic matter, the fungi, actinomycetes, and various heterotrophic bacteria synthesize an extensive protoplasm. For this purpose, they assimilate the nitrates and ammonium compounds present in the soil and thus compete with higher plants.

The conclusion may be reached that the phenomenon of denitrification is of no economic significance in well-aerated, not too moist soils, in the presence of moderate amounts of organic matter or nitrate. In soils kept under water for some time, as rice soils, however, addition of nitrates may prove injurious because of the formation of toxic nitrite. It may be added here that there is also no distinct parallelism between plant communities, the geological substrate, and the presence and activities of denitrifying bacteria.

Selected Bibliography

1. Barritt, N. W., The liberation of elementary nitrogen by bacteria, *Biochem. J.*, 25: 1965–1972, 1931.

2 Bonazzi, A, On nitrification V The mechanism of ammonia oxidation, *J Bact*, 8 343–363, 1923
3 Bright, J W, and Conn, H J, Ammonification of manure in soil, *N Y Agr Expt Sta Tech Bull* 67, 1919
4 Corbet, A S, The formation of hyponitrous acid as an intermediate compound in the biological or photochemical oxidation of ammonia to nitrous acid, *Biochem J*, 28 1575–1582, 1934.
5 Dhar, N R, Bhattacharya, A. K, and Biswas, N N, Influence of light on nitrification in soil, *J Indian Chem Soc*, 10 699–712, 1933, *Nature*, 133 213–214, 1934
6 Dhar, N R, and Rao, G G, Nitrification in soil and in atmosphere A photochemical process, *J. Indian Chem Soc*, 9 81–91, 1933
7 Doryland, C J T, The influence of energy material upon the relation of soil microorganisms to soluble plant food, *N Dakota Agr Expt Sta Bull* 116, 1916
8 Gainey, P L, Parallel formation of carbon dioxide, ammonia, and nitrate in soil, *Soil Sci*, 7 293–311, 1919
9 Kluyver, A J, *The Chemical Activities of Microorganisms*, University of London Press, 1931
10 McLean, H. C, and Wilson, G. W., Ammonification studies with soil fungi, *N J Agr Expt. Sta. Bull* 270, 1914
11 Neller, J R, Studies on the correlation between the production of carbon dioxide and the accumulation of ammonia by soil organisms, *Soil Sci.*, 5.225–242, 1918.
12 Osborne, T B, *The Vegetable Proteins*, Longmans, Green & Co, London, 1924.
13 Rao, G. G, and Dhar, N R, Photosensitized oxidation of ammonia and ammonium salts and the problem of nitrification in soils, *Soil Sci*, 31.379–384, 1931, 38.143–159, 183–189, 1934
14 Taber, S, The production of saltpeter in the south during the Civil War, *Science*, 96 535–536, 1942
15 Temple, J C, Nitrification in acid or non-basic soils, *Georgia Agr Expt Sta Bull* 103, 1914
16 Thorne, C E, *Farm Manures*, Orange Judd Publishing Co, New York, 1914
17 Voorhees, E B, and Lipman, J G, A review of investigations in soil bacteriology, *U S Dept Agr Office Expt Sta Bull* 194, 1907
18 Waksman, S A, and Lomanitz, S, Contribution to the chemistry of decomposition of proteins and amino acids by various groups of microorganisms, *J Agr Research*, 30 263–281, 1924
19 Waksman, S A, and Starkey, R L, The decomposition of proteins by microorganisms with particular reference to purified vegetable proteins, *J Bact*, 23 405–428, 1932
20 Werkman, C H, and Wood, H G, On the metabolism of bacteria, *Botan Rev*, 8 1–68, 1942

·8·

Nitrogen Fixation—Nonsymbiotic

Nitrogen Fixation in Nature

The supply of fixed nitrogen in the soil is very limited, ranging normally from less than 0.1 to 0.2 per cent, and higher in exceptional cases. Rainfall brings down small quantities of nitrogen that have been fixed by electric discharges in the atmosphere. These are chiefly in the form of nitrogenous oxides. The chemical and physicochemical fixation of nitrogen, through the agency of sunlight, for example, may also be considered of very limited importance. The major part of the elementary nitrogen that finds its way into the soil and that is used for synthesis of plant and animal life is due entirely to its fixation by certain groups of microorganisms.

Two major groups of bacteria, usually designated as nonsymbiotic and symbiotic forms, are primarily concerned in this process. Aside from these, there is also a limited fixation of nitrogen by a variety of different bacteria and fungi, and especially by blue-green algae. The capacity of nonsymbiotic bacteria to fix atmospheric nitrogen and the amount of nitrogen fixed depend largely upon the nature and concentration of the available energy. Since soil humus cannot be used as a source of energy and since nitrogen fixation is inhibited by the presence of available forms of nitrogen in the soil, the significance of the nonsymbiotic organisms in normal soil is still a matter of speculation. On the other hand, the fixation of nitrogen through the symbiotic action of leguminous plants and bacteria that grow in the plant roots and produce nodules is of great economic importance in agriculture.

The root-nodule associations were the first to be recognized for their ability to fix atmospheric nitrogen. The ability of leguminous plants to improve the soil by increasing its supply of available nitrogen has been known for more than two thousand years. The role of the bacteria in the process was established more than six decades ago, but it is only within the last decade or two that the true biological nature of the process has been established. Numerous other claims concerning the ability of various organisms to fix atmospheric nitrogen have been questioned. An organism is considered unable to fix nitrogen if no increase in combined nitrogen can be demonstrated by chemical analysis Even then, if such an increase can be demonstrated, the importance of the reaction in the soil itself may still be open to question

Berthelot claimed in 1885 to have demonstrated that, when a soil is exposed to the air, its nitrogen content gradually increases and the fixation of nitrogen is biological in nature. This claim was not substantiated. It was not until six years later that the capacity for nitrogen fixation by nonsymbiotic organisms was established by Winogradsky. *Clostridium pasteurianum*, an anaerobic organism belonging to the group of butyric acid bacteria, was the first organism to be found capable of bringing about an increase in the amount of combined nitrogen in the medium An available source of energy was required for this purpose. A definite ratio was found to exist between the carbohydrate consumed and the amount of the nitrogen fixed

Following Winogradsky's work, Beijerinck demonstrated in 1901 that nonsymbiotic nitrogen fixation can be carried out by aerobic bacteria belonging to the genus *Azotobacter* Other organisms, designated as *Granulobacter*, were also found capable of fixing atmospheric nitrogen In addition to these, numerous other bacteria in the soil were found capable of fixing small amounts of nitrogen on artificial culture media especially when freshly isolated from the soil

It has been claimed that various other organisms, in addition to the bacteria, have been found capable of fixing varying amounts of atmospheric nitrogen These organisms ranged from different groups of algae and fungi to a variety of animal forms Most of these claims have remained unsubstantiated However, some of the blue algae and some of the purple (nonsulfur) bacteria have been found capable of fixing molecular nitrogen

Classification of Nitrogen-Fixing Organisms

The nitrogen-fixing bacteria require sources of energy that they are able to obtain from certain organic compounds of carbon, which are also used for cell synthesis These organisms can be classified on the basis of their ability to utilize the available sources of energy in a nonsymbiotic manner. Other organisms are able to obtain the carbon for their energy and for cell synthesis from the growing plant with which they live symbiotically. These organisms are not obligate, so far as the nitrogen is concerned, since they are also able to obtain their nitrogen from organic or inorganic compounds

I Nonsymbiotic nitrogen-fixing bacteria
   1 Anaerobic organisms
      a *Clostridium pasteurianum,* comprising the group of non-starch-fermenting type of clostridia.
      b *Bacillus saccharobutyricus,* comprising the starch-fermenting clostridia and occasional plectridia.
      c *Plectridium* group, including the starch-fermenting *Plectridium,* which differ from the plectridia of the previous group by forming long, slender, often curved rods, with thick oval spores as their extreme ends, and by being more proteolytic and less fermentative in nature
      d. Butyl-alcohol-forming group, morphologically related to the second group of starch-fermenting clostridia
   2 Aerobic organisms
      a *Azotobacter,* comprising five distinct species. *Az chroococcum, Az beijerinckii, Az vinelandii, Az agilis,* and *Az indicum.*
      b *Diplococcus pneumoniae, Aerobacter aerogenes,* and other non-spore-forming bacteria
      c *Bacillus asterosporus* and other spore-forming bacteria
II Symbiotic nitrogen-fixing bacteria.
   1 Bacteria living in the roots of leguminous plants
   2 Bacteria living on and in the roots of nonleguminous plants
   3. Bacteria living in the leaves of certain plants
III Nitrogen fixation by blue-green algae

Anaerobic Bacteria

The nitrogen-fixing capacity is well distributed among the anaerobic butyric acid bacteria but to a varying degree

The number of nitrogen-fixing clostridia in the soil has been found to be greater than 100,000 per gram. They are much more abundant than the members of the *Azotobacter* group. This led various investigators to conclude that the genus *Clostridium* rather than *Azotobacter* is the most important group of nonsymbiotic nitrogen-fixing bacteria. Duggeli reported 100–1,000,000 anaerobic bacteria and 0–100,000 aerobic nitrogen-fixing bacteria per gram of soil Plots receiving sodium nitrate as a source of nitrogen contained 10,600–12,000 cells of *Clostridium* and 4,900–6,300 *Azotobacter.* Plots receiving no nitrogen, but potassium and phosphorus fertilizers, contained 1,120,000 *Clostridium* and 98,700 *Azotobacter* cells per gram of soil.

It is essential to keep in mind that, out of a hundred living cells of *Cl pasteurianum* found in a culture, only very few are able to develop into colonies or give positive growth on artificial culture media For this reason, the abundance in the soil of anaerobic bacteria capable of fixing atmospheric nitrogen must be considered very extensive Further, *Cl. pasteurianum* is found in soils that are much too acid for the favorable development of *Azotobacter*, in the growth of which an acid reaction becomes a limiting factor This tends to add further weight to the claim of the potentially greater importance of the anaerobic than the aerobic bacteria as nonsymbiotic nitrogen-fixing organisms in the soil

When freshly isolated from the soil, the clostridia fix more nitrogen than after they have been cultivated for a long time in artificial media. Cultures kept in collections for a long time can be invigorated by growing them in liquid media to which enough ammonium sulfate is added to offer the organism less nitrogen than is needed for the complete decomposition of the sugar By transferring such cultures, when gas formation ceases, to fresh media, normal growth and nitrogen fixation are obtained.

Nitrogen fixation was shown by Bredemann to be a common property of the butyric acid bacilli. Some of these organisms are strict anaerobes, whereas others are less sensitive to oxygen. Although more tolerant of acidity than *Azotobacter*, they have a definite optimum at approximately neutral reaction. In pure cultures, 2–3 mg nitrogen is fixed per gram of sugar decomposed, although some strains may fix as much as 5 to more than 6 mg. The mechanism of fixation is explained as a direct reduction of elementary nitrogen to ammonia by nascent hydrogen. *Bacillus asterosporus* is a facultative anaerobe It was found capable of fixing small amounts of nitrogen, 1–3 mg per gram of sugar

Aerobic Bacteria

When a simple medium containing tap water, 0 02 per cent K_2HPO_4, and 2 per cent glucose is inoculated with soil and incubated, anaerobic and certain other bacteria are obtained When the glucose is replaced by mannitol or by propionate of potassium or sodium, aerobic bacteria predominate Beijerinck first isolated one of these organisms, which he described as *Azotobacter chroococcum.* It is found in soils and manures. On repeated transfer to fresh lots of sterile media, the organism was gradually purified from most of the contaminating forms and was finally isolated in pure culture on mannitol agar.

Although five species of *Azotobacter* are now known, Löhnis and Smith recognized only two species, *Az. chroococcum* and *Az. agilis*. They considered *Az. beijerinckii* Lipman and *Az. vitreum* Löhnis to be varieties of *Az. agilis*. Kluyver has shown, however, that *Az. agilis*

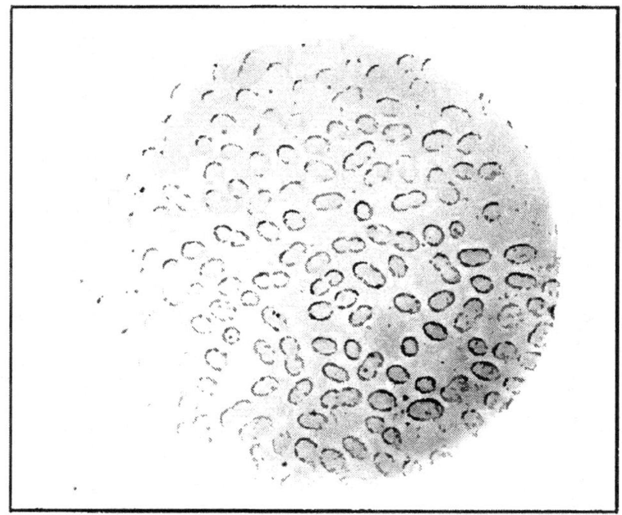

Fig. 81. *Azotobacter chroococcum*, young culture (from Beijerinck).

is quite distinct from *Az. vinelandii* and is found only in canal waters, whereas the latter is characteristic of soil. Winogradsky proposed the name *Azomonas* for the noncystogenic organisms found in waters. *Azotobacter indicum* is certainly a distinct form.

Azotobacter represents a highly interesting group of strictly aerobic organisms. Its temperature range lies between 10°C and 40°C, with an optimum at 30–35°C. It is highly sensitive to acidity, with an optimum at *p*H 7–8. A large number of organic compounds can be used as sources of energy and carbon. They include fatty acids and oxyacids, higher and lower alcohols, and mono-, di-, and polysaccharides.

The fixation of nitrogen by *Azotobacter* is brought about by a system of enzymes designated as "azotase." Nitrogenase, one of the components of this system, is capable of combining directly with elementary nitrogen. This enzyme complex has not been isolated, although there is found in the literature a statement by Bach that such enzyme complexes can be obtained. Apparently the production and activity of this enzyme are inseparably linked with the synthesis of cell substance. Burk designated the enzyme as "growthbound," for which the name "phyo-enzyme" was suggested. The enzyme nitrogenase requires a certain concentration of calcium (or strontium) for its activity. It is incapable of exerting any effect at reac-

FIG. 82. *Azotobacter agilis,* showing flagella stain (from Beijerinck).

tions below pH 6. It is strongly activated by minute concentrations of molybdenum and to a lesser degree by vanadium.

The primary product of nitrogen fixation is not fully known, as shown later. Winogradsky reported it to be ammonia. Virtanen and others have said that an oxime compound seems involved. Most of the fixed nitrogen is present in the cultures as cell material. Small quantities of combined nitrogen may be secreted into the medium as long as growth takes place. When the medium is exhausted of nutrients and growth has ceased, a rapid production of ammonia from the cell material sets in, because of the lytic processes that take place.

Azotobacter can also assimilate various combined forms of nitrogen, such as nitrate, ammonia, and simple amino compounds. The presence of these compounds in the medium represses the fixation of free nitrogen. This appears to be due not so much to preferential assimilation, as to the inactivation of the nitrogenase. Burk and

Lineweaver observed this effect in concentrations of 0.5 mg NO_3-N or NH_4-N per 100 ml of medium.

Azotobacter transforms the carbon compounds into carbon dioxide, water, and cell substance. The amount of nitrogen fixed is about 10

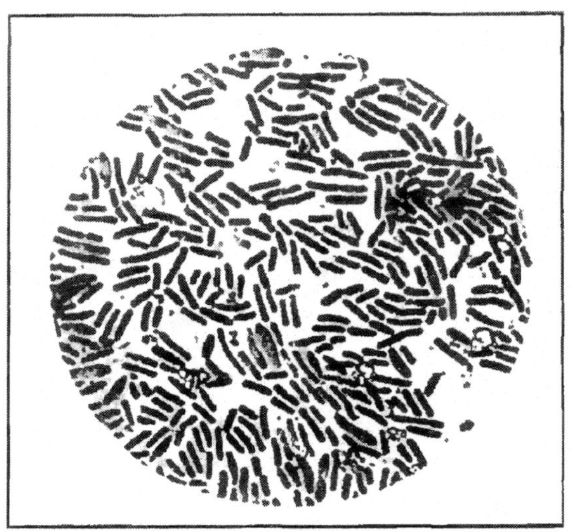

Fig. 83. *Clostridium pasteurianum* (from Winogradsky).

mg per gram of sugar consumed. Other carbon compounds are utilized in proportion to their availability, as shown in Table 41. The

Table 41. Nitrogen Fixed by *Azotobacter chroococcum* with Different Sources of Energy

Milligrams of nitrogen fixed per 100 gm of carbon available.

Pine needles	57.3	Plant roots and stubble	596.8
Oak leaves	126.9	Lupines	711.5
Maple leaves	89.5	Alfalfa	319.5
Wheat straw	325.4	Clover	1237.9
Corn stover	280.3	Glucose	1456.5

efficiency of nitrogen fixation also depends upon the type of organism, experimental conditions, and presence of contaminants, as shown in Tables 42 and 43.

Azotobacter is widely distributed in the soil, although only a relatively limited number of cells are found in any one soil. The reaction of the soil, the abundance of organic matter, the concentration of certain mineral elements, notably phosphate, and the absence of

TABLE 42 NITROGEN FIXATION BY STRAINS OF *Azotobacter* WITH AND WITHOUT A CONTAMINANT (from Lind and Wilson)

Hours	Strain No *	Nitrogen Fixed † Pure Culture of *Azotobacter*	Plus Contaminant
Azotobacter and *Bacillus* from Mixed Culture			
21	1	6.9	11.1
	2	9.5	16.2
	3	8.2	16.2
12	1	7.0	19.8
	2	6.7	27.2
	3	8.3	26.4
12	1	5.0	20.1
	2	8.9	22.3
	3	7.3	21.7
41	1	16.5	31.4
	2	20.0	32.5
	3	18.9	32.5
12	2	10.8	18.8
	3	10.4	26.7
Azotobacter and *Clostridium pasteurianum*			
12	2	6.7	19.5
12	3	8.9	21.0

* Strain 1 was *Azotobacter* stock culture, strains 2 and 3 were pure isolates of *Azotobacter* from mixed culture

† Values in milligrams N per 100 ml, this includes nitrogen in inoculum, which was 1 ml in 15 ml.

antagonistic or competing agents are among the factors that control the presence and abundance of this organism in the soil

Out of 105 soil samples examined, Burri found *Azotobacter* missing in 34, chiefly heavy clay soils. Jones and Murdoch isolated *Azotobacter* from 9 out of 17 soil types examined, and from 22 out of 29 soil samples representing 9 types The maximum number of *Azotobacter* cells found per gram of soil was 18. Rossi reported an average of 1,815 cells per gram of Italian soil, the number ranging from 0 to 21,400 Swaby found *Azotobacter* in 26 per cent of all soil samples examined, usually 30 cells per gram of soil *Clostridium butylicum* was found, however, in most of the soils, usually 100 spores per gram

TABLE 43 EFFECT OF SOURCE OF IRON ON NITROGEN FIXATION BY PURE AND MIXED CULTURES OF *Azotobacter* (from Lind and Wilson)

Source of Iron	Hours	Nitrogen Fixed * Pure Culture	Nitrogen Fixed * Plus Contaminant
New humate	8	1.9	1.6
	17	10.3	9.8
	23	18.4	23.8
Old humate	16	5.9	14.0
New humate	16	13.4	16.4
Old humate	18	6.5	13.4
Old humate	23	10.5	25.8
		9.8	25.3
Old humate + Fe		26.6	27.8
		27.2	26.7

* Values in milligrams N per 100 ml, this includes nitrogen in inoculum, which was 1 ml in 15 ml

Azotobacter usually cannot develop in a soil having a *p*H of less than 6.0. As soon as the reaction of the soil is adjusted by means of lime, so that the *p*H becomes higher than this minimum, a typical *Azotobacter* flora will develop. The carbonate-phosphate ratio in soil was found to influence markedly the development of this organism in soils of different reaction. In Malayan soils, however, certain strains of *Azotobacter* have been found capable of growing at a wide *p*H range, 3.6 being the limit on the acid side. Starkey and De isolated an organism (*Az. indicum*) capable of growing at reactions lower than *p*H 6.0.

Abundance of *Azotobacter* in the soil was found to be influenced by cropping and by fertilizer treatment, the numbers being higher in unfertilized than in fertilized soils.

Azotobacter may live symbiotically with algae, especially with *Nostoc* and *Anabaena*, as well as with other bacteria. The quantities of nitrogen fixed by this association are frequently considerable, as pointed out in Tables 42 and 43. The symbiotic action between *Cl. pasteurianum* and *Azotobacter*, whereby the latter uses up the oxygen, making conditions favorable for the former, has also been demonstrated. The various acids produced by *Clostridium* are neutralized by the soil bases and can be utilized by *Azotobacter* as sources of energy; this symbiotic action leads to a maximum economy in the utilization of energy. In the presence of *Rhizobium leguminosarum*, *Azotobacter* was found to fix more nitrogen than alone. Symbiosis between pure cultures of cellulose-decomposing and nitrogen-fixing bacteria has also been reported.

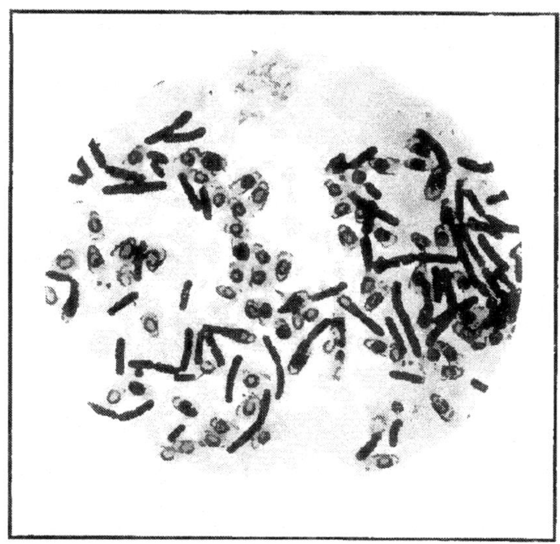

Fig. 84. *Clostridium pasteurianum*, showing spore formation (from Winogradsky).

Blue-Green Algae

The ability of blue-green algae to fix atmospheric nitrogen is now definitely established. Drewes first observed this phenomenon in 1928 for species of *Anabaena* and *Nostoc*. His discovery was confirmed by Allison and Morris in 1930. Certain strains of Myxophyceae, isolated from nitrogen-deficient warm springs, were also found to be capable of utilizing atmospheric nitrogen. A species of *Nostoc punctiforme* was isolated from different host plants and found capable of fixing up to 1.95 mg of nitrogen per 50 ml of culture solution, in presence of a suitable sugar source. A culture of *Nostoc muscorum* isolated from the soil was found capable of obtaining both its carbon and its nitrogen from the air; it fixed as much as 10 mg of nitrogen in 45 days and 18 mg in 85 days per 100 ml of medium from carbohydrate; in the dark, it fixed 10–12 mg of nitrogen per 1 gm of glucose consumed.

Mechanism of Nitrogen Fixation

The amount of nitrogen fixed by various bacteria depends upon the nature of the energy source, the presence of available nitrogen and minerals, the soil reaction and other environmental conditions, and the presence of various specific bacteria. Some species utilize one source of energy more readily than another. Lipman recorded

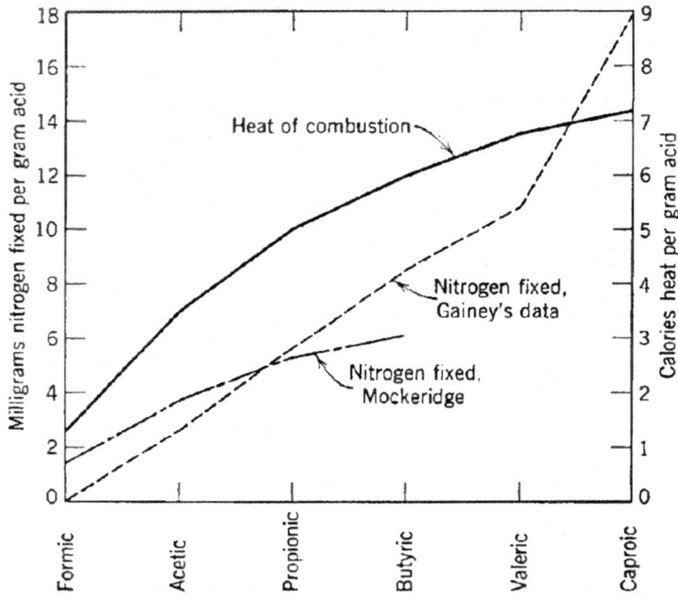

FIG. 85. Comparison between nitrogen fixation and heat of combustion per gram of organic acid, used as a source of energy (from Gainey).

an increase in the amount of nitrogen fixed with an increase in molecular weight of fatty acids, in the form of sodium salts, including acetic, propionic, and butyric; the next number of the homologous series (valerianic acid) presented a poor source of carbon; the sodium salts of succinic and citric acids were not utilized at all.

With glucose as a source of energy, *Az. chroococcum* was reported to liberate 70 per cent of the carbon as CO_2; 12 per cent was assimilated in the bacterial cells, and 18 per cent was left among the various decomposition products other than CO_2. These were made up of ethyl alcohol, aldehyde, and formic, acetic, lactic, tartaric, and other acids. The bacterial cells contained 30 per cent protein, a considerable amount of fat, and phosphatides.

Kostytschev and Winogradsky demonstrated that ammonia is produced in cultures of *Azotobacter*. They concluded that this ammonia is the first stage in the fixation of nitrogen by bacteria Burk found that ammonia was present in the older cultures and concluded, therefore, that it is rather a secondary decomposition product The inability to find ammonia in young cultures of the organism speaks against its being the first step in the fixation process.

Blom suggested the following reactions as explanations of the mechanism of the fixation of nitrogen, through the hydroxylamine stage This was produced by cultures of *Az agilis*, iron serving as a catalyst.

1 $N{=}N$ (atmospheric) $\rightleftharpoons$ $N{=}N$ (solution)

2 $2(\text{Cat } Fe^{++}) + N{\equiv}N \rightleftharpoons (\text{Cat } Fe^{++})_2\ N{\equiv}N.$

3 $(\text{Cat } Fe^{++})_2\ N{\equiv}N + 2H_2O \rightleftharpoons$
$(\text{Cat } Fe^{++})_2\ HONH{-}HNOH$

4 $(\text{Cat. } Fe^{++})_2\ HONH{-}HNOH + 2H^+ \rightleftharpoons$
$2(\text{Cat } Fe^{+++}) + 2HONH_2.$

5 $(\text{Cat } Fe^{+++}) + H \rightleftharpoons (\text{Cat } Fe^{++}) + H^+$

The hydroxylamine, once produced will interact with oxalacetic acid to give rise to oximes, which are changed to aspartic acid, as shown later

According to Winogradsky, both anaerobic and aerobic bacteria produce ammonia out of the nitrogen gas and nascent hydrogen with which they come in contact. In the case of the anaerobes, the hydrogen is formed during the butyric acid fermentation In the case of *Azotobacter*, an enzyme, azohydrase, concerned in the ammonia synthesis is believed to be produced A part of the ammonia is immobilized by the growing cells, and a part is excreted into the medium The molecular nitrogen acts as a hydrogen acceptor the action of the enzyme continuing even after the death of the cells

Wieland also considered that the action of the hydrogen acceptors formed in the cells of nitrogen-fixing bacteria does not depend upon oxygen for hydration, but rather upon the molecular nitrogen with which the hydrogen forms ammonia, perhaps through the hydrazine stage in a manner similar to the Haber synthesis

Virtanen found aspartic acid in young cultures of *Azotobacter* before ammonia could be detected, this led him to conclude that amino acid is the first product of nitrogen fixation. This is brought out in the following series of reactions:

$$N_2 \rightarrow ? \rightarrow \underset{\text{Hydroxylamine}}{NH_2OH}$$

$$+ \qquad \rightarrow$$

$$C_6H_{12}O_6 \rightarrow \underset{\text{Oxalacetic acid}}{HOOC \cdot CO \cdot CH_2 \cdot COOH}$$

$$\underset{\text{Oxime}}{HOOC \cdot C(NOH) \cdot CH_2 \cdot COOH} \rightarrow \underset{\text{Aspartic acid}}{HOOC \cdot CH(NH_2)CH_2 \cdot COOH}$$

$$\underset{\text{Aspartic acid}}{HOOC \cdot CH(NH_2)CH_2 \cdot COOH} + \underset{\text{Pyruvic acid}}{H_3C \cdot CO \cdot COOH} \rightarrow$$

$$\underset{\text{Oxalacetic acid}}{HOOC \cdot CO \cdot CH_2 \cdot COOH} + \underset{\text{Alanine}}{CH_3 \cdot CH(NH_2) \cdot COOH}$$

The first step in the reaction has also been presented by Virtanen as follows:

$$N_2 \xrightarrow{2H_2O} \underset{OH}{HN}—\underset{OH}{NH} \xrightarrow{H} \underset{OH}{NH_2} \quad \text{or} \quad N_2 \xrightarrow{2H} HN{=}NH \xrightarrow{H_2O} NH_2OH$$

According to Wilson and his associates, the biochemical nitrogen fixation by *Azotobacter* has much in common with that of the legumes. The following points were recognized.

1. Hydrogen and carbon monoxide are specific inhibitors for both types of fixation.

2. Aspartic acid, possibly with an oxime as a precursor, occupies a key position.

3. Molybdenum acts as a specific catalyst in *Azotobacter* and appears to have a similar effect in legumes.

4. *Azotobacter* produces a hydrogenase which seems to be connected with the nitrogen fixation; this enzyme is not found in nodules or in cultures of the nodule bacteria *in vitro*.

5. Nitrogen fixation by *Azotobacter* has, except in one species, an optimum at *p*H 7.0–7.5, and ceases at *p*H 6.0, which seems to represent the normal reaction of the nodule tissue and therefore presumably also the optimum for the symbiotic process of fixation.

6. *Azotobacter* fixes nitrogen only during active cell multiplication, and uses virtually all the fixed nitrogen for cell synthesis. This does not seem to apply to the legumes, where the fixation appears more like a kind of respiration process which results in a steady transfer of some 80–90 per cent of the fixed nitrogen from the nodules to the

rest of the host plant. Therefore, symbiotic nitrogen fixation requires a much smaller expenditure of energy. *Azotobacter* consumes at its optimal rate of growth at least 40–50 units of carbohydrate, and usually twice as much, per unit of nitrogen fixed, whereas Bond calculated that the corresponding figure for the root-nodule bacteria in

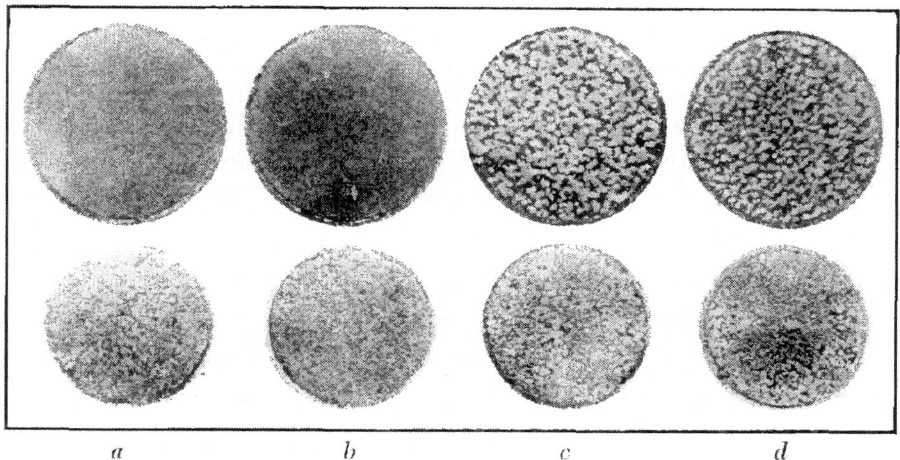

Fig. 86. Growth of *Azotobacter* in soils treated with starch to test for deficiencies in available nutrient elements. *Upper row*, soil deficient in phosphate; *lower row*, soil not deficient in either potash or phosphate. *Left to right, a*, check, nothing added; *b*, potash added; *c*, phosphate added; *d*, phosphate and potash added (from Sackett).

soybeans is only about 15 units, and that the total respiration of the nodules consumes some 16 per cent of all the carbohydrate produced in photosynthesis (Jensen).

Effect of Humus on Nitrogen Fixation

The beneficial action of humus on nitrogen fixation is frequently ascribed to its inorganic constituents, particularly to its content of aluminum and silicic acid. This assumption is confirmed by the following two facts: (*a*) artificial humus has no such effect; (*b*) the source of the natural humus influences markedly the degree of its beneficial action. The claim that the action of the humus is due to its inorganic constituents has been further substantiated by the fact that purified humates do not possess any stimulating effect. The role of the colloid is probably due chiefly to its catalytic action and its protective action against poisons; the protective action of the colloid has also been ascribed to the distribution of the phosphorus and to the buffering effect upon the reaction of the medium.

Burk concluded that the favorable effect of humus upon the nitrogen-fixation process is due entirely to its iron content. According to Birch-Hirschfeld soil extract contains several components that have a favorable effect upon growth and nitrogen fixation by *Azotobacter*. These components are of both an organic and an inorganic nature, the growth stimulation being due to the organic complex. Molybdenum cannot take the place of soil extract, although both favor about alike the amount of nitrogen fixed per unit of sugar consumed.

Burema and Wieringa demonstrated that the role of molybdenum in the fixation of nitrogen is that of a reducing agent. Less molybdenum is required for the reduction of nitrate than for the reduction of free nitrogen. Jensen reported that *Az. indicum* requires molybdenum for nitrogen fixation, molybdenum could not be replaced by vanadium.

The nitrogen fixed through nonsymbiotic processes can at best restore only a part of the losses of nitrogen from soil by crop removal and by leaching. The common estimates are 20–50 pounds fixed per acre annually, but the actual amounts may be much smaller.

The frequently expressed opinion that soils from arid climates have an extraordinary nitrogen-fixing power and may be employed, by the use of crop residues by nonsymbiotic nitrogen-fixing organisms, for cereal cultivation without depletion of nitrogen, has been denied by Jensen. In Australian wheat soils no gain at all is usually expected, and only under exceptionally favorable circumstances was a fixation obtained corresponding to one-third of the nitrogen requirements of the crops on wheat land worked on the usual wheat-fallow rotation. The activity of nonsymbiotic nitrogen fixation in nature appears to be largely confined to uncultivated soils where no crops are carried away and the vegetable debris is allowed to decompose.

Jensen further concluded that the practice of growing wheat alternating with fallow and without use of nitrogenous fertilizers is to be regarded as a gradual consumption of the nitrogen reserves of the soil, from which some nitrate is produced during fallowing. The nonsymbiotic nitrogen fixation and the effect of the rain will compensate for this loss only incompletely. If continued, it must in time lead to permanent loss of fertility. The growth of leguminous crops in the rotations and the judicious application of nitrogenous fertilizers are the logical correctives.

Further information on the inability of nonsymbiotic nitrogen-fixing bacteria to supply available nitrogen when natural plant residues high in cellulose are added to the soil is found in Tables 44 and 45.

TABLE 44 INFLUENCE OF SUGAR UPON CROP YIELD AND NITROGEN CONTENT OF CROP (from A. Koch)

	Control	Glucose *	Sucrose	Sucrose
Grams of dry substance per pot, for 18-year period				
Crop yield	120 5	180 7	192 2	542.6
Excess over control		60 2	72 7	122 1
Milligrams of Nitrogen in Crop				
Nitrogen	2 363	2,916	3,000	3,640
Excess over control		553	637	1,283

* 360 gm of sugars added, over the 18-year period, to the treated pots

TABLE 45 INFLUENCE OF CELLULOSE UPON CROP YIELD (from A Koch)

Grams of dry substance per pot, for 3-year periods

Years	Control	Paper, 120 gm	Paper, 120 gm + Manure Infusion	Manure Infusion Alone
1911–13	68 3	12 8	17 9	67 0
1914 16	60 0	81 7	87 3	62 8
1917–19	66 0	77 4	82 8	69 9
1920–21	65 2	71 1	72 8	67 0
Total crop	259 5	243 0	260 8	266 7

With glucose and sucrose as sources of energy, considerable nitrogen was fixed With cellulose, on the other hand, there was no increase in the nitrogen supply even after 11 years' treatment Unfortunately, plant residues that usually find their way into the soil are poor in sugar and rich in cellulose

Selected Bibliography

1 Allison, F. E, Hoover, S R, and Morris, H J, Physiological studies with the nitrogen-fixing alga *Nostoc muscorum*, *Botan Gaz*, 98 433–463, 1937
2 Bond, G, Quantitative observations on the fixation and transfer of nitrogen

in the soybean with special reference to the mechanism of transfer of fixed nitrogen from bacillus to host, *Ann Botany*, 50 559–578, 1936, Symbiosis of leguminous plants and nodule bacteria I Observations on respiration and on the extent of utilization of host carbohydrates by the nodule bacteria *Ann Botany*, N S, 5 313–337, 1941

3 Burk, D, and Horner, C K, The origin and significance of ammonia formed by *Azotobacter*, *Soil Sci* 41 81–132, 1936

4. Burk, D, and Burris, R H, Biochemical nitrogen-fixation, *Ann. Rev Biochem*, 10 587–618, 1941

5 Jensen, H L, Contributions to the nitrogen economy of Australian wheat soils, with particular reference to New South Wales, *Proc Linnean Soc N S Wales*, 15 1–122, 1940.

6 Jensen, H L, Symbiotic nitrogen-fixation, *Austral J Sci*, 6 162–165, 1944

7 Jones, D H and Murdoch, F G, Quantitative and qualitative bacterial analysis of soil samples taken in fall of 1918, *Soil Sci*, 8 259–267, 1919

8 Kluyver, A J., and van Reenen, W J, Über *Azotobacter agilis* Beijerinck, *Arch Mikrob*, 4 280–300, 1933

9 Lind, C J, and Wilson, P W, Nitrogen-fixation by *Azotobacter* in association with other bacteria, *Soil Sci*, 54 105–111, 1942

10 Starkey, R L, and De, P K, A new species of *Azotobacter*, *Soil Sci*, 47. 329–343, 1939

11 Stumbo, C R, and Gainey, P L, An apparent induced loss of nitrogen-fixing ability in *Azotobacter J Agr Research*, 57 217–227, 1938

12 Van Niel, C B, A note on the apparent absence of *Azotobacter* in soils, *Arch Mikrob*, 6 215–218, 1935

13 Virtanen, A I, *Cattle Fodder and Human Nutrition, with Special Reference to Biological Nitrogen Fixation*, Cambridge University Press, 1938

14 Virtanen, A I, Biological nitrogen-fixation, *Ann Rev Microb*, 2 485–506, 1948

15 Wilson, P W, *The Biochemistry of Symbiotic Nitrogen Fixation*, University of Wisconsin Press, Madison, Wis, 1940

16 Wilson, P W, and Lind, C J, Carbon monoxide inhibition of *Azotobacter* in microrespiration experiments, *J Bact*, 45 219–232, 1943

·9·

Nitrogen Fixation—Symbiotic

Early Observations

Many centuries before the discovery was made that bacteria exist in the root nodules of leguminous plants and that these bacteria live in symbiosis with the plants, thus enriching the soil with combined nitrogen, the practical agriculturist came to consider the growth of legumes on his land as equivalent to manuring or fertilizing the soil for the succeeding crop The use of leguminous plants for green manuring was described in great detail by Greek and Roman writers, notably Virgil, Varro, and Columella. Directions were given for preparing the soil and for sowing, cultivating, and harvesting the crop Lupines, vetches, and alfalfa were frequently mentioned in these books as specific crops to be turned over when the plants were young

With the beginning of the nineteenth century, when the basis was laid for modern agricultural science, more accurate information gradually began to accumulate. Sir Humphry Davy, in his book *Agricultural Chemistry,* published in 1813, observed· "Peas and beans in all instances seem well adapted to prepare the ground for wheat . . . they contain a small quantity of a matter analogous to albumen, but it seems that the azote which forms a constituent part of this matter is derived from the atmosphere"

These observations were fully borne out in the classical studies of Boussingault, published in 1837–1838 This French agronomist and chemist was the first to develop systematically the idea of nitrogen nutrition of leguminous and cereal plants. A typical field experiment on crop rotation is shown in Table 46. Boussingault established the fact that, when clover is grown in unmanured soils, there is a considerable gain of nitrogen; wheat, on the other hand, showed no gain or loss of nitrogen He suggested that leguminous plants assimilate nitrogen from the atmosphere, whereas cereal plants cannot do so

TABLE 46 CROP-ROTATION EXPERIMENT OF BOUSSINGAULT

Rotation						Nitrogen		Gain	
1	2	3	4	5	6	In Crop *pounds per acre*	In Manures Used *pounds per acre*	Total *pounds per acre*	Per Year *pounds per acre*
Potatoes	Wheat	Clover	Wheat	Turnips		229	185	44	9
Mangel beets	Wheat	Clover	Wheat	Oats		231	185	46	9
Potatoes	Wheat	Clover	Wheat	Peas	Rye	323	223	100	17
Fallow	Wheat	Wheat				80	76	4	1
Alfalfa	Alfalfa	Alfalfa	Alfalfa	Alfalfa	Alfalfa	980	205	775	130

Boussingault made an effort to repeat these experiments under more carefully controlled conditions. He ignited the sand, thereby killing the bacteria, and found that neither cereals nor legumes were capable of assimilating nitrogen from the atmosphere.

The German chemist Liebig (1843) could not accept the idea that atmospheric nitrogen can be assimilated by plants. The beneficial effects of leguminous plants were explained by the fact that the plants form a large leaf surface and thus expose a greater area for absorption of ammonia from the atmosphere. The results of Boussingault's rotation experiments, which occupied sixteen years, were considered to be due to errors in the analysis of the manure. Since the farm manure was dried in a vacuum at 110°C before being analyzed for nitrogen, at least half the ammonia nitrogen could have been volatilized. Liebig suggested that, had such errors been taken into account, the results would lose much of their significance.

To prove or disprove Liebig's ideas, Lawes, Gilbert, and Pugh, of the Rothamsted Experimental Station, began in 1857 a series of crucial experiments. They were so careful in handling the soil that they destroyed the organism fixing the nitrogen symbiotically with leguminous plants. They thus failed to become the discoverers of the symbiotic fixation process. In absence of bacteria, the legume behaved like cereals. This phenomenon was later confirmed by a number of other investigators who showed that legumes do not fix nitrogen when the soil has been ignited but do fix nitrogen in unignited soil. Schulz-Lupitz grew lupines for fifteen consecutive times, without application of nitrogen fertilizer and without diminishing yields. Much higher yields were obtained when cereals followed lupines than when the cereals were grown on the same soil not preceded by a leguminous crop; the nitrogen content of the soil was thereby found to increase.

Role of Bacteria in Fixation Process

The presence of nodules on the roots of leguminous plants was known long before their significance was recognized. At first they

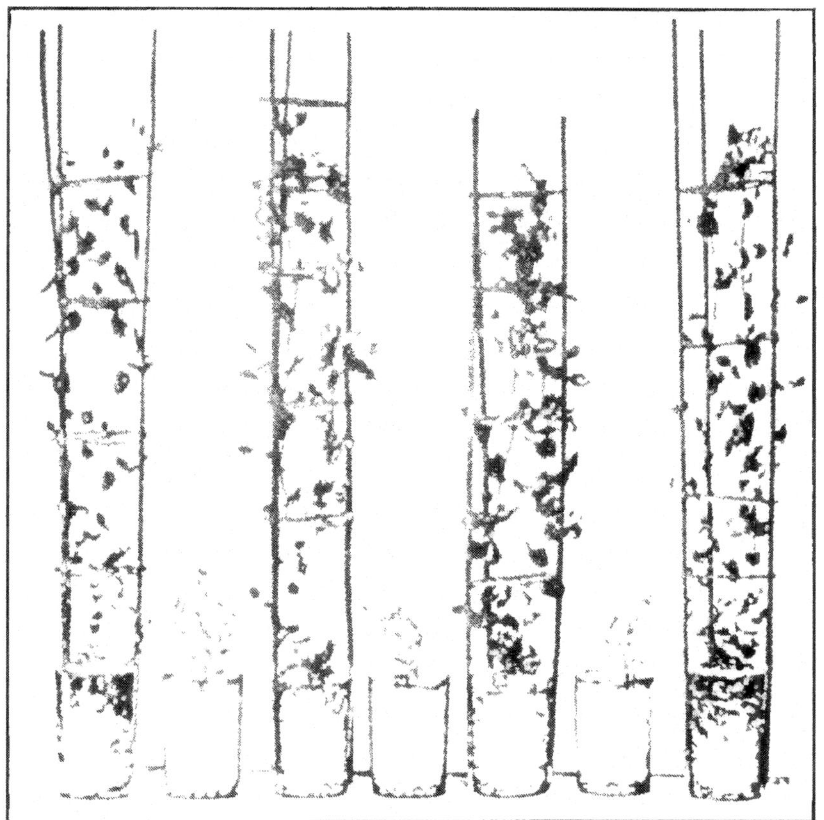

Fig. 87. Influence of the legume organisms on growth of peas. All are growing in sterilized sand, but in the four pots placed alternately, which show good growth, extract of garden soil has been added (from Hellriegel and Wilfarth, after Russell).

were looked upon as root galls. Although Lachmann observed in 1858 that motile bacteria cause the formation of the nodules and that these are responsible for nitrogen fixation, Woronin, who also found in 1866 that the nodules consist of bacteria, considered the nodules pathological outgrowths. In 1879, Frank demonstrated that the formation of nodules can be prevented by sterilization of soil; he suggested that the nodules are caused by outside infection.

Atwater and Woods, working in Connecticut, recognized in 1884 the possibility that both plants and bacteria are factors in the process of fixation of atmospheric nitrogen. Soon afterward, Hellriegel and Wilfarth in Germany demonstrated that the nodules on the roots of leguminous plants are due to bacterial infection, and that this is a

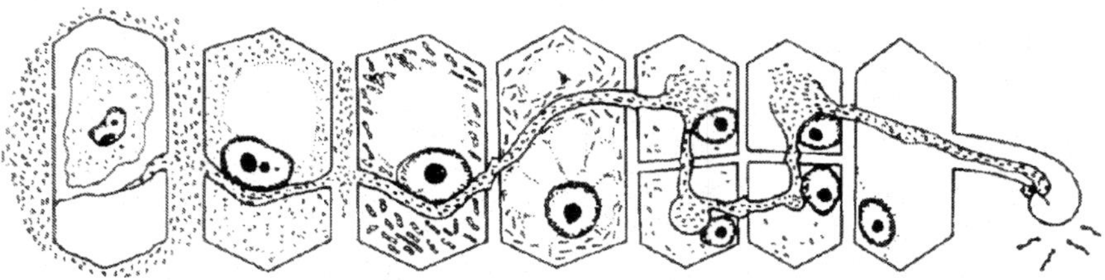

FIG. 88. Life history of root-nodule bacteria in the tissue of the alfalfa nodule (from Thornton).

beneficial process, since within these nodules the bacteria fix the atmospheric nitrogen. Plants could be grown on artificial soils containing only traces of combined nitrogen, provided the mineral elements necessary for the nutrition of the plant were present and nodules were formed. In absence of nodules, the plants were unable to utilize the atmospheric nitrogen for their growth. When sterilized soil was treated with a suspension of fresh soil, nodules were formed and the plants grew normally. The growth of the cereals depended, however, on the nitrate content of the soil. These results were soon confirmed by Lawes and Gilbert and others.

The causative organism responsible for nitrogen fixation in pure culture was isolated in 1888 by Beijerinck, who named it *Bacillus radicicola*. He described three stages in the development of the organism:

1. The bacterium is present in the soil in the form of small rods which can penetrate the root hairs of the leguminous plants and from there are transferred to the "infectious tissue."

2. The organism later changes into a motile form.

3. Within the plant tissues, the cells are transformed into bacteroids, which function as the symbiotic mechanism.

The mechanism of root infection by the legume organism was studied in detail by Prazmowski in 1889. The amounts of nitrogen obtained by the association of the plant and the bacterium were worked out by Schloesing and Laurent. Leguminous plants were grown in sterile glass cylinders containing sterile sand and watered with sterile water. The composition of the gas in the cylinder was determined. It was found that the uninoculated plants showed a gain of only 0.6 mg of nitrogen and no nodule formation; the inoculated plants, however, showed a gain of 34.1 and 40.6 mg of nitrogen and abundant nodule formation. These results were confirmed by numerous investigators. It is sufficient to cite those obtained by Virtanen (Table 47).

TABLE 47 GROWTH OF RED CLOVER IN QUARTZ SAND (from Virtanen)

*p*H 6.5, 10 plants in each pot, age of plants, 106 days.

N Nutrition	Inoculation	Dry Weight of Plants
		gm
KNO_3	Not inoculated	23.78
KNO_3	Not inoculated	24.07
$(NH_4)_2SO_4$	Not inoculated	22.32
$(NH_4)_2SO_4$	Not inoculated	18.00
N-free medium	Inoculated	31.38
N-free medium	Inoculated	30.27

Different plants vary greatly in the amount of nitrogen fixed, as shown by Wilson (Table 48).

TABLE 48 DAILY UPTAKE OF NITROGEN BY VARIOUS LEGUMINOUS PLANTS (from Wilson)

Plant	Milligrams of N per Plant			Milligrams of N per Gram of Dry Weight of Nodule
	Minimum	Maximum	Average	
Horsebean	14.0	27.7	17.1	38
Pea	5.6	10.3	8.7	98
Bean	6.9	9.8	7.8	67
Lupine	3.4	8.4	5.8	65
Vetch	3.0	3.4	3.2	80
Alfalfa	1.0	1.5	1.2	67
Red clover	0.9	1.0	1.0	55

Strain of Organisms and Nodule Formation

Numerous studies were made of strain variations of bacteria as influencing the fixation of nitrogen It is sufficient to cite the results of Fred, Baldwin, and McCoy

1. Different isolations of organisms from a nodule or from the soil may vary widely in their ability to benefit the host plant through the fixation of nitrogen even though nodules are readily formed. A strain that fixes little nitrogen in association with the host is called "poor," and one that is beneficial is considered a "good" strain.

2 The nodules formed by poor strains are usually small, round, and white and are scattered over the entire root system. Nodules from a good strain are fewer in number but much larger, they are pink in color and elongated, and are located near the main roots. This is true of certain legumes but not necessarily of others

3 The plant species determines largely whether a given strain is poor or good Cultivation on certain media often causes a good strain to lose its effectiveness Successive passage through a host plant modifies the effectiveness of a strain A poor strain may improve, and a good one may deteriorate

4 Many of the strains found in the natural habitat, either in the soil or in the nodules of wild legumes, are of the poor type

5 Although a given host may possess nodules of both effective and ineffective types, plants already infected with one strain of the organism resist infection of a contrasting strain to a greater degree than do nodule-free plants

The plants exert a chemotactic effect upon the bacteria, which congregate around the plant roots, the bacteria, in their turn, secrete a substance of the nature of an auxin, which causes the curling of the root hairs of the plant. During the early stages of growth of the plant the bacteria act as parasites and enter the host through the root hairs or through ordinary epidermal cells When nitrates are present, formation of nodules is repressed The plant may also form a substance which inhibits the growth of the bacteria and causes their destruction, which may explain the inefficiency of certain bacterial strains On entering the root, the bacteria multiply, forming a thread of infection, which branches out into the parenchymatous cells of the root The bacteria elaborate certain stimulating substances which cause the cells to enlarge On reaching the inner cells of the roots, the bacteria favor the multiplication of the surrounding cells. This leads to the formation of a young nodule, which produces a swelling on the side of the root by pushing out the overlying cortical parenchyma and epidermis

In some plants, bacterial infection results in a rapid division of the infested cells, which give rise to bacteroidal tissue In these plants the nodules usually arise in the cambium layers

A third type of infection is known, in which the intercellular zoogloea plays the important part The bacteria which enter the root change into rods and multiply rapidly in the slime filament or in the zoogloeal mass. Many of these rods change into bacteroids

Wilson reported three types of plant response with respect to nitrogen fixation

1. The association of certain strains of bacteria with all the species of host plant tested

2 The association of certain strains of bacteria with only one species of host, not with another

3 The association of certain strains of bacteria with certain species of plants, producing erratic responses due to the carbohydrate-nitrogen relationship in the plant.

Morphology and Life Cycle of Nodule Bacteria

The bacteria responsible for the formation of root nodules vary greatly in size and shape Beijerinck described the small, oval forms as "swarmers" In the young nodules, there are present normal rods together with large club-shaped or branching forms (bacteroids). In old decomposing nodules, the branching forms are vacuolated, showing small, oval, deep-staining bodies within, which are the motile swarmers or the branching form dividing into bacilli

The organism produces short Gram-negative rods, motile by means of flagella when young The bacteroids may also be formed on artificial media, when such substances as acid phosphate, sodium succinate and glycerol, caffeine and cumarine are present Caffeine and other vegetable alkaloids, like guanidine, pyridine, and chinoline, will stimulate the formation of involution forms in pure culture It was suggested, therefore, that the formation of the bacteroids in root nodules is due to the presence of alkaloids in the plant The bacteroids are produced in the medium or in the nodule as a result of specific nutrition or of unfavorable conditions According to Zipfel, the branching forms are not degeneration forms, but may be looked upon as normal and necessary stages in the life cycle of the organism with specific biological functions. Some investigators question, however, the reproducibility of the bacteroids.

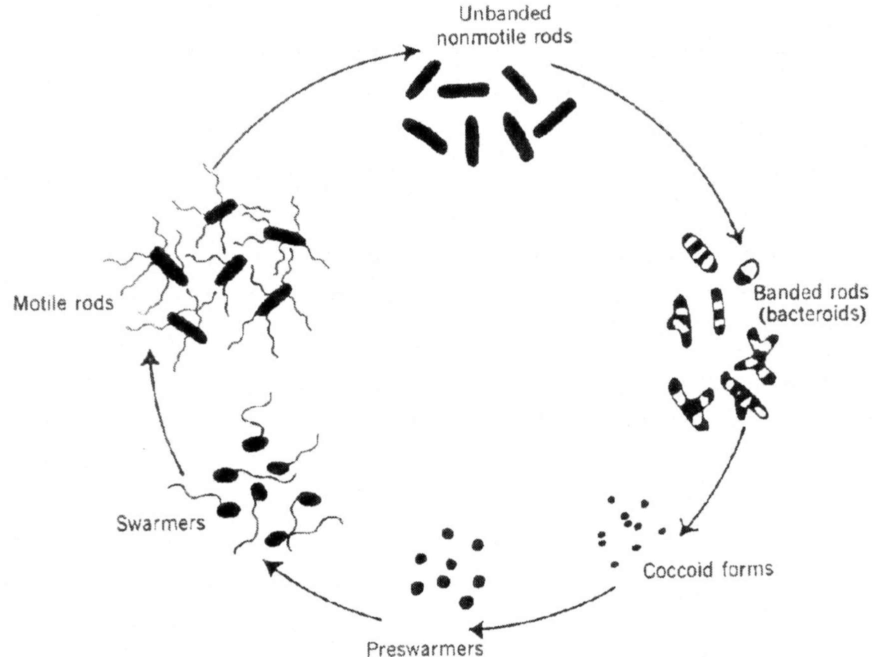

FIG. 89. The life cycle of *Bacillus radicicola* (from Thornton and Gangulee).

Five stages in the life cycle of the root-nodule organism are now recognized:

1. Nonmotile, preswarmer stage, observed in cultures kept in a neutral soil solution.
2. Larger, nonmotile coccus, obtained in the presence of certain carbohydrates and phosphates.
3. Motile, swarmer stage, the cell becoming ellipsoidal and developing high motility.
4. Rod form, resulting from the further elongation of the swarmer, with decreasing motility.
5. Vacuolated stage produced in absence of carbohydrates, the chromatin dividing into a number of bands. These bands become rounded and escape from the rod as the coccoid preswarmer.

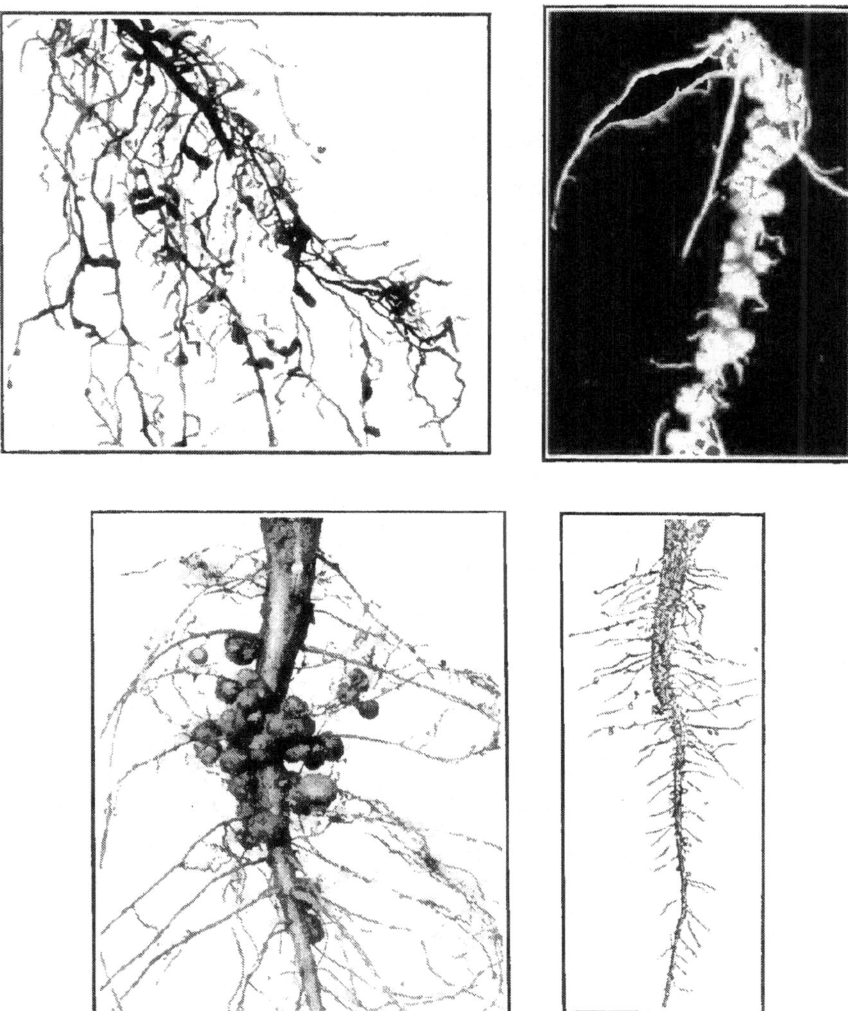

FIG. 90. Different types of nodules of leguminous plants.

SPECIFIC DIFFERENTIATION

Three groups of methods are usually employed for the specific differentiation of the root-nodule bacteria: (1) plant inoculation, (2) morphological and cultural studies, (3) serological and immunological reactions.

Zipfel made agglutination tests and concluded that the various root-nodule bacteria do not represent merely varieties of the same species but are distinct species. He recognized six groups of organisms capable of infecting (1) *Lupinus*, (2) *Trifolium*, (3) *Medicago*, (4) *Pisum*, (5) *Faba*, and (6) *Phaseolus*. Other investigators recognized nine groups of legume bacteria on the basis of serological investigations: (1) *Lupinus* and *Ornithopus*, (2) *Melilotus*, *Medicago*, and *Trigonella*, (3) *Vicia* (*V. sativa*), (4) *Pisum*, (5) *Vicia faba*, (6) *Trifolium pratense*, (7) *Phaseolus*, (8) *Glycine* (*Soja*), and (9) *Onobrychis sativa*.

Bergey placed the root-nodule organism in a separate genus, *Rhizobium*, and divided the different forms into two species: (1) *Rh. leguminosarum* Frank, inoculating *Pisum*, *Vicia*, *Lathyrus*, etc., and (2) *Rh. radicicola* Beij., producing nodules on *Trifolium*, *Phaseolus*, and others.

Fred, Baldwin, and McCoy classified these bacteria into seven groups: (1) alfalfa group, *Rh. meliloti*, (2) clover group, *Rh. trifolii*; (3) pea group, *Rh. leguminosarum*, (4) bean group, *Rh. phaseoli*; (5) lupine group, *Rh. lupini*, (6) soybean group, *Rh. japonicum*; (7) cowpea group, *Rhizobium* sp.

Within each species, there are various strains, which differ primarily in their effectiveness, or ability to fix free nitrogen in association with the proper host plant. Various explanations have been suggested for the specificity of the root-nodule organisms, based on soil reaction and climate. It was at first believed that this is a case of specific enzymes produced by the bacteria or of differences in the root sap. The various members of each cross-inoculation group are closely related with respect to protein characteristics of their seeds.

It was at first believed that some plants will interact with several strains of *Rhizobium*, whereas other plants are limited to particular strains. Cross-pollinating plants were said to be inoculated by more bacterial strains than are self-pollinating plants. The application of serological reactions brought out the fact that various strains of bacteria may form nodules on the same host plant, but only one type is found in the same nodule. That not all strains of the organism are capable of inoculating one type of plant suggests the existence of various biotypes even for the same plant. Two types of the organism can form nodules on the soybean plant. Both are identical morphologically, but they are different physiologically and serologically.

Physiology of Nodule Bacteria

The various strains of *Rhizobium* are strictly aerobic. They are unable to fix atmospheric nitrogen when grown in artificial media. Different carbohydrates can be used as sources of energy, maltose, sucrose, glucose, and mannitol being best; cellulose, pectin, or starch cannot be utilized. Laurent found that *Rhizobium* can be cultivated on nitrogen-free media containing 0.1 per cent KH_2PO_4, 0.01 per cent $MgSO_4$, and 5–10 per cent of an available energy source. Beijerinck insisted, however, that a source of nitrogen is also required. Some of these strains produce considerable acidity, whereas others do not, the acid producers giving rise to peritrichous flagellation. Some of the strains grow very fast, others very slowly, requiring 3–4 weeks. The slow growers produce gum (Table 49).

Table 49 Rate of Fixation of Nitrogen by Various Leguminous Plants

Period of Growth	Fixation of Atmospheric Nitrogen: Per Plant	Per Day	Per Gram Dry Weight of Nodules per Day	Per Cent of Nitrogen Transferred to Plant	Data Reported by
days	*mg*	*mg*	*mg*		
Soybeans					
35–43	3.98	0.50	27.6	80	Bond
49–63	12.30	0.88	15.4	83	
70–84	14.34	1.39	10.3	87	
99–108	19.50	2.16	8.1	89	
108–125	23.09	1.36	4.5	92	
125–141	0.80	0.05	0.2	350	
Soybeans					
25–31	12.04	2.01	33.5	84	Wilson and Umbreit
38–48	27.55	2.76	21.2	88	
48–60	54.08	4.51	19.6	90	
25–29	2.98	0.75	10.7	69	
35–41	34.08	3.84	29.5	87	
Cowpeas					
14–22	4.96	0.62		71	Whiting
30–41	26.84	2.44		82	
41–58	63.32	3.73		93	

The optimum reaction for the growth of *Rhizobium* is pH 5.5–7.0, with limiting reactions of pH 3.2–5.0, on the acid side, and pH 9.0–10.0, on the alkaline. Mazé was the first to draw attention to the fact that the nodule bacteria comprise both acid-resistant and acid-sensitive types The alfalfa organism is most sensitive to acidity, and the lupine organism most resistant.

The limiting temperatures for the growth of nodule bacteria are 0° and 50°C The thermal death point is at 60–62°, and the optimum varies between 18° and 28°C. The bacteria are not injured by diffused sunlight and can readily withstand direct sunlight. Drying is injurious but not fully destructive As a result of direct and rapid drying of soil, the numbers of *Rhizobium* diminish rapidly, as determined by the plate method. The organism can persist in the soil for several years, even in absence of the host plant, however, it is seldom found in soils where specific plants have not grown. *Rhizobium* is not found in manures The bacteria move through the soil very slowly, and are largely distributed by seed, soil, and ground waters.

The rate of photosynthesis of the plant and the available supply of combined nitrogen have an important effect upon nitrogen fixation When photosynthesis is suppressed by permanent darkness, nitrogen fixation ceases and the bacteria become parasitic upon the host plant. With moderately rapid photosynthesis, nitrogen fixation reaches its maximum and may even exceed the rate of protein synthesis, so that excretion of combined nitrogen takes place At an excessive rate of photosynthesis, nitrogen fixation is again depressed Optimum fixation depends on a balance between the supplies of carbohydrate and nitrogen, under these conditions the fixation process is stimulated by nitrate, which otherwise is inhibitive In the fixation of nitrogen, nitrate has two functions (*a*) it counteracts the deformation of the root hairs, which is necessary for entrance of the bacteria, thus reducing the number of nodules, (*b*) it affects the activities of the nodules already formed by reducing the volume of bacterial tissue and by influencing the carbohydrate-nitrogen balance in the host plant.

The fixation of nitrogen depends on certain relations between the bacteria and the host plant The bacteria may produce on one host plant nodules of abnormal nature and yield little or no fixed nitrogen, in a host of a different species, normal nodule formation and nitrogen fixation may occur Clovers may show this phenomenon of "host-plant specificity," a concept which has recently come into prominence and which takes the place of the separation of bacterial strains into the "effective" and the "ineffective" Chen and Thornton (1940) showed that nodules produced by "ineffective" bacteria contain a small volume of rapidly degenerating bacterial tissue, the quantity of nitrogen fixed per unit volume of bacterial tissue, however, is the same in "effective" and "ineffective" nodules. An "ineffective" or "poor" strain is not one, therefore, which lacks the power of causing nitrogen fixation, but one which in a given host plant evokes the formation of specific substances inhibitory to the development of the bacterial tissue, as pointed out by Jensen Certain strains may be effective, however, on some species and not on other, closely related species

Nodule Formation by Nonleguminous Plants

In addition to leguminous plants, certain nonlegumes, such as *Ceanothus* (redroot), *Elaeagnus* (silver berry), *Alnus* (alder), and *Myrica* (sweet gale), are also capable of forming nodules on their roots. These nodules are perennial and branch in all directions, finally developing round aggregates of considerable size

These nodules were at first believed to be of fungus origin. It was shown later that they are caused by bacteria closely resembling the *Rhizobium* group, and that they are capable of causing fixation of nitrogen. Burrill and Hansen emphasized, however, that some of the nodules are not caused by *Rhizobium* The concept of their ability to fix atmospheric nitrogen was not considered conclusive In some plants (*Myrica*) the organism seems to be of the nature of an actinomyces *Coriaria japonica* produces nodules similar to those of *Alnus,* due also to an actinomyces (*A. myricae* of Peklo). This plant, when it forms nodules, is able to grow vigorously and accumulate nitrogen in a medium free from combined nitrogen The plants free from such nodules show signs of nitrogen starvation

The presence of *Rhizobium, Azotobacter,* and certain algae (*Anabaena, Nostoc*) was noted in the roots of *Cycas.* The ability of most of these plants to fix nitrogen is still questionable, although it is reported that some, like *Casuarina,* are able to grow readily in poor sandy soil There is no doubt that some of these bacteria found in the roots of the plants are responsible for symbiotic nitrogen fixation The production of a growth-promoting substance by the bacteria has also been suggested

There are also certain leguminous plants that do not form nodules. These include various members of the Caesalpinaceae, such as *Gymnocladus, Cercis,* and *Gleditsia.*

FIG. 91. Soybeans grown in sand culture. *Left,* no humus; *right,* abundant supply of humus. Note how humus has stimulated root and plant growth (from Blair).

Mechanism of Nitrogen Fixation by Leguminous Plants

The mechanism of nitrogen fixation by the leguminous plants has long been, and still is, a subject of controversy. These plants fix atmospheric nitrogen through their roots and not through their leaves, as was first assumed for some plants. In the early stages of growth, the roots contain the larger part of the nitrogen in the plant; at the time of harvest, however, 74 per cent of the nitrogen is found in the tops. The fixation of the nitrogen takes place in the early stages of growth of the seedling. The mechanism of the fixation process has been elucidated by Virtanen as follows

$$
\begin{array}{ccccccccc}
 & & & & N_2 \text{ (atm nitrogen)} & & & & \\
 & & & & \downarrow & & & & \\
 & & & & NH & & & & \\
 & & COOH & & \| \text{ (di-imide)?} & & COOH & & COOH \\
 & & | & & NH & & | & & | \\
 & & CO & & \downarrow & & CNOH & & CHNH_2 \\
C_6H_{12}O_6 & \rightarrow & | & + & NH_2OH & \rightarrow & | & \rightarrow & | \\
 & & CH_2 & & & & CH_2 & & CH_2 \\
 & & | & & & & | & & | \\
 & & COOH & & & & COOH & & COOH \\
\text{Carbohydrates in plants} & & \text{Oxalacetic acid} & & \text{Hydroxylamine} & & \text{Oximinosuccinic acid} & & l\text{-Aspartic acid}
\end{array}
$$

The presence of various amino acids and amides in leguminous plants has been used as substantiation of the above concept. These acids are believed to be excreted from the plant into the soil and are made available for the growth of nonleguminous plants The data presented in Table 50 tend to substantiate these conclusions, with which Wilson, however, could not fully agree.

TABLE 50. GROWTH AND NITROGEN CONTENT OF RED CLOVER, PEAS, BARLEY, AND WHEAT PLANTS IN QUARTZ SAND (from Virtanen)

N Nutrition	Dry Weight	Nitrogen in Plant
	gm	*mg*
Red clover		
KNO$_3$	2.329	50.0
Aspartic acid	4.428	90.9
Without N nutrition	0.028	0.14
Peas		
KNO$_3$	1.402	40.1
Aspartic acid	1.474	40.0
Without N nutrition	0.325	6.2
Barley *		
KNO$_3$	0.433	13.3
Aspartic acid	0.049	1.9
Without N nutrition	0.063	0.7
Wheat		
KNO$_3$	2.143	35.3
Aspartic acid	0.113	3.7
Without N nutrition	0.117	0.8

* Culture of barley harvested at much earlier stage than other cultures

Inoculation of leguminous plants increases the protein content of the plant, often without increasing the crop yield. Plants that depend largely upon the bacteria for their nitrogen show a high alkaloid content. When the plants obtain their nitrogen from inorganic compounds, they are poor in alkaloids. This is especially true of lupines.

Molybdenum is said to have an important effect on nitrogen fixation by leguminous plants. This subject was investigated recently in detail by Jensen, who concluded that nitrogen fixation by alfalfa and white clover in agar culture is not stimulated by additions of molybdenum in quantities exceeding 0.03–0.05 γ per plant. As much as 37,000 parts of nitrogen could be fixed per part of molybdenum present. A relatively small but significant response was found to 1 part of molybdenum per 80,000 parts of nitrogen fixed. At a ratio of molybdenum to nitrogen of 1:20,000, further addition of molybdenum had no effect. The root nodules of leguminous plants grown at low molybdenum concentration contained 5–15 times more molybdenum than did the roots, and the latter were richer in molybdenum than the tops. Alfalfa plants took up more molybdenum when fixing free nitrogen than when utilizing combined nitrogen. These results suggested that molybdenum stimulates the process of symbiotic nitrogen fixation and is undoubtedly required for general metabolism. Vanadium cannot replace molybdenum.

Bacteriophage

Root-nodule bacteria are subject to the action of phage, which is quite specific for the different organisms. This phenomenon represents a complicating factor in the host-bacteria relationship. The phage is widely distributed. It has been isolated from nodules, roots, and stems of leguminous plants, as well as from soils in which legumes have grown. Demolon and Dunez found the bacteriophage in the neighborhood of the roots of leguminous plants, but not a few inches away from the roots. As in the case of other phages, resistant strains can easily be obtained. This is complicated by the fact that different phages vary in their ability to cause the lysis of a given sensitive strain. Vandecavaye and Katznelson isolated a phage which caused lysis in a dilution of 10^{-11}. According to Demolon and Dunez, phages from clovers, lupine, and pea are able to lyse preferentially the particular species of bacteria, but some phages seem to be more general in their effectiveness upon different strains of rhizobia. When a large number of legumes were planted on an alfalfa field suffering from "fatigue," believed to be due to the presence of the bacteriophage, the nodules of all species contained abnormal, vacuolated forms of the organisms as well as the specific phage. The importance of the phage in the phenomenon of fatigue may still be considered questionable, however According to Katznelson, a phage for alfalfa was absorbed from suspensions only by members of the alfalfa-sweet-clover cross-inoculation group, thus suggesting a technique which may be useful in distinguishing members of the different species of *Rhizobium*

Excretion of Nitrogen by Legumes

The first demonstration that nonleguminous plants are able to benefit from association with a legume was presented by Lipman He suggested that the beneficial effect was due to nitrogenous compounds excreted by the leguminous plants and consumed by the nonlegumes. Lipman used a half-and-half mixture of peas and oats grown in a medium consisting of soil plus sand The total nitrogen and dry weight of the oats associated with the peas exceeded those of the crop of oats grown alone. The yields of oats and peas in the mixture were greater than those of the crops grown alone.

Lipman further demonstrated in a series of experiments that the benefit to the associated nonlegume arises from excretion of nitrogen by the leguminous plant. He used as the medium a pure quartz sand treated with all the necessary plant nutrients except nitrogen and placed a small pot within a larger one so that the two plants grew in separate containers Whenever the inner pot was porous, or would allow the passage of substances in solution, the nonlegume developed normally and, on analysis, showed considerable quantities of nitrogen If the inner pot was glazed, the nonlegume grew poorly and contained little nitrogen On the basis of these results, Lipman suggested that nonlegumes benefit from association with legumes as a result of the excretion of nitrogen by the latter This work was repeated by many others, some quite independently of the above experiments

Virtanen observed in 1927 that oats grown in association with peas on a nitrogen-free quartz sand developed as though combined nitrogen had been supplied Similar results were later obtained with other combinations of legumes and nonlegumes. The fact that legumes can excrete nitrogen from the nodule is substantiated by the following evidence:

1. The quantity of nitrogen excreted is too large to be explained by the sloughed-off nodules and portions of the roots. Frequently 50 per cent or more of the total nitrogen fixed is excreted, more nitrogen than is usually present in the entire root system.

Fig. 92. Influence of a legume (peas) on growth of a nonlegume (oats). Oats in inner pot, peas in outer. Porous inner pot on left, glazed inner pot on right (from Lipman).

2. Virtanen grew the plants under bacteriologically controlled conditions. Excretion took place, thus proving that the origin of the nitrogen is the legume bacteria and not other soil microorganisms.

3. Nitrogen compounds were excreted even in the absence of nonlegumes. They were identified as comprising largely aspartic acid and beta-alanine. The formation of the beta-alanine was ascribed to decarboxylation of the excreted aspartic acid by the root-nodule organisms. If the nitrogen originated from sloughed-off portions of the plant, the presence of more than one amino acid would be expected.

4. Excretion may occur fairly early in the development of the plant, before sloughing of nodules or roots would be expected.

Wilson further developed this concept by considering the effect of length of day upon the excretion of nitrogen by the leguminous plant, as measured by absorption by the nonlegume (Table 51).

TABLE 51. INFLUENCE OF LENGTH OF DAY UPON FIXATION OF NITROGEN (from Wilson)

	Nitrogen Fixed	
	Short Day	Long Day
	mg	*mg*
Canada field pea	36.2	52.3
Associated barley	43.8	50.1
Canada field pea	30.1	37.0
Associated barley	47.8	51.1
Associated barley control	36.7	19.8

IMPORTANCE OF SYMBIOTIC NITROGEN FIXATION IN THE SOIL

Though the amounts of nitrogen fixed nonsymbiotically under field conditions are still subject to doubt, the symbiotic fixation of nitrogen is of great economic importance. The amount of nitrogen added to the soil by leguminous plants depends entirely upon the abundance of available nitrogen in the soil. The poorer the soil is in nitrogen and the richer it is in lime, phosphorus, and potash, the greater will be the gain in nitrogen from the growth of legumes. The nature of the legume, soil conditions, and season will affect the amount of nitrogen fixed (Table 52).

TABLE 52. INFLUENCE OF $CaCO_3$ UPON NITROGEN FIXATION BY ALFALFA GROWN IN SAND (from Jensen)

	Total N in Plants		Gain of N per Gram Dry Nodule	
Days	$-CaCO_3$ *	$+CaCO_3$ †	$-CaCO_3$	$+CaCO_3$
	mg	*mg*	*mg*	*mg*
60	16	36		712
85	127	144	1,298	1,506
100	175	258	1,209	2,321

* *p*H of sand 5.1. † *p*H of sand 7.2.

Warington demonstrated in 1891 that an increase of about 350 pounds of nitrogen per acre may be obtained as a result of the growth of inoculated clover. All the subsequent reports point to large increases in soil nitrogen due to the growth of leguminous plants in the presence of specific bacteria. Poor soils usually show larger

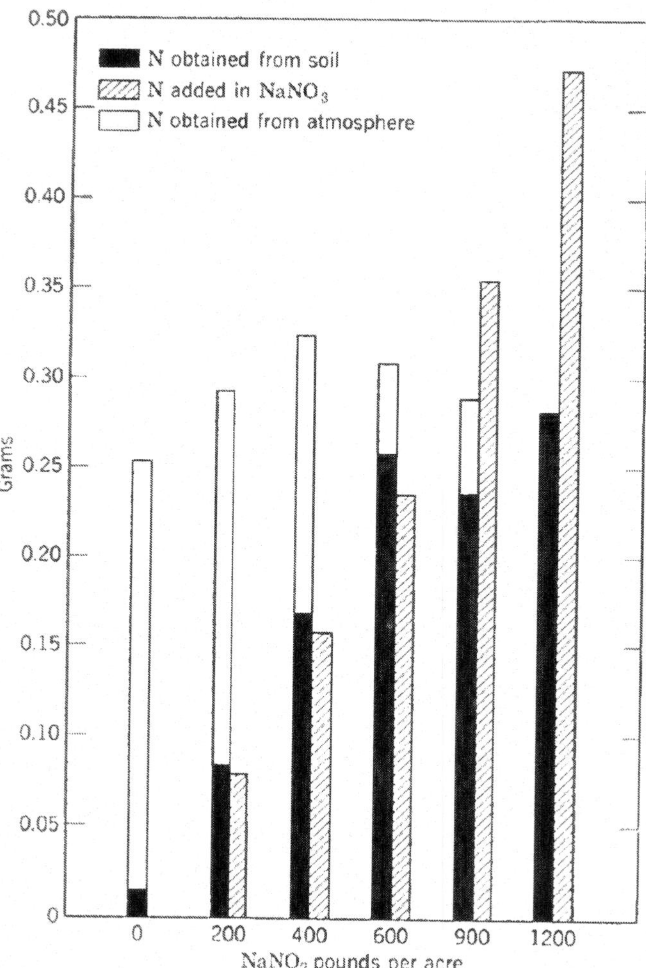

Fig. 93. Relation between soil and atmospheric nitrogen obtained by a crop of inoculated alfalfa growing on soil variously treated with sodium nitrate (from Giobel).

gains than rich soils. Soils to which lime and phosphorus compounds have been added show greater increases in combined nitrogen than do soils in which these are lacking. Inoculated soils give higher increases than uninoculated, especially if the particular legume has not been grown previously on the same soil. Hiltner obtained by inoculation an increase of 1.7–31 times the yield for lupines and 15–80 times for serradella. On the average, there may be a gain of 50–100 pounds of nitrogen per acre of soil due to the growth of legumes Lipman and Blair obtained a gain of 54 pounds annually over a period of 7 years from the growth of legumes in rotation with corn, potatoes, oats, and rye in cylinders

Hopkins reported that a 3-ton crop of cowpea hay adds 86 pounds of nitrogen per acre, a 25-bushel crop of soybeans with 2.25 tons of straw adds 106 pounds, a 4-ton clover crop adds 106 pounds, and a 4-ton alfalfa crop adds 132 pounds On the average, about two-thirds of the nitrogen in the legumes grown in the soil is obtained from the air Under optimum conditions and on a relatively poor soil, as much as 400 pounds of nitrogen may be added per acre yearly. In a light sandy soil, clover was reported to produce an annual gain of 50 pounds of nitrogen. If the crop is removed, the nitrogen content of the soil may not be greatly increased, since the amount fixed may be just sufficient to fulfill the need of the tops. Perennial legumes, like alfalfa, may not show an increase in soil nitrogen, although the nitrogen is higher than in the same soils upon which grains are grown.

Because of the associated bacteria, the economic importance of legumes in agriculture is so great that it has been said many times that, had the whole subject of soil microbiology contributed nothing more of practical value than a knowledge of the legume bacteria, it would have more than fully justified itself

Selected Bibliography

1 Allen, E. K, and Allen, O N, Biochemical and symbiotic properties of the rhizobia, *Bact Revs*, 14 273–330, 1950
2. Allison, F E, and Ludwig, C A, The cause of decreased nodule formation on legumes supplied with abundant combined nitrogen, *Soil Sci*, 37 431–443, 1934
3. Bond, G, Quantitative observations on the fixation and transfer of nitrogen in the soy bean, *Ann Botany*, 50 559–578, 1936
4 Chen, H K, and Thornton, H G The structure of "ineffective" nodules and its influence on nitrogen fixation, *Proc Roy Soc London*, B, 129 208–229, 1940

5. Fred, E. B., Baldwin, I. L., and McCoy, E., *Root Nodule Bacteria and Leguminous Plants*, University of Wisconsin Press, Madison, Wis., 1932.
6. Graebel, G., The relation of the soil nitrogen to nodule development and fixation of nitrogen by certain legumes, *N. J. Agr. Expt. Sta. Bull.* 436: 125, 1926.
7. Jensen, H. L., Nitrogen fixation in leguminous plants, I–VI, *Proc. Linnean Soc. N. S. Wales*, 67:98–108, 1942; 68:207–220, 1943; 69:229–237, 1944; 70:203–210, 1946.
8. Jones, F. R., and Tisdale, W. B., Effect of soil temperature upon the development of nodules on the roots of certain legumes, *J. Agr. Research*, 22:17–32, 1921.
9. Lipman, J. G., and Conybeare, A. B., Preliminary note on the inventory and balance sheet of plant nutrients in the United States, *N. J. Agr. Expt. Sta. Bull.* 607, 1936.
10. Thornton, H. G., The influence of the host plant in inducing parasitism in lucerne and clover nodules, *Proc. Roy. Soc. London*, B, 106:110–122, 1930.
11. Thornton, H. G., and Nicol, H., Reduction of nodule numbers and growth, produced by the addition of sodium nitrate to lucerne in sand culture, *J. Agr. Sci.*, 26:173–188, 1936.
12. Virtanen, A. I., *Cattle Fodder and Human Nutrition, with Special Reference to Biological Nitrogen Fixation*, Cambridge University Press, 1938.
13. Virtanen, A. I., and Laine, T., Investigations on the root nodule bacteria of leguminous plants. XXII. The excretion products of root nodules. The mechanism of N-fixation, *Biochem. J.*, 33:412–427, 1939.
14. Wilson, P. W., *The Biochemistry of Symbiotic Nitrogen Fixation*, University of Wisconsin Press, Madison, Wis., 1940.
15. Wilson, P. W., and Burris, R. H., The mechanism of biological nitrogen fixation, *Bact. Revs.*, 11:41–73, 1947.
16. Wilson, P. W., Hull, J. F., and Burris, R. H., Competition between free and combined nitrogen in nutrition of *Azotobacter*, *Proc. Natl. Acad. Sci.*, 29:289–294, 1943.
17. Wyss, O., Lind, C. J., Wilson, J. B., and Wilson, P. W., Mechanism of biological nitrogen fixation. 7. Molecular H_2 and pN_2 function of *Azotobacter*, *Biochem. J.*, 35:845–854, 1941.

· 10 ·

Transformation of Mineral* Substances in Soil by Microorganisms

Through their roots, plants take up from the soil a number of different elements in the form of salts These are frequently classified as essential and minor or trace elements. The first group includes sulfur, phosphorus, potassium, calcium, magnesium, iron, manganese, and sodium. The second group includes zinc, molybdenum, cadmium, chlorine, aluminum, boron, copper, silicon, and a variety of others. In the transformation of these elements in the soil, microorganisms frequently play a direct part, though often their effect upon the various elements is merely indirect. Even such inert elements as silicon may be essential in the growth of certain bacteria and of various algae, notably the diatoms. Molybdenum has been found to play a role in the fixation of atmospheric nitrogen. Other elements are found to have a neutralizing effect upon plant toxins. Still others, like cobalt, may influence the growth of the cell to retard multiplication Some of the elements, notably phosphorus, are essential constituents of the cell nucleus and its cytoplasm Still others, like sulfur, may serve as sources of energy to various bacteria and also form essential constituents of certain amino acids.

Transformation of Sulfur

Sulfur is one of the elements essential for plant growth. This element makes up about 0 11 per cent of the earth's crust Phosphorus occurs in about the same concentration It appears from analyses of river water that sulfur is removed from the soil faster than any other element, however, since its ions, SO_4, tend to dissolve in the water, whereas the PO_4 ions tend to precipitate in the soil

* The term "mineral" is used to designate all elements and compounds not containing carbon or nitrogen

The removal of sulfur by farm crops may be far greater than has usually been assumed; it may be entirely out of proportion to the reserve of this element in the soil. It has been suggested that the depletion of sulfur may, in time, have an important effect on soil fertility. The annual loss of sulfur from unlimed soil through crop-

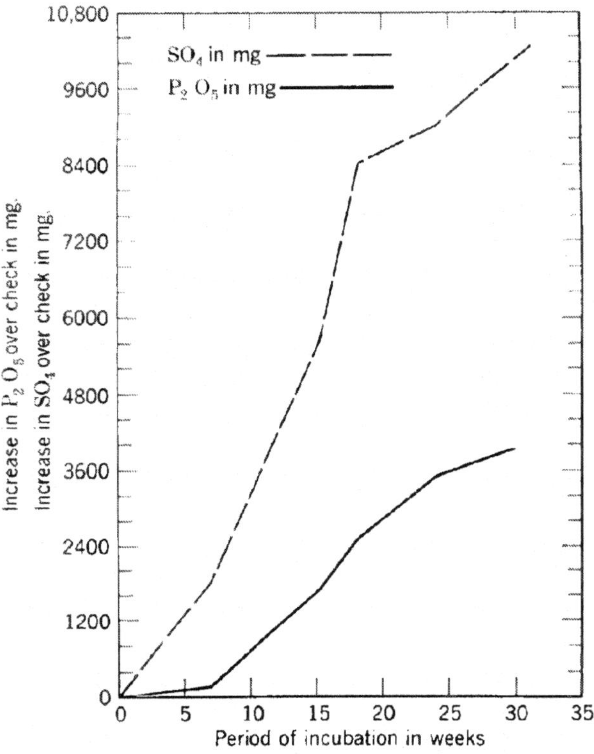

Fig. 94. Course of accumulation of citrate-soluble P_2O_5 and SO_4 in composts of soil, rock phosphate, and sulfur (from Lipman, McLean, and Lint).

ping and drainage has been reported to amount to 44 pounds per acre. This loss was increased by applications of lime. One-half to two-thirds of the sulfur applied to the soil in the form of potassium sulfate was found to be removed in the drainage water.

Sulfur is added or finds its way into the soil in a number of different forms: (*a*) in certain organic compounds, which form constituent parts of the plant and animal residues added to or left on the soil; (*b*) as elementary sulfur, which is usually added to the soil as a fertilizer or which is continuously brought down in the rain water, (*c*) as sulfates, which are added to the soil in certain mineral fertilizers, such as superphosphates and gypsum

The sulfur content of plant materials varies from a small fraction of 1 per cent, as in rye straw, to almost 1 per cent, as in turnip tops

Sulfur and sulfur compounds in the soil are subject to numerous transformations resulting directly or indirectly from the activities of different groups of microorganisms When plant and animal residues undergo decomposition, whether in the soil or in the compost, the sulfur-bearing constituents, notably the proteins and certain glucosides, are hydrolyzed The proteins give rise to the sulfur-bearing amino acid cystine, the glucosides yield mustard oil and other sulfur compounds

The chemical structure of two typical sulfur-bearing compounds may be presented as follows·

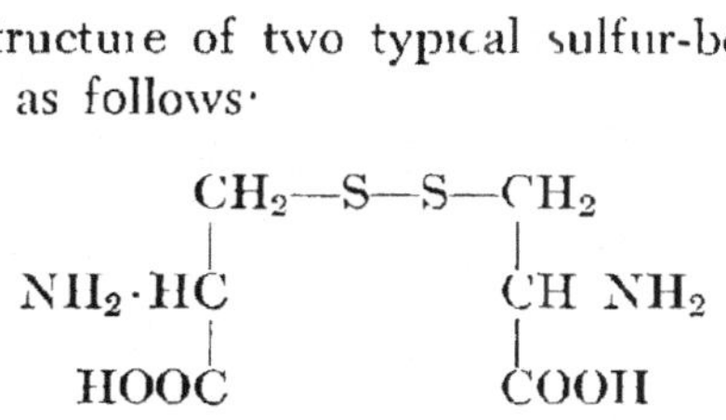

$$\begin{array}{lcl} & CH_2\text{—}S\text{—}S\text{—}CH_2 & \\ NH_2\cdot HC & & CH\ NH_2 \\ HOOC & & COOH \end{array}$$

Cystine

$$\begin{array}{l} CH_2\ SO_2OH \\ | \\ CH_2\ NH_2 \end{array}$$

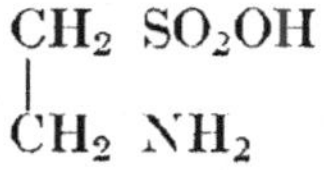

Taurine

In recent studies on antibiotic products of microbial metabolism, sulfur has also been found as an essential constituent of such important compounds as penicillin

These compounds can be attacked by various bacteria and other microorganisms. Only a small part of the sulfur is consumed by these organisms Most of it is liberated as hydrogen sulfide Under anaerobic conditions, other sulfur compounds, such as mercaptans, may also be produced These are largely responsible for the pungent odor which is always present when animal residues and certain protein-rich materials undergo decomposition in absence of available oxygen Under aerobic conditions, both hydrogen sulfide and mercaptans are rapidly oxidized further to sulfates.

Among the bacteria responsible for the transformation of sulfur in nature, those that are able to oxidize the elemental sulfur and simple compounds of sulfur are of particular interest These bacteria are known as "sulfur bacteria" They belong to different morphological and physiological groups, some being small, a micron or so in size Others are large and filamentous Some are obligate autotrophic, that is, they depend on the energy liberated in the oxidation of sulfur, and others are facultative autotrophic, or are also able to derive their energy from organic compounds.

The most numerous of these bacteria in the soil population are the autotrophic organisms. They function in a manner somewhat similar to green plants, though the latter use the energy of sunlight (photosynthesis), whereas the autotrophic bacteria are able to utilize the chemical energy liberated in the oxidation process (chemosynthesis) Both the bacteria and the green plants use the carbon dioxide of the atmosphere as sources of carbon for cell synthesis.

The following chemical reactions are involved in the oxidation of sulfur and its compounds by bacteria

$$2H_2S + O_2 = 2H_2O + S_2$$

$$S_2 + 3O_2 + 2H_2O = 2H_2SO_4$$

$$Na_2S_2O_3 + 2O_2 + H_2O = Na_2SO_4 + H_2SO_4$$

$$2Na_2S_2O_3 + O_2 = 2Na_2SO_4 + S_2$$

The rate of oxidation of the sulfur and its simple compounds to sulfuric acid and to sulfates is influenced not only by the nature of the organism but also by the environmental conditions (Table 53)

TABLE 53 OXIDATION OF ELEMENTARY SULFUR TO SULFURIC ACID BY *Thiobacillus thiooxidans* (from Waksman and Starkey)

Incubation	Amount of Culture in Flask	Control Flask		Inoculated Flask		Elementary Sulfur Disappeared	Increase in Sulfate
		Sulfur	Sulfate	Sulfur	Sulfate		
days	*ml*	*mg S*	*mg S*	*mg S*	*mg S*	*mg S*	*mg S*
15	100	1,001	86.4	788	302.1	213	215.7
30	100	992	90.5	735	354.0	257	263.5
15	300	3,002	112.2	2,496	633.0	506	520.8
30	300	2,997	126.5	1,971	1,168.0	1,023	1,011.5

Of particular importance is the reaction of the soil or substrate, salt concentration, and presence of organic materials

Each of the above reactions can be brought about by different types of bacteria The first reaction, which results in the precipitation of sulfur, takes place largely in water basins and in peat bogs and can be carried out by a great many bacteria. This type of reaction has recently attracted much attention as an outgrowth of an effort to increase the supply of available sulfur by utilizing the waste products In well-aerated soils, however, sulfur does not accumulate as a result of oxidation of hydrogen sulfide, but is rapidly oxidized further to sulfate, as shown by the second reaction.

When elementary sulfur is the starting point, only very few bacteria are able to bring about its oxidation to sulfuric acid The acid interacts with the bases and other buffering substances present in the soil to give rise to various sulfates. When it is desirable to reduce the alkalinity of certain soils, such as black alkali soils, or when it is advisable to make the soil more acid for control of certain disease-producing organisms, such as potato scab, addition of sulfur, and its resultant oxidation to sulfuric acid, may become of great economic importance This reaction can be summarized as follows

$$Ca_3(PO_4)_2 + 2H_2SO_4 = 2CaSO_4 + Ca(H_2PO_4)_2$$

Among the other transformations of sulfur compounds in the soil and in other natural substrates, the reduction processes are of great significance. The reduction of sulfate to hydrogen sulfide is brought about by certain specific bacteria, usually designated as sulfate-reducing organisms One of these organisms has been designated by Beijerinck as *Microspira desulfuricans*, and more recently by Starkey as *Sporovibrio desulfuricans* The reduction process takes place in the presence of a suitable source of energy as follows

$$CaSO_4 + CH_3\ COOH = H_2S + CaCO_3 + CO_2 + H_2O$$

Anaerobic conditions, or absence of free atmospheric oxygen, is essential for this reaction, and a form of organic matter must be available The sulfate is used by the bacteria as a source of oxygen for the oxidation of the organic substances, the energy liberated in the oxidation process is partly consumed in the reduction of the sulfate. The hydrogen sulfide produced in this reaction is characteristic of certain water basins, of peat bogs, and of other water-saturated environments, where there is a lack of free oxygen In the presence of iron, black iron sulfide is produced which is characteristic of the organic muds laid down under anaerobic conditions This reaction may lead to corrosion of iron in steel pipes, which may become of considerable economic importance.

The hydrogen sulfide formed in the reduction of sulfates may again be oxidized to sulfate upon coming in contact with an oxygen source and in the presence of the specific sulfur-oxidizing bacteria

Transformation of Phosphorus

Phosphorus is continuously added to the soil in organic residues and in fertilizers It is also found in untreated soil in a number of

Table 54 Phosphorus and Potassium Content of Some Typical Soil Bacteria

	Ash	Total P_2O_5	Total K_2O
	per cent	*per cent*	*per cent*
Az chroococcum	8.2–8.6	4.93–5.2	2.41–2.65
B mycoides	7.5	4.07	2.27
Ps fluorescens liquefaciens	6.48	5.32	0.83

different forms. Briefly these forms of phosphorus may be classified as follows

1 Organic compounds present in plant and animal residues added to the soil They are also abundant in the microbial cell substance which is synthesized in the soil Organic compounds of phosphorus also form a constituent part of the humus complexes of the soil.

2 Rock phosphate and other insoluble phosphates are usually present in the native rocks from which the soil is derived They are also frequently added to the soil in the form of various fertilizers as well as in the bones of dead animals (Table 55)

Table 55 Effect of Nitrification on the Solubility of Tricalcium Phosphate in Soil (from Kelley)

Materials Added	After 28 Days			After 57 Days		
	NO_3-N	Ca	P_2O_5	NO_3-N	Ca	P_2O_5
	ppm	*ppm*	*ppm*	*ppm*	*ppm*	*ppm*
Control	20.0	45.0	13.1	25.5	50.6	11.0
$CaCO_3$	22.0	56.5	11.9	29.0	70.8	13.2
$Ca_3(PO_4)_2$	21.0	53.5	21.2	28.0	58.8	25.0
$CaCO_3 + Ca_3(PO_4)_2$	22.0	59.1	17.3	28.0	70.1	22.4
$(NH_4)_2SO_4$	98.0	219.4	18.5	99.0	225.4	19.4
$(NH_4)_2SO_4 + CaCO_3$	97.0	254.4	18.5	98.0	270.5	7.4
$(NH_4)_2SO_4 + Ca_3(PO_4)_2$	99.0	217.7	52.1	99.0	229.6	38.0
$(NH_4)_2SO_4 + CaCO_3 + Ca_3(PO_4)_2$	100.0	253.4	26.6	101.0	230.4	13.9
Dried blood	91.0	107.7	9.7	90.0	113.9	10.0
Dried blood + $CaCO_3$	89.0	107.2	9.8	90.0	140.2	11.5
Dried blood + $Ca_3(PO_4)_2$	82.0	111.7	24.3	88.0	117.7	22.2
Dried blood + $CaCO_3 + Ca_3(PO_4)_2$	81.0	118.2	19.5	87.5	138.1	18.3

3 Soluble inorganic phosphates, like those of sodium, potassium, calcium, and magnesium, are added to the soil in fertilizer materials and in plant and animal residues

Among the organic phosphorus compounds which find their way into the soil, lecithin, nucleic acids, and phytin occupy a prominent place

Lecithin contains 9.39 per cent P_2O_5, 1 6 per cent N, and 65 36 per cent C. It contains two fatty acid radicals, such as palmitic and stearic or oleic acids, as shown by the following structural formula

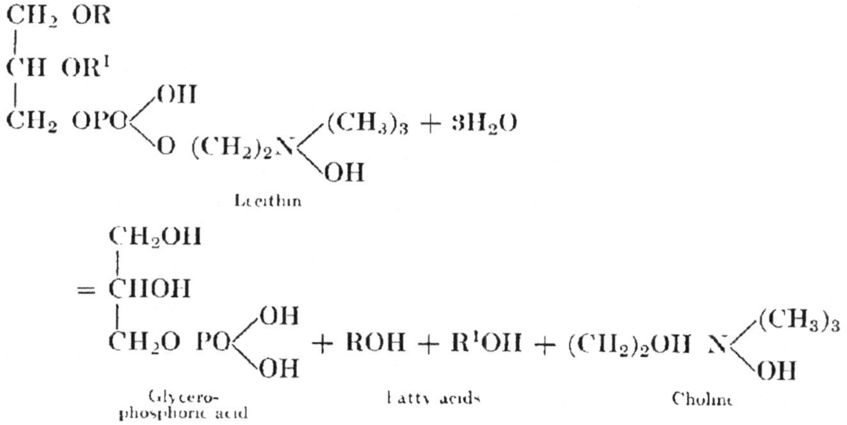

$$\begin{array}{l} CH_2\ OR \\ | \\ CH\ OR^1 \\ | \\ CH_2\ OPO \begin{cases} OH \\ O\ (CH_2)_2N \begin{cases} (CH_3)_3 \\ OH \end{cases} \end{cases} + 3H_2O \end{array}$$

Lecithin

$$= \begin{array}{l} CH_2OH \\ | \\ CHOH \\ | \\ CH_2O\ PO \begin{cases} OH \\ OH \end{cases} \end{array} + ROH + R^1OH + (CH_2)_2OH\ N \begin{cases} (CH_3)_3 \\ OH \end{cases}$$

Glycero-phosphoric acid — Fatty acids — Choline

Nucleic acids are found abundantly in the microbial cell substance In their decomposition, some of the groups are broken down more readily than others. In the presence of readily available sources of carbon and nitrogen, various bacteria and fungi are capable of breaking down both lecithin and nucleic acids and liberating the phosphorus as phosphate As much as 66 per cent of the lecithin phosphorus was transformed into soluble phosphate in 60 days The rest of the phosphorus was assimilated by the bacteria for the synthesis of cell material

Phytin is a hexaphosphate, which occurs abundantly in plant materials, notably in the seeds It contains about 26 per cent phosphorus in the form of phytic acid, $C_6H_{24}O_{27}P_6$. This compound is acted upon by fungi and bacteria by means of an enzyme, designated as "phytase," with the result that the organic phosphorus is transformed into phosphate

$$C_6H_{24}O_{27}P_6 + 6O_2 = 6H_3PO_4 + 6CO_2 + 3H_2O$$

Nucleoproteins contain 7–9 per cent phosphorus and 13–14 per cent nitrogen When attacked by microorganisms, they give rise to phosphoric acid, sugar, purine and pyrimidine bases These compounds are decomposed further by a variety of bacteria and fungi Certain bacteria, designated as the *Nucleobacter* group, have been found to be specifically concerned in the decomposition of nucleins, through the nucleic acid stage, into phosphoric acid

A number of other organic phosphorus compounds, notably inosite monophosphate ($C_6H_{13}O_9P$), which is found in wheat bran, are commonly added to the soil Their decomposition is similar to the transformation of phytin and nucleic acids

The insoluble phosphates added to the soil are subject to the activities of microorganisms largely in an indirect manner The various organic and inorganic acids produced by microorganisms interact with the insoluble phosphates, giving rise to soluble compounds This is illustrated by the following reactions:

$$Ca_3(PO_4)_2 + 2HNO_3 = 2CaHPO_4 + Ca(NO_3)_2$$

$$Ca_3(PO_4)_2 + 4HNO_3 = Ca(H_2PO_4)_2 + 2Ca(NO_3)_2$$

$$Ca_3(PO_4)_2 + H_2SO_4 = 2CaHPO_4 + CaSO_4$$

The relation between sulfur oxidation and phosphate solubilization is brought out in Fig 95

Gerretsen presented evidence that the intake of phosphorus by plants from basic slag is markedly improved by the activity of soil microbes. The solvent action of the soil microorganisms on insoluble phosphates was obtained with the aid of glass plates, covered with an agar film, in which calcium phosphate was precipitated, and buried aslant in the culture vessels Clear solubilization zones were observed in distinct spots, especially underneath root tips and young branches In sterile cultures these solubilization zones were absent, proving that the solvent action of the roots was negligible. When the roots excrete organic substances with a low C N quotient, there is a possibility that phosphates may be precipitated by microbiological activity

In the decomposition of organic matter by microorganisms, usually not all the phosphorus is liberated as phosphate, a certain amount being assimilated by the organisms for the synthesis of fresh cell material When the organic complexes contain little or no phosphorus, the bacteria and fungi are able to remove from the soil some of the soluble phosphate that they require for their cell synthesis. This is similar to the needs of the microorganisms for nitrogen, although the amounts of phosphorus required for this purpose are less.

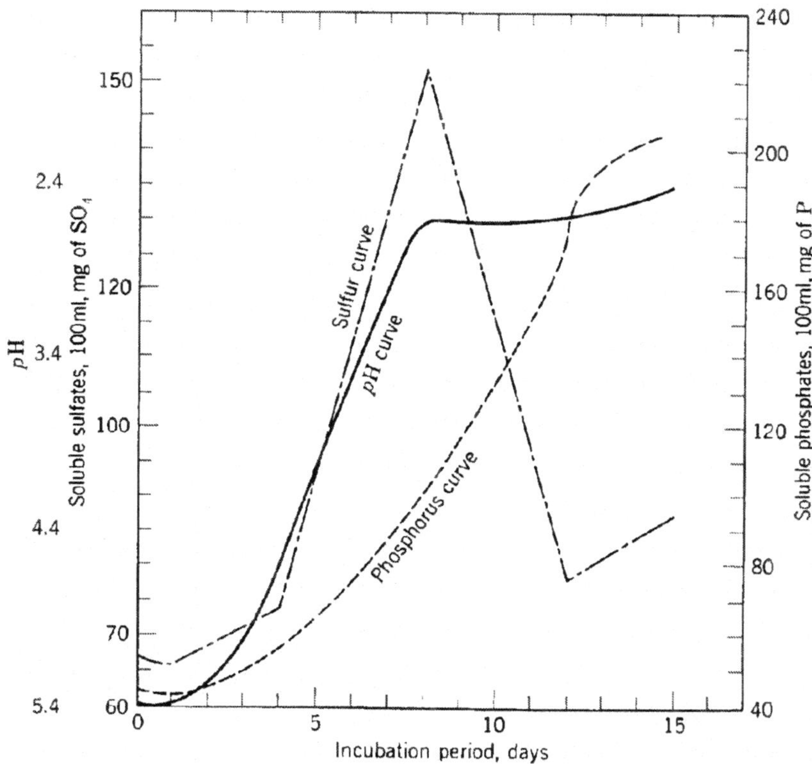

Fig. 95. Course of sulfur oxidation and transformation of insoluble phosphate into soluble forms by *Thiobacillus thiooxidans* in liquid media (from Waksman and Joffe).

The estimation of available phosphate in the soil, or the potential response of a crop to a dressing of phosphate, is complicated by several factors, notably the root system of the plant, the depth of penetration of the root system, and rainfall. The favorable effect of addition of available phosphate to the soil will be an increase in the root system, which leads to a greater uptake of the soil phosphate. The ability of the roots of plants to absorb the less easily available phosphates depends on the phosphate nutrition of the plant and its root system. Some plants excrete organic acids from their roots. All plants have certain concentrations of carbon dioxide around their roots, because of respiration of the microbiological population of the soil, especially in the rhizosphere This results in greater availability of insoluble phosphates and may result in a transfer of some of the phosphate thus made available to the roots of the crop Soil conditions, especially aeration, are of great importance in this connection

The methods now in use for estimating the available phosphate in the soil are based upon treatment of the soil with a suitable solvent, such as citric or acetic acid or ammonium fluoride, and determination of the amount of phosphate in the extract A number of biological methods are also in use. These include measuring the amount of phosphate taken up by rye seedlings, or the amount of growth made by phosphate-requiring bacteria, such as *Azotobacter*, or fungi, such as *Aspergillus*, with soil as the only source of phosphorus These methods allow a proximate evaluation of the availability or shortage of phosphate in the soil No single method, however, is sufficient for evaluating the potential responsiveness of soils to a given crop treated with a certain amount of phosphate, since different crops vary greatly in their ability to extract phosphate from the soil

The microbiological methods for evaluating the available phosphorus in the soil are based upon the fact that a certain parallelism has been observed between microbial cell synthesis and phosphate consumption This observation has been used to advantage in determining the available phosphate present in the soil Various bacteria, notably *Azotobacter chroococcum*, and fungi, such as *Aspergillus niger*, *Cunninghamella*, *Trichoderma*, and *A oryzae*, are utilized as test organisms

The method of analysis is usually carried out as follows A certain quantity of the soil in question is added to a sugar-salt solution free from phosphorus and nitrogen and is inoculated with a suitable strain of *Azotobacter* After incubation for 14–30 days at 28°C, the amount of nitrogen fixed is determined The fixed nitrogen is a measure of *Azotobacter* growth, which is controlled by the available phosphorus Since the ratio of cell nitrogen to cell phosphorus is 2 1, the amount of phosphorus consumed can be calculated from the amount of nitrogen fixed, thus giving the available phosphorus in the soil sample added to the solution.

This method has been variously modified. In one of these modifications a carbohydrate (sugar, starch, mannitol) is added to the soil in question Some $CaCO_3$ is also added if the soil is acid The soil is then inoculated with *Azotobacter* and packed into small dishes, the surfaces of which are smoothed out. The amount of available phosphorus in the soil is measured by the growth of *Azotobacter* on the surface of the soil, as determined by the appearance of slimy colonies. The available phosphorus in a given soil is measured from the actual amount of growth of the *Azotobacter* colony.

Some of the methods are based upon the use of fungi. These methods are similar to the above, except that available nitrogen is also added to the solution or to the soil. The fungus growth is used as a measure of the available phosphorus.

Transformation of Potassium, Calcium, Magnesium, and Iron

In addition to the elements already discussed, others that are required for plant and animal nutrition and that are present in or introduced into the soil are also subject, directly or indirectly, to activities of microorganisms. Some of these elements, including po-

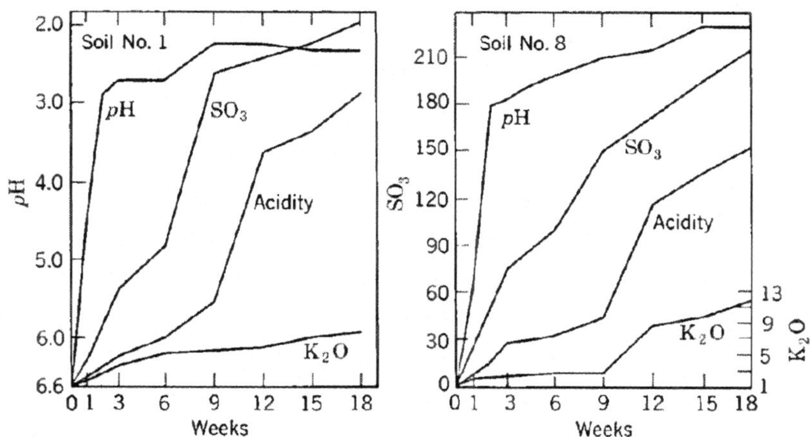

Fig. 96. Relation between sulfur oxidation and water-soluble potassium in composts containing sulfur and greensand marl (from Rudolfs).

tassium, calcium, magnesium, and iron, are utilized for the metabolism of the soil organisms. They are used either as nutrients or as catalysts and are, therefore, required in very small amounts. Their transformation by microorganisms and their role in microbial metabolism depend on the nature of the element, on the nature of the organism, and on soil conditions.

Potassium is found in soil both in organic forms and in the form of zeolitic and nonzeolitic silicates. It is added to the soil in soluble inorganic forms, notably salts of sulfates, chlorides, and phosphates, in insoluble inorganic form, known as marl; and in the form of stable manures and plant residues. The K_2O content of plant residues ranges from 0.5 to 2.0 per cent. Fresh manure contains 0.288–0.504 per cent K_2O. Its concentration in the ash content of bacterial cells is 4.0–25.6 per cent, and in that of fungus mycelium, 8.7–39.5 per cent. The presence and activities of microorganisms influence greatly the availability of potassium in soil to plant growth. Microbial activities may lead to an increase in the available potassium, as when organic matter is decomposed by microorganisms and when acids interact with the zeolites, liberating the potassium. Orthoclase interacts with certain microbial products to give soluble potassium salts:

$$Al_2O_3 \cdot K_2O \cdot 6SiO_2 + 4H_2SO_4 = Al_2(SO_4)_3 + K_2SO_4 + 6SiO_2 + 4H_2O$$

$$Al_2O_3 \cdot K_2O \cdot 6SiO_2 + Ca(HCO_3)_2 = Al_2O_3 \cdot CaO \cdot 6SiO_2 + 2KHCO_3$$

Potassium compounds present in the soil or in culture are assimilated by bacteria and fungi and stored away in the cell material. When the latter is decomposed, the potassium again becomes available. The potassium replaces in the soil the zeolitic bases Ca, Mg, and Na. The concentration of available potassium in the soil is thus controlled not only by the total concentration of the element, but also by the form in which it is present in the soil, by the degree of saturation of the soil zeolites, by the soil reaction, by the available organic matter, and finally by the activities of various groups of microorganisms.

The *Azotobacter* method has often been used to determine the concentration of available potassium in the soil, which was found to vary between 2 and 30 per cent of the total, depending upon the fertility of the soil.

Calcium and *magnesium* are also essential in the nutrition of soil microorganisms. In addition, they play important parts as buffering substances for neutralizing the organic and inorganic acids formed in the soil.

Iron may undergo in the soil a variety of transformations through the activities of microorganisms. It is essential for cell synthesis. Certain bacteria are capable of oxidizing ferrous salts to ferric compounds and of utilizing the energy liberated for the assimilation of carbon dioxide, in a manner similar to the action of nitrifying and sulfur-oxidizing bacteria, according to the following reaction:

$$2FeSO_4 + 3H_2O + 2CaCO_3 + O = 2Fe(OH)_3 + 2CaSO_4 + 2CO_2$$

Iron interacts with the humus compounds of the soil to give rise to iron humates. It is more readily available in this form to plants growing in alkali soils when it is not precipitated out as inorganic phosphate.

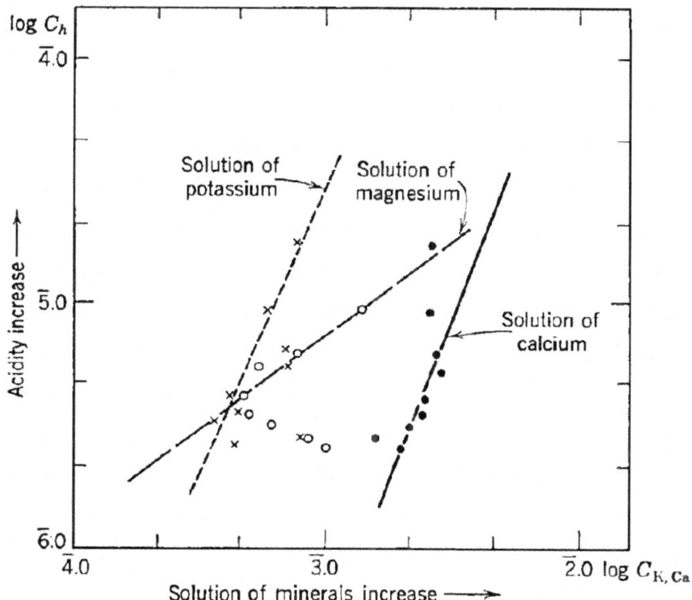

Fig. 97. Influence of acidity created by growth of *Azotobacter* on solution of calcium, magnesium, and potassium from the mineral biotite (from Wright).

The Role of Microorganisms in the Transformation of Rare or Trace Elements

Molybdenum, copper, zinc, cobalt, boron, and certain other elements act primarily as catalyzers for the activities of different soil organisms. Molybdenum is essential for the fixation of nitrogen by *Azotobacter*, a fact utilized for determining the concentration of available molybdenum in the soil. Boron is highly essential to the growth of legume bacteria, though high concentrations are injurious. Copper is essential for a variety of microbial processes, but high concentrations of this element, too, are injurious. Its concentration in the soil can be determined by the use of certain fungi and bacteria. Zinc and cobalt form essential constituents of certain enzyme and vitamin systems. Zinc also favors growths of fungi and represses spore formation.

Transformation of Arsenic and Selenium

Arsenic is widely distributed in nature. It is rarely found, however, in toxic amounts in the soil. Although arsenic has come into general use in various insecticides, only small amounts find their way into the soil. In some cases, however, as when arsenical dust is applied to combat certain insects, the amounts left in the soil may result in the stunting or dwarfing of the succeeding crop. This is true also of soil in coniferous nurseries where lead arsenate is used to combat insect larvae. Microbial activities in the soil may be affected unless this arsenic is rendered inactive or insoluble.

Certain soil fungi have the capacity to volatilize arsenical substances by reducing them to arsine. Cultures of such fungi readily give off the odor of arsine from arsenic-containing media. Members of the genus *Scopulariopsis* or *Penicillium brevicaule,* certain aspergilli, notably *A. sydowi, A. fumigatus,* and *A. ochraceus,* species of *Fusarium,* and various dematiaceae are responsible for these activities.

The transformation of selenium by microorganisms in the soil is of importance in connection with the selective absorption of this element by crop plants. Certain geological formations contain selenium. Plants grown in these areas accumulate the element in their cell material. Various bacteria and fungi have the capacity of volatilizing selenium, producing markedly offensive odors. These are readily detected in culture tubes and in pot experiments in the greenhouse. When selenium-containing plants undergo decomposition, the activities of the various microorganisms result in the production of strong odors. Microbiological activities in the soil render the selenium-containing substances available to green plants under conditions in which the plants are not otherwise able to obtain selenium. The organisms concerned in the volatilization of selenium include most of the arsenic fungi, especially the *Scopulariopsis brevicaule* group, and certain soil bacteria, notably *Pseudomonas fluorescens.*

Selenium compounds are subject to a variety of other bacterial activities, in the reduction of selenates to selenites and in the oxidation of elementary selenium.

Transformation of Other Elements

In addition to the above elements, a variety of others either are subject to transformation by microorganisms or play a part in their metabolism It is sufficient to mention hydrogen, oxygen, and silicon

Hydrogen enters into the composition of microbial cells in the form of water It forms an important part of the various organic and inorganic constituents of the microbial cell It is subject also to characteristic oxidation reactions by specific bacteria, considerable energy being liberated in this reaction.

$$H_2 + O = H_2O$$

Oxygen is highly important in all biological reactions, including both anaerobic (fermentation) and aerobic (respiration) processes It is important in cell synthesis and in organic matter decomposition Without it, no life would exist

Silicon is present abundantly in the mineral framework of the soil. It is found extensively in the cell substance of many soil organisms, notably the diatoms, certain protozoa, fungi, and bacteria Silicon undergoes various transformations as a result of the direct and indirect activities of microorganisms When plant residues are decomposed, silicon is liberated as silica and is allowed to accumulate Silica may be rendered soluble through the action of carbon dioxide and through the organic and inorganic acids produced by microorganisms This plays an essential role in rock weathering and soil formation

The action of microorganisms on silica has been little studied, even though a high silica content is found in the stems of various plants In the cereals the rigidity of the straw is largely due to silica An abundance of sodium nitrate added to the soil was found to depress the silica content of straw

Selected Bibliography

1 Fred, E B, and Haas, A R C, The etching of marble by roots in the presence of bacteria, *J Gen Physiol*, 1 631–638, 1919

2 Gerretsen, F C, Manganese deficiency of oats and its relation to soil bacteria, *Ann Botany*, N S, 1 207–230, 1937

3 Hopkins, C. G., and Whiting, A. L., Soil bacteria and phosphates, *Ill. Agr. Expt. Sta. Bull.* 190, 1916.

4 Jensen, C. A., Effect of decomposing organic matter on the solubility of certain inorganic constituents of the soil, *J. Agr. Research*, 9:253–268, 1917.

5 Joffe, J. S., The role of sulfur in agriculture, *N. J. Agr. Expt. Sta. Bull.* 374, 1922.

6 Joffe, J. S., and McLean, H. C., Alkali soil investigations, *Soil Sci.*, 17:395–409, 1924; 18:13–30, 133–149, 237–251, 1924.

7 Kelley, W. P., Effect of nitrifying bacteria on the solubility of tricalcium phosphate, *J. Agr. Research*, 12:671–683, 1918.

8 Lipman, J. G., McLean, H. C., and Lint, H. C., Sulfur oxidation in soils and its effect on the availability of mineral phosphates, *Soil Sci.*, 2:499–538, 1916.

9 Rudolfs, W., and Helbronner, A., Oxidation of zinc sulfide by microorganisms, *Soil Sci.*, 14:459–464, 1922; *Compt. rend.*, 174:1378–1380, 1922.

10 Teakle, L. J. H., Phosphate in the soil solution as affected by reaction and cation concentrations, *Soil Sci.*, 25:143–162, 1928.

11 Waksman, S. A., and Joffe, J. S., The chemistry of the oxidation of sulfur by microorganisms to sulfuric acid and the transformation of insoluble phosphates into soluble forms, *J. Biol. Chem.*, 50:35–45, 1922.

12 Waksman, S. A., and Starkey, R. L., On the growth and respiration of sulfur-oxidizing bacteria, *J. Gen. Physiol.*, 5:285–310, 1923.

13 Whiting, A. L., Inorganic substances, especially aluminum, in relation to the activities of soil organisms, *J. Am. Soc. Agron.*, 15:277–289, 1923.

14 Wright, D., Equilibrium studies with certain acids and minerals and their probable relation to the decomposition of minerals by bacteria, *Univ. Calif. Publ. Agr. Sci.*, 4:247–337, 1922.

· 11 ·

Higher Plants and Soil Microorganisms

The microorganisms of the soil exert a variety of effects on the growth of higher plants. Most of these effects are beneficial, but a few can be injurious. Higher plants, on the other hand, influence the growth of microorganisms in different ways, both stimulating and injurious. The mutual interrelations between the higher plants and the microorganisms may be summarized under the following groups of reactions:

1. Microorganisms favor the growth of higher plants by affecting the availability of various nutrient elements essential for plant growth, notably carbon as carbon dioxide, nitrogen, and phosphorus.

2. Microorganisms favor plant growth through the production of specific growth-stimulating or growth-regulating substances, such as auxins and phytohormones.

3. Certain groups of microorganisms form a variety of symbiotic relationships with higher plants.

4. Different microorganisms may compete with higher plants for some of the nutrients present in the soil.

5. Some microorganisms have injurious effects upon higher plants, either by directly attacking them as plant parasites, or by producing certain toxic substances.

6. Certain viruses, notably bacteriophages, have the capacity to attack useful bacteria and may thus prove to be indirectly injurious to plant growth.

The plants, in turn, supply microorganisms with various nutrients in the form of plant residues and excretion products. They also offer a favorable medium for the growth of various groups of microorganisms, either in the immediate vicinity of the roots or directly upon the roots. By the excretion of toxic products, plants may also exert various injurious effects upon the growth of microorganisms.

The Concept of Rhizosphere

In 1904 Hiltner introduced the concept of the "rhizosphere" to express the zone of increased microbiological activity immediately around the roots of higher plants. This term came, in time, to designate the intimate relations between soil microorganisms and the root systems of higher plants. More recently, two zones of influence of plant roots upon the microbiological population came to be recognized, the root surface and the rhizosphere, both being often grouped under the term "root region." Although considerable information has now accumulated concerning the mutual effects of these two biological systems, we are still lacking a clear idea of the importance of this phenomenon in the growth of higher plants.

These relationships may be considered midway between those of true symbiosis, on the one hand, as in the case of the root-nodule bacteria and the leguminous plants and of some of the mycorrhiza formations, and, on the other, of the phenomena of parasitism. Some of the relationships, like the utilization by the plants of the metabolic products of microorganisms, are no doubt highly beneficial, others, such as the possible curling and even more toxic effects of certain antibiotics on the leaves of some plants, may be injurious.

The rhizosphere can be studied conveniently by means of the contact slide method of Rossi and Cholodny. This consists in burying glass slides or cover glasses in contact with the plant roots, these slides or cover slips are removed at various intervals, stained, and examined microscopically. This method allows us to study the effect of root growth upon the development of specific microorganisms. Unfortunately, the larger forms like the nematodes and protozoa do not adhere to the slides. This method established the fact, however, that various bacteria, actinomycetes, and fungi find the root zone a highly favorable medium for their development.

The nature of the plant and its age and the nature of the soil and its treatment will influence considerably the nature and abundance of the organisms. Starkey showed that alfalfa roots had only a slight stimulating effect upon filamentous fungi, whereas eggplants had an appreciable effect; sugar beet and corn were least effective. Legumes exerted a particularly marked effect upon bacteria. Starkey was able to distinguish two sources of nutrients provided by roots: (*a*) soluble excretions, (*b*) sloughed-off dead root cells. Although root excretions and detritus are the principal cause of the rhizosphere effect,

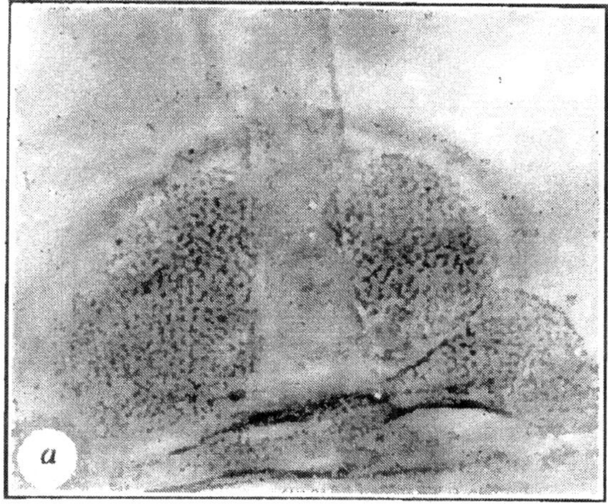

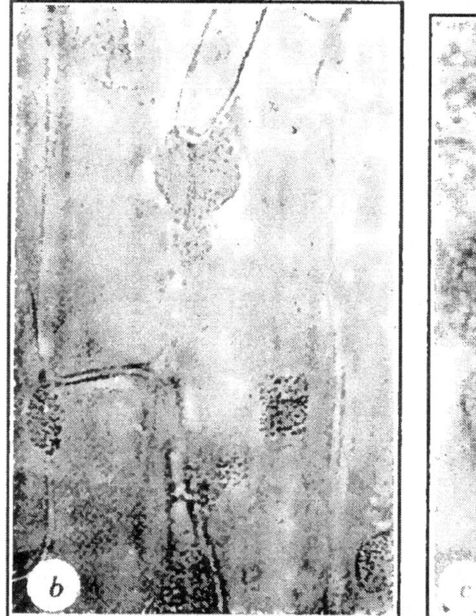

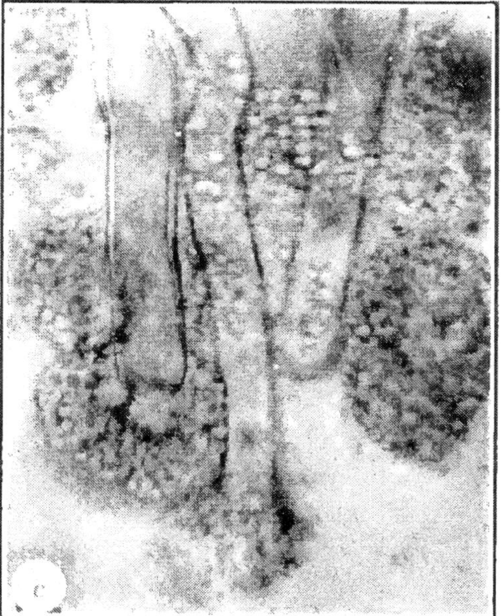

FIG. 98. Microorganisms photographed on roots processed with formalin-acetic-alcohol and lactophenol with acid fuchsin: *a*, optical section of a massive bacterial colony completely encircling the base of a lettuce root hair; *b*, bacterial colonies distributed over young maize root; *c*, relatively large spherical to ovoid cells of undetermined nature clustered on pineapple root hairs (from Linford).

other possible causes were considered, namely, lowering of the concentration of certain mineral nutrients in the soil due to absorption, partial desiccation of the soil by absorption of water, increase in soil carbonates following root excretion of carbon dioxide, contribution of microbial foods by sloughed-off root portions or excretions.

Thom and Humfeld found that alfalfa, rye, and vetch stimulated

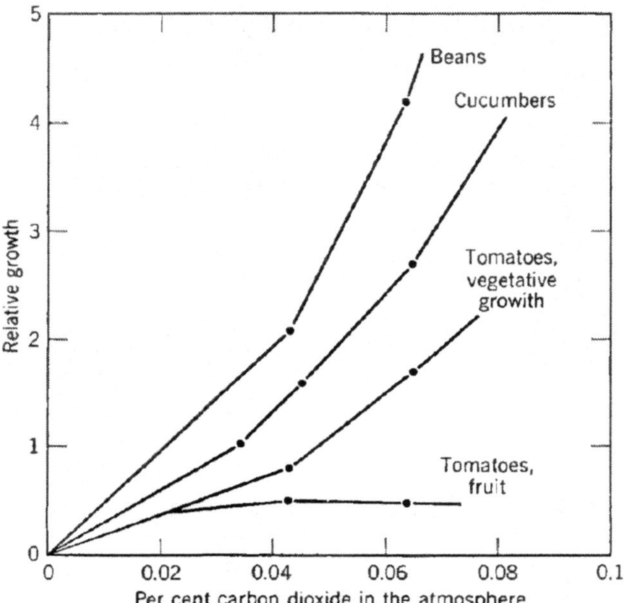

Fig. 99. Influence of concentration of carbon dioxide in the atmosphere on growth of plants (from Lundegårdh).

the bacteria more than the fungi, and the latter more than the actinomycetes. In other studies, the rhizosphere population of manured soil was reported to be much greater than that of unmanured soil, although the effect of manuring was much greater upon the nonrhizosphere population.

Garrett emphasized that it is necessary to distinguish between rhizosphere effects characteristic of living roots and the increase in the microflora of the root region in diseased roots and in healthy but senescent roots; the latter phenomena are associated with the initial stages of the microfloral succession occurring in moribund and dead roots, whether a pathogen is the primary colonizer or not. Thom and Humfeld observed a marked increase in numbers of root surface microorganisms in a root-rot-susceptible variety of tobacco grown in infective soil, as compared with the same variety of tobacco grown in healthy soil, similar effects for wheat were also demonstrated Starkey illustrated the intense development of microorganisms in and about senescent and dying roots or portions of roots

According to West and Lochhead, there exists in every soil investigated a balance between two general nutritional classes of bacteria On the one hand are bacteria capable of rapid growth on a single substrate, and in opposition to them are others dependent for their development on an ample supply of certain specific compounds. If conditions favor an increase in one group the incidence of the other must correspondingly fall These two workers demonstrated striking differences in distribution of these nutritional groups between rhizosphere and control soils· in the rhizosphere soil, the percentage incidence of organisms capable of growth on the basal medium alone declined, whereas that of organisms with more complex growth requirements increased The increase in percentage incidence of the group requiring growth factors was especially marked It was found later that a requirement for amino acids, and not for growth factors, was the most important characteristic of the rhizosphere population Fertile soil is usually well supplied with growth factors, and the growth factor heterotrophy does not, therefore necessarily limit growth of a microorganism in soil

Influence of Soil Microorganisms upon Plant Growth

Among the numerous soil processes that are carried out by microorganisms and that directly affect the growth of higher plants, the following may be analyzed in further detail

Microorganisms decompose the plant and animal residues added to the soil and the organic matter or humus in the soil itself. They thus liberate the nitrogen and minerals necessary for the growth of higher plants and produce considerable quantities of CO_2, which is essential for plant growth

Microorganisms oxidize and otherwise transform into forms readily available to plants various minerals either introduced into the soil, such as ammonium salts and sulfur or formed there in the decomposition of the organic residues

Microorganisms synthesize a variety of organic substances from the inorganic compounds in the soil and thus compete with higher plants for available nutrients, notably the nitrogen and the minerals

Since the soluble materials tend to leach from the soil, this process favors conservation of the nutrients in the soil in the absence of a growing crop.

Under certain conditions, microorganisms reduce various oxidized

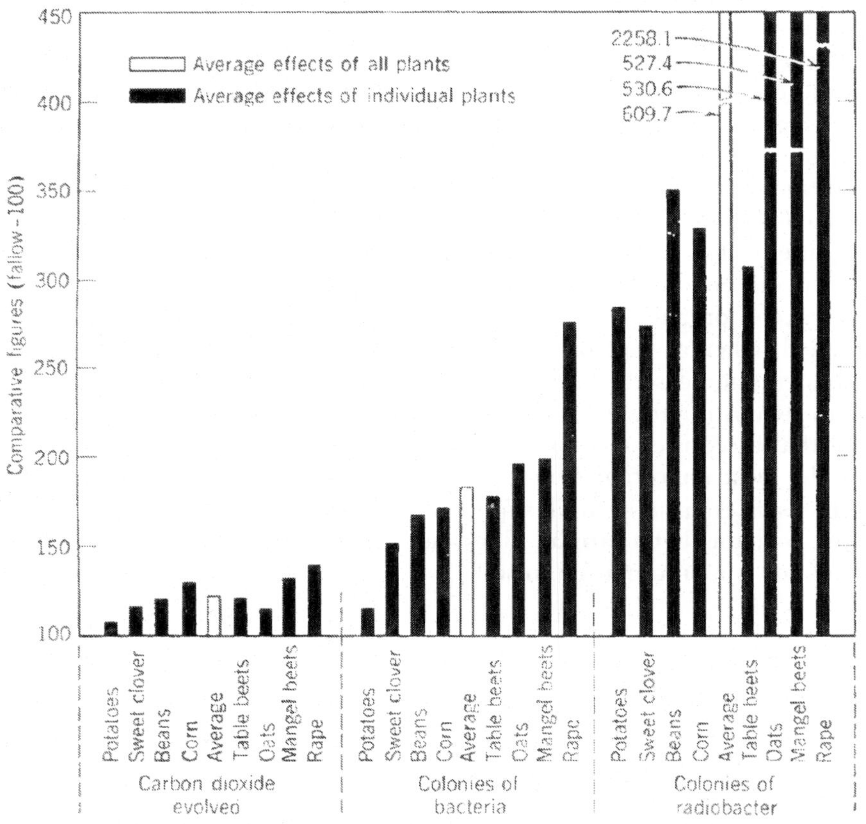

FIG. 100. Influence of plants upon the growth and activities of bacteria in soil (from Starkey).

substances, like sulfates and nitrates, to substances which may be toxic to higher plants or which result in losses of available elements.

Microorganisms enter into various associations with plants that are highly important in the growth of the plants. The growth of leguminous plants is directly affected by the symbiotic nodule-forming bacteria, making these plants independent of the supply of soil nitrogen. The growth of many trees and other plants depends largely upon the fungi that form mycorrhiza on their roots. This represents a phenomenon of symbiosis or of commensalism, whereby the fungi favor in some way the growth of the plants It has even been suggested that fungi play a role in tuberization in plants as well as in protein formation in certain seeds, as in legume association or mycorrhiza formation

Various groups of bacteria, fungi, and actinomycetes are capable of penetrating the roots of plants and developing there, or of living in close proximity, giving rise to a rhizosphere effect. It has been suggested that certain soil organisms are capable of bringing about a decided stimulation of the development of plant roots, either through the production of hormones or through some other mechanism

The formation by microorganisms of CO_2 and various organic acids results in a greater solubility of the soil minerals, particularly the carbonates and phosphates, and some of the zeolites The various inorganic acids produced as a result of bacterial action, including nitrous, nitric, and sulfuric acids, are also known to exert marked effects in the solubilization of minerals in the soil Since microorganisms influence the concentration of gases in the soil atmosphere notably oxygen and CO_2, root development of higher plants may thus be appreciably affected.

Gerretsen found that, in sterile sand cultures with $Ca_3(PO_4)_2$ as the source of phosphorus, more of this element was absorbed when the sand was inoculated with 1 per cent of garden soil Various experiments indicated that microorganisms play a highly important role in making phosphorus available to the plants When plant roots were placed on an agar medium containing tricalcium phosphate, the microorganisms developing about the roots caused the solution of the phosphate. The factors affecting this process are the nature and quantity of root excretions, presence and number of phosphate-dissolving microorganisms in the soil, chemical composition of the phosphate, and *p*H and temperature of the soil.

Microorganisms have often been reported to exert a highly favorable effect upon the germination of plant seeds and their subsequent growth This relation was even said to be symbiotic in nature More careful studies, however, established the fact that the normal microflora of the seed is essentially that derived from the soil, and that none of the organisms are specific for the seeds themselves Seeds and soil microorganisms are associated in an indirect way, but they are physiologically unrelated The growth and activities of the two do not depend on one another, although some studies seem to indicate that certain seeds, at least, may carry a typical microbiological population. More recent studies tend to indicate that microorganisms may produce substances which have a direct beneficial effect upon plant growth, due to production of hormones, auxins, or similar substances.

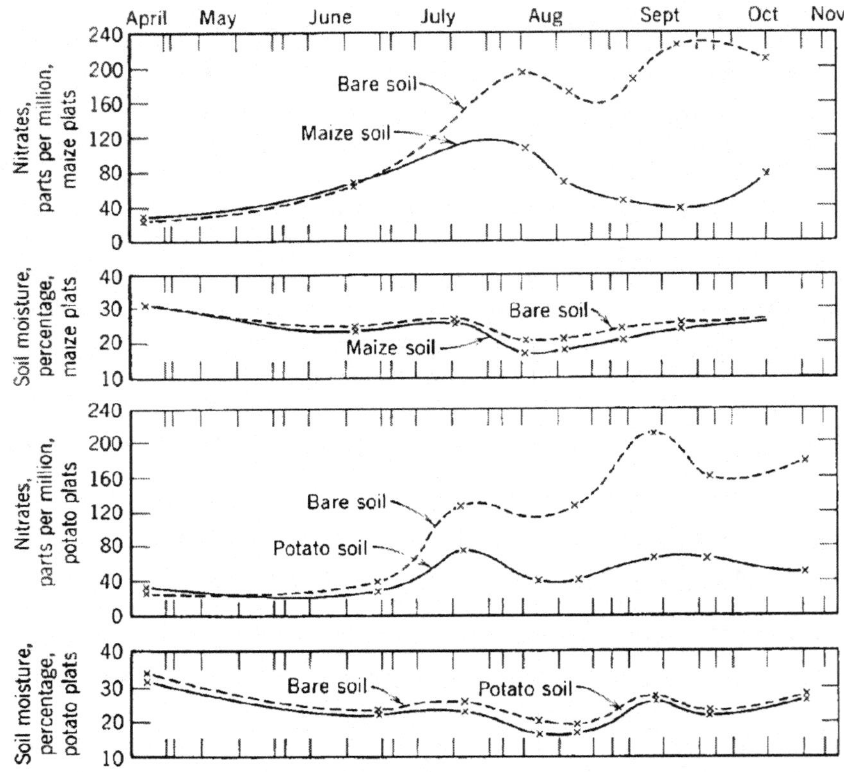

Fig. 101. Influence of crop upon nitrate content of the soil (from Lyon and Bizzell).

When a green manure crop is turned under and seeds are planted immediately, the seedlings may be injured, partly by the action of microorganisms, and partly by the presence in decomposing plant residues of certain substances toxic to seedlings or germinated seeds. As a result of the decomposition of the young plants, numerous fungi develop, some of which are destructive to seedlings. The rapid evolution of CO_2 and consumption of oxygen also produce conditions unfavorable to oxidation, a phenomenon essential for the germination of the seeds. When seeds are planted two weeks after the plowing of the green manure, there is no serious injury to germination

Various attempts have been made to explain the unproductiveness of certain soils by the presence of substances that are injurious to plant growth. These substances, designated as soil "toxins," were believed to be formed in the soil as a result of activities of certain groups of microorganisms The "toxin" theory of soil fertility was based upon the injurious action of such substances on the growth of higher plants. The treatment of soil by heat, volatile antiseptics, or simple liming was believed to overcome this injurious effect

Under certain conditions, the presence of decomposed organic residues and of microbial cell substance has a favorable effect upon the growth of plants and microorganisms Whether this is due to the production by microorganisms of plant-stimulating substances, in the nature of auxins, "auximones," or "phytohormones," or to the "buffering" or "poising" effect upon the oxidation-reducing potential of the medium, or to the production of stimulating substances, whatever their nature may be remains to be determined

Krassilnikov and his associates have shown that various bacteria and fungi may exert a highly stimulating or inhibiting effect upon the growth of isolated roots of plants, depending on the nature of the organism and of the plant The inhibitory action may be due to competition for nutrients, to injurious action of high concentrations of growth-stimulating substances, or to the physical effect of bacterial slimes in preventing the roots from obtaining sufficient nutrients.

Influence of Plants upon Microorganisms

The growing plant exerts a variety of influences upon the activities of the microorganisms in the soil These can be briefly summarized as follows.

1 Plants secrete soluble organic and inorganic compounds that offer a favorable medium for the growth of microorganisms Among the chemically defined products, it is sufficient to mention formic, oxalic, and malic acids, certain reducing and nonreducing sugars, phosphatides, and various nitrogenous compounds All these favor the growth of many soil fungi and bacteria

2. Plants supply large amounts of energy for the growth of microorganisms, in the form of dead roots and root hairs, root cap cells, epidermal cells, and other waste products of plants

3 Through their roots, growing plants continuously remove from the soil various soluble minerals, including nitrates, phosphates, and

potassium salts. This results in a change in the composition of the soil solution and in a modification of the activities of microorganisms.

4. Plants excrete considerable CO_2 into the soil. This tends to change the reaction of the soil. It also increases the solubility of certain inorganic soil constituents and changes the composition of the soil atmosphere.

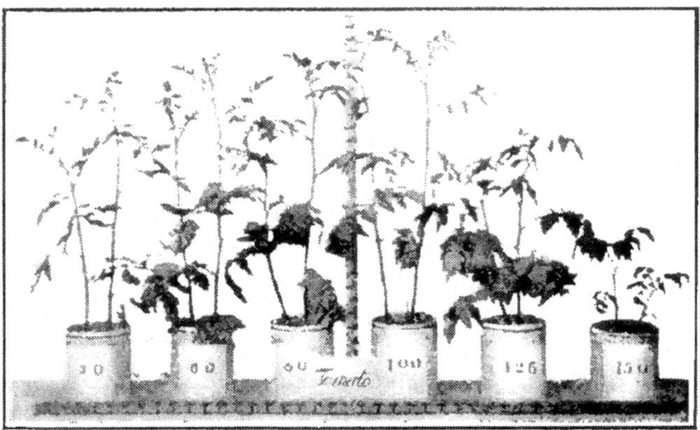

FIG. 102. Influence of partial sterilization by heat upon growth of tomatoes. The soils in the pots from left to right were heated as follows before planting: 30°C, 60°C, 80°C, 100°C, 125°C, 150°C for 2 hours (from Pickering).

5. Plants remove from the soil considerable moisture, thus exerting an injurious influence upon the growth of microorganisms.

6. Plants modify the structure of the soil and thereby produce a medium that is more favorable for the development of microorganisms.

7. Plants remove the nitrates from the soil, leaving the bases behind and thereby affecting the reaction of the soil.

To measure the influence of plants upon microbiological activities in the soil, certain well-defined procedures may be utilized. These comprise some of the common measures of the microbiological state of the soil, such as (*a*) the numbers of microorganisms, (*b*) nitrate accumulation or nitrifying capacity of the soil, (*c*) oxidizing power of the soil as expressed in terms of oxygen absorption or CO_2 production, (*d*) a variety of other biological activities. It is often difficult to differentiate between the direct influence of the growing plant and the influence of the plant products.

Among the bacteria which are particularly influenced by growing plants, the *Radiobacter* group occupies a prominent place. A crystal violet medium is used for plating out the soil. The dye inhibits the growth of the actinomycetes and the Gram-positive bacteria, but not of the Gram-negative bacteria. *Radiobacter* colonies are raised, smooth, glistening, with opaque centers and transparent edges. When legumes are grown in a given soil, there is an increase in the number of *Radiobacter* in that soil. The greatest numbers of this group of organisms are found close to the plant, but frequently none at all one foot away from the plant. Cowpeas, field peas, vetch, and soybeans stimulate these bacteria, the increase being accompanied by an increase in the consumption of nitrates and in the evolution of CO_2.

When a single type of plant is continuously grown in a soil, it leaves residues that may result in a change in the chemical composition of the soil, which in turn influences the bacterial population. Some kinds of plant species favor certain types of bacteria and inhibit others, and thus bring about a change in the bacterial equilibrium in the soil. The new bacterial population produces a change in the composition of the soil which may subsequently affect plant growth, whereby some plant species are favored and others are retarded. The continuous growth of a single type of plant, such as wheat, flax, or clover, will bring about the development of fungi pathogenic to this plant, making the soil "sick" for the particular plant.

Starkey has shown that higher plants may affect some groups of microorganisms differently from other groups, the extent of the influence of various plants upon different organisms may vary. The greatest increase appears to be brought about in the *Radiobacter* group, although some striking effects may be observed upon the general bacterial population. Potato increased the numbers of bacteria only to a slight extent, whereas rape produced some striking changes. The influence of various plants upon the soil population as measured by the number of *Radiobacter* per gram of soil depends upon the stages of growth of the plant (Table 56). Slight effects are observed in the early stages. The maximum occurs when plants reach considerable size. Because of their longer growing period, biennials show a much more prolonged effect upon the soil organisms than do annuals. The effect of higher plants upon the microbiological population of the soil may be an important factor in bringing about the seasonal fluctuations of microorganisms.

Neller measured the total CO_2 liberated from oxidation processes taking place in the soil during plant growth. He found much more

TABLE 56 INFLUENCE OF DEVELOPMENT OF HIGHER PLANTS UPON ABUNDANCE OF *Radiobacter* (from Starkey)

Plant	Number of *Radiobacter*, thousands per gram of soil					
	44 Days	63 Days	86 Days	138 Days	173 Days	Average of All Periods
Fallow	540	920	900	320	420	620
Oats	780	7,800	6,320	860	670	3,290
Corn	680	2 020	3,180	3 340	960	2 040
Beans	1,980	2,540	4,400	360	1,640	2,180
Potatoes	780	980	5,340	1,200	500	1,760
Table beets	840	1,540	3,560	2,180	1 380	1,900
Mangel beets	1,400	6,400	3,160	4 000	1,400	3,270
Rape	46,600	8,600	6 360	5,120	3,640	14,060
Sweet clover *	1,140	2,000	1,900	620	2,820	1,700

* For the sweet clover, the sampling periods were 25, 44, 67, 119, and 154 days

rapid oxidation in a soil in which plants were growing than in the corresponding uncropped soil kept under the same conditions of moisture, aeration, and temperature. The growing roots exerted a direct influence upon the decomposition of the organic matter in the soil This also brought about a greater liberation of available plant nutrients and thus stimulated further plant growth Neller suggested that a symbiotic relationship exists between the growing plant and the oxidizing organisms in the soil The influence of nature of crop upon the numbers of bacteria and evolution of CO_2 from soil is illustrated in Table 57

TABLE 57 INFLUENCE OF PLANT UPON THE NUMBERS OF BACTERIA AND EVOLUTION OF CO_2 (from Neller)

Plant	Bacteria per Gram Soil	Soil Reaction	CO_2 Produced by 1 Kg Soil in 24 Hours at 20°C
	millions	pH	*mg*
Triticum vulgare	49	6 75	69 4
Secale cereale	42	6 44	68 2
Avena sativa	45	6 42	79 0
Beta vulgaris	78	6 89	74 3
Medicago sativa	120	6 89	86 8
Trifolium pratense		6 66	82 4

According to Starkey, the evolution of CO_2 is greater from soils in which plants are growing than in unplanted soil. The course of formation of the CO_2 during the growing season is different for each of the plants There is a parallel influence of the plants on the formation of CO_2 and changes in the bacterial population in the soil. This is expressed by a slight effect in the early stages of growth of the plants, and by a greater effect with advance in vegetative development and fruiting, the effect becomes less when the plants begin to degenerate and die. The oxidation of the soil nitrogen to nitrate was affected in a somewhat similar manner

The fact that the roots of plants are surrounded by a film of bacteria actively respiring was taken as explaining the formation of CO_2 about the roots

Grass growing in the vicinity of trees is usually observed to have a harmful effect upon the trees This was explained by the fact that the surface roots of the trees are deprived of combined nitrogen by the grass roots Furthermore, by producing a soil atmosphere rich in CO_2, the grass causes the surface roots to grow down and thus suffer from lack of oxygen It has frequently been suggested that the injurious effect is due to the formation of a toxin by the grass, however, no evidence of this has been presented.

The root residues, in the form of sloughed-off portions and finer rootlets, may influence greatly the nature of the population developing in their neighborhood This is likewise true of the excretion products of the plants Plants also produce a variety of gases which greatly influence the nature of the organisms developing in the particular area Further evidence of the marked influence of growing plants on the microbiological population of the soil is found in the fact that a given soil decomposes cellulose with varying rapidity according to the nature of the plants that have been growing in it The nature of the organisms taking part in the decomposition of cellulose in a given soil varies with the plants grown in the soil.

It thus seems to be definitely established now that larger numbers of microorganisms find a more favorable condition for their development in close proximity to plant roots than at a distance Nitrogen-fixing and cellulose-decomposing bacteria are particularly prominent This may be because the plants excrete or leave in the form of residues a certain amount of available energy, this would favor the development of the nitrogen-fixing organisms There is no evidence, however, that fixation of nitrogen is increased around the roots. The cellulose-rich residues would naturally favor the development of cellulose-decomposing bacteria and fungi in the soil. The nature of these organisms depends upon the nature of the residues, the nature of the soil, and the environmental conditions.

BACIERIZATION

The term "bacterization" has been applied to soil and seed inoculation with bacteria and other microorganisms either to stimulate plant growth or to combat the attack on plants by various pathogenic fungi and bacteria. There is no doubt of the favorable effect upon the growth of leguminous plants of seed or soil inoculation when properly adapted cultures are used. This is true also of certain mycorrhiza fungi upon nursery plants, especially on trees not previously grown in a given area. The favorable effect, however, upon wheat or other cereal plants or upon sugar beets of inoculation with *Azotobacter* or other bacteria has not been established. In summarizing these results, Jensen questioned the premise of nitrogen fixation by *Azotobacter*, although he was inclined to accept the favorable effect of growth factors elaborated by bacteria. Allison, as well, submitted to severe criticism the value of the experiments on the use of *Azotobacter* as a seed inoculant. He examined in detail the claims made for the beneficial effects of such inoculation, that (*a*) nitrogen is fixed by the bacteria living in the rhizosphere, largely on the root excretions, (*b*) the added bacteria protect the plants against pathogenic microorganisms either by discouraging their growth or by destroying them, (*c*) the bacteria stimulate plant growth through the production of hormones, auxins, vitamins, and other growth accelerators or regulators. The last claim was considered the only plausible one that may be of any significance as regards seed inoculation.

Selected Bibliography

1 Allison, F. E., *Azotobacter* inoculation of crops. I. Historical, *Soil Sci.*, 64:413–429, 1947.

2 Clark, F. E., Soil microorganisms and plant roots, *Advances in Agron.*, 1:241–288, 1949.

3 Crafts, A. S., Movement of viruses, auxins, and chemical indicators in plants, *Botan. Rev.*, 5:471–504, 1939.

4 Garrett, S. D., Ecology of the root-inhabiting fungi, *Biol. Revs.*, 25:220–254, 1950.

5 Gerretsen, F. C., The influence of microorganisms on the phosphate intake by the plant, *Plant and Soil*, 1:51–81, 1948.

6 Gustafson, F. G, Inducement of fruit development by growth-promoting chemicals, *Proc Natl Acad Sci*, 22 628-636, 1936

7 Harley, J L, Mycorrhiza and soil ecology, *Biol Revs*, 23 127–158, 1948

8 Jensen, H L, Bacterial treatment of non-leguminous seeds on agricultural practice, *Austral J. Sci*, 4.117–120, 1942

9 Katznelson, H, Lochhead, A G, and Timonin, M I, Soil microorganisms and the rhizosphere, *Botan Rev*, 14 543–587, 1948

10 Linford, M B, Methods of observing soil flora and fauna associated with roots, *Soil Sci*, 53 93–103, 1942

11 Lipman, J G, A method for the study of soil fertility problems, *J Agr Sci*, 3 297–300, 1909

12 Lochhead, A G, and Thexton, R H, Qualitative studies of soil microorganisms VII The "rhizosphere effect" in relation to the amino acid nutrition of bacteria, *Can J Research*, C, 25 20–26, 1947

13 Neller, J R, The influence of growing plants upon oxidation processes in the soil, *Soil Sci*, 13 139–159, 1922

14 Nicol, H, *Plant Growth Substances*, Chemical Publishing Co, New York, 2nd Ed, 1941

15 Parker-Rhodes, A F, Preliminary experiments on the estimation of traces of heteroauxin in soils, *J Agr Sci*, 30 654–671, 1940

16 Schreiner, O, and Skinner, J J, Nitrogenous soil constituents and their bearing on soil fertility, *U S Dept Agr Bur Soils Bull* 87, 1912

17 Starkey, R L, Some influences of the development of higher plants upon the microorganisms in the soil VI Microscopic examination of the rhizosphere, *Soil Sci*, 45 207–249, 1938

18 West, P M, and Lochhead, A G, Qualitative studies of soil microorganisms IV The rhizosphere in relation to the nutritive requirements of soil bacteria, *Can J Research*, C, 18 129–135, 1940, *Soil Sci*, 50·409–420, 1940

19 West, P M, and Wilson, P W, Biotin = co-enzyme R as a growth stimulant for the root-nodule bacteria, *Enzymologia*, 8 152–162, 1940

20 Wilson, J K, and Lyon, T L, The growth of certain microorganisms in planted and in unplanted soil, *N Y (Cornell) Univ Agr Expt Sta Mem* 103, 1926

· 12 ·

Associative and Antagonistic Effects of Soil Microorganisms

Microorganisms live in the soil, not in the form of pure cultures, but as complex populations. Each particle of soil, no matter how small, contains more than one type of organism. Many of these organisms depend upon one another for direct and indirect nutrients, some compete with one another for energy sources and for the elements and compounds used as nutrients. This results in the formation of numerous associations among the soil microorganisms in which various relationships exist, some favorable to one another and others injurious. The abundance, in the complex soil population, of each type of organism, the rate of its multiplication, and its physiological activities are greatly influenced by the presence and abundance of other organisms.

What Is a Soil Microbiological Population?

The quantitative and qualitative composition of a complex population is controlled by the nature and availability of the nutrients, the physical, chemical, and biological nature of the habitat, and the environmental conditions, especially aeration, temperature, and moisture supply. This is also true of the soil microbiological populations (Table 58). The examination by suitable methods of a sandy or clay soil, which is as free from organic materials as possible, will reveal a microbiological population that is very limited in numbers and types. Snow, for example, made a study of the abundance of microorganisms in wind-blown soils. She found as few as 17,000 organisms per gram of soil containing about 0.3 per cent organic matter, these organisms were largely bacteria, together with some (10–15 per cent) actinomycetes and a few (0.56–2.0 per cent) fungi. Another soil with 0.45 per cent organic matter gave, on the average,

59,666 organisms per gram, with only 0.61 per cent actinomycetes and 0.27 per cent fungi. These organisms even in such low numbers, were found to be made up of various distinct types, as brought out by differences in pigmentation, staining reactions, and spore formation. The limited quantity of nutrients brought in by subterranean drainage or rainfall, by localized growth of a plant or an animal, will result in formation and liberation of small amounts of nutrients for keeping the microbial population alive. The organisms capable of living in this environment find comparatively little competition.

TABLE 58. INFLUENCE OF GROWING PLANTS ON NUMBER OF MICROORGANISMS IN SOIL (from Starkey)

Plant	Sample of Soil Taken	Microorganisms Found *		
		Bacteria	Actinomycetes	Fungi
Rye	Near roots	28,600	4,400	216
	Away from roots	13,200	3,200	162
Corn	Near roots	41,000	13,400	178
	Away from roots	24,300	8,800	134
Sugar beet	Near roots	57,800	15,000	222
	Away from roots	32,100	12,200	176
Alfalfa	Near roots	93,800	9,000	268
	Away from roots	17,800	3,300	254

* In thousands per gram of soil.

Among these organisms, the autotrophic bacteria are of prime importance. These are highly specialized forms, capable of using as sources of energy the traces of ammonia brought down by the rain or the traces of hydrogen and methane found in the atmosphere. Although very little fixed nitrogen is available to the autotrophic bacteria, the traces produced by atmospheric discharges and brought down by the rainfall will suffice, since energy is the all-important limiting factor, and nitrogen-fixing bacteria are hardly able to exist under these conditions until specialized higher plants become established or complex forms of energy are made available. Microbial life is thus at a minimum under these conditions and competition is limited, since the carbon source required for cell synthesis, CO_2, is all-abundant. Only upon death of the microorganisms, when they become themselves nutrients for other organisms, does competition set in. A certain amount of association is possible, as when nitrate-forming bacteria utilize the nitrite produced by ammonia-oxidizing forms.

The next step in the development of a microbial population comes when organic materials are made available. To simplify the reactions involved, it is sufficient to consider the effect of the various chemical constituents of plant life upon the growth of a complex population. Since 80–99 per cent of the organic matter in plant materials is made up of carbohydrates and lignins, the effect is a group of important reactions. One may take, for illustration, three groups of the non-nitrogenous constituents, the glucose, the cellulose, and the lignin.

The simple carbohydrate can be attacked by many types of organisms. When the nitrogen supply is low, only organisms capable of fixing nitrogen of the atmosphere will be able to grow and utilize glucose. Under these conditions there is very little competition, since the two groups of bacteria capable of bringing this process about, in the absence of the green plant, are aerobic forms (*Azotobacter*) and anaerobic types (*Clostridium*). These can only supplement one another, the first assisting the second by consuming the oxygen, and the second helping the first by breaking down its waste products. Thus it has been shown that collaboration of these two groups of organisms leads to greater fixation of nitrogen.

The cellulose leads to the development of totally different groups of organisms, since it cannot be utilized directly by nitrogen-fixing bacteria. Its decomposition is, therefore, controlled entirely by the amount of available nitrogen. The abundance and nature of the nitrogen and the nature of the environment influence greatly the nature of the organisms developing at the expense of the cellulose. A variety of associative and competitive phenomena may result. The first is manifested when the cellulose is broken down by some organisms to dextrin-like compounds or to simple carbohydrates. These are transformed by other organisms to organic acids, which are finally broken down by still other organisms to CO_2 and water or to CO_2 and methane. Competitive processes result when the cellulose is attacked by bacteria, lower or higher fungi, actinomycetes, or even invertebrate animals. Whether one group or another becomes dominant depends on the reaction of the soil, nature and amount of available nitrogen, oxygen supply, and temperature (Table 59).

Finally, lignin presents a different problem in regard to microbial development. This substance, the chemical nature of which is still in dispute, is more resistant to decomposition than most other organic compounds synthesized by plant or by animal life. Although it is known that various fungi, such as certain basidiomycetes, certain actinomycetes, and certain bacteria, are capable of decomposing lignin, very little is known concerning the mechanism of its breakdown. This is due primarily to the inability of most organisms to attack isolated lignin, which has apparently been changed chemically in the process of its isolation, and to the changing nature of lignin with the growth of the plant and in different types of plants

TABLE 59 DECOMPOSITION OF ALFALFA BY PURE AND MIXED CULTURES OF MICROORGANISMS

Organism	Total Alfalfa Decomposed	Hemicelluloses Decomposed	Cellulose Decomposed	NH_3-N Produced
	per cent	*per cent*	*per cent*	*mg*
Trichoderma	9.3	4.7	0	61
Rhizopus	6.6	12.8	2.9	53
Trichoderma + *Rhizopus*	13.7	22.6	10.6	63
Trichoderma + *Cunninghamella*	15.0	15.4	5.7	47
Trichoderma + *Ps fluorescens*	10.5	14.5	6.4	32
Streptomyces 3065	16.6	43.0	23.2	52
Trichoderma + *Streptomyces* 3065	12.5	14.6	4.8	56
Soil infusion	28.4	40.9	50.8	21

These few illustrations will suffice to emphasize the fact that the composition of a microbiological population is influenced by the composition of the plant residues and by the environmental factors It leaves considerable room for numerous types of interrelationships among the organisms making up this population

The general interrelationships among living systems, as influenced by environment and available foods, are frequently expressed by the terms "biotic populations," "ecologic relationships," and "struggle for existence." In most instances, only scanty consideration has thus been given to microbial populations This is due, on the one hand, to the dominant interest that has centered upon higher forms of life, and, on the other, to the fact that most knowledge gained from the study and utilization of microorganisms, especially their physiological activities, has been derived largely from pure cultures rather than mixed populations Although the microbiological population of soils and of water basins offers unusual opportunities for the study of such relationships, the student of these tried to steer clear of the complicated problems thus involved, and concerned himself as much as possible with single organisms and with specific processes brought about by them The problem was considered nearly solved, once a pure culture was obtained. On the other hand, the investigator who worked with the soil population as a whole usually polluted it to such an extent by the addition of an excess of a single type of material that any natural relationship among microorganisms was thereby erased The information gained from studies of "pure" and "mixed" cultures was patched together to fit the complex natural processes occurring in soils or in water basins, with the result that often a "crazy quilt" arrangement resulted rather than a clear picture of the natural processes This was due entirely to failure to recognize that many of the processes carried out by microorganisms, and often the very existence of these organisms, are greatly modified in the natural environment as compared with their growth in pure cultures and in the test tube

The study of the associative and antagonistic interrelationships among microorganisms, especially the marked interest that has recently been centered upon the production by these organisms of antibiotic substances, has resulted in the accumulation of many facts that permit more systematic generalization dealing with the subject under consideration

Associative Effects

The associative influences among microorganisms living in the soil are numerous They may be classified briefly as follows:

1. Effect of aerobic organisms upon the growth of anaerobes The aerobes consume the free oxygen in the soil atmosphere, thus creating conditions that are favorable for the growth of organisms not requiring oxygen, the anaerobes

2. Preparation of an essential nutrient or substrate by one organism for the growth of another. This type of relationship is very common in the soil Nitrite-forming bacteria oxidize ammonia to nitrite, thus producing a substrate which is required for the activities of the nitrate-forming bacteria, since the latter are not able to use any other source of energy. Proteolytic bacteria hydrolyze proteins to amino acids, thereby producing substances which are essential for the activities of peptolytic bacteria or of organisms that cannot attack native proteins. Cellulose-decomposing bacteria give rise to organic acids and other intermediary products essential for the activities of various organisms which themselves cannot attack cellulose.

3. Production by certain organisms of specific substances which are essential for the growth of other organisms These are frequently designated as growth-promoting substances or as vitamins

4. Utilization and destruction by various microorganisms of the metabolic waste products of other organisms In this process, the former organisms create conditions which are favorable for the continued growth of the latter.

5. Dependence of certain organisms upon others for carrying out life activities, this association becomes one of symbiosis. Miscellaneous associative relationships exist among microorganisms, for example, the living together of algae and *Azotobacter*, the former synthesizing carbon compounds and the latter fixing nitrogen. This is true of associations of leguminous plants with root-nodule bacteria, of coniferous trees and other higher plants with mycorrhiza fungi, of insects with fungi and bacteria, in the association between an insect and an actinomyces, the latter provides some growth substance for the former.

Antagonistic Effects

Antagonistic interrelationships are also very common among members of the soil population, whereby one organism, directly or indirectly, affects injuriously the activities of another organism. These interrelationships may also be briefly summarized

1. Competition among microorganisms for available nutrients. This may occur between organisms belonging to the same group, as between two types of bacteria, or between organisms belonging to different groups, as between bacteria and fungi

2 Creation by one organism of conditions which are unfavorable for the growth of another, as by changing the reaction of the medium to acid, by the production of inorganic (nitric, sulfuric) or organic (citric, oxalic, fumaric, butyric, lactic) acids

3 Production by one organism of specific substances which are injurious to growth of other organisms (Table 60). Here belong such well-defined compounds as alcohols and quinones, as well as the numerous antibiotics These substances are frequently classified as soil toxins, the exact nature of most of which still remains undefined (Table 61)

4 Direct parasitism of one organism upon another. Here belong the various effects of fungi upon bacteria, of bacteria upon fungi, of fungi and nematodes upon insect larvae One of the significant as-

pects of parasitism among soil microorganisms is the attack of various bacteria and fungi upon plant-parasitic insects and nematodes.

5. Predaceous effects, or the feeding of one organism upon an-

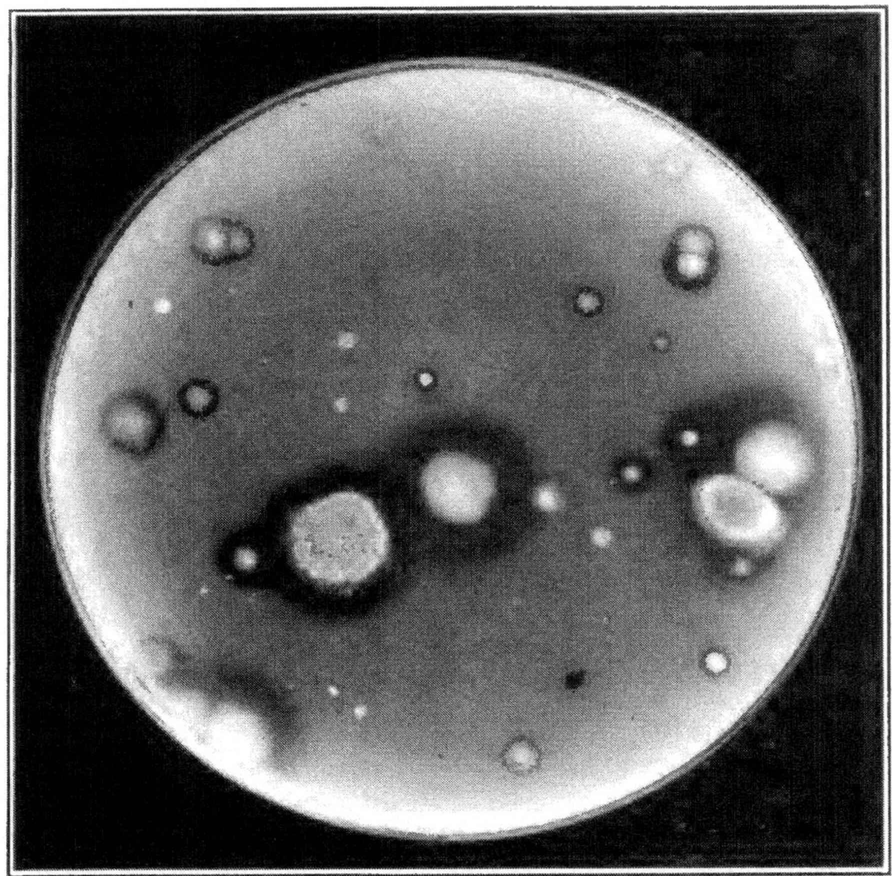

FIG. 103. Development of antagonistic fungi on bacterial-agar plate (from Waksman and Horning).

other, as in the consumption of bacteria by protozoa, of fungi by insects, of nematodes by one another.

Many organisms are capable of producing substances that are injurious to their own development (*isoantagonistic*) or to the growth of other organisms in close proximity (*heteroantagonistic*). This is largely the reason why certain fungi and bacteria are capable of growing in virtually pure cultures even in a nonsterile environment. It is sufficient to cite the production of lactic and butyric acids by

TABLE 60. ANTAGONISTIC ACTION OF *Pseudomonas fluorescens* UPON VARIOUS MICROORGANISMS (from Lewis)

Organism	Percentage of Aged Medium in the Agar									
	0.5	1.0	2.5	5.0	10	15	20	30	40	50
B. cereus	—	—	+							
B. mycoides	—	—	+							
B. anthracis	—	+								
B. vulgatus	—	—	+							
B. subtilis	—	—	+							
B. megatherium	—	+								
R. cinnebareus	—	+								
R. roseus	—	—	+							
M. flavus	—	—	—	+						
N. catarrhalis	—	—	—	+						
Ps. aeruginosa	—	—	—	—	—	—	—	—	—	—
Ps. fluorescens	—	—	—	—	—	—	—	—	—	—
S. lutea	—	—	—	+						
S. marcescens	—	—	—	—	—	+				
S. albus	—	—	+							
S. aureus	—	—	—	+						
S. citreus	—	—	+							
K. pneumoniae	—	—	—	+						
V. comma	—	+								
Ch. violaceum	—	+								
E. typhi	—	—	+							
Sh. paradysenteriae	—	—	+							
S. enteritidis	—	—	—	+						
S. suipestifer	—	—	—	+						
S. pullorum	—	—	—	+						
E. coli	—	—	—	—	—	—	+			
A. aerogenes	—	—	—	—	—	—	+			
Ph. bowlesii	—	—	+							
Sac. marianus	—	—	—	—	—	—	—	—	—	—
Sac. ellipsoideus	—	—	—	—	—	—	—	+		
Sac. pastorianus	—	—	—	—	—	—	—	—	+	
Zygosac. priorianus	—	—	—	—	—	—	—	+		
Torula sphaerica	—	—	—	—	—	—	—	—	—	—
A. niger	—	—	—	—	—	—	—	—	—	—

+ denotes complete inhibition.

TABLE 61. SURVIVAL OF *Escherichia coli* IN SOIL AND DEVELOPMENT OF ANTAGONISTS (from Waksman and Woodruff)

Numbers of organisms in thousands per gram dry soil.

Incubation of Soil	Number of Enrichments with *E. coli*	*E. coli* Cells	Total Number of Bacteria	Number of Antagonists *
days				
0	..	Few	9,100 †	.
5	1	6,800	......	.
33	5	130	......	....
127	11	0	40,000	5,700

* An antagonistic colony is one surrounded by a halo of dissolved *E. coli* cells on the plate.

† Control soil, not receiving any enrichments.

the corresponding bacteria; of citric, oxalic, and gluconic acids by *Aspergillus niger;* of fumaric and lactic acid by *Rhizopus nigricans;* of a number of alcohols by various yeasts, bacteria, and fungi; and of certain phenols and quinones by various fungi. These substances, as well as a great number of other compounds which, for lack of

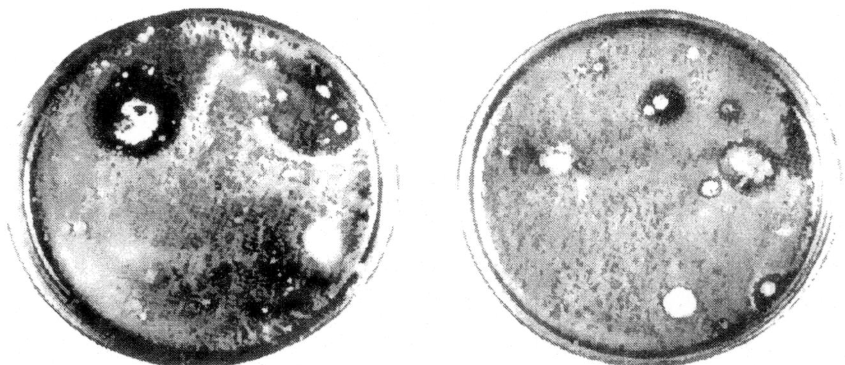

FIG. 104. Bacterial plates made from soil, showing clear zones surrounding colonies of antagonistic organisms (from Stokes and Woodward).

more exact information, are usually designated as "lethal," "toxic," or "growth-inhibiting" compounds, and more recently as "antibiotics," have frequently been looked upon as protective metabolic products formed by microorganisms in "their struggle for existence." Some may play a highly significant part in the life of many organisms; the role of others is still a matter of speculation.

Microbial Equilibrium

The numerous microorganisms inhabiting the soil are living largely in a state of mutual equilibrium. Any modification of this equilibrium results in a number of changes in the nature and abundance of the microbiological population The numerous interrelationships among these organisms permit not only an understanding of their specific ecological nature under a certain set of conditions, but also a better understanding of the metabolic products resulting from the activities of this population Since the complex nature of this population does not permit its treatment as a whole, certain relationships among different organisms may be isolated and examined separately. Attention may be directed, for example, to the relations between the non-spore-forming bacteria in the soil and the spore-formers, of the actinomycetes and the bacteria, of some fungi and other fungi, of bacteria and fungi, of nonpathogenic organisms and pathogens, and of protozoa and bacteria.

Conn and Bright found that, when *Bacillus cereus* and *Pseudomonas fluorescens* were inoculated simultaneously into sterile manured soil, the former failed to develop, whereas the latter grew abundantly Lewis reported that *Ps. fluorescens* repressed the growth of *B. mycoides* and of other spore-forming bacteria and micrococci, however, *Aerobacter aerogenes* and *Serratia marcescens* were highly resistant; fungi were not inhibited; yeasts were inhibited only to a limited extent, and actinomycetes were more sensitive. Lewis also confirmed results of other investigators that the production of bactericidal and inhibitory substances by bacteria depends on the amount of available oxygen; these substances were found to be thermostable and were adsorbed by charcoal and by soil

Greig-Smith demonstrated that various actinomycetes are capable of producing substances toxic to bacteria The fact that actinomycetes grow rather slowly suggested to him the possibility that they comprise the factor limiting bacterial development in the soil. Certain actinomycetes were later found to be antagonistic to *S. pyogenes* and to spore-forming bacteria, but not to *Ps aeruginosa* The latter, because of its capacity to produce pyocyanase, was believed to be capable of vaccinating the substrate against the growth of other microorganisms.

The antagonistic activities of microorganisms have received particular attention as potential agents for suppressing the growth and even for destroying bacteria and other microorganisms capable of producing human and animal diseases, and possibly also fungi and bacteria causing plant diseases. A number of theories have been proposed at various times in an effort to explain the mechanism of

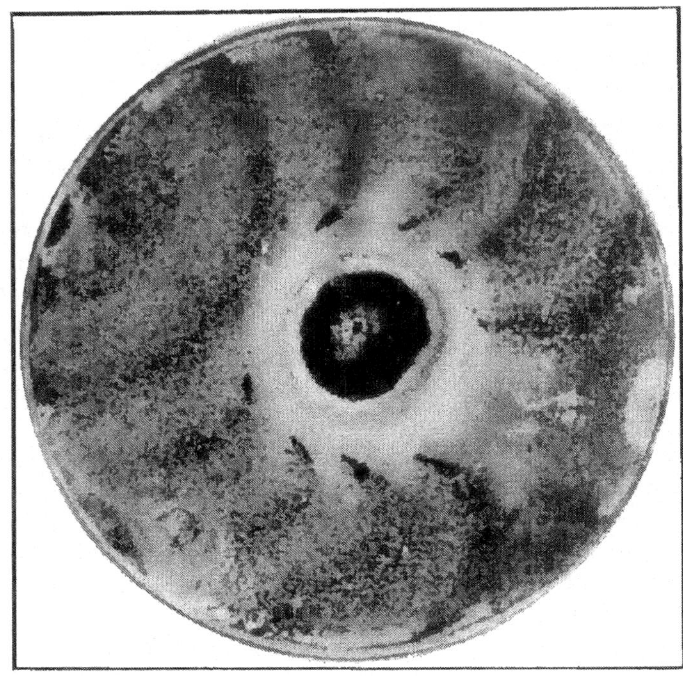

Fig. 105. Antagonistic effect of one fungus, *Pseudeurotium zonatum* (*center*), upon another, *Trichoderma lignorum* (from Goidanich *et al.*).

antagonism of one organism to another. These theories may be summarized as follows:

1. Exhaustion of available nutrients in the medium or substrate.
2. Physicochemical changes, produced by growing one organism in a certain medium, which affect the activities of another. These include changes in osmotic pressure, surface tension, oxidation-reduction potential, and reaction.
3. Certain types of reactions, such as radiation effects, which may be designated as action at a distance.
4. Space antagonism or competition for available space in a given medium.
5. Production of specific enzymes, either by the antagonist itself or as a result of autolysis of the antagonized cells, which have the capacity of lysing or dissolving the cells of other organisms.

6. Destruction of certain organisms by others, as that of bacteria by protozoa, or the parasitizing of some organisms upon others, as of certain nematodes upon Japanese beetle larvae.

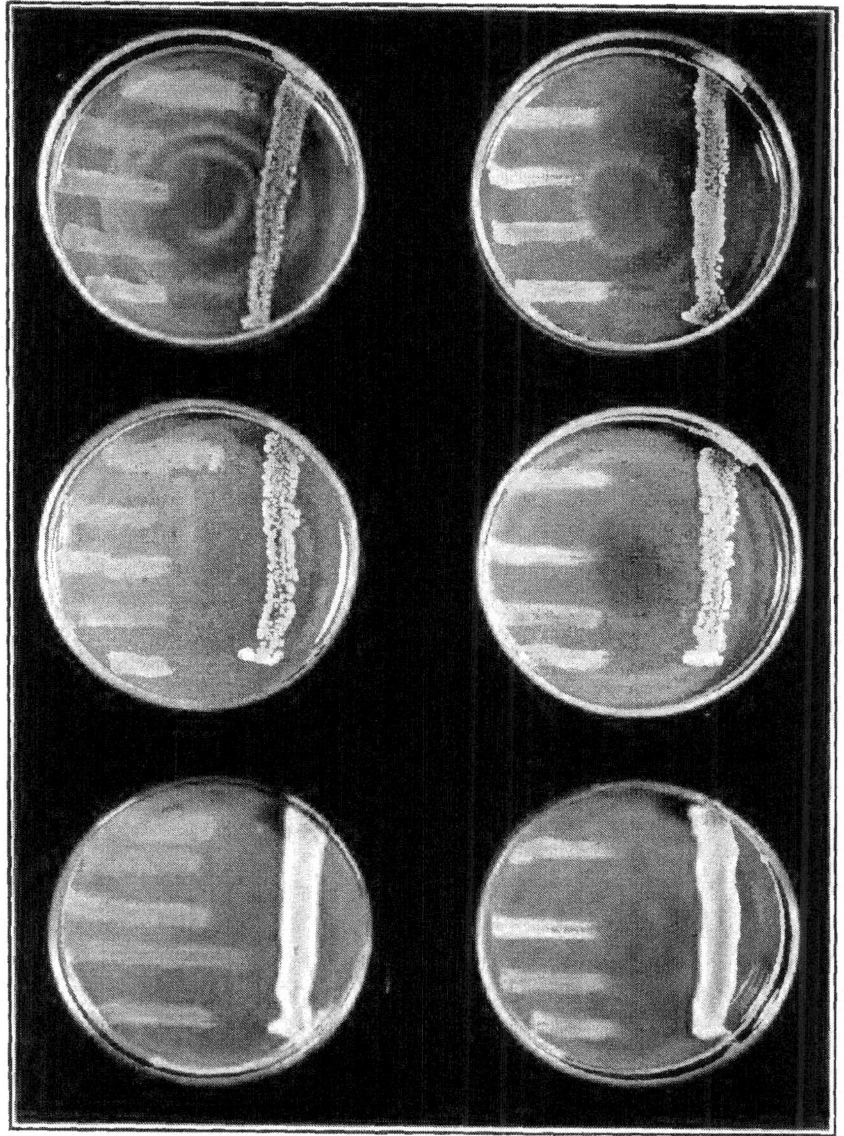

FIG. 106. Cross-streak method for testing production of antibiotic substances.

7. Production by certain microorganisms and liberation of specific substances that have a selective bacteriostatic and bactericidal effect, or fungistatic and fungicidal action, or both, namely, antibiotics.

Of these theories, only the last two deserve careful consideration from the point of view of soil microbiological processes and their effect upon plant growth

Effect of Protozoa upon Soil Bacteria

"The protozoan theory of soil fertility" was suggested by Russell and Hutchinson. It was based upon the belief that the capacity of protozoa to consume some of the bacteria is responsible for the infertility of certain soils.

The results of later and more detailed investigations on the relation of protozoa to bacteria, however, fail to support this theory When protozoa are added to cultures of specific bacteria concerned in known important soil processes, such as ammonia-forming and nitrogen-fixing bacteria, they are able to feed upon these bacteria and to bring about considerable reduction in their numbers This capacity is not necessarily accompanied by a detrimental effect upon the specific processes for which these bacteria are responsible, the effect of the protozoa may actually be beneficial. It has, therefore, been suggested that the presence of protozoa in the soil, even if accompanied by the consumption of bacteria, may result in keeping the latter at a level of maximum efficiency

The theory that protozoa play a controlling part in soil fertility was based upon the changes in bacterial numbers and activities as a result of partial sterilization When the protozoa were destroyed by heat or chemicals, the bacteria were found to multiply rapidly. This was believed to lead to more active decomposition of the organic matter, to greater liberation of nitrogen, and to improvement in soil fertility This explanation was based upon several assumptions which were not fully justified It was assumed, for example, that bacteria are the only important soil organisms responsible for the decomposition of organic matter; actually it has been repeatedly shown that fungi, actinomycetes, and other organisms are also capable of bringing about this process It was further assumed that protozoa, by consuming some of the bacteria, especially those decomposing organic matter and forming ammonia, restrict bacterial development and, *ipso facto,* organic matter decomposition. The fact was overlooked that fungi and actinomycetes of the soil could bring about, just as well as the bacteria, the decomposition of soil humus and liberate the nitrogen as ammonia a process which could thus take place even with the elimination of all the bacteria

When protozoa were found to exert a favorable effect upon various processes brought about by bacteria in controlled laboratory experiments, it was assumed that similar action is exerted in the soil. The protozoa were thus found to be not injurious but actually favorable to soil processes This assumption, however, may also be open to question, no consideration is given to the fact that the presence of numerous other organisms in the soil modifies considerably the activities of the protozoa. The use of artificial media may give a one-sided concept of the significance of protozoa in soil processes.

Direct microscopic methods of soil examination have revealed the fact that protozoa make up only a small portion of the soil population, both in numbers and in the total amount of active cell substance Their ability to reduce bacterial numbers in normal soil is very slight. The indirect method of studying protozoa in solution media, where the types developing and the activities resulting are quite different from those occurring in the soil, has been largely responsible for the exaggerated importance attached to these organisms. Certain observations have also been made on the toxic action of different bacteria upon protozoa In some cases protozoa were able to develop a certain resistance to the action of bacterial products.

It is now generally agreed that partial sterilization of soil brings about the destruction of most parasitic insects and fungi In this process, a large amount of organic matter is made available for the surviving bacteria (Table 62). These soon begin to develop at the expense of the available organic matter and bring about the liberation of large amounts of nitrogen as ammonia This ammonia accumulates in the soil, since it cannot be nitrified, because of the destruction of the nitrifying bacteria by the treatment It favors increased plant growth.

The effect of organisms destructive to pathogens and their use in controlling various plant diseases offer great practical potentialities

Production of Antibiotic Substances by Microorganisms

Tremendous interest has been aroused in recent years in the subject of antibiotic substances, especially from the point of view of their possible utilization as chemotherapeutic agents. These substances are produced largely by soil-inhabiting microorganisms They are classified on the basis of the organisms producing them, such as penicillin, actinomycin, or streptomycin, or on the basis of

Table 62. Survival of Bacteria Added to Soil and Their Effect upon the Soil Microbiological Population

Inoculum	Incubation		Organisms Recovered *	
	Time	Temperature	Total	Coliform Bacteria
	days	°C		
Control soil	5	28	21,400	200
E. coli added †	5	28	25,600	6,800
E. coli added ‡	5	28	39,700	3,500
E. coli added	5	37	22,800	4,700
Control soil	33	28	5,900	10
E. coli added	33	28	22,100	130
E. coli added ‡	33	28	17,600	140
E. coli added	33	37	23,000	10

* In thousands per gram of soil.
† Washed suspension of *E. coli* cells added at start and after 5 days.
‡ $CaCO_3$ added to soil.

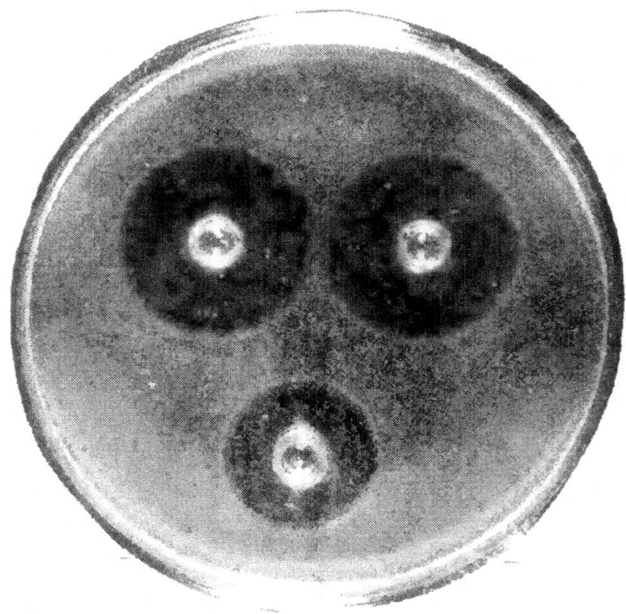

Fig. 107. Cup method for quantitative measurements of concentration of antibiotics.

the organisms affected by them, such as mycocidin, or on the basis of their chemical composition, such as chloramphenicol. They differ greatly in their chemical properties, toxicity to animals, and *in vitro* vs. *in vivo* activities.

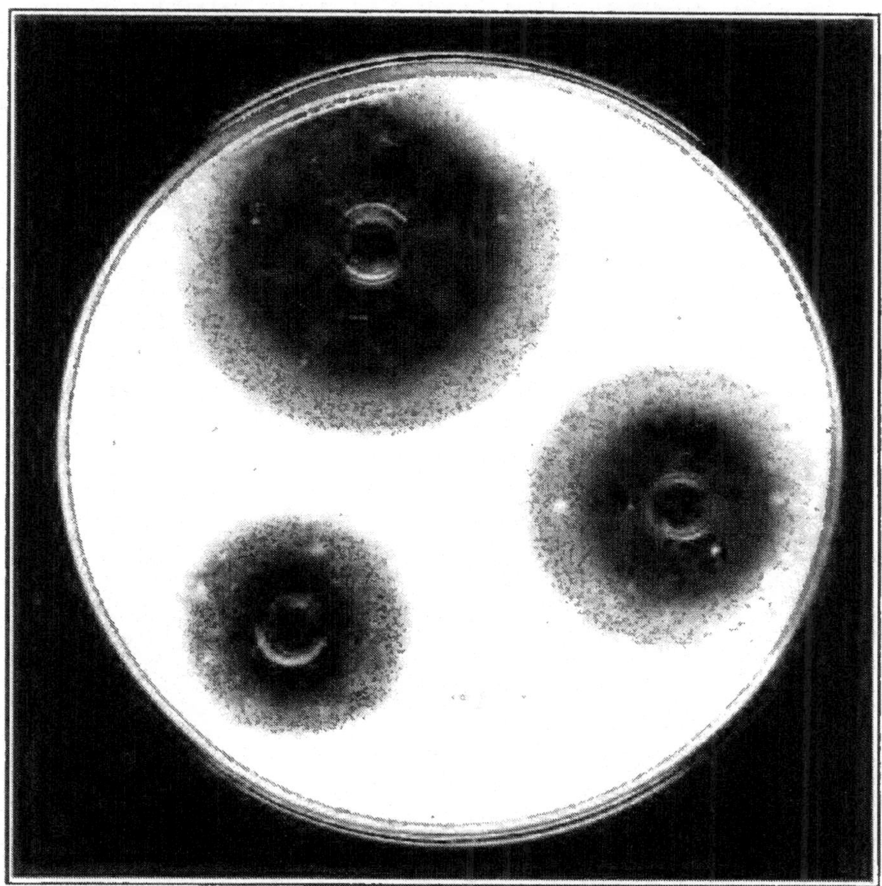

FIG. 108. Cup method against fungi.

Many microorganisms isolated from the soil have been found capable of producing antibiotics. Among the actinomycetes, for example, 10–50 per cent of all organisms tested were found to have such properties. Both spore-forming bacteria and non-spore-formers are able to produce antibiotics. Those produced by the spore-formers include tyrothricin, bacitracin, subtilin, and polymyxin; those produced by the non-spore-formers include pyocyanase, pyocyanin, prodigiosin, nisin, and colicines. The soil fungi have yielded a large number of antibiotics, most important of which is penicillin; others include mycophenolic acid, gliotoxin, clavacin, gladiolic acid, che-

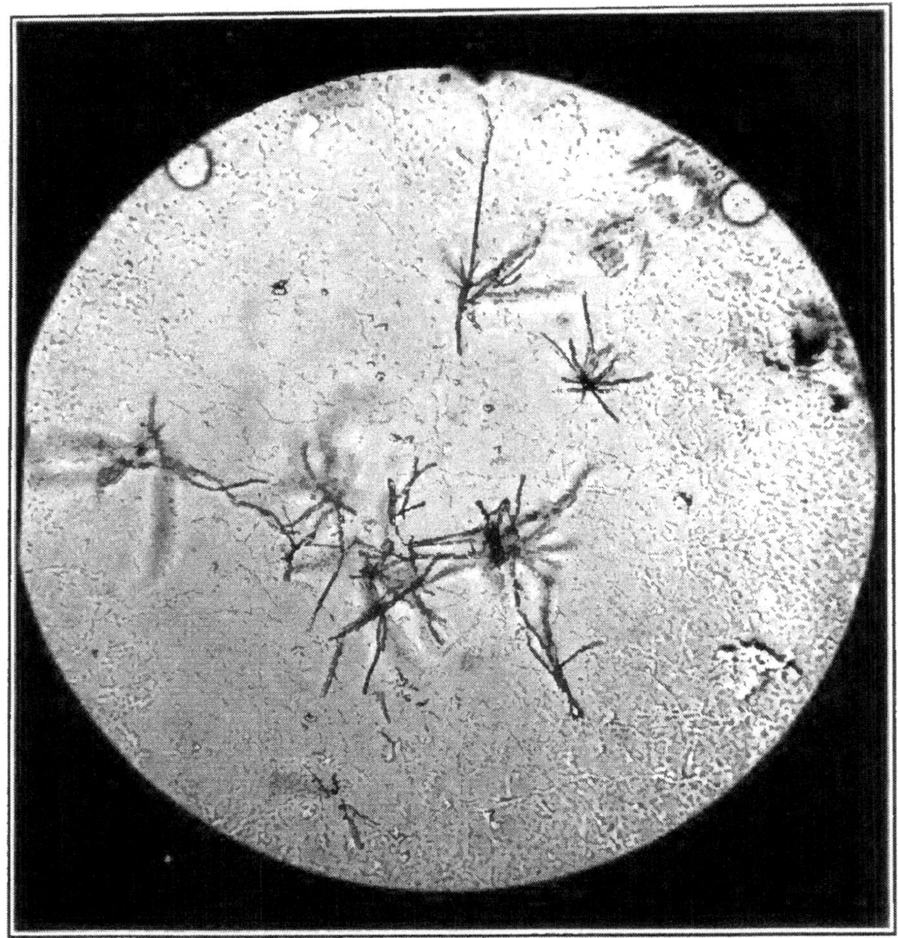

Fig. 109. *Streptomyces griseus*, streptomycin-producing strain. Vegetative and aerial mycelium.

tomin, penicillic acid, fumigatin, and fumigacin (Table 63). The actinomycetes have already yielded more than seventy antibiotics, some of which, notably streptomycin, chloramphenicol, aureomycin, terramycin, and neomycin, have found extensive practical application. Others include actinomycin, streptothricin, actidione, streptocin, xantomycin, viomycin, antimycin, fungicidin, and fradicin.

TABLE 63. ANTAGONISTIC INTERRELATIONSHIPS AMONG DIFFERENT FUNGI

Antagonist	Organisms Affected
Acrostalagmus sp.	*Rhizoctonia*
Alternaria tenuis	*Ophiobolus*
A. clavatus	Various fungi
A. flavus	*Peziza*
A. niger	*Peziza, Rhizoctonia*
Botrytis allii	*Monilia, Botrytis*, etc.
Botrytis cinerea	*Rhizoctonia*
Cephalothecium roseum	*Helminthosporium*
Cunninghamella elegans	*Monilia*
Fusarium lateritium	*Rhizoctonia*
Fusarium sp.	*Deuterophoma*
Gliocladium sp.	*Helminthosporium, Mucor*, etc.
Helminthosporium sp.	*Colletotrichum, Fusarium, Botrytis*, etc.
H. teres	*Fusarium, Ustilago, Helminthosporium*, etc.
H. sativum	*Ophiobolus*
Mucor sp.	*Ophiobolus, Mucor*
Penicillium sp.	*Peziza, Rhizoctonia, Ophiobolus, Fusarium*
Peziza sclerotiorum	*Mucor, Trichothecium, Dematium*, etc.
Peziza trifoliorum	*Peziza*
Sclerotium rolfsii	*Helminthosporium*
Sterigmatocystis sp.	*Alternaria*
Thamnidium elegans	*Mucor*
Torula suganii	*Aspergillus, Monascus*, etc.
Torulopsis sp.	Blue-staining fungi
T. lignorum	*Rhizoctonia, Armillaria, Phytophthora, Pythium*, etc.
Verticillium sp.	*Rhizoctonia*

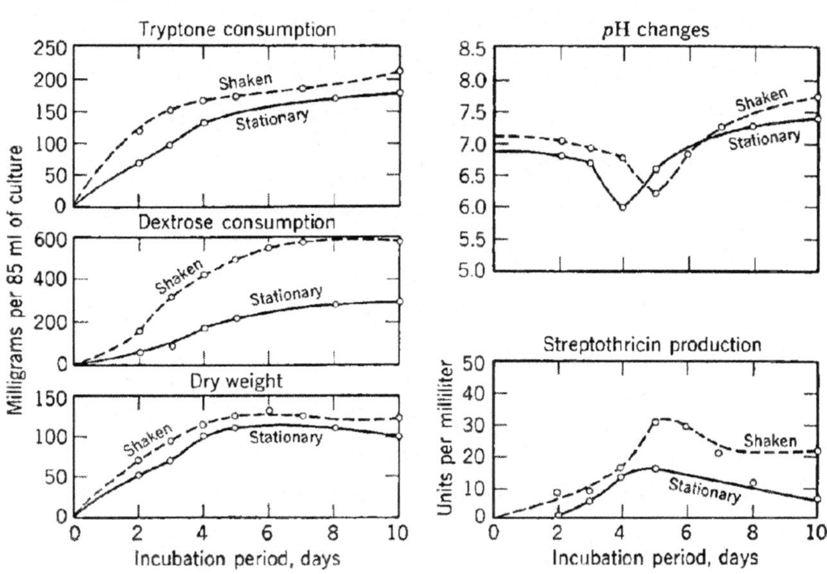

FIG. 110. Metabolism of *S. lavendulae* and production of streptothricin (from Woodruff and Foster).

In view of the fact that the organisms producing antibiotics are of soil origin, the question has naturally been raised of what importance these substances are in soil processes. It has been established, for example, that various bacteria, both beneficial and harmful, are affected by certain antibiotics; the former include the root-nodule bacteria and *Azotobacter,* and the latter include bacteria causing various blights and other plant infections.

Fig. 111. Electron micrograph of actinophage, type I, of streptomycin-producing *Streptomyces griseus* ×31,000 (courtesy of Squibb Institute for Medical Research).

The effect of antibiotics upon the soil microbiological population has given rise to various speculations.

On the one hand, certain claims have been put forth that this phenomenon is of only minor importance in soil processes. The following reasons have been presented to substantiate this view:

(*a*) the production of antibiotics is dependent upon the presence of specific nutrients which usually are not found in normal soil, (*b*) some antibiotics are readily destroyed by different soil-inhabiting microorganisms; (*c*) the soil organisms exposed to the action of antibiotics tend rapidly to develop resistance to them, (*d*) the survival or predominance of various microorganisms in the soil does not appear to be correlated with the capacity of such organisms to produce antibiotics.

On the other hand, claims have been made which tend to suggest that, under certain conditions at least, antibiotics may play a part in soil processes. These are based on the following observations (*a*) the presence of small amounts of antibiotic substances in the soil, (*b*) the formation of antibiotics by various pure cultures of microorganisms in sterile soil; (*c*) the persistence of certain antibiotics added to the soil, (*d*) the capacity of various soil-inhabiting organisms to inhibit the growth of plant pathogens, (*e*) the favorable effect upon the control of certain plant pathogens exerted by stable manures, green manures, and other materials which favor the development of antibiotic-producing organisms Claims, not fully confirmed, have been made that inoculation of soil with antagonistic organisms will result in a depression in the development of the pathogens.

The presence in soil of substances toxic to plant growth has also been definitely established. It is not known whether these are related to the antibiotics. It is known that some antibiotics, like actinomycin and glutinosin, have the capacity of causing certain plant diseases, such as curly tips. There are not enough established facts, however, to permit generalizations concerning the importance of antibiotic substances, or of the organisms producing them, in the control of soil fertility

Selected Bibliography

1. Baron, A L, *Handbook of Antibiotics*, Reinhold Publishing Corp, New York, 1950
2. Florey, H W, Chain, E, Heatley, N G, Jennings, M A, Sanders, A G, Abraham, E. P, and Florey, M E, *Antibiotics, a Survey of Penicillin, Streptomycin, and Other Antimicrobial Substances from Fungi, Actinomycetes, Bacteria, and Plants*, 2 vols, Oxford University Press, New York, 1949.

3 Karel, L., and Roach, E. S., *A Dictionary of Antibiosis,* Columbia University Press, New York, 1951.

4 Pratt, R., and Dufrenoy, J., *Antibiotics,* J. B. Lippincott Co., Philadelphia, 1949.

5 Waksman, S. A., *Microbial Antagonisms and Antibiotic Substances,* The Commonwealth Fund, New York, 1947.

6 Waksman, S. A., *et al. Streptomycin,* Williams & Wilkins Co., Baltimore, 1950.

·13·

Disease-Producing Microorganisms in the Soil and Their Control

Survival of Human and Animal Pathogens in the Soil

Microbes capable of causing various human and animal diseases find their way into the soil and into water basins in very large numbers, either in the excreta of the infected host or in the dead and infected residues of the latter If one considers the millions of years that animals and plants have existed on this planet, one can only surmise the great numbers of microbes causing the numerous diseases of all forms of life that must have thus been introduced into soils and surface waters What has become of all the bacteria causing typhoid fever, dysentery, cholera, diphtheria, pneumonia, bubonic plague, tuberculosis, and leprosy in man, mastitis and abortion in cattle, and numerous diseases of other animals? This question was first raised by medical bacteriologists in the eighties of the last century The soil was searched for the presence of bacterial agents causing infectious diseases and responsible for epidemics. The results obtained established beyond doubt that, with very few exceptions, organisms pathogenic to man and to animals do not remain alive in the soil for very long

A few disease-producing microorganisms, however, are able to survive in the soil for considerable periods One need only mention the organisms causing tetanus, gas gangrene, skin infections, actinomycosis and blackleg in cattle, coccidiosis of poultry, hookworm infections, trichinosis, enteric disorders in man. To these must be added diseases caused by various other bacteria, actinomycetes, and fungi. This is also true of numerous plant diseases, such as potato scab, root rots, take-all of cereal crops, and the damping-off diseases of vegetables The great majority of disease-producing microorganisms, notably the human and animal pathogens listed above, are able to remain in an active and reproducible state in the soil for only very short periods. It is also important to cite the fact that typhoid and dysentery bacteria, which are known to contaminate watersheds and water supplies, sooner or later disappear. No one now raises the question concerning the role of the soil as the carrier of these disease-producing agents or as the cause of severe or of even minor epidemics. This rapid disappearance of disease-producing bacteria may be due to several factors, such as unfavorable environment, lack of sufficient or proper food supply, destruction by predaceous

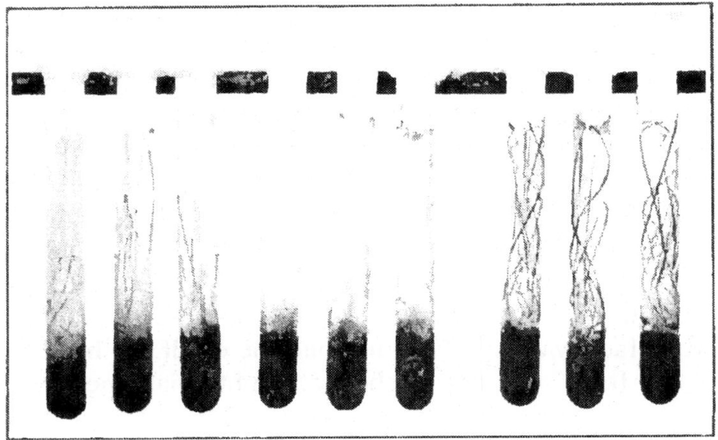

FIG. 112. Effect of soil organisms against parasitism by *P. volutum* on *Agrostis* (from van Luijk).

agents, such as protozoa and other animals, and destruction by various saprophytic bacteria and fungi considered antagonists.

Jordan and his associates found that *Eberthella typhosa* survived in sterilized tap water for 15–25 days, as against 4–7 days in fresh water; it died off even more rapidly (in 1–4 days) in raw river or canal water. The degree of survival of this organism in water was found to be in inverse ratio to the degree of contamination of the water, the saprophytic bacteria being directly responsible for the destruction of the pathogen. Freshly isolated organisms survived a shorter time than laboratory cultures, and higher temperatures were more destructive than lower ones.

The presence of certain bacteria in water is often found to hinder the survival of *E. typhosa*. When *Pseudomonas aeruginosa*, on the other hand, is present in drinking water, it may not be accompanied by any other bacteria. Media inoculated with this organism and with *Escherichia coli* gave, after 13 days' cultivation, cultures of only *Ps aeruginosa;* however, the two organisms can coexist in sterilized water *Vibrio cholerae* does not survive very long in fresh water, although long enough to cause occasional epidemics

The addition of typhoid bacteria to a well-moistened and cultivated soil brings about rapid destruction of the organisms. The same phenomenon occurs when a culture of these organisms is added to that of a soil microbe An antagonistic relation is often found to exist in some soils but not in others; this is traced to the presence of specific bacteria. Frost reported a marked reduction in numbers of typhoid bacteria added to the soil, 98 per cent of the cells being killed in 6 days. It was suggested that in the course of a few more days all these cells would have disappeared from the soil On the other hand, under conditions less favorable to the antagonists, the typhoid organism survived not only for many days, but even for months.

Escherichia coli is rapidly crowded out by other organisms in manure piles and in soil The dysentery and typhoid organisms disappear rapidly, in 12 and 16 hours, in sea water, the paratyphoid organisms have been found to survive for 21 and 23 days. Sea water appears to contain an agent, other than its salts, which exerts a bactericidal effect.

Under conditions prevailing in southern England, *Mycobacterium tuberculosis* was found to remain alive and virulent in cow's feces, exposed on pasture land, for at least 5 months during winter, 2 months during spring, and 4 months during autumn, in summer, no living organisms were demonstrated even after 2 months; under protection from direct sunlight, the survival period was longer Bovine tubercle bacteria have been detected in soil and manure, and on grass up to 178 days after infection, but not later When *M. tuberculosis* was added to nonsterile soil, it was slowly destroyed, the plate count was reduced to about one-sixth of the original in 1 month *Brucella melitensis* survived in sterilized tap water for 42 days, as compared to 7 days in unsterilized water, it survived in sterilized soil 72 days, as compared to 20 days in unsterilized soil

In addition to the above pathogenic organisms, others which have the capacity of causing infections or of producing potent toxins in human foodstuffs under proper conditions are found abundantly in the soil. These include the tetanus and gas gangrene organisms, on the one hand, and the botulinus, on the other These organisms may be present even in virgin soils.

Clostridium tetani appears to be also universally distributed in soils fertilized with animal manures and subject to the dust of the streets. Nicolaier demonstrated the presence of this organism in more than 50 per cent of the soils examined, an observation later confirmed by others. Of 100 Scottish soils examined, 4 gave cultures producing botulinus toxin and 5 tetanus toxin. It was even suggested that the tetanus organism develops in rotting straw or manure, taking a part in processes of decomposition. The presence of this organism in the soil has also been ascribed to fecal excretions, because of its development in the intestine.

The subject of the gas-gangrene-producing bacteria has received special consideration in connection with the study of war wounds and trench fever. Spores of *Cl. sporogenes, Cl. welchii, Cl. tertius, Cl. oedematiens, Cl. bifermentans, Cl. cochlearius, Cl. tetani,* and of other bacteria have been found in all soils of Central Europe.

The nature of the soil, or its physical, chemical, and biological conditions, have a marked influence upon the survival of these organisms in the soil. The bacterium causing fowl typhoid (*Shigella gallinarum*) will not remain in the soil for more than a week at a reaction of *p*H 6.2–6.4 or lower. At a *p*H of 6.7–7.0, however, the organism does not seem to be affected and will survive in the soil for 40–70 days. The organism causing white diarrhoea in chickens (*Sh. pullorum*) shows somewhat greater susceptibility to acid soils than *Sh. gallinarum*, it survived for more than 64 days in soils of *p*H 7.0. In moist soils, the organism was more viable and less susceptible to lower *p*H than in dry soils, it survived for 8 days in soils of *p*H 6.2–7.0. *Mycobacterium tuberculosis* will survive in the soil for many years, without losing its virulence.

The causative agents of human and animal actinomycotic diseases are often claimed to be brought about by soil organisms or forms harbored upon plants. Klinger drew attention to the fact that none of the aerobic actinomycetes commonly found on grasses and in straw infusion (also in soil) were isolated by him in any actinomycotic case. Only anaerobic forms were obtained from the latter, these developed on most media at temperatures above 30°C, and only seldom were cultures obtained which made a scant growth under aerobic conditions. Mixed infections consisting of anaerobes growing at body temperature together with aerobes are often obtained. We have to do here with species which have adapted themselves to a symbiosis with warm-blooded animals, and which have almost nothing in common with aerobic saprophytes. There is no doubt, however, that some aerobic actinomycetes are capable of causing infections of men and animals.

The hookworm disease, caused by *Ancylostoma duodenale* and *Necator americanus*, is primarily due to soil pollution. The larvae were found to develop for as long as 6 months in soil protected by

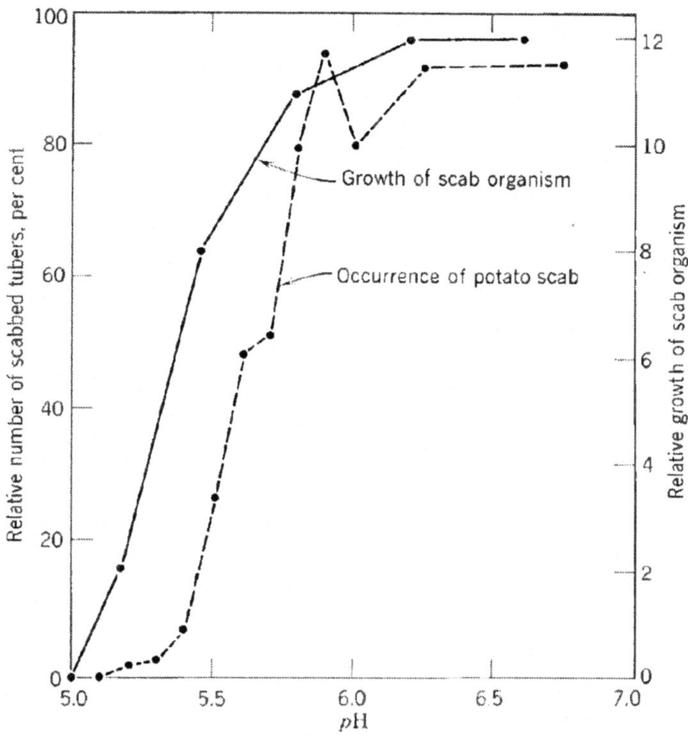

Fig. 113. Relation of soil reaction to the growth of scab organism and occurrence of potato scab (from Dippenaar).

vegetation. The physical, chemical, and biological soil conditions have a very important influence upon the development of hookworm larvae from infected feces and upon the continued life of these larvae in the soil. The larvae are found largely in the capillary film of moisture surrounding the soil particles.

In spite of the gradual and even rapid destruction of some pathogenic microorganisms in the soil, the survival of others presents important problems to farmers raising hogs, cattle, poultry, and other domestic animals. To overcome this condition, rotation of crops is usually practiced; several years are generally required to render infected pastures safe for use. A better understanding of the antagonists that are responsible for the rapid destruction of pathogenic organisms in the soil may throw light upon this problem and improve the methods of control.

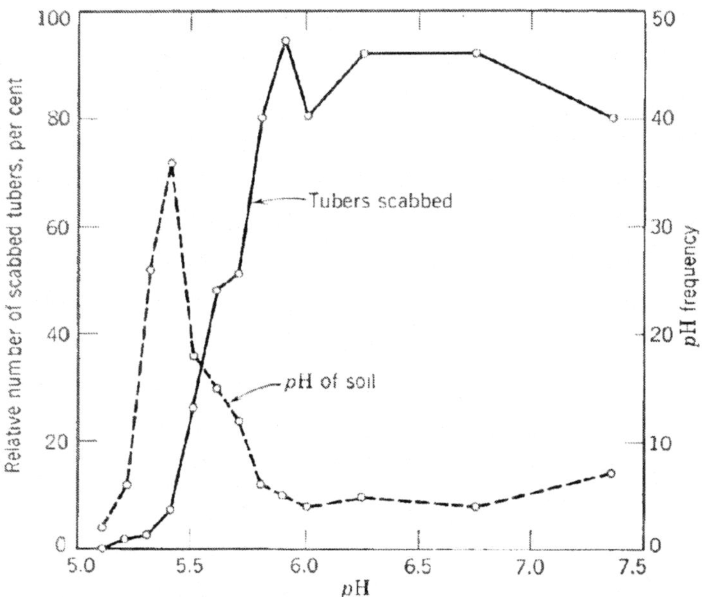

FIG. 114. Influence of the hydrogen-ion concentration on the incidence of potato scab (from Dippenaar).

Survival of Plant Pathogens in the Soil

The organisms causing plant diseases can be divided into five distinct groups: fungi, actinomycetes, bacteria, animal forms, and viruses. They are all found in the soil, and most are able to survive there for long periods, especially in the presence of the host plant. The fungi are by far the largest and most important group.

These fungi belong to the Myxomycetes (*Plasmodiophora brassicae*, causing club root of cabbage), Phycomycetes (*Phytophthora infestans, Aphanomyces laevis, Synchytrium endobioticum, Pythium debaryanum*), Ascomycetes (*Botrytis cinerea, Sclerotinia trifoliorum, Corticium vagum*), Fungi Imperfecti (*Phoma betae, Verticillium alboatrum, Helminthosporium gramineum, Fusarium lini, Fusarium vasinfectum*), and finally certain Basidiomycetes, including smuts.

Various fungi have been isolated from both cultivated and virgin soils on which the particular host plant has never been grown before. *Fusarium radicicola* and *Rhizoctonia solani,* known to be parasitic on the Irish potato, were isolated from soils never cropped with potatoes and from virgin desert lands. Disease-free seed planted on new lands frequently yielded a diseased product. Soils in which clover or grain was previously grown are better adapted to the production of disease-free potatoes than is virgin land. Some plant-pathogenic fungi are able to persist in soil for many years;

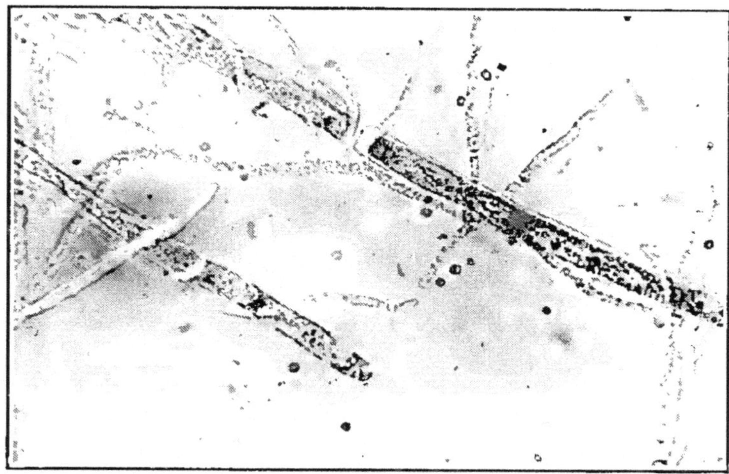

Fig. 115. An antagonistic fungus, *Trichoderma,* attacking a plant pathogenic fungus, *Sclerotium rolfsii,* showing one break of a septum (from Weindling).

flax, for example, must be grown only on new soils. Various species of *Phytophthora* can withstand low winter temperatures without much injury; they can also resist some desiccation; *Ph. infestans* can live saprophytically in soil, growing on old, partly decomposed plants. The pathogenicity of these fungi is not diminished by living in the soil. Many plants are infected by fungi, the spores of which may not live in the soil but may adhere to the seeds and produce a mycelium, which, on the germination of the seed, is able to attack the seedlings.

Many of these fungi are facultative parasites, since they are able to grow in soil in absence of the host plant. The spores of *Sclerotinia trifoliorum* can give rise to a mycelium which is at first saprophytic and then becomes facultative parasitic. These spores germinate on the vegetable residues in the soil; the mycelium spreads over the soil at a rate which depends on environmental conditions.

The soil fusaria have been divided into true soil inhabitants and soil invaders. The latter are dependent on the host for their continued existence in the soil; once the host plant is removed, the fungus gradually dies out.

Cabbage- and tomato-sick soils may show as many as 40,000 colonies (on plate) of the parasitic organisms per gram of soil. *Trichoderma koningi* and *T. lignorum,* two common saprophytic soil fungi, are known to cause rots of stored sweet potato, as well as "ring

Fig. 116. Sweet-orange seedlings in nonsterilized soil: *A*, control; *B*, *Rhizoctonia* inoculated into soil layer in bottom of jar; *C*, *Rhizoctonia* as in *B*, plus *Trichoderma* in top layer of peat (from Weindling and Fawcett).

rots." The common soil and dust fungus *Rhizopus nigricans* is known to be the cause of soft rot of sweet potatoes.

The plant-pathogenic actinomycetes are represented in the soil by several species, the most important of which is *Streptomyces scabies,* the causative agent of potato scab. The limiting reactions for growth of these organisms are *p*H 5.5–6.0 and 9.0, with an optimum at *p*H 7.0–7.5. A greater acidity, *p*H 5.0 or less, either controlled or reduced the disease but did not eliminate the organism. At *p*H 4.8 or lower, the potato plant as well was injured. An examination of some 100 fields for the presence of scab organisms in Nebraska gave no field free from scab, 24–30 per cent causing decided infection of the tubers. Previous cultivation of the soil, frequent growth of potatoes, heavier soil, and larger numbers and percentages of actinomycetes in soil corresponded with a higher percentage of scab.

Comparison of a large number of strains of actinomycetes isolated from scabby potatoes shows that one is dealing here not with a single species, but with a large group of organisms. As many as thirty species of actinomyces have been described, these are believed to be causative agents of potato scab, the type of lesion being influenced by the species The existence of more than one type of actinomyces capable of causing mangel-beet scab has also been suggested.

The formation of "pox" on sweet potatoes was shown to be due to an actinomyces found in the soil This organism has been designated as *Actinomyces poolensis*.

Bacteria capable of causing plant diseases include *Bacillus tumefaciens,* the crown-gall organism, *B campestris,* causing black rot of cruciferae, and a number of other bacteria causing bacterial rot of potatoes and other plants

Among the plant and animal pests present in the soil, we find also protozoa, nematodes, wireworms, crustaceans, myriapods, and insects. The plant-parasitic nematodes include *Heterodera schachtii,* causing the disease of mangels, *Tylenchus tritici* on wheat, *Het radicicola,* causing swellings or knots on roots of tomatoes and cucumbers, *Tylenchus dipsae,* causing the root knot on oats, tulip root, and clover; *Aphelenchus olesistus,* causing leaf blight, and *Tylenchus dipsaci,* capable of causing galls on stems, leaves, and tubers of potatoes.

The plant-parasitic insects include a number of Coleoptera, Lepidoptera, and Diptera. Wireworms may cause considerable damage to crops, as when old meadows are plowed under and planted to corn or potatoes These worms are capable of traveling considerable distances below the surface of the soil The nematodes and other worms, as well as the various insect pests, are favored by the addition of organic matter.

There is an association between the intensity of plant disease caused by *Het schachtii* and the cyst content of the soil, in those cases where the disease was observed recently. The nematode disease may be due to an association between the fungus *Rhizoctonia solani* and *Het schachtii* Infestation of soil with Phylloxera has been found to be most frequent in heavy-textured soils and less frequent in sandy soils

There is also a possibility that the soil harbors organisms which are parasitic upon plant and animal parasites, as was shown to be true of a nematode parasitic on the Japanese beetle, *Popillia japonica*, which spends a large part of its life cycle in the soil.

The mosaic disease of tobacco, caused by a filterable virus, may persist in the soil Tomato mosaic was also found to be able to live for 4–6 weeks in field soils, but there was no evidence of overwintering of the virus

Different soil-borne parasites are affected very differently by environmental factors High soil temperatures stimulate the development of the *Fusarium* disease of cabbage, and low temperatures inhibit it. *Thielavia* root rot of tobacco is checked in warm soils and is seriously injurious only in cool soils. Jones emphasized this seasonal contrast. Of two successive summers one was very cool, with a midsummer soil temperature averaging about 5°C lower than that of the succeeding summer, the root rot of tobacco was unusually severe, whereas cabbage remained relatively free from disease. The succeeding year with its warm midsummer period caused destruction of the cabbage crop because of the yellows disease, whereas the tobacco was free from root rot. High soil temperatures favor vascular diseases, including flax wilt, tomato wilt, and cabbage yellows High temperature (25–27°C) also favors *Sclerotium rolfsii* and certain other plant-pathogenic fungi

Soil moisture also exerts an important influence on many plant parasites Sanford found dry soils favorable and wet soils inhibitory to potato scab. Soil fungi causing "damping off" are favored by high moisture, wet soils, even to the saturation point, favor the club-root parasite of cabbage Powdery scab develops best in periods of damp, rainy, and cloudy weather and is favored by poor drainage.

The amount of organic matter present in the soil influences plant infection, since it offers a source of energy for the saprophytic existence of the organisms. Certain pathogens cannot infect the host plant in pure sand, but will do so in the presence of organic matter, which allows the mycelium to exist for some time. Clay soils are more favorable to infestation than are sandy soils. The root rot of peas is not disseminated by the seed, but spreads through the soil and is especially favored by a high content of organic matter The cotton and alfalfa root rot spreads through the soil radially with a growth similar to fairy rings, it is favored by heavy soils, humid weather, and dense cover crops. Addition of organic matter to soil also favors development of nematodes and rainworms In some instances, the application of organic matter has helped to check the spread of a disease, for example, cotton rot

In addition to organic matter, the use of artificial fertilizers, especially nitrogen and phosphorus, and the nature of the soil have a considerable influence on the development of different organisms causing plant diseases. The other most important treatments which have a significant effect are those leading to changes in soil reaction.

Organisms Antagonistic to Plant-Disease-Producing Microbes

The antagonistic action of soil organisms to fungi causing plant diseases results in a modification of the virulence of the pathogens that find a temporary or permanent habitat in the soil Various bacteria capable of inhibiting the development of the corn smut have been isolated These bacteria are able to destroy the smut fungi The widespread distribution of such bacteria in the soil was believed to check the multiplication of the pathogen Some of the antagonistic bacteria produce enzymes which have the capacity to dissolve the chemical constituents of the cell walls of the fungi Chudiakov isolated two bacteria which lysed different species of *Fusarium* and other pathogenic fungi. These bacteria were widely distributed in the soil, but were absent in certain flax-sick soils. When the pathogen was introduced into soils containing active antagonistic bacteria, it did not develop, and no disease was produced

The virulence of the root rot of cereals caused by *Ophiobolus graminis* received special attention. It was believed that this organism could be completely controlled by the activities of various soil-inhabiting microorganisms, filtrates of these organisms were nearly as effective in repressing the pathogen as were the living organisms. The fact that potato scab can be reduced by plowing under a green rye crop has also been explained by the development of other organisms, such as saprophytic actinomycetes, which suppress the growth of the pathogenic S *scabies.*

The "biological control' of various soil-borne diseases was thus suggested. This method consists in modifying the soil so as to encourage the maximum development of the antagonizing saprophytic soil population Inoculation of sterilized soil with the saprophytic fungus *Trichoderma,* for example, was found to prevent infection of citrus seedlings by the pathogenic *Rhizoctonia* (Table 64)

The spoilage of fruits can also be suppressed by inoculation with mixtures of known organisms According to Potter, the organism causing rot of turnips produces a potent, heat-resistant toxin, which is also destructive to the pathogen itself. Spraying turnips with this

TABLE 64 EFFECT OF *Trichoderma lignorum* ON GERMINATION AND GROWTH OF BARLEY INFECTED WITH *Helminthosporium sativum* IN STERILIZED SOIL (from Christensen)

Strain of *H sativum*	Percentage of Plants								
	Emerged			Stunted			Contorted Leaves		
	H *	H + T	H + SI	H	H + T	H + SI	H	H + T	H + SI
21	84	94	94	46	12	6	52	32	15
22	88	94	98	33	8	6	57	27	14
23	86	88	96	25	17	8	78	31	21
24	88	98	94	10	4	3	17	15	10

* H = *Helminthosporium*, T = *Trichoderma*, SI = soil infusion

bacterial product checked the disease The same principle was found to hold true for oranges infected with *Penicillium italicum* The injurious action of certain common soil bacteria upon *Pseudomonas citri,* the cause of citrus canker, has also been reported Wheat seedlings were protected from infection by *Helminthosporium* and flax seedlings from *Fusarium* by use of antagonistic bacteria A watermelon disease caused by *Phymatotrichum omnivorum* was reduced when certain fungi (*Trichoderma lignorum*) and bacteria were present in the soil together with the pathogen The severity of the seedling blight of flax, caused by *F lini,* was diminished when the pathogen was accompanied in the soil by certain other fungi The pathogenicity of *H. sativum* on wheat seedlings was suppressed by the antagonistic action of *Trichothecium roseum,* which is believed to produce a toxic substance

The role of microbiological antagonism in the control of soil-borne plant diseases has been outlined as follows The soil population is in a dynamic biological equilibrium When a certain crop is grown continuously, various parasites capable of attacking the roots of that crop multiply Organic manures stimulate the development of various saprophytes in the soil These multiply at the expense of the pathogens and are able to check their activity, either by preventing their growth or by attacking and destroying the mycelium of the parasites. The biological control of plant diseases is particularly effective against those organisms which have become highly specialized to a parasitic form of life

Van Luijk obtained biological control of plant parasites by inoculation of soil with microorganisms selected for their antagonistic capacity, or by addition of their growth products. Broadfoot emphasized that antagonism of a saprophyte to a plant pathogen, as measured by growth on artificial media, is not necessarily a measure of the actual control that may be exerted upon the parasite in the soil Inoculation of soil with an antagonistic organism, such as *T. lignorum*, may have only a temporary effect in changing the microbiological balance of the soil population. Weindling and Fawcett attempted to control *R solani* by use of *T lignorum*, and Cordon and Haenseler by use of *B simplex*, with similar effects Daines reported that *T. lignorum* produces a substance toxic to *S scabies*. This substance is rapidly destroyed in the soil on aeration It was, therefore, believed doubtful that the fungus could be of much assistance in combating potato scab.

Fellows obtained field control of the take-all disease of wheat (*O graminis*) in Kansas by application of chicken and horse manure, alfalfa stems and leaves, and other organic materials Garrett attempted to prove that the factor chiefly controlling the spread of the pathogenic fungus along the roots of the wheat plant was associated with the accumulation of carbon dioxide and a corresponding lowering of the oxygen tension. This could best be maintained by additions of organic manures. Organic matter low in nitrogen was more effective than high-nitrogenous materials, it was, therefore, suggested that the soil microflora uses the mycelium of the pathogen as a source of nitrogen Addition of nitrogenous materials, either in an organic or in an inorganic form, protected the parasite by offering a more readily available source of nitrogen Differences in the microflora associated with the decomposition of various composts are believed to be largely responsible for differences in persistence and virulence of pathogens causing root rots of cereals

Green manures, when added to soil before planting, cause considerable reduction in slime disease of tomato plants Organic materials high in nitrogen, and supplementary additions of nitrogen sufficient for complete decomposition of the organic material, are most effective. Thom and Morrow found that organic matter, during the period of its active decomposition is most effective in depressing pathogenic fungi. Inactivation of pathogenic fungi in the soil by use of the antagonistic action of soil microorganisms has been variously attempted Organic manures were added to the soil to control *Phymatotrichum omnivorum*, the root rot of irrigated cotton under continuous cultivation in Arizona With the Rossi-Cholodny slide technique, it was possible to demonstrate that microbiological antagonism represents the true mechanism of the control process. Development of saprophytic organisms was most profuse in the slides buried in the manured plots, whereas the mycelium of *P. omnivorum* was most abundant on the slides in the unmanured plots King suggested that parasitism of the fungal strands by bacteria is one of the reasons for the decline of the pathogen in manured soils Henry believed that the biological control by the soil microflora could even be directed against internal seed infection, since appreciable infection of surface-sterilized flaxseed was found to occur in sterilized but not in unsterilized soil.

Attention has already been called to the fact that numerous observations have been made concerning the favorable effect of bacteria in depressing various plant diseases This is true, for example, of the addition of bacteria to unsterilized soil exhausted by growing flax; the percentage of plants diseased by *F. lini* was thereby lowered. The term "bacterization" was applied to the process of treatment of seed with active bacteria to support the plant against pathogenic fungi It has been suggested that the effect of bacteria on germinating seeds is due to the liberated bacterial products capable of depressing the development of parasitic fungi. Although not in all cases conclusive, the results fully justify the hope that a better knowledge of the soil antagonists may lead, if not to complete control, at least to a certain amount of control over the numerous plant diseases caused by pathogenic fungi, especially those that persist for a time in the soil.

Methods of Control of Plant Diseases

The methods of treatment of soil for the control of injurious microorganisms are divided into five distinct groups.

1. Proper rotation, or withholding of the host plant, since various parasites accumulate as a result of continuous growth of the same or closely related plants, use of resistant plant varieties.

2. Special physical methods of soil treatment, such as soil cultivation, change of soil reaction, use of organic matter, use of specific fertilizers

3 Partial sterilization of soil

4. Use of chemicals for the destruction of specific disease-producing organisms

5 Biological control or introduction of organisms destructive to the parasites.

Crop Rotation

In practicing crop rotation, one should remember that many of the disease-producing organisms can persist in the soil for a number of years and some are capable of leading there a normal saprophytic existence. A rotation of at least 5–6 years should be practiced against the club root of cruciferous plants and the sugar-beet nematode

Physical and Chemical Methods of Soil Treatment

Among the most efficient methods of control of soil-borne infections is the adjustment of the soil reaction, by the use of either alkali-forming (lime) or acid-forming (sulfur, ammonium sulfate) materials Addition of sulfur or inorganic acids to soils having a reaction of *p*H 5.9 or above is recommended; the amount of sulfur or acid to be applied depends, of course, on the initial reaction and buffer content of the soil. However, the action of sulfur in controlling the wart disease of potatoes depends not alone upon the acidity produced, but also upon some other mode of action of the sulfur, probably thiosulfuric acid produced at an early stage of oxidation of the sulfur

For the control of potato scab, sulfur is effective. Sweet-potato scurf and pox can also be checked by the application of sulfur Lime, which reduces the acidity of the soil, and stable manure favor the development of scab The addition of fertilizers (acid phosphate) to make the soil reaction acid tends to decrease the development of scab According to Millard, sufficiently liberal dressings of green manure added to the soil will inhibit the disease. This is probably due to the temporary increase in soil acidity, as a result of the decomposition of the organic matter by the soil fungi, and to an increase in soil moisture Scab is much more prevalent in dry seasons, since actinomycetes are much less active in very moist soils Sanford suggested that the soil reaction may not be the important factor in controlling the development of potato scab in the soil. Moisture was found to be directly or indirectly the main factor, a high moisture content controlling the disease, whereas abundant

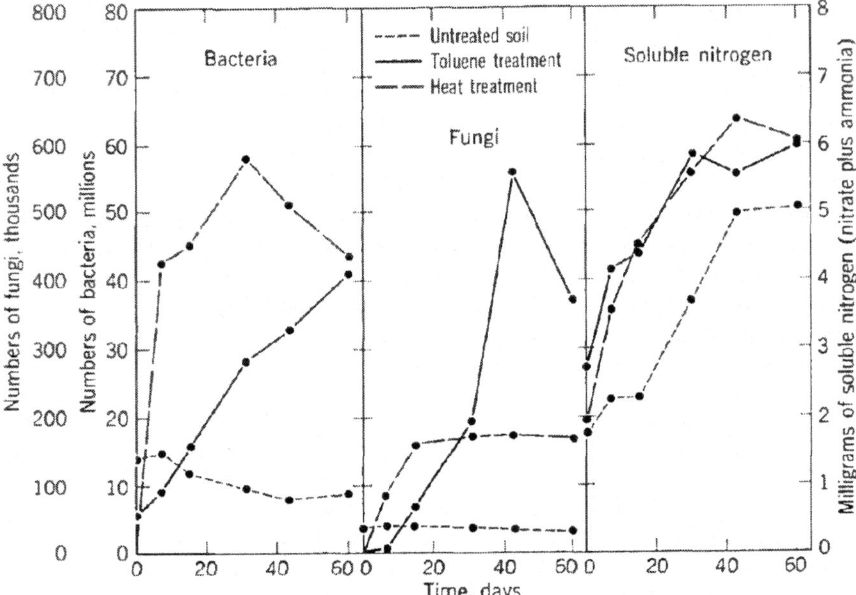

FIG. 117. Influence of toluol and heat upon the numbers and activities of micro-organisms in soil (from Waksman and Starkey).

scab was formed in dry soils. The development of scab is influenced also by the temperature of the soil, the optimum for scab being 22°C.

Soil Sterilization and Partial Sterilization

The soil may be sterilized completely or only partially, whereby not all the organisms are destroyed, but only certain groups. Complete sterilization is difficult to accomplish in the field or in the greenhouse, since the soil readily becomes reinfected again; it is not even desirable. In the laboratory, it often becomes necessary to sterilize a soil for growing pure cultures of organisms, for testing the purity of certain strains, and for invigorating laboratory-kept cultures. To sterilize a soil, it is placed in glass or clay containers and heated under pressure, at 15–20 pounds, for 2–3 hours. By using flowing steam for 1–2 hours, on 6 consecutive days, complete sterilization can also be obtained. The sterility of the soil thus treated must be carefully checked.

Though we know little about transmission through the soil of virus diseases of animals, we do know that various virus diseases of plants may be thus transmitted; for example, mosaic virus of wheat. To inactivate the virus, the soil, according to Johnson, must be heated for 10 minutes at 50–60°C.

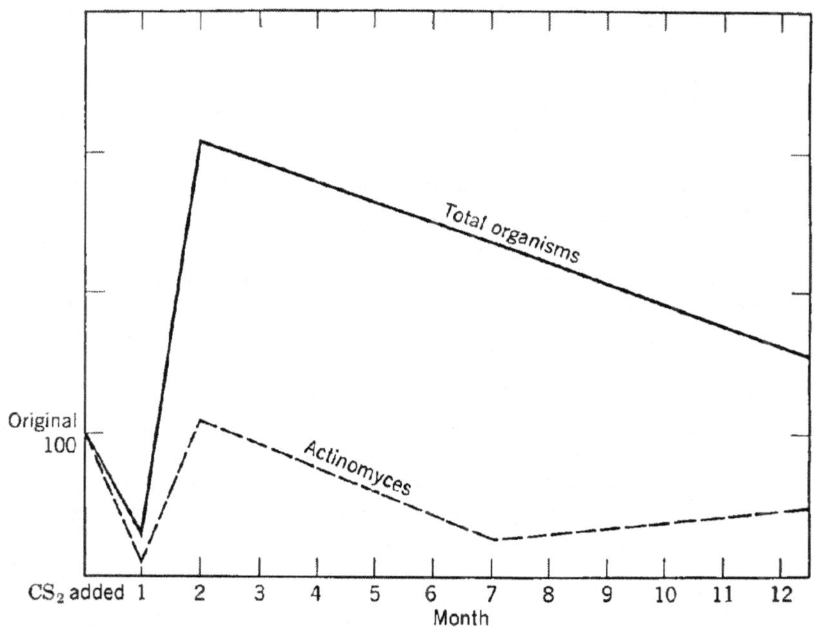

FIG. 118. Influence of CS_2 upon the numbers of bacteria and actinomycetes in soil (from Hiltner and Störmer).

It often appears necessary to partly sterilize the soil to destroy certain injurious insects or pathogenic fungi, but not to kill the whole soil population. Such partial sterilization can be brought about by use of heat, as by steam and dry heat, or by means of various volatile and nonvolatile antiseptics, the first comprising carbon bisulfide, toluol, formaldehyde, and hydrocyanic acid; the second including phenol, cresol, and chloropicrin. These disinfectants do not accumulate in the soil, but are either lost by volatilization or destroyed by soil organisms. The treatments have a selective effect upon the soil microbiological population, affecting particularly the fungi, many of the protozoa, and certain bacteria, such as the nitrifying organisms.

Many bacteria are able to resist these treatments and soon begin to multiply rapidly after the disinfectant has been removed. Active multiplication of these bacteria results in extensive decomposition of the soil organic matter, which is accompanied by abundant liberation of ammonia. The latter is used by plants, resulting in increased plant growth. Partial sterilization of soil may, therefore, be compared to fertilization with nitrogen. The effect of partial sterilization of soil with toluol and heat upon the bacterial and fungus populations, as well as upon the liberation of the nitrogen in an available form, is shown in Fig. 117.

Several theories have been proposed to explain the effect of partial sterilization in increasing the fertility of the soil. It has been asserted by some that disinfectants, when used in small amounts, have a direct stimulating effect upon microorganisms and plant roots, others have assumed that the toxins of the soil are destroyed by such treatments, still others have emphasized the destruction of plant-pathogenic fungi and bacteria in the soil. The theory that has received the greatest consideration, in an attempt to explain the phenomenon of partial sterilization, is the "protozoan theory of soil fertility," discussed previously.

Use of Special Chemicals for Treatment of Soil

A number of chemical compounds have been recommended for control of various fungi and nematodes in the soil. The saturation of soil with formaldehyde to prevent spreading of disease-producing organisms has often been practiced. Formaldehyde in concentrations of 0.045–0.05 per cent was found to give very good results in combating the sugar-beet nematodes. It is difficult to reach the nematodes at a depth lower than 60 cm, and it is difficult to cause the poison to penetrate the whole mass of soil. The nematodes present in the lower depths of soil and in the form of cysts can be made to develop and come nearer the surface by the use of catch crops and chemical stimulants. In absence of the host plant, the nematode larvae die off. Formalin, sometimes following crude benzol treatment for control of potato wart, mercury bichloride and other disinfectants are recommended for control of various plant diseases. The treatment of soil with a 1:1,000 or 1:1,200 solution of mercuric chloride was found to be effective in controlling root maggot, black rot, club root, and damping-off diseases.

Arsenic, mixed with ashes for soil dressing, is rather widely employed in China for destruction of worms, a similar practice is used for golf greens. Acetic acid (1.2 per cent), applied 10 days before planting, has also been recommended for destruction of soil-infesting damping-off fungi.

Various other soil fungicides and volatile antiseptics, like carbon bisulfide and toluol, have been frequently employed for destruction of pathogenic fungi. Carbon bisulfide can be used with success against a number of disease-producing fungi. This disinfectant should be applied to the soil free from plants; otherwise the chemical

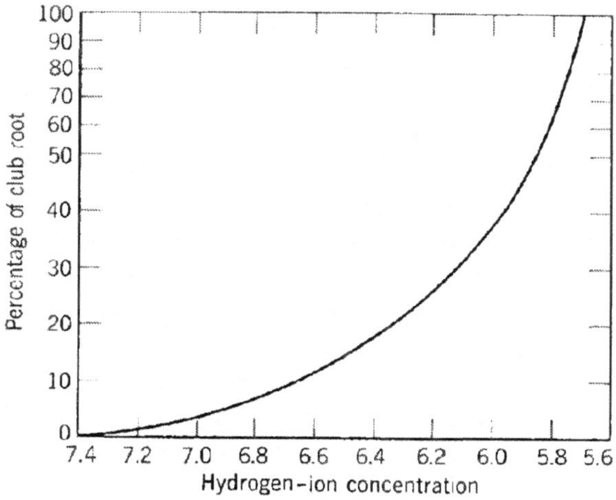

FIG. 119. Effect of soil acidity on the percentage of club root (from Chupp).

will result in plant injury. Good results have also been obtained with toluol in controlling various diseases.

It is impossible to sterilize the soil completely, especially by the use of high doses of disinfectants, without injuring the plants. The amount of disinfectant necessary to destroy the pathogenic organisms in the soil is considerably less than that necessary to sterilize the soil as a whole. Various chemicals vary greatly in this respect. Mercuric chloride is far more active than organic mercuriates; the microbicidal dose for mercury compounds is about the same as the antiseptic dose, whereas for copper salts the antiseptic dose is much lower than the microbicidal.

When soil is sterilized, the fungi and other plant and animal parasites are readily destroyed. Once certain parasitic organisms are introduced, however, they may develop readily in the treated soil and even cause a larger amount of infection. Treatment of soil with a disinfecting agent followed by inoculation with saprophytic fungi may prove to be most efficient in increasing the value of the treatment. Whether the saprophytic fungus uses up the available nutrients rendered soluble on steaming of soil or whether the favor-

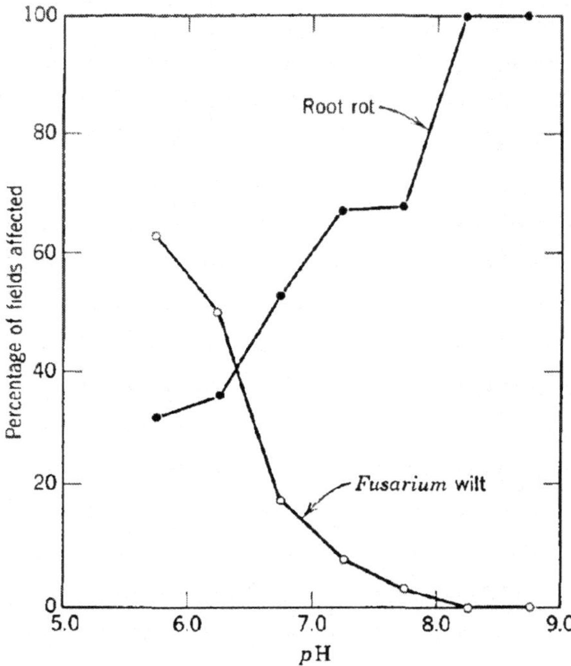

FIG. 120. Effect of *p*H upon occurrence of root rot and wilt (from Taubenhaus *et al.*).

able effect is due to the production of a substance directly injurious to the plant pathogen, remains to be determined.

USE OF SOIL INOCULANTS

The methods of biological control of disease-producing organisms are still insufficiently studied. Here belong the introduction of birds and other higher animals, as well as of certain insects feeding upon specific injurious insects and worms, or the use of predaceous nematodes against plant-pathogenic nematodes, or of entomogenous fungi and bacteria parasitic upon insects. The phenomena of antagonism may also be listed here.

Numerous attempts have been made to inoculate the soil with antagonistic organisms for the purpose of controlling plant diseases. These efforts have proved to be, in most instances, complete failures, as pointed out previously. This is largely because, unless the conditions of the soil are modified by supplying more nutrients to the antagonists or by creating a favorable reaction, the antagonists will not develop The introduction of organic materials, such as green manures and stable manures, may correct such a condition, thus favoring development of the antagonists, which bring about, directly or indirectly, suppression of the disease-producing agent.

Selected Bibliography

1 Daines, R H , Control of plant diseases by use of inorganic soil amendments, *Soil Sci* , 61 55–66, 1946
2 Johnson, F , Heat inactivation of wheat mosaic virus in soils, *Science*, 95 610, 1942
3. Garrett, S D , *Root Disease Fungi*, Chronica Botanica, Waltham, Mass , 1944
4 Newhall, A G , Volatile soil fumigants for plant disease control, *Soil Sci* , 61 67–82, 1946
5 Sanford, S B , Some soil microbiological aspects of plant pathology, *Sci Agr* , 13 638, 1933, *Soil Sci* , 61 9, 1946
6 Waksman, S A , *The Actinomycetes*, Chronica Botanica, Waltham, Mass , 1950.
7. Weindling, R , Microbial antagonism and disease control, *Soil Sci* , 61 23–30, 1946

14

Stable Manures, Composts, and Green Manures

Nature of Stable Manures

A large part of the plant residues removed from the land in the form of harvested crops is returned to the soil as various waste materials, ranging from factory to kitchen and farm wastes, or after the plant residues have been used for bedding purposes and been partly consumed by animals, or after they have passed through the digestive system of these animals

Stable manures consist of three groups of components: (*a*) bedding or litter, (*b*) solid excreta of animals, (*c*) liquid excreta or urine. The nature and relative concentration of these components vary greatly in different manures, depending on the animals and the methods of feeding and handling the animals. Since the various components of the manures also differ considerably in chemical composition it is natural to expect that the composition of different manures should vary

Plant residues used for bedding purposes are usually high in carbohydrates, especially in cellulose, and low in nitrogen and minerals Urine is high in nitrogen and minerals and has very little, if any, carbohydrate material Solid excreta contain considerable amounts of proteins, and thus tend to give a more balanced medium for the growth of microorganisms The chemical composition of three different types of stable manures is shown in Table 65 Sheep manure is high in protein, in cold-water-soluble organic materials, and in ash, it is low in cellulose. Horse manure is low in protein and high in cellulose and hemicelluloses Cow manure falls between these two A comparison of the nitrogen and mineral composition of a number of manures is given in Table 66. Chicken and pigeon manures are highest in nitrogen, phosphorus, and potassium,

TABLE 65 CHEMICAL COMPOSITION OF VARIOUS FRESH MANURES (from Waksman and Diehm)

On basis of dry, litter-free material

Chemical Constituents	Sheep Manure *	Horse Manure †	Cow Manure *
	per cent	*per cent*	*per cent*
Ether-soluble substances	2 8	1 9	2 8
Cold-water-soluble organic matter	19 2	3 2	5 0
Hot-water-soluble organic matter	5 7	2 4	5 3
Hemicelluloses	18 5	23.5	18 6
Cellulose	18 7	27 5	25 2
Lignin	20 7	14 2	20 2
Total protein	25 5	6 8	14 9
Ash	17 2	9 1	13 0

* Solid and liquid excreta
† Solid excreta only

or the most important nutrients required for plant growth. Cattle and horse manures contain the lowest quantities of these essential ingredients.

On the basis of numerous analyses, stable manure is found to contain, in a fresh state, about 70–80 per cent water, 0 3–0 6 per cent nitrogen, 0 1–0 4 per cent phosphorus as P_2O_5, 0 3–1.0 per cent potassium as K_2O. A ton of fresh manure thus carries about 400–600 pounds of dry matter, about 10 pounds is nitrogen, 6 pounds P_2O_5, and 10 pounds potash About half the nitrogen and a large part of the other two elements are in water-soluble forms and are thus immediately available for plant growth

Cow manure and horse manure are about equal in nutritive value to plants and as sources of humus To eliminate certain undesirable characteristics of fresh stable manure, to destroy the weed seeds

TABLE 66 CHEMICAL NATURE OF DIFFERENT MANURES (from Jenkins)

Manure	Moisture	Composition of Dry Matter		
		Nitrogen	P_2O_5	K_2O
	per cent	*per cent*	*per cent*	*per cent*
Cattle	80	1 67	1 11	0 56
Horse	75	2 29	1 25	1 38
Sheep	68	3 75	1 87	1 25
Pig	82	3 75	3 13	2 50
Hen	56	6 27	5 92	3 27
Pigeon	52	5 68	5 74	3 23

that may be present, and to obtain a product which can be readily pulverized, such manures are sometimes composted before their introduction into the soil. Although stable manures contain appreciable amounts of plant nutrients, their value as sources of humus increases their importance in soil A large part of the organic matter in some of the manures decomposes rapidly and, therefore, has a relatively short period of effectiveness. Poultry manure and sheep manure particularly are frequently used as organic fertilizers and not as sources of soil organic matter As fertilizers they are generally expensive, they are applied to the soil directly or mixed with certain proportions of peat or soil.

Decomposition of Stable Manures

When placed in a compost that is kept under conditions of favorable moisture and aeration, the various organic constituents of stable manures are immediately attacked by a great variety of microorganisms, including not only fungi, actinomycetes, and aerobic and anaerobic bacteria but also protozoa and other forms of life These organisms do not attack the manures as a whole or all the chemical constituents of the manures at the same rate. The decomposition of the compost and the various changes brought about in its specific organic constituents depend to a large extent upon the nature and composition of the manure and upon the conditions under which the decomposition of the manure is taking place.

The microorganisms bringing about the decomposition of stable manures either inhabit the manures or are derived from the soil These microorganisms bring about a rapid destruction of the carbohydrates and some of the proteins, this is accompanied by synthesis of considerable microbial cell substance. Although the various processes involved in the decomposition of stable manures are closely interrelated, they may be considered from three distinct angles. (*a*) the decomposition of the organic matter as a whole in the manures and the formation of humus, (*b*) the liberation, oxidation, reduction, and synthetic processes involving the nitrogen complexes, (*c*) the influence of the microorganisms found in the manures upon the microbiological population of the soil and upon soil processes

The transformation of the nitrogen in the manures, leading to its final liberation in a form available for the growth of higher plants, or as ammonia, is closely connected with the general processes of decomposition of the organic constituents in the manures. The nature and activities of the microorganisms in the manures are also

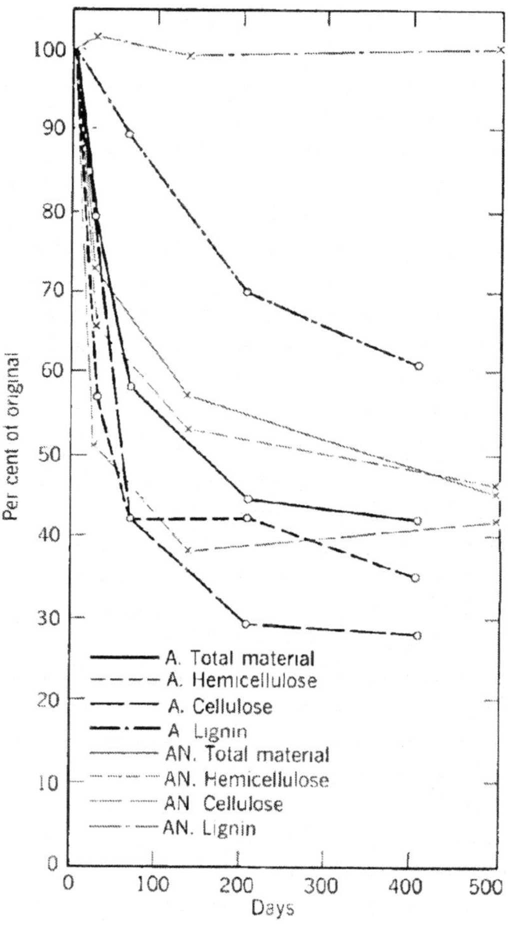

Fig. 121. Course of decomposition of alfalfa plant: A = aerobic, AN = anaerobic (from Tenney and Waksman).

dependent on and are closely connected with the transformation of the organic and inorganic complexes. The rate of decomposition of stable manures, the liberation of the nitrogen into available forms, and the formation of humus, all depend upon the nature and abundance of the three components of the manures; namely, the bedding or litter, solid excreta, and urine.

According to Déhérain, the function of the litter in manure consists in absorbing the liquids excreted by the animals and in supplying celluloses, substances which characterize the nature, decomposition processes, and products resulting from the manure, and which give the manure its special value for soil improvement. A knowledge of

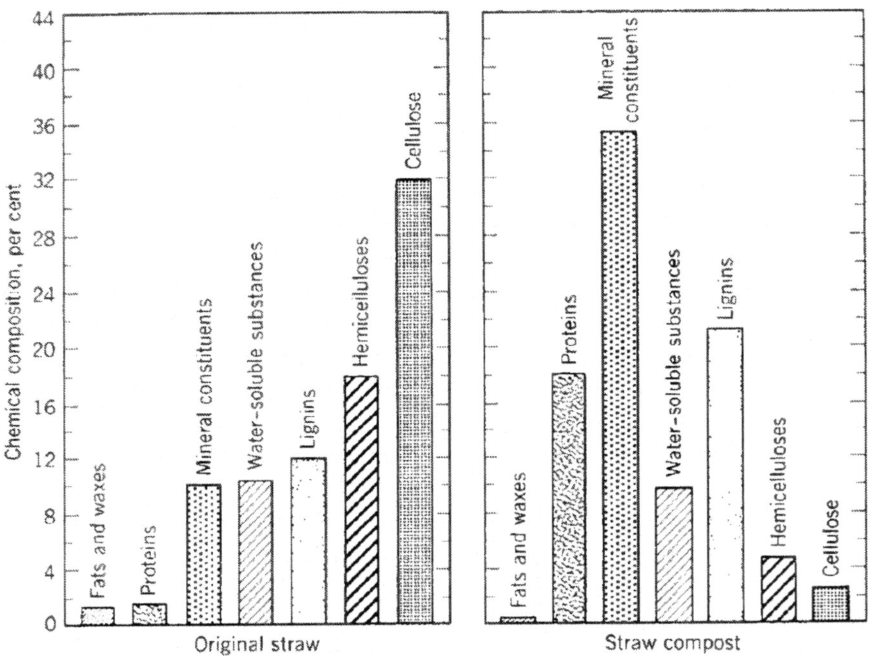

Fig. 122. Comparative chemical composition of oat straw and of a compost prepared from it (from Waksman and Gerretsen).

the chemical composition of the litter was, therefore, considered to be of great importance. König emphasized that decomposition of stable manures involves, first of all, the transformation of carbon compounds present in the manures, and that 75 per cent of the carbon disappears within a year after application of the manure to the soil. The decomposition is more rapid during the warmer periods of the year than during the colder periods.

Among the organic constituents of the manure, the pentosans and cellulose are decomposed more rapidly than the total organic matter, whereas the lignins are decomposed more slowly. Decomposition of manure is thus accompanied by a rapid reduction in the carbohydrates and a gradual enrichment in the lignins. Both the total and easily soluble nitrogenous compounds in the manure diminish rapidly after its application to the soil This was originally believed to be due either to denitrification or to a removal of the nitrogen to the subsoil. It was later found that large parts of these soluble forms of nitrogen are transformed into insoluble forms by the microorganisms responsible for the decomposition of the carbohydrates Only about a third of the nitrogen and a third of the phosphoric acid in the manure were found to be made available to the growing crops during the first 2 years after application of the manure, 70 per cent of the potash was made available in that time

Barthel and Bengtsson freed stable manure from ammonia by distillation. When the manure thus treated was added to the soil, no nitrate was formed, this tended to prove that ammoniacal nitrogen and urea nitrogen in the manure, but not the nitrogen present in the form of organic compounds, undergo active nitrification The organic nitrogen was believed to be tied up in the manure in a form unavailable for growth of higher plants. According to Egorov, one-half to two-thirds of the nitrogen in the solid excreta of the manure is in the form of microbial cell substance. By fixing the nitrogen in their cells, during the process of decomposition of manure, fungi and other microorganisms are thus able to reduce the losses of nitrogen. Moisture and aeration exert an important effect upon the rapidity and nature of the decomposition This is illustrated in the composting of fresh horse manure (Fig 54)

Although fresh stable manure contains an extensive population of characteristic microorganisms, especially bacteria and protozoa (coprophilic forms), many of these organisms die out in the process of composting and are replaced by others which are characteristic of the compost or of the soil. Among these, the thermophilic microorganisms, comprising various fungi, actinomycetes, and bacteria, occupy a unique place They develop in the composts after the temperature has reached 50–60°C Some of them are able to grow even at 65–75°C, bringing about active decomposition of the organic constituents of the manure These organisms are quite distinct from the typical soil population This has bearing upon the various reports that manure should be considered a source of bacteria for soil inoculation

Conservation of Stable Manures

A number of processes are utilized in the treatment of manures, to conserve the nutrients and render the manures highly beneficial for soil fertilization and soil improvement. Each of the processes has certain distinct advantages and disadvantages. The major objective of such conservation is prevention of the nitrogen losses which usually take place in the decomposition of manures. These losses can be threefold: (*a*) volatilization of the nitrogen as ammonia, (*b*)

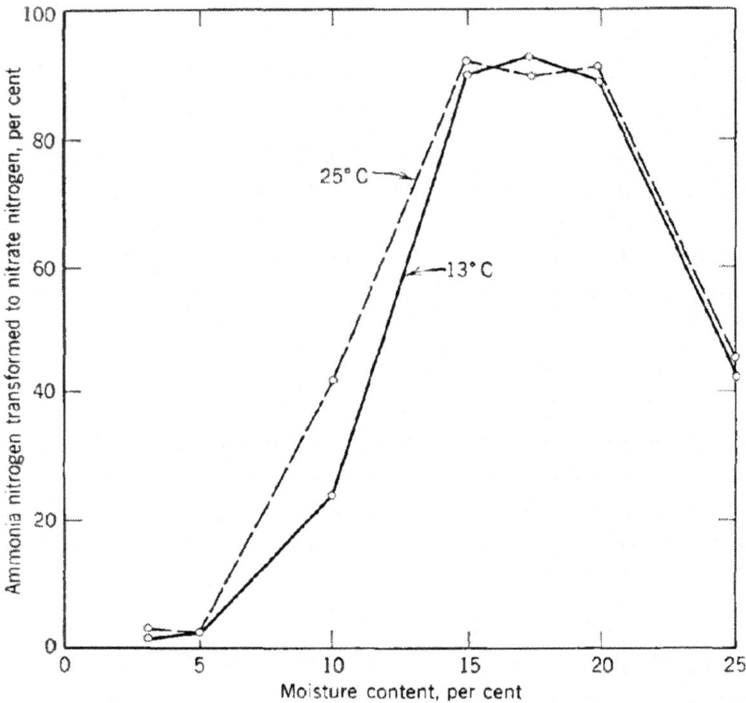

Fig. 123. Influence of moisture upon nitrate formation (from Traaen).

losses of nitrogen by denitrification of the nitrate to atmospheric nitrogen, (*c*) losses of nitrogen by leaching of the nitrate and of soluble organic forms. Some of the phosphate and potassium in the manure may also be lost by leaching, as a result of careless handling. Another purpose in devising special methods of treating manures is conservation of as much of the organic matter as possible (Table 67).

Among the different processes of conserving manures, those designated as "hot manure" and "cold manure" are the most common. The "hot fermentation" process has recently received particular attention. When the manure is first permitted to undergo aerobic decomposition for a few days, to allow a rapid rise in temperature, and

TABLE 67 LOSSES FROM EXPOSURE OF MANURE IN THE OPEN YARD (from Salter and Schollenberger)

Constituent	New Jersey,* 2½ Months, Early Summer, Cow Manure	Canada † 3 Months, Apr.-July, One-Half Horse, One-Half Cow	Ohio,‡ 3 Months, Jan.-Apr., Steer	New York, § 6 Months, Apr.-Sept.	
				Horse	Cow
	per cent	*per cent*	*per cent*	*per cent*	*per cent*
Organic matter		60	39		
Nitrogen	31	29	30	60	41
Phosphoric acid	19	8	24	47	19
Potash	43	22	59	76	8

* Thorne, C. E., *Farm Manures*, p. 146. Orange Judd Publishing Co., New York, 1914.

† Shutt, M. A., Barnyard manure, *Can. Dept. Agr. Cent. Expt. Farm Bull.* 31, 1898.

‡ Thorne, C. E., *et al.*, The maintenance of soil fertility, *Ohio Agr. Expt. Sta. Bull.* 183, 1907.

§ Roberts, I. P., and H. H. Wing, On the deterioration of farmyard manure by leaching and fermentation, *Cornell Univ. Agr. Expt. Sta. Bull.* 13, 1889.

is then compressed to produce anaerobic conditions, a compost is formed which behaves differently from the commonly composted manure. Hot fermented manure has also the advantage that many of the disease-producing organisms carried in the manure are destroyed.

In the decomposition of stable manures, both in composts and in soils, considerable quantities of humus are formed. The processes involved are similar to the general processes of decomposition of plant and animal residues discussed previously. Because of the specific nature of the manure and because of the particular conditions under which the decomposition may take place in composts, a number of special problems are involved. Most important among these are the conservation of the nitrogen in the manure, as pointed out above, hygienic treatment of the solid human excreta to prevent epidemics and infectious diseases, and maximum production of humus. It is believed by many that, when equal amounts of nutrient elements are added to the soil in the form of mineral fertilizers, on the one hand, and of stable manures, on the other, the resulting equal increases in plant growth tend to prove that the manure is not superior to the fertilizer. The fact is frequently overlooked that manure may not give immediate superior effects because it does not contain sufficient concentrations of available nitrogen. Further, insufficient consideration is usually given to the importance of the

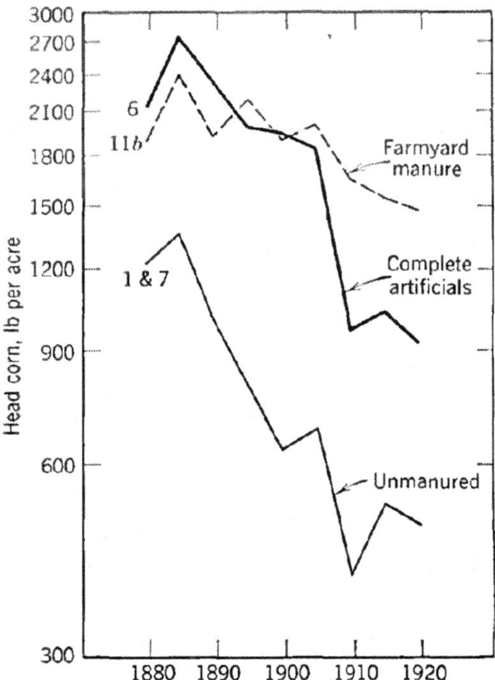

FIG. 124. Influence of manures upon the conservation of soil fertility (from Russell).

TABLE 68. MANURE SPREAD ON FIELD COMPARED WITH MANURE LEFT IN PILES (from Salter and Schollenberger)

	Relative Value in Increasing Crop Yields
Manure spread and plowed under immediately	100
Manure spread 2 days before plowing	71
Manure in piles 2 days before spreading and plowing	80
Manure spread 14 days before plowing	49
Manure in piles 14 days before spreading and plowing	55

residual effect of manure in building up the humus content of the soil (Table 68).

EFFECT OF STABLE MANURES UPON PLANT GROWTH AND SOIL FERTILITY

The important role of stable manures in plant growth and in soil fertility has been variously ascribed to six distinct factors: (1) Manures offer a readily available supply of nitrogen, phosphoric acid, and potash for growth of higher plants. (2) In the decomposition of the carbon complexes in the manures by microorganisms, considerable carbon dioxide is liberated, which is essential for plant growth. (3) The organic matter of the manures replenishes the supply of soil humus (4) Manures exert an important influence upon the microbiological activities in soil (5) Because of their bacterial content, stable manures are important for their inoculating properties. (6) Manures influence the colloidal properties of soil and the state of its aggregation

The phosphorus and potassium in stable manures are present largely in forms readily available to higher plants, as are inorganic salts The nitrogen in the manure is only about one-third to one-half as available as that of inorganic fertilizer; this has been brought out in numerous field tests as well as by nitrification experiments. There is little justification, therefore, for comparing the availability of the nitrogen in organic manures and in inorganic fertilizers, without considering the cumulative effects of the manure on the fertility of the soil and especially on its physical condition; this error has been frequently made in fertilizer trials, where only given crop yields for one year have been measured Stable manures were found to give particularly significant results, as compared with inorganic fertilizers, in dry years and on light soils (Table 69).

TABLE 69 COMPARATIVE CUMULATIVE EFFECTS OF MANURE AND CHEMICAL FERTILIZERS (from Salter and Schollenberger)

Ohio Agricultural Experiment Station, Wooster, Ohio, 5-year rotation fertility experiment

Plot	Treatment	Average Increase in Total Produce per Rotation *		Increase as Per Cent of That for Chemicals	
		First 10 Years	Entire 43 Years	First 10 Years	Entire 43 Years
		pounds	*pounds*	*per cent*	*per cent*
18	Manure	6,142	11,120	79	106
12	Chemicals	7,731	10,528	100	100
20	Manure	4,024	6,231	68	86
14	Chemicals	5,891	7,263	100	100

* Averages for limed and unlimed soils

Artificial Manures

With the introduction of machine power to replace horse and other animal power, the amount of stable manure available to the farmer was appreciably reduced. Furthermore, the growth of large urban areas required intensive truck-garden systems which consumed large quantities of the available manure. This resulted in a decrease in the amount left for use in fields and gardens. Recourse was had, therefore, to composting plant residues with mineral fertilizer, resulting in a product similar in every respect to that obtained from stable manures. To distinguish such composts of plant residues from composts of stable manures, the former are usually designated as "artificial manures."

To prepare artificial manures similar in chemical composition and in their effects upon the soil to composts commonly obtained from stable manures, cereal straw or other plant residues are utilized. These are supplemented with an inorganic source of nitrogen and to some extent also with available phosphorus and lime. When they are properly moistened, decomposition of the composts sets in immediately and is accompanied by a rise in temperature. The microbiological population and the chemical processes of decomposition involved are similar to those which commonly are found in like composts of stable manures. The value of inoculating such composts with active microorganisms is still debatable. Some fresh garden soil or actively decomposing stable manure is occasionally used for inoculation, with very satisfactory results.

The rapidity of decomposition of the plant materials in the compost and their transformation into humus depend upon the nature of the materials, their chemical composition, the amount and nature of the inorganic nutrients added, especially the nitrogen, the moisture content of the compost, its proper aeration, and temperature. These factors also influence the chemical nature of the humus produced in the compost and its effect upon soil processes. The nature of the plant residues and the conditions and extent of decomposition are particularly important. The humus of a compost produced from cereal straw will therefore, vary from that formed from corn stalks, or from oak leaves, or from pine needles, or from soybean stover (Table 70).

The compost is usually turned several times, especially after a temperature of 65–80°C has been attained. The turning must be

Table 70 Chemical Composition of Plant Residues, Manures, and Soil Humus (from Pichard)

Per cent of total organic matter

Constituents	Cereal Straw	Artificial Manures		Horse Manure for Mushrooms	Humus in Peat	Humus in Mineral Soil
		1	2			
Fatty substances	1.90	0.73	0.91	0.14	1.12	12.00
Resins	4.48	1.95	4.83	3.93	2.24	0.44
Pentosans	28.40	23.57	11.26	11.47	4.72	3.44
Hexosans	5.05	10.81	4.80	3.48		
Cellulose	37.35	29.66	19.59	13.17	2.77	2.98
Lignin	14.35	20.76	15.54	29.60	16.42	13.65
Soluble "humic acids"		3.56	16.62	19.25	26.98	27.46
"Humins"		4.25	5.50	3.50	16.95	6.21
Nitrogen	0.41	0.56	1.36	2.42	3.37	2.15

frequent enough for proper aeration, which favors development of aerobic fungi, actinomycetes, and bacteria. The moisture content of the compost must be adjusted to 75–80 per cent. If excess water is added, anaerobic conditions, which will retard decomposition, are created. With insufficient water, especially in loose, open heaps, nitrogen losses may result, and an inferior product is obtained.

Figure 122 gives the relative composition of artificial manure and of the original plant material from which it was prepared. Oat straw was allowed to decompose for 273 days at 37°C in the presence of added inorganic nutrient salts. In that time, the cellulose disappeared almost completely, the hemicelluloses and fats were markedly reduced, the lignin increased appreciably in relation to the other constituents, and the relative amounts of ash and protein increased to an even larger extent. The increase in the ash content is due to its gradual accumulation, resulting from destruction of the organic constituents. The increase in protein content is relatively greater than the increase in ash; this is due both to the relative accumulation of the protein parallel to the destruction of the carbohydrates and to the synthesis of microbial proteins from the inorganic nitrogen added to the compost. The lower the original nitrogen content of the plant material used in the preparation of the compost, the greater the amount of nitrogen required, and the greater the amount of protein subsequently synthesized. The lignin in the compost also increases during the process of decomposition, but to a relatively smaller degree than the increase in ash and protein; this increase in

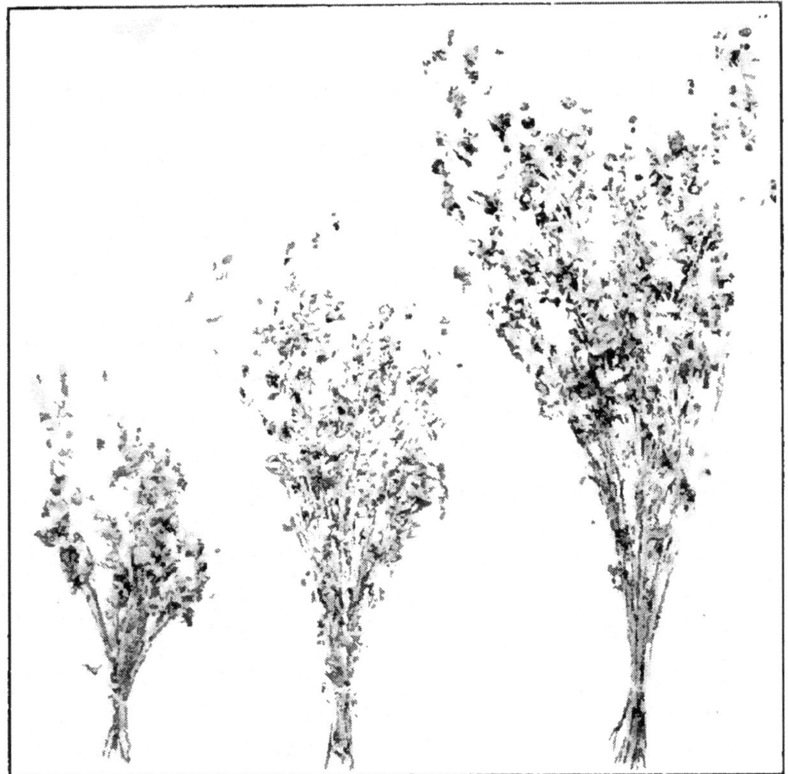

FIG. 125. Effect of artificial manure on growth of alsike clover. *Left to right,* lime and acid phosphate; lime, acid phosphate, and straw; lime, acid phosphate, and artificial manure (from Albrecht).

lignin content is due to the greater resistance of lignin than of the other plant constituents to microbial decomposition. The temperature and moisture content of the compost have an important influence upon the rapidity of decomposition of the straw and upon the formation of the humus.

A number of formulas have been suggested for supplementing straw and other plant residues to obtain a good artificial compost. Two such formulas follow:

Formula 1

Ammonium sulfate	67.5 pounds
Acid phosphate	22.5
Ground limestone	60

Use 150 pounds of this mixture per ton of straw.

Formula 2

Ammonium sulfate	60 pounds
Acid phosphate	30
Ground limestone	50
Potassium nitrate	25

Use 165 pounds of this mixture per ton of straw.

Other sources of nitrogen may be employed, such as urea, calcium cyanamide, or ammonium phosphate. The amounts of phosphate

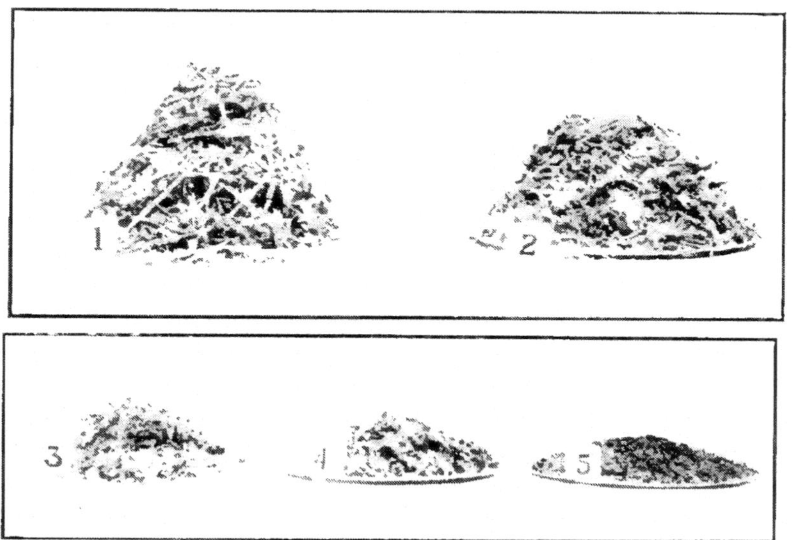

Fig. 126. Effect of temperature upon composting: 1, 7°C; 2, 7°C; 3, 18°C; 4, 27°C; 5, 37°C. All except 1 received supplementary additions of nitrogen and mineral salts (from Waksman and Gerretsen).

and lime added are adjusted according to the nature of the nitrogen source used.

When the moisture content of a heap of plant residues is not high enough to allow normal decomposition and is not low enough to prevent it, a phenomenon known as self-heating may occur. Animal manures as well as plant residues, especially hay, kept in heaps, may undergo limited decomposition; this may lead to the formation of certain volatile substances, which, on coming in contact with the air, ignite spontaneously. This is also true of heaps of peat. The heap acts as an insulator, preventing radiation of heat from the inside and penetration of oxygen from the outside. The lack of sufficient moisture prevents absorption of the heat. A low moisture, a high temperature, and a lack of oxygen penetration may thus create conditions favorable for spontaneous heating. Losses of organic matter during spontaneous heating of alfalfa were found to be largely at the expense of the fats, sugars, and hemicelluloses, and to a lesser degree of the cellulose and protein; lignin suffered no loss at all. Absorption of oxygen by the lignin, accompanied by a rise in tem-

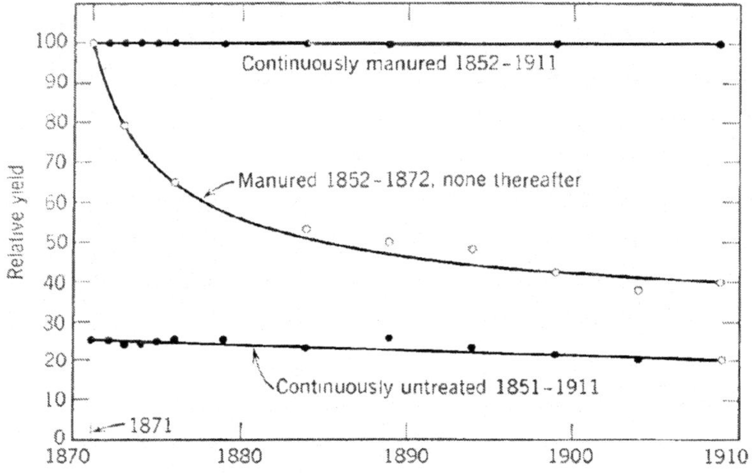

FIG. 127. Residual effects of heavy applications of manure (from Hall).

perature to the ignition point, was believed to lead to the actual ignition. It has been suggested that addition of salt to moist alfalfa hay will inhibit bacterial development and thus delay the process of decomposition long enough to permit curing.

GREEN MANURES

Green manures comprise plant crops grown in a given soil to a certain stage of development and plowed under while still green. Both leguminous and nonleguminous plants are utilized for this purpose. The nature of the plant to be selected for green manuring depends upon the soil and the climate and upon farming practice.

Green manures serve several distinct purposes for plant growth and soil improvement: (1) To increase the supply of total and available nitrogen in the soil. Various leguminous plants are utilized for this purpose. The nature of the legume thus selected depends largely on the geography of the region, the season of the year when the land is free from a crop, the nature of the soil, and the rotation system. (2) To prevent the nutrient elements of the soil, especially the nitrates, from leaching out during the part of the year when no cultivated crops are being grown on the soil. (3) To increase the supply of organic matter in soil. (4) To protect the soil against erosion.

The plants used for green manuring are high in water-soluble constituents, in nitrogen, and in minerals, they are comparatively low in cellulose and in lignin. As a result, decomposition of a green manure crop plowed into the soil sets in very rapidly. This is accompanied by rapid liberation of the nitrogen and the minerals in available forms, comparatively little humus is produced. Figure 48 illustrates the difference between the chemical composition of young plants and of mature plants and the influence that this has upon the decomposition of the various organic constituents of these materials. As the plants grow older, their ash and nitrogen contents decrease, and their cellulose and lignin contents increase. Decomposition of younger plants results in liberation of some of the nitrogen as ammonia, the younger the plant and the higher the nitrogen content, the more rapidly is ammonia liberated and the greater is the amount liberated. Beyond a certain stage, no ammonia will be liberated; actually nitrogen may have to be added to hasten decomposition, as already shown.

The plants grown for green manuring and plowed into the soil can be divided into three categories. (1) those that contain a certain balanced proportion of available carbohydrates to nitrogen; (2) those that contain an excess of nitrogen, or more than is required for decomposition of the carbohydrates, and (3) those that contain an excess of carbohydrates and lignin over nitrogen. The third group, comprising both legumes and nonlegumes, decompose more slowly than the plants of the other two categories.

Table 71 shows the relative amounts of total plant material and nitrogen in a number of plants used for green manuring, and the effect of such manures on crop growth and loss of humus from soil, as compared to the plowing under of weeds only. Vetch and crimson clover produced the largest amounts of growth, contained the highest amounts of nitrogen, and gave the highest crop yields of corn after plowing under of the green manure. Wheat and rye used as green manures gave the highest percentages of plant material in the roots, the lowest nitrogen contents in the plant material, and the poorest effects upon the corn crop, they also resulted in the smallest loss of humus. Whereas the humus loss for the weed plot was 0.08 per cent of the carbon, losses for the wheat and rye plots were only 0.01 per cent. It is important to note that, even with heavy applications of green manures for 5 years, the humus content of the soil decreased.

TABLE 71. YIELDS AND COMPOSITION OF GREEN MANURE CROPS SEEDED IN STANDING CORN AND PLOWED UNDER THE FOLLOWING SPRING (from Sprague)

Nature of Plant Used as Green Manure	Weight of Crop, 5-Year Average		Nitrogen Content of Tops and Roots, 2-Year Average	Total Nitrogen per Acre in Green Manure	Yields of Shelled Corn Following Green Manure Crops	Loss in Soil Humus as Carbon
	Total Dry Weight per Acre *pounds*	Per Cent of Dry Weight in Roots	*per cent*	*pounds*	*per cent*	*per cent*
Winter vetch	3,812	20.8	3.49	133.0	127.8	0.02
Crimson clover	3,049	21.3	3.03	92.4	115.6	0.10
Red clover	1,786	17.8	2.82	50.4	114.7	0.05
Sweet clover	1,436	19.7	2.75	39.5	113.7	0.07
Alsike clover	1,983	20.6	2.68	53.1	104.4	0.11
Winter wheat	2,089	39.3	1.63	34.1	99.7	0.01
Winter rye	2,463	35.5	1.29	31.8	95.3	0.01
Weeds only	1,263	7.6	1.50	18.9	100.0	0.08

When comparatively young plant materials are used as green manures, there is danger of a loss of nitrogen through volatilization as ammonia, the loss depending upon the amount of total nitrogen, as well as of readily decomposing nitrogen compounds in the green plant material. Young plants, low in lignin and in cellulose, but high in water-soluble substances and in nitrogen, decompose much more rapidly than do mature plants; they leave a much smaller residue in the form of humus, and only a small part of the original nitrogen is stored away in this humus. In the case of more mature plants, a considerably larger amount of humus is left in the soil, because of slower decomposition of the plant material and because of the higher lignin content, smaller quantities of the plant nutrients are liberated in decomposition of these materials. In many instances, considerable time may elapse before the nutrient elements, especially the nitrogen, are liberated in forms available for plant growth. The age of the plant used for green manuring exerts an important influence upon the amount and rapidity of liberation of the nutrient elements in available forms and upon the chemical nature and abundance of the humus produced. The extent of the liberation of the nutrients and the amount of humus produced can thus be controlled by proper selection of plants for green manuring and of the time when these plants are plowed under.

The humus left from the decomposition of green manures does not completely replace the humus lost from the soil as a result of cultivation Mooers has shown that, when cowpeas were grown on a soil and the whole crop was turned under annually, there was a loss of 0.11 per cent of humus, or a total of 2,200 pounds per acre during a 20-year period. When the cowpea crop was removed and only the stubble turned under, the loss of humus from the soil was considerably greater. at the end of the 20 years, the total loss was 0 24 per cent, or 4,800 pounds per acre. As a result of the turning under of 20 annual crops of cowpea hay containing about 20 tons of dry matter, there was left in the soil 2,600 pounds of humus, that is, only 6.5 per cent of the total plant material. Stable manure, on the other hand, not only could fully replace the losses of humus from the soil but actually brought about an increase in humus content. When the soil received stable manure, at the rate of 4 tons per acre annually for 20 years, a gain of 0 11 per cent of humus took place.

Use of green manures is recommended where an available supply of nitrogen and carbon dioxide is required but where the amount of humus left is not of great importance When it is essential to increase the supply of humus in the soil, stable manures or mature plant residues are to be preferred, either after they have been composted or when supplemented with available nitrogen and phosphorus upon addition to the soil.

Selected Bibliography

1 Albrecht, W A, Artificial manure production on the farm, *Univ Missouri Agr. Expt Sta Bull* 258, 1927
2 Albrecht, W A, Methods of incorporating organic matter with the soil in relation to nitrogen accumulations, *Univ Missouri Agr Expt Sta Bull* 249, 1936
3 Barnette, R M, Jones, H W, and Hester, J B, Lysimeter studies with the decomposition of summer cover crops, *Univ Florida Agr Expt Sta Bull* 327, 1938
4 Daji, J A, The decomposition of green manures in soil, *J Agr Sci*, 24 15–27, 1934
5 Dunn, L E, and Wheeting, L C, Utilization of barnyard manure for Washington soils, *Wash State Coll Agr Expt. Sta Bull* 395, 1941.
6. Humfeld, H, and Smith, N R, The decomposition of vetch green manure in relation to the surrounding soil, *J Agr Research*, 44 113, 1932
7 Jenkins, S H, *Organic Manures*, Imperial Bureau of Soil Science, Harpenden, England, 1935
8 Jensen, H L, The microbiology of farmyard manure decomposition in the soil I Changes in the microflora and their relation to nitrification, *J Agr Sci*, 21 38–80, 1931
9 Leukel, W A, Barnette, R M, and Hester, J B, Composition and nitrification studies on *Crotalaria striata, Soil Sci*, 28 347–371, 1929
10 Mooers, C A, Effects of liming and green manuring on crop yields and on soil supplies of nitrogen and humus, *Univ Tenn Agr. Expt. Sta Bull* 135, 1926
11 Piper, C V, Green manuring, *U S Dept Agr Farmers' Bull* 1250, 1922
12 Salter, R M, and Schollenberger, C J, Farm manure, *Ohio Agr Expt Sta Bull* 605, 1939
13 Smith, F B, Stevenson, W H, and Brown, P. E, The production of artificial farm manures, *Iowa State Coll. Agr Bull.* 126, 1930.
14 Smith, F B, and Thornton, G D, Production of artificial manure, *Univ Florida Agr Expt Sta Bull* 415, 1945
15 Sprague, H B, The value of winter green manure crops, *N J Agr Expt Sta Bull* 609, 1936
16 Thorne, C E, *Farm Manures*, Orange Judd Publishing Co, New York, p 146, 1914
17. Turk, L M, The composition of soybean plants at various growth stages as related to their rate of decomposition and use as green manure, *Univ Missouri Agr Expt Sta Bull* 173, 1932
18 Waksman, S A, Chemical and microbiological principles underlying the decomposition of green manures in the soil, *J Am Soc Agron*, 21 1–18, 1929

19. Waksman, S A , *Humus, Origin, Chemical Composition and Importance in Nature*, Williams & Wilkins Co , Baltimore, 2nd Ed , 1938
20 Waksman, S A , Tenney, F G , and Diehm, R A , Chemical and microbiological principles underlying the transformation of organic matter in the preparation of artificial manures, *J Am Soc Agron* , 21 533–546, 1929

· 15 ·

Microorganisms and Soil Fertility

Domestication of Microorganisms

The control of a given reaction that occurs in nature and the application of such reaction or system for the benefit of man and his economy, especially when this involves complex biological processes, gradually lead to the domestication of this system and these processes. Men learned to domesticate animals and plants in prehistoric times. Only very few animals and very few plants have been introduced into human economy since history began. In the case of microorganisms, the picture is quite different. The ability of man to domesticate microorganisms, including those living below ground and those living above it, those that are able to control diseases and those that bring about useful processes, may be looked upon as one of the greatest triumphs of modern civilization. This has been accomplished in the brief span of less than about three-quarters of a century. Some of these domestications have been brought about only within the last decade, as in the manufacture of antibiotics. Soil microorganisms have contributed their share to the growing family of domesticated forms of life which man has placed under his control.

Within this category, by far the most important group of organisms, from the point of view of soil processes and crop production, are the root-nodule or legume bacteria, or those organisms that form nodules on the roots of leguminous plants. The solution of the problem of soil inoculation and development of an understanding of the strain specificity of the organisms concerned in the inoculation of specific plants have in many instances revolutionized agricultural practice. Such organisms have come to occupy a highly important place in rural economy and also in soil conservation and soil improvement.

In addition to root-nodule bacteria, various other microorganisms have been utilized for soil inoculation. Although but seldom is a soil found to be so lacking in specific organisms that their introduction is required to bring about a particular soil process, occasionally the growth of certain crops and the need for specific reactions in the soil make such inoculation desirable This is true, for example, of the growth of various forest trees, for which certain mycorrhiza fungi are required It is also true for certain types of orchids and other plants. In addition, the use of sulfur bacteria in very specific cases and of nitrifying organisms in others nearly exhausts the occasional needs for artificial introduction of organisms into the soil. All other claims for the favorable effects obtained by inoculation of soil with various bacteria or fungi, ranging from *Azotobacter* and spore-forming bacteria, namely, the "all-crop inoculants," to certain fungi or earthworms, are exaggerated claims, based more on hope than on fact, and always with an eye on the immediate benefit to the seller of those cultures

Among the other important processes in which considerable improvement has resulted from knowledge of the microbiological population, the preparation of composts, discussed in the preceding chapter, the preservation of manures and the conservation of soil deserve particular attention

Preservation of Manures

When stable manures or plant residues supplemented with inorganic fertilizer are placed in composts and conditions are made favorable to the activities of microorganisms, through proper aeration and sufficient moisture, numerous microbiological reactions immediately set in These are accompanied by a rapid rise in temperature. Among the major chemical changes that take place during the process of composting, the reduction of the cellulose and hemicelluloses and the relative increase in ash, lignin, and protein are most significant The latter occurs at the expense of the water-soluble forms of nitrogen, which are utilized by the microorganisms for their synthetic needs and are thereby converted into complex organic forms There is hardly any need for specific inoculation Plant residues and soils carry enough organisms which will immediately become active when favorable conditions are established Addition of a few more organisms will scarcely modify the many changes set in motion by the microorganisms already present

One of the major economic problems involved in the preservation of stable manures is the loss of nitrogen, which may amount to as much as 20–50 per cent of the total nitrogen present in the manure Various procedures have been utilized for preventing such losses. One of the simplest principles is to hasten the activities of the microorganisms which bring about the destruction of the cellulose and the hemicelluloses in the manure If conditions are favorable, an active microbiological population will bring this about during the early stages of decomposition, thereby transforming the soluble forms of nitrogen in the manure into complex organic forms The supplementary addition of superphosphate will often tend to neutralize the ammonia liberated, thus preventing its volatilization

If the decomposition of the manure has been allowed to proceed too far and if oxidation of the nitrogen to nitrate has begun, there is great danger of this nitrate's being reduced to atmospheric nitrogen. A compost offers ideal conditions for such a reaction. To prevent such losses, the compost must be made anaerobic, so as to hinder the activities of the nitrifying bacteria, thus avoiding the conversion of the ammonia into nitrate and the subsequent reduction of the latter to gaseous forms of nitrogen

Evaluation of Soil Fertility by Measuring Microbiological Activities

Numerous attempts were made during the first decade of this century, beginning with Remy and Lohnis and followed by Lipman and Brown and many others, to interpret the fertility potential of a soil on the basis of its microbiological activity Several methods of approach were usually followed, of which these may serve as illustrations.

1. A small amount of a given soil was added to a nutrient solution of known composition and, after a few days' incubation, a single biological change was measured. The reactions most commonly studied were the formation of ammonia from peptone, or ammonification, the formation of nitrate from ammonium salt, or nitrification, the destruction of nitrate, or denitrification, and the fixation of nitrogen

2. A chemical substance, simple or complex in nature, was added to a given quantity of soil, the moisture of which was adjusted to 60 or 70 per cent of water-holding capacity. The soil was incubated at 20–30°C for 7–30 days, and changes, similar to those listed above, were measured.

3. An examination was made, by the plate or other suitable method, of the abundance of certain organisms in the soil. An attempt was then made to evaluate the fertility of the soil on the basis of the numbers and biochemical potentialities of these organisms.

4. Microorganisms were used for determining the concentration of certain important plant nutrients in the soil.

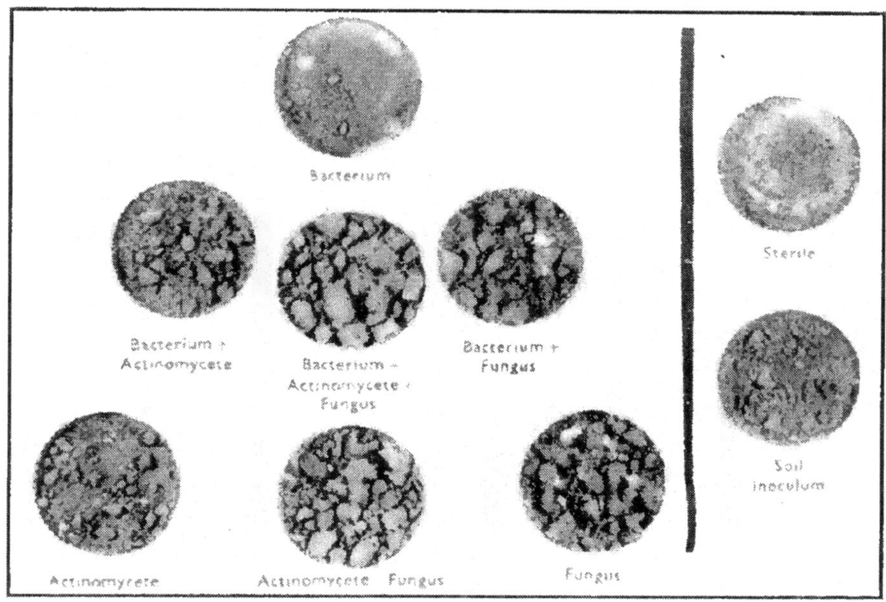

Fig. 128. Effect of microorganisms on soil aggregation (from Swaby).

Without analyzing the voluminous literature that dealt with this subject, it is sufficient to say that none of these methods yielded results that could meet the test of severe criticism. They are now largely abandoned, in spite of the fact that certain very definite correlations have often been reported between the results obtained by these methods and the fertility of soils. The major difficulty involved in the use of such methods was that reactions brought about by microorganisms in the soil under natural conditions are subject to too many variables. These comprise not only inherent differences in soil conditions, but also the effects of climate and soil management. Not all these could possibly be taken into consideration in the various laboratory studies. As long as a knowledge of the effects of these variables was lacking, the information obtained by microbiological procedures was limited in scope and had little application to practical agriculture.

Microorganisms and Soil Conservation

The role of microorganisms in improving the physical condition of the soil, notably soil aggregation, has recently received consider-

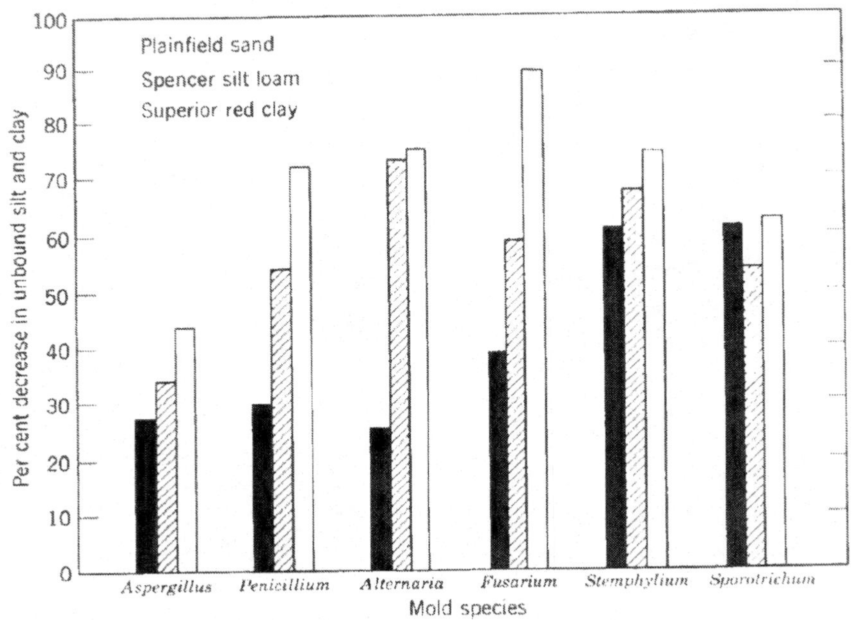

Fig. 129. Influence of specific fungi on aggregation of three soils treated with alfalfa (from Gilmour, Allen, Truog).

able attention. The structure of the soil is greatly affected by the mycelium of fungi and the slimy cells of bacteria, as well as by their metabolic products. The effect of these consists in binding the loose soil particles into water-stable aggregates. Various microorganisms vary greatly in this respect. Whereas some bacteria have very little effect, certain fungi, by means of their long hyphae, entangle the soil particles into stable aggregates. The slimy substances, of a hemicellulose or polyuronide nature, produced by various bacteria are also highly effective in this respect.

Addition of organic materials to the soil, notably glucose, starch, straw, clover, and stable manures, favors greatly the state of aggregation by favoring development of various groups of microorganisms.

According to Swaby, pure cultures of *Absidia glauca* and *Aspergillus nidulans* growing in sterilized soil enriched with glucose produced 242 and 374 meters of mycelium per gram, as measured by methods of Jones and Mollison. They entangled, respectively, 96.5 and 80.3 per cent of soil into stable aggregates. Fresh soil contained 38.8 meters of hyphae per gram. The presence of 38 per cent of aggregates in such soil could thus be ascribed to the function of fungus mycelium (Fig. 129). This is also brought out in Table 72. The

TABLE 72. THE INFLUENCE OF MOLD SPECIES AND ALFALFA ON THE DISPERSION RATIOS OF THREE SOILS (from Gilmour *et al.*)

Mold Species Added	Dispersion Ratios					
	Plainfield Sand		Spencer Silt Loam		Superior Red Clay	
	No Organic Matter Added	Alfalfa Added	No Organic Matter Added	Alfalfa Added	No Organic Matter Added	Alfalfa Added
None	41.5	37.2	43.5	30.4	38.0	20.0
A. niger	42.6	29.7	26.4	27.5	18.1	10.5
Penicillium sp.	41.4	28.8	24.7	21.4	16.8	9.2
Alternaria sp.	40.1	29.9	27.3	11.6	21.3	8.2
Fusarium sp.	42.6	25.0	28.2	18.2	35.3	2.9
Helminthosporium sp.	42.6	24.8	25.2	27.5	36.7	9.9
Curvularia sp.	40.1	22.8	28.4	12.6	37.6	4.1
Stemphylium sp.	44.7	15.7	29.6	11.2	35.0	8.2
Sporotrichum sp.	41.5	15.7	28.4	21.4	34.8	11.8

aggregating effect of bacteria was calculated to be only about 2 per cent of the total.

That microorganisms differ greatly in their soil-aggregating properties and that the products of some of these organisms are excellent soil-binders have also been brought out by Martin, McCalla, and others. Fungi and certain polysaccharide-forming bacteria were found to be more effective than actinomycetes, which in turn were better than yeasts; certain bacteria were least effective.

Many of the soil-aggregating substances and even the mycelium and cells produced by microorganisms are later destroyed by other microorganisms, thus producing an effect of disaggregation. Microbial associations alone could not account for the formation of permanent crumbs, especially when no fresh organic materials were added; this suggests the probability that other cementing substances, such as clay and humus, play essential roles in this process, as shown recently by Swaby.

The inoculation of soil with fungi, such as *Trichoderma lignorum*, to improve soil structure has been recommended. Such inoculation is effective, however, only when accompanied by addition of freshly decomposable organic matter to the soil.

TABLE 73. AGGREGATING EFFECT OF MICROORGANISMS UPON VARIOUS SILT AND CLAY FRACTIONS OF COLLINGTON SANDY LOAM WITH COMPLEX ORGANIC MATERIALS AS ENERGY SOURCES (from Martin and Waksman)

Incubation period, days		20			50			90		
Fraction, μ		<50	<20	<5	<50	<20	<5	<50	<20	<5
Inoculation	Energy Source *	Ag †	Ag	Ag	Ag	Ag	Ag	Ag	Ag	Ag
A. niger	Control	0	0	0	0	0	0	0	0	0
	Alfalfa	49	45	31	57	52	36	52	46	30
	Manure	24	22	10	29	41	31	32	36	40
	Peat	4	9	3	19	31	30	15	23	34
Soil suspension	Control	0	0	0	0	0	0	0	0	0
	Alfalfa	57	61	61	71	77	74	68	68	64
	Manure	32	41	27	44	54	56	40	47	50
	Peat	8	17	18	15	29	34	13	20	25

* All organic materials used in 2 per cent concentration.
† Ag = Percentage aggregation.

Gilmour, Allen, and Truog concluded that inoculated soils to which no organic materials had been added underwent only a slight to moderate degree of aggregation. On the other hand, the addition of oat straw and alfalfa decreased considerably the percentages of unbound silt and clay in the soils studied. When no fungi were present, there were lesser decreases in the unbound fractions. In the presence of alfalfa and fungi, there was a marked reduction in the susceptibilities of the soils to erosion. The effectiveness of fungi in the aggregation process was related to the effectiveness of the individual organisms, the type of organic matter, and the physical composition of the soil.

TABLE 74 INFLUENCE OF FUNGI ON SOIL AGGREGATION (from Swaby)

Aggregation	Mean Weight of Aggregates, >1 Mm/50 Gm Soil	Total Number of Strains	Growth on Agar, Number of Strains	
			Woolly	Prostrate
	gm			
Excellent	37–45	21	18	3
Very good	29–37	15	10	5
Good	21–29	11	3	8
Fair	13–21	3	0	3
Totals		50	31	19

SOIL INOCULATION

It often becomes necessary to introduce into the soil bacteria and certain other microorganisms that may be lacking there Among these, root-nodule bacteria occupy a pre-eminent place, as brought out previously. At first, soil in which the legume was grown successfully was used for inoculation Soon after, however, artificial cultures in liquid and solid media were substituted for the soil In recent years, peat material has been utilized as a carrier for legume bacteria.

Although soils in which legumes have once grown contain for some time the organisms responsible for formation of nodules on the corresponding plants, it was found that these bacteria may deteriorate in the soil, either by loss of vitality or through the effect of antagonistic microorganisms It may, therefore, become advisable to inoculate a soil frequently for a certain legume The existence of various strains of bacteria, which vary greatly in activity, the formation of bacteriophages active against the specific bacteria, and the potential effect of antibiotics produced by other microorganisms lead more and more to recognition of the importance of repeated inoculation of soils with vigorous cultures of organisms

On a much smaller scale, but of potential importance, are the mycorrhiza fungi These are capable of producing associations with various higher plants, notably certain evergreens, resulting in increased plant growth It has been found advisable to inoculate nursery beds with a small amount of soil from an old bed in which the corresponding trees have been grown successfully. So far, no pure cultures of fungi have been utilized for this purpose. In certain soils, however, it seems to have been established beyond doubt that the presence of fungi is essential for normal tree development.

In addition to these two groups of microorganisms—the legume bacteria and mycorrhiza fungi—it has also been found that occasionally inoculation of soils with other organisms may result in increased plant growth. Among these organisms, it is sufficient to mention the nitrifying bacteria, sulfur-oxidizing bacteria, bacteria pathogenic to Japanese beetles or other insects, and nematodes parasitic upon insects or destructive to other injurious nematodes. In some cases the advisability of microbial inoculation of soil is questionable, unless accompanied by certain soil treatments. This is true of the use of certain saprophytic fungi which are believed to act as a check upon the development of pathogenic fungi, of fungi for improving soil structure, and of "all-soil inoculants" (Azotogen).

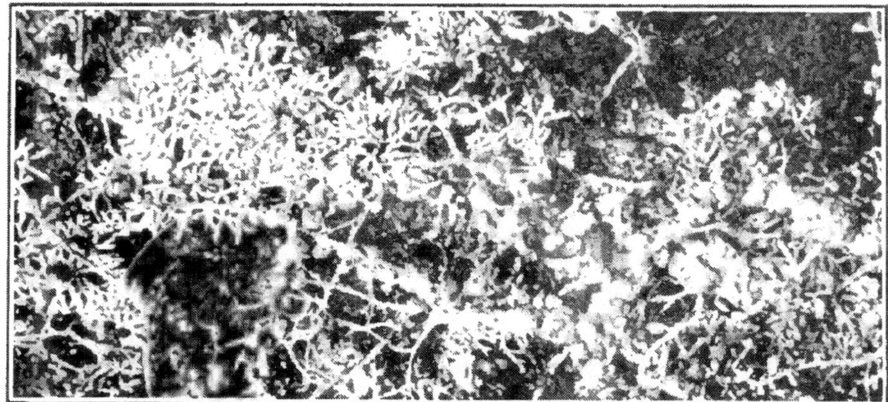

Fig. 130. Ectotrophic mycorrhiza developing on roots of *Pinus sylvestris* (from Melin).

Enrichment of the soil with organisms not present there originally may lead to development of antagonists, which bring about the destruction of the introduced bacteria.

Modification of Soil Reaction and Microbiological Activities

There is no one particular reaction which is favorable alike to all groups of soil microorganisms. When the soil is acid, especially at a reaction less than pH 6.0, it may become injurious to the growth of many bacteria, notably the nitrifying and the nitrogen-fixing types, and favorable to the development of fungi. This may be because the competition of the bacteria for the available nutrients in the soil is repressed by increased acidity On the other hand, a less acid or slightly alkaline reaction of the soil may become unfavorable to the development of fungi and have a favorable effect upon many of the soil bacteria Thus, when conditions are made unfavorable to the development of one group of organisms in the soil, another group may be favored.

Addition of calcium carbonate to an acid soil was found to stimulate greatly the multiplication of bacteria, accompanied by an increase in the decomposition of the soil organic matter This is shown in Table 75. Addition of excess calcium carbonate and especially of magnesium carbonate, however, may become injurious to many of the soil bacteria

TABLE 75 INFLUENCE OF $CaCO_3$ ON EVOLUTION OF CO_2 FROM SOIL (from Konig)

$CaCO_3$ Added	CO_2 Evolved per Day
per cent	*mg*
0	181 3
0 04	223 6
0 10	308 4
0 20	416 4
0 40	455 4

EFFECTS OF CULTIVATION AND FERTILIZATION

Cultivation of soil, which results in conservation of the soil moisture, is favorable to the development of various groups of microorganisms It brings about an increased production of nitrate because of improved soil aeration By favoring the development of aerobic organisms, cultivation stimulates greater decomposition of

TABLE 76 INFLUENCE OF TILLAGE UPON ABUNDANCE OF BACTERIA IN SOIL (from Chester)

Numbers in thousands per gram.

Period of Time	Bacteria
At start	2,040
After 7 days	5,495
After 9 days	6,171
After 14 days	11,326
After 24 days	12 600

the organic matter, leading to increased carbon dioxide evolution and greater liberation of the nitrogen as ammonia. This explains the favorable effect of fallowing upon the activities of the soil microbiological population The "ripening" of soil in spring is a result of treatments that are favorable to the activities of soil microorganisms.

Fertilization and crop rotation also have an important effect upon the microbiological population The nature of the fertilizer, the residual effect upon the reaction of the soil, the nature of the crop grown, and the treatment of the crop will influence in one way or another the nature and abundance of microorganisms of the soil This is true especially of the addition of available energy in the plant residues, the excretion by plants of substances favorable to microbial development, the increase in soil nutrients, and the improvement in the buffering capacity and physical condition of the soil

Microorganisms and Plant Growth

Plants and microorganisms exert numerous effects upon one another. Plants supply to the microorganisms most of the energy and nutrients in the form of the numerous residues in the roots and stubble. They also secrete soluble substances which affect in various ways the growth of microorganisms Plants control the chemical composition of the soil solution, thus modifying the nature of the medium in which most of the activities of microorganisms take place. By removing some of the nutrients from the soil, plants may exert an injurious effect upon the growth of microorganisms, or may actually compete with them for some of these nutrients Plant roots influence the structure of the soil and bring about an improvement in soil aeration, thus affecting greatly the growth of microorganisms.

Microorganisms, in their turn, exert numerous influences upon the growth of higher plants By decomposing the plant and animal residues in the soil, thus bringing about their mineralization, microorganisms liberate the nutrients required for plant growth, especially the carbon dioxide, nitrate, phosphate, and sulfate. The symbiotic nitrogen-fixing bacteria, through their association with the roots of leguminous plants, effect the fixation of large quantities of nitrogen. Plants and microorganisms form a variety of other symbiotic associations, designated as mycorrhiza (roots and fungi) and bacteriorrhiza (roots and bacteria). Although the importance of mycorrhiza in plant development has been definitely established, the effect of the bacteriorrhiza formations is still under discussion.

Various microorganisms are believed to produce plant-growth-stimulating substances, including vitamins and hormones. Although this is still open to debate, the fact remains that plants may benefit considerably from addition of certain hormones and vitamins to the soil. To what extent bacteria and other organisms are responsible for the production of such substances has not been established as yet. There is no doubt, however, that addition of organic matter, especially stable manures, to the soil results in favorable effects upon plant growth, which cannot be ascribed to the mere inorganic fer-

TABLE 77. INFLUENCE OF PLANT DEVELOPMENT UPON THE ABUNDANCE OF MICROBES AND THEIR ACTIVITY IN SOILS AT DIFFERENT DISTANCES FROM THE PLANT ROOTS *
(from Starkey)

Plant	Region of Sampling	Bacteria *millions*	Actinomycetes *millions*	Fungi *thousands*	CO_2 Formed *mg*
Bean	15 inches from main roots	18.6	7.6	24.6	9.7
Bean	9 inches from main roots	32.8	10.0	21.6	12.0
Bean	3 inches from main roots	36.2	8.0	20.0	12.0
Bean	Close to main roots	55.4	6.2	19.2	15.1
Bean	Superficial layer of the roots	199.4	12.6	35.2	
Beet	15 inches from main root	18.6	10.0	25.8	11.2
Beet	9 inches from main root	27.0	11.4	25.0	13.6
Beet	3 inches from main root	33.4	10.4	25.8	14.9
Beet	Close to main root	57.4	6.8	30.0	18.2
Beet	Superficial layer of the roots	427.4	10.6	136.0	
Corn	15 inches from main root	22.8	8.4	29.6	10.3
Corn	9 inches from main root	26.2	11.8	23.2	15.2
Corn	3 inches from main root	44.8	8.8	29.6	15.2
Corn	Close to main root	93.2	10.2	49.6	25.0
Corn	Superficial layer of the roots	653.4	8.6	278.0	

* Age of plants, 113 days.

tilizer constituents of the manure. The favorable action, resulting from decomposition of the organic residues, upon plant growth must be definitely ascribed to the activities of microorganisms.

The effect of antibiotics produced by microorganisms upon plants is another debatable question. Certain compounds, like actinomycin and clavacin, are formed in artificial media by soil-inhabiting microorganisms. These compounds have a toxic effect upon plant growth, resulting in a type of wilting. The question remains, however, to what extent these substances are produced in the soil itself and how their activities are modified by the inorganic and organic soil colloids.

Soil Population as a Whole

The numerous interrelationships existing in the soil between plants and microorganisms, on the one hand, and between soils and microorganisms, on the other, demonstrate the manifold activities of the extensive microbiological population inhabiting the soil. These microorganisms are responsible for numerous chemical reactions taking place in the soil. The organisms do not exist and multiply in the soil in a fixed manner. Their growth and activities are constantly modified, depending upon the nature of the soil, its treatment, the crop grown, and various changes in environmental conditions. The microbiological population of any soil at a given moment, may be in a state of equilibrium. Any modification of this equilibrium will bring about a marked change, both in qualitative composition and in quantitative interrelations, among the constituent members of this population.

Under natural conditions, modifications of this equilibrium take place constantly. The freezing of soil in winter, the melting of snow and the thawing of ice in spring, the frequent wetting and drying of soil in summer and in fall, the addition of leaves, roots, and other plant stubble from the growing vegetation, will continuously modify the soil population by changing the conditions of the soil. The nature of the crop and the treatment of the soil, especially cultivation and fertilization, further influence in many ways the nature and composition of the soil microbiological population.

Aside from those modifications, man has learned to influence the soil population through various specific treatments, such as addition of lime or of acid-reacting fertilizers, air-drying or steam-sterilization, or treatment with various antiseptics. This is true particularly of greenhouse soils and of nursery beds. All these treatments bring about marked changes in the composition of the microbiological population.

Selected Bibliography

1. Ensminger, L. E., and Gieseking, J. E., Resistance of clay-adsorbed proteins to proteolytic hydrolysis, *Soil Sci.*, 53 205–209, 1942.
2. Geltser, F. Y., Influence of the type of organic matter on soil structure, *Trans. Sov. Sect. Intern. Soc. Soil Sci.*, 5 115–120, 1936.

3. Gilmour, C M, Allen, O N, and Truog, E, Soil aggregation as influenced by the growth of mold species, kind of soil, and organic matter, *Proc Soil Sci Soc. Am*, 13 292–296, 1949

4 McCalla, T M, Influence of microorganisms and of some organic substances on soil structure, *Soil Sci*, 59 287–297, 1945

5 McCalla, T M, Influence of some microbial groups on stabilizing soil structure against falling water drops, *Proc Soil Sci Soc Am*, 11 260–263, 1946

6 Martin, J P, Microorganisms and soil aggregation I Origin and nature of some aggregating substances, *Soil Sci*, 59 163–174, 1945, II Influence of bacterial polysaccharides on soil structure, *Soil Sci*, 61 157–166, 1946

7 Myers, H E, and McCalla, T M, Changes in soil aggregation in relation to bacterial number, hydrogen-ion concentration, and length of time soil was kept moist, *Soil Sci*, 51 189–200, 1941

8 Swaby, R J, The relationship between microorganisms and soil aggregation, *J Gen Microb*, 3 236–254, 1949

·16·

Recent Developments in Soil Microbiology

General Trends

Soil microbiology is a borderline science. It deals with microorganisms and their importance in soil processes It involves problems in ecology, physiology, and biochemistry Since it is concerned with soils as the natural substrate for the growth of microorganisms, it embraces physical, chemical, and biological phenomena An understanding of the relationships of microorganisms to higher plants and of the effect of microorganisms upon the activities of other microorganisms is essential.

Soil microbiology has certain theoretical and practical considerations It involves (*a*) knowledge of the microscopic, ultramicroscopic, and near-microscopic populations of the soil, as influenced by the nature and composition of the soil, by climatic and environmental conditions, and by plant growth, (*b*) knowledge of the activities of these microorganisms, which result in a variety of processes and in the formation of numerous metabolic products, influencing directly or indirectly the nature and composition of the soil and the growth of cultivated and uncultivated plants; (*c*) methods of control of microbiological activities, and their domestication, thus harnessing them for the service of man as well as of those plants and animals upon whom man has come to depend for his existence

Although the numerous groups of microorganisms inhabiting the soil form only a very small part of the soil mass, they are responsible for many of the chemical transformations, and even for some of the physical changes, that take place in the soil They result in making the soil a living system rather than a mass of dead debris The microbiological population is largely distributed through the upper layers of the soil mass, where the living plants send down their roots and where they obtain the necessary nutrients. When the roots die, they are rapidly attacked by the soil organisms, with the result that some of the nutrient elements are returned to circulation and made available again for the growth of new roots and new plants. In this process, the microorganisms build up extensive cell material, comprising bacterial cells and slimy substances produced by bacteria, mycelium of fungi and of actinomycetes and their products, as well as numerous other living and dead bodies of microscopic forms of life. All these contribute to the formation of soil humus. They not only serve as reservoirs for further activities of microorganisms, but also exert various physical and chemical effects upon the soil, as by binding the soil particles and interacting with the various cations and anions of the soil organic and inorganic constituents.

As a result of these microbiological activities in the soil, a continuous stream of carbon dioxide, ammonia, nitrate, phosphate, and other nutrient elements is made available for plant growth. The humus supply of the soil may either increase or be gradually destroyed, depending on the rate of formation of new plant material and its decomposition. This dark-colored, amorphous, highly characteristic soil constituent possesses certain important physical and chemical properties which give to the soil its specific characteristics. The formation and disintegration of humus are closely bound with the activities of the microbiological population of the soil, on the one hand, and with soil conditions and plant growth, on the other.

Many attempts have been made to develop inocula for various nonleguminous plants; these comprise the so-called all-crop soil inocula, and the inocula of nonsymbiotic nitrogen-fixing bacteria. All these have failed to accomplish useful results. The suggestion that the favorable effect of small amounts of stable manures upon plant growth is due to the introduction of large numbers of bacteria into the soil has likewise remained unsubstantiated. When soil conditions are not favorable to the development of particular organisms, mere introduction of these organisms will not result in their establishment in the soil. When conditions are made favorable for the development of new organisms, as by drainage of salt lands and peat bogs, by liming of acid soils, and by planting specific host crops, certain organisms may be introduced to advantage. This is particularly true of the legume bacteria, and occasionally of nitrifying bacteria, sulfur-oxidizing bacteria, and mycorrhiza fungi.

The preparation of composts represents another important process in which considerable improvement has resulted from knowledge of the microbiological population. When stable manures or plant residues supplemented with inorganic fertilizer are placed in a compost and conditions made favorable to the activities of aerobic microorganisms, as by proper aeration and provision of sufficient moisture, numerous reactions immediately take place These are accompanied by a rapid rise in temperature, which may serve as a measure of the rapidity of the decomposition process. The microbiological population of the compost changes with a change in temperature and with the nature of the materials undergoing decomposition Among the major chemical reactions that take place during the process of composting, the destruction of the cellulose and hemicelluloses, and the resulting increases in ash, lignin, and protein contents are most significant. Protein synthesis is brought about by the activities of the microorganisms

One of the major economic problems involved in the preservation of stable manures is the potential loss of nitrogen, as pointed out previously Various methods have been utilized for the conservation of the manure, the major purpose being the prevention of these losses. One of these methods consists in hastening the activities of microorganisms which bring about the destruction of the cellulose and hemicelluloses in the manure, if the microbiological population is sufficiently active to bring this about during the early stages of composting, the soluble forms of nitrogen in the manure will be rapidly transformed into complex insoluble organic forms.

The survival in the soil of organisms causing plant and animal diseases has also received considerable attention Among the plant diseases, the root rots, take-all diseases of cereals, soft rots, scabs, club roots, and numerous others brought about by fungi, actinomycetes, and bacteria are particularly important. To these should be added the many insect pests which pass a part of their life cycle in the soil, and the various diseases caused by worms and other animal forms. Numerous methods of control have been developed, ranging from partial sterilization by heat and chemicals to the introduction of bacteria, fungi, and nematodes destructive to the parasite

The fate of bacteria causing epidemics of animal diseases, and that of fungi and actinomycetes causing less widespread outbreaks of skin diseases and deep-seated diseases, have received considerable attention. The study of antagonistic organisms found in the soil and their formation of substances destructive to the pathogens is now making rapid progress

Recent trends in soil microbiology have thus centered upon a better understanding of the nature and complexity of the soil population, the conditions which influence its quantitative and qualitative composition, the activities of these organisms in the soil, and the utilization of these activities for soil improvement, soil conservation, plant productivity, and combating of plant and animal pathogens

The Soil as a Living System

Because of the extensive microbiological population inhabiting it, the soil must be considered not merely a dynamic or even a biological system, but a living system. This assumption can be substantiated as follows (*a*) living organisms, belonging both to plant and to animal systems, have taken an active part in the processes of rock weathering and soil formation; (*b*) these organisms have contributed to the formation and accumulation of one of the most important and characteristic soil constituents, humus, which is largely responsible for differentiating a soil from a mere mass of inorganic debris, (*c*) the soil processes are continuous both in summer and in winter, and are affected by temperature, aeration, moisture, and supply of fresh plant and animal residues, (*d*) the extensive flora and fauna representing numerous forms of life that inhabit the soil range from the smallest bacteria to the large burrowing animals and the roots of higher plants

The Soil Microbiological Population

One could discover in the soil most forms of life, within proper dimensions of size and space, if one would only search for them long enough and develop the proper methods for their demonstration. Exclusive of higher plants, which find in the soil a support and a medium for their growth and from which they derive most of their nutrients, and exclusive of the numerous animals that spend the whole or a part of their life cycle in the soil, there exists in the soil an extensive population of microorganisms. This comprises forms which are characteristic of the soil and which seldom live in a natural state under other conditions, as well as forms which find in the soil only a temporary habitat

The soil population also varies considerably, both in kind and in abundance, depending upon the nature of the soil, its treatment, and various environmental conditions. This can easily be demonstrated by comparing the population of an undisturbed virgin soil with that of the same soil after it has been cultivated and has received various added organic and inorganic substances. In the virgin soil, the microorganisms are in a state of equilibrium, where the relative abundance of the various bacteria, fungi, actinomycetes, and protozoa depends upon the nature of the soil and its condition. In the treated soil, however, this equilibrium is often disturbed, and certain organisms develop in great abundance, out of all proportion to the others The specific nature of these organisms depends either upon the chemical nature of the material added or upon the nature of the changes produced in the soil by the treatment. The disturbance thus brought about in the microbiological equilibrium may be of a lasting nature, whereby one group of organisms may become predominant, to be followed later by the rapid development of other groups, or it may be only temporary, that is, after a short time the interrupted equilibrium may become re-established on the same quantitative basis or in a modified form.

The changing activities brought about by the microbiological population of the soil can be best illustrated by following the course of decomposition in the soil of fresh plant and animal residues Protein-rich materials lead to an extensive development of bacteria and actinomycetes, cellulose-rich materials bring about extensive development of fungi and certain bacteria Among the fungi, the Phycomycetes may come first when fresh plant residues are added, they are followed by Ascomycetes and Fungi Imperfecti, and finally by Basidiomycetes. A large part of the synthesized fungus mycelium will be gradually destroyed by bacteria The bacteria may be followed by protozoa. This sequence of forms does not follow under all conditions. Many of the microorganisms are specific and are adapted to one process; others are omnivorous and are capable of performing a number of functions. The nature of the material undergoing decomposition, environmental conditions, and incidental occurrence of specific microbial types will influence the predominance of certain forms over others

The changing numbers and types of organisms in the complex soil population, particularly when influenced by a number of soil and environmental factors, do not lend themselves readily to ordinary statistical treatment Under these conditions, one is likely to overlook the forest because attention is focused upon single trees Statistics alone, when not properly interpreted, may tend to overemphasize certain members of the population, frequently of very little significance in soil processes, and to overlook others of much greater importance

Interrelationships of Members of the Soil Population

The interrelations of members of the soil population, on the one hand, and of higher plants and other soil microorganisms, on the other, have received considerable attention. Of particular interest are the antagonistic and associative effects among microorganisms. The antagonistic effects have received recognition by those interested in combating soil-borne plant diseases. The specific effects of fungi, bacteria, and actinomycetes in depressing various disease-producing fungi, such as cotton root rot, various root diseases of cereals, and damping-off diseases of other plants, have been ascribed to the production of toxic substances by saprophytes or to the competition with the parasites for the available food. In some cases, the depression of the parasite has been brought about by controlling the activities of specific soil saprophytes. Potato scab may be controlled by addition of sulfur, which is oxidized by specific bacteria to sulfuric acid, the resulting acidity becomes unfavorable to the actinomyces producing the scab.

An attempt has been made to interpret the ability of certain organisms to produce antibiotic substances in terms of survival of certain microorganisms in the struggle for existence in nature, and especially in the soil. One cannot, of course, deny the fact that certain substances produced by some organisms are toxic to others, and may thus tend to control the development or even the survival of the latter in the soil. If one considers, however, the artificial conditions under which antibiotics are produced by various selected strains of organisms, the fact that these antibiotics are selective in their action upon other organisms, and that these can readily develop strains which are resistant to the action of antibiotics, one wonders how effective these substances are in controlling the soil population under natural conditions. Penicillin, produced by various species of *Penicillium* and *Aspergillus*, offers a good illustration. It is produced only in highly specific media, of which the soil is hardly a type. It is readily destroyed by various organisms inhabiting the soil. It has but little activity upon the fungi and most of the bacteria living in the soil.

Effect of Changing Conditions

The numerous bacteria and fungi living in the soil will not always react in a similar manner to a change in conditions of nutrition and environment. Many of the important soil bacteria, such as the nitrifying organisms, the nonsymbiotic nitrogen-fixing forms, and some of the cellulose-decomposing organisms, are highly sensitive to acidity and will usually fail to grow at a pH less than 6.0, other bacteria, however, such as some of the sulfur-oxidizing forms and the facultative anaerobic bacteria, seem to be able to withstand considerable acid concentration. The same is true of the response of different bacteria to the addition of specific organic substances, to a change in soil aeration, and to other soil changes. The fungi also show considerable variation in response to changing soil or nutrient conditions: some are more sensitive than others to increasing acidity or to diminished aeration, some attack the water-soluble substances more readily, others attack by preference the cellulose, and still others prefer the lignins and the proteins. There is also considerable variation in response to changes in environment and in food supply among the various actinomycetes and protozoa.

The stimulation of specific groups of organisms, whereby the normal microbiological equilibrium in the soil is interrupted and one particular type or group, previously present only in limited numbers or even in a latent state, becomes predominant, is due to the specialization of various microorganisms. Usually the energy source introduced into the soil can be utilized only by the particular organism under specific soil conditions, or the soil is modified to such a degree as to favor the development of one organism in preference to others. Winogradsky distinguished between the "autochthonous" bacteria, or those organisms which attack primarily the organic substances of the soil, and the "zymogenic" forms, or those which develop rapidly as a result of addition of fresh organic substances.

When complex plant and animal materials are added to the soil, the stimulating effect upon the development of various bacteria or fungi is difficult to analyze, because of the changing nature of the organisms with the progress of the decomposition process. The chemical composition of the material added, which varies with the nature of the material and the degree of its maturity in the case of a plant substance, the chemical and physical soil conditions, and the environmental factors, all modify the microbiological response to such treatments. As a plant matures, it contains smaller quantities of water-soluble substances, such as sugars and amino acids, and it becomes poorer in nitrogen and minerals and richer in cellulose and lignin. The addition to the soil of residues of a young plant will favor an abundant development of many bacteria, including the lactic acid forms, which attack the sugars and other water-soluble substances, mature plant residues favor extensive development of fungi, especially when available nitrogen is present in the soil or is added to it.

To illustrate further the effect of changing conditions upon the development of specific microorganisms, the population of a compost may be examined in further detail If a compost is kept at 28°C, the population will consist largely of bacteria, fungi, protozoa, and nematodes; actinomycetes develop only to a limited degree; aerobic cellulose-decomposing bacteria, especially members of the *Cytophaga* group, are most active At 50°C, where the rate of decomposition is highest, certain thermophilic fungi and actinomycetes predominate, bacteria are also present but they are not the most abundant forms: and the animal population is almost completely lacking At 65°C, the fungi are eliminated entirely, certain actinomycetes, belonging to the *Micromonospora* type, and the thermophilic bacteria are most abundant, cellulose decomposition is brought about by anaerobic, spore-forming thermophilic bacteria. At 75°C, decomposition is limited and takes place largely at the expense of the proteins and hemicelluloses, cellulose is not attacked at all; certain bacteria of the *Plectridium* type and certain species of *Micromonospora* make up the population The most rapid decomposition of the manure takes place first at 65°C. At this temperature, the nitrogen is completely consumed The inoculation of hot composts with an active thermophilic population has been found to hasten the process of decomposition Animal pathogens present in the manure are also destroyed at the high temperature.

Role of Microorganisms in Soil Processes

The role of microorganisms in the mineralization of waste materials in soils, water basins, and composts no longer requires emphasis One need not dwell upon the function of microorganisms in bringing about the liberation of nitrogen in an available form, as ammonia, and in the oxidation of the ammonia to nitrate. It is now universally recognized that the growth of legumes and their associated bacteria are of tremendous economic significance to agriculture Numerous other microbiological reactions have been elucidated and are at present well understood It is sufficient merely to mention the oxidation of sulfur by bacteria, a process which frequently becomes of considerable importance, the reduction of sulfates, nitrates, and arsenates, processes which involve the activities of various groups of microorganisms and may have, under certain conditions, great economic significance, the composting of stable manures and plant residues for the production of artificial composts, which involves the activities of large microbial populations, and the growth of plant and animal parasites, involving fungi, actinomycetes, bacteria, nematodes and various other worms, and insect larvae, resulting in conditions which require radical modification of soil management

The importance of microorganisms in a number of other soil processes is still a matter of dispute, if not of mere speculation Here belong the activities of nonsymbiotic nitrogen-fixing bacteria, in spite of the fact that the occurrence and physiology of these organisms have been studied extensively The specific effect upon plant growth of various substances produced by microorganisms, including vitamins, hormones, and other growth-promoting substances, is also still a matter for speculation. The effect of the saprophytic population of the soil upon plant and animal parasites which live in or find their way into the soil is still insufficiently understood The influence of microorganisms and of their metabolic products upon the physical condition of the soil, especially in aggregating the finer soil particles, a problem of great importance in soil conservation, is becoming more and more clearly recognized. The mycorrhizal relationships, in spite of the progress made during the last few years, are still to be unraveled, and the processes involved are yet to be understood and utilized for practical purposes.

These and numerous other processes resulting from the activities of the soil-inhabiting microorganisms are frequently complicated and involved So far, only very few of them have been recognized and still fewer utilized. Further progress will undoubtedly result with the development of new methods and with the growing appreciation of the interlocking activities of the complex microbiological population of the soil

Soil microbiology has made only a beginning. It is still facing open vistas for further investigation A highly complex population active in a most complex medium, the soil and bringing about a number of most complicated processes, fully deserves the interest not only of the soil microbiologist and of the soil chemist, but also of the agronomist, the botanist, the zoologist, the pedologist, and the biochemist, in finding the answers to some of the riddles which Mother Earth still propounds for us.

Index

Lightning Source UK Ltd.
Milton Keynes UK
UKOW04f1920031016

284377UK00001B/28/P